UNCORKING THE PAST

UNCORKING THE PAST

THE QUEST FOR WINE, BEER, AND OTHER
ALCOHOLIC BEVERAGES

PATRICK E. MCGOVERN

UNIVERSITY OF CALIFORNIA PRESS

BERKELEY   LOS ANGELES   LONDON

University of California Press, one of the most
distinguished university presses in the United States,
enriches lives around the world by advancing scholarship
in the humanities, social sciences, and natural sciences. Its
activities are supported by the UC Press Foundation and
by philanthropic contributions from individuals and
institutions. For more information, visit www
.ucpress.edu.

University of California Press
Berkeley and Los Angeles, California

University of California Press, Ltd.
London, England

© 2009 by The Regents of the University of California

Library of Congress Cataloging-in-Publication Data
McGovern, Patrick E.
    Uncorking the past : the quest for wine, beer, and other
alcoholic beverages / Patrick E. McGovern.
        p.   cm.
    Includes bibliographical references and index.
    ISBN: 978-0-520-25379-7 (cloth : alk. paper)
    1. Alcoholic beverages—History.   2. Alcoholic
beverages—Social aspects.   3. Drinking of alcoholic
beverages—History.   4. Drinking of alcoholic
beverages—Social aspects.   I. Title.
GT2884.M36   2009
394.1'3—dc22   2009010512

Manufactured in the United States of America
18 17 16 15 14 13 12 11 10 09
10 9 8 7 6 5 4 3 2 1

This book is printed on Cascades Enviro 100, a 100% post
consumer waste, recycled, de-inked fiber. FSC recycled
certified and processed chlorine free. It is acid free,
Ecologo certified, and manufactured by BioGas energy.

*To the innovative fermented-beverage
makers of our species*

CONTENTS

ILLUSTRATIONS

FIGURES

COLOR PLATES FOLLOW PAGE 128

PREFACE

AT THE END OF MY BOOK *ANCIENT WINE,* I posed a question: Why have cultures around the world had a millennia-long love affair with wine? My short answer then was that alcohol has been the universal drug, and that wine provides the highest concentration of this simple organic compound (ethanol) available in nature. Humans throughout history have been astounded by alcohol's effects, whether it is imbibed as a beverage or applied to the skin. The health benefits are obvious—alcohol relieves pain, stops infection, and seems to cure diseases. Its psychological and social benefits are equally apparent—alcohol eases the difficulties of everyday life, lubricates social exchanges, and contributes to a joy in being alive.

Perhaps most profoundly, alcohol's mind-altering effects tap into mystical, unseen realms of the human brain. Wherever we look in the ancient or modern world, we see that the principal way to communicate with the gods or the ancestors involves an alcoholic beverage, whether it is the wine of the Eucharist, the beer presented to the Sumerian goddess Ninkasi, the mead of the Vikings, or the elixir of an Amazonian or African tribe.

Briefly put, alcoholic beverages are unique among all the drugs that humans and our early hominid ancestors have exploited on this planet for more than four million years. Their preeminence and universal allure—what might be called their biological, social, and religious imperatives—make them significant in understanding the development of our species and its cultures.

To appreciate this strong coupling between alcoholic beverages and human bioculture, I propose a journey of exploration that extends farther back than the beginnings of grape wine in the Middle East. We will start out at the center of our galaxy, move on to the beginnings of life on this planet, and then follow humankind's preoccupation with and ingenious concoction of alcoholic beverages from continent to continent, as our species spread out from Africa across the Earth. We will examine the most recent archaeological discoveries, chemical analyses of residues on ancient pottery, and advances in the analysis of DNA. These new findings can be interpreted by drawing on ancient art and writings, the ethnography of more recent traditional beverage making, and experimental archaeology, in which we attempt to re-create the ancient beverages. The result is a rewriting of the prehistory and history of ancient alcoholic beverages, including wine, beer, and some strange mixtures I call "extreme beverages" that combine many different ingredients. Because this book picks up where *Ancient Wine* left off, the interested reader should consult it for more details of archaeological excavations and finds related to wine.

Some readers might already be thinking that my approach to alcoholic beverages does not take account of their darker side. The initial stimulant effect of an alcoholic beverage, as exhibited by euphoria or easy sociability, can of course turn into anger or self-hatred with excessive drinking. The depressant properties of the drug then kick in, as a person loses balance, slurs speech, and may even begin to hallucinate; the world spins out of control, and the expressions on the faces of one's drinking companions take on a strange remoteness. The drinker may finally succumb to unconsciousness, with only disjointed fragments of the episode remembered the next day amid a ferocious hangover.

The naysayers and prohibitionists tell us that alcoholic beverages have been an unmitigated blight on humanity. They have caused untold property damage, disrupted families, led to every kind of vice and violence, and destroyed individuals' lives. I agree that alcohol consumed in excess can be extremely detrimental to the individual and community. But any substance (especially food), activity (such as running, dancing, music making, or sex), or powerful idea (such as religious conviction) can activate appetitive and pleasure centers in our brains (see chapter 9) and lead to compulsive, addictive behavior. Because drugs such as alcohol impinge directly on the brain, they are particularly potent and need to be used with caution.

Despite its risks, few substances have earned the praise that alcohol has. The psychologist William James perhaps expressed it best in his landmark book, *The Varieties of Religious Experience:*

The sway of alcohol over mankind is unquestionably due to its power to stimulate the mystical faculties of human nature, usually crushed to earth by the cold facts and dry criticisms of the sober hour. Sobriety diminishes, discriminates, and says no; drunkenness expands, unites, and says yes. It is in fact the great exciter of the *Yes* function in man. It brings its votary from the chill periphery of things to the radiant core. It makes him for the moment one with truth. Not through mere perversity do men run after it . . . it is part of the deeper mystery and tragedy of life that whiffs and gleams of something we immediately recognise as excellent. (377–78)

Accolades from famous artists, musicians, writers, and scholars through the ages echo James's sentiments. Louis Pasteur, who first observed wine yeast and tartaric acid crystals under the microscope, rhapsodized that "the flavor of wine is like delicate poetry," picking up on the sentiments of the Roman poet Horace (Epode 11), who wrote that wine "brings to light the hidden secrets of the soul."

So, is wine a mocker or does it gladden the heart of man? Have so many exceptional people simply been deluded about how alcohol fueled their creativity? Did Dylan Thomas, Jackson Pollock, Janis Joplin, and Jack Kerouac drink themselves into their graves in vain?

To be sure, much remains to be discovered on every front, from understanding the effects of alcohol on the human brain to filling out the history of ancient alcoholic beverages around the world. I have only touched on some of the high points in this millennia-long quest, as occasioned by the accidents of discovery and sampling. We still know little about the early use of alcohol in vast areas of Central Asia, India, Southeast Asia, the Pacific islands, Amazonia, Australia, and even some areas of Europe and North America, and we can expect surprises. For example, it has often been claimed that, among all animals, only humans overindulge in alcoholic beverages. Recently, however, it has been shown that Malaysian tree shrews, among the earliest primates on the planet, binge each night on fermented palm nectar.

The title of this book might be viewed as something of a misnomer. After all, our earliest evidence for the use of cork to seal a container of an alcoholic beverage—grape wine in this instance—is early fifth-century

B.C. Athens, where a neatly rounded and beveled piece, looking much like the corks we are accustomed to, was wedged into the mouth of a wine jug and made flush with the top of the rim. A hole through the center of the cork might appear to have defeated the purpose, but perhaps it had already been removed, with some forerunner of the corkscrew, and then reinserted before the jar came to rest in the ancient well of the Agora. The excavator believed that a string had been tied through the hole so that the jar could be lowered into the well and the wine cooled.

About the same time that the Athenian wine was being drunk, an Etruscan ship went down off the coast of the French Riviera, near the island of Grand Ribaud. Its hull was filled with hundreds of wine amphoras, stacked at least five layers deep. When found recently, many of these vessels, cushioned by grapevines, were still stoppered with their original cork closures. The corks were inserted into the narrow mouths of the jars as proficiently as any modern corking machine could do it.

But the substance first known to have been stored in a vessel stoppered with cork is honey, the principal concentrated source of sugar in nature. A bronze amphora, dated ca. 540–30 B.C., was filled with liquid honey (still sticky and redolent of its characteristic aromas when it was found), closed up with cork, and deposited in a completely walled-up subterranean chamber in the ancient Italian city of Paestum, in Campania. It was intended not for making mead but as an offering to the chief goddess of the city and of the Greek pantheon, Hera, with one of the valued healing substances of antiquity. A couch at the center of the chamber might have represented the sacred marriage of the goddess, who was associated with the underworld, to her consort and brother, Zeus. As we will see later, the sacred marriage (*hieros gamos*) ceremony was a long-standing tradition in the Near East and was often preceded by the sharing of an alcoholic beverage.

It seems likely that earlier examples of vessels sealed with cork existed, especially in the parts of the western Mediterranean where the cork oak thrives. Wherever the practice originated, however, the goal was generally to preserve a precious liquid for future quaffing. Before the cork took on this role, our human ancestors had to make do with wood, stone, vegetal matter, or leather. With the advent of pottery around 10,000 B.C. in east Asia, raw clay began to be molded into stoppers. If a vessel was stored on its side, as was happening as early as 3500 B.C. in the Zagros Mountains of Iran, the clay absorbed liquid from the contents and expanded to keep out oxygen, just like cork, and prevented the wine from turning to vinegar. As Pliny the Elder so eloquently observed of methods to prevent wine disease in his *Natural History* of the first century A.D., "There is no department of man's life on which more labor is spent."

Uncorking the bottle represents the grand finale to the preservation and aging process—whether that entails pulling away a heavy slate stone covering a hollow tree trunk full of prehistoric fermented grape juice or honey mead, chopping off the clay stopper of an ancient Egyptian wine jar with a carefully placed blow so as to not contaminate the elixir, or opening a vintage port by searing off the neck of the glass bottle with hot tongs. As the champagne cork pops or the hollow tree trunk bubbles over, we anticipate celebratory, exuberant sensations.

ONE

HOMO IMBIBENS

I Drink, Therefore I Am

ASTRONOMERS PROBING OUR GALAXY WITH powerful radio waves have discovered that alcohol does not exist only on the Earth. Massive clouds of methanol, ethanol, and vinyl ethanol—measuring billions of kilometers across—have been located in interstellar space and surrounding new star systems. One cloud, denoted Sagittarius B2N, is located near the center of the Milky Way, some 26,000 light-years or 150 quadrillion miles away from the Earth. While the distant location ensures that humans will not be exploiting extraterrestrial ethanol any time soon, the magnitude of this phenomenon has excited speculation about how the complex carbon molecules of life on Earth were first formed.

Scientists hypothesize that the vinyl ethanol molecules in particular, with their more chemically reactive double bonds, might have been held in place on interstellar dust particles. As in making a vinyl plastic, one vinyl ethanol molecule would couple to another, gradually building up ever more complex organic compounds that are the stuff of life. Dust particles, with their loads of these new carbon polymers, might have been transported through the universe in the icy heads of comets. At high velocities, the ice would melt, releasing the dust to seed a planet like Earth with a kind of organic soup, out of which primitive life forms emerged. It is a gigantic leap from the formation of ethanol to the evolution of the intricate biochemical machinery of the simplest bacteria, not to mention the human organism. But as we peer into the night sky, we might ask why there is an alcoholic haze at the center of our galaxy, and what role alcohol played in jump-starting and sustaining life on our planet.

CREATING A FERMENT

If alcohol permeates our galaxy and universe, it should come as no surprise that sugar fermentation (or glycolysis) is thought to be the earliest form of energy production used by life on Earth. Some four billion years ago, primitive single-celled microbes are hypothesized to have dined on simple sugars in the primordial soup and excreted ethanol and carbon dioxide. A kind of carbonated alcoholic beverage would thus have been available right from the beginning.

Today, two species of single-celled yeasts (*Saccharomyces cerevisiae* and *S. bayanus*), encompassing a large group of wild and domesticated strains, carry on in this grand tradition and serve as the workhorses that produce the alcohol in fermented beverages around the world. Although hardly primitive—they have most of the same specialized organelles as multicellular plants and animals, including a central nucleus which contains the chromosomal DNA—these yeast thrive in oxygen-free environments, such as we imagine existed on Earth when life began.

If we accept this scenario, then the alcohol generated by these first organisms must have been wafting across the planet for millennia. It and other short-chained carbon compounds eventually came to signal the presence of a convenient, high-energy sugar resource. The pungent, enticing aroma of alcohol announced to later sugar-loving animals of the world, ranging from fruit flies to elephants, where the banquet was to be found. When fruit-bearing trees appeared around 100 million years ago (mya), during the Cretaceous period, they offered an abundance of both sugar and alcohol. The sweet liquid that oozes out of ruptured, ripened fruit provides the ideal combination of water and nutrients that allows yeast to multiply and convert the sugar into alcohol.

Animals became superbly adept at exploiting the sugary cocktail of fruit trees, which in turn benefited from the animals' dispersal of their seed. The close symbiosis between a tree and the animals that pollinate its flowers, eat its fruit, and carry out a host of other mutually advantageous functions is astonishing. Take the fig tree, with some eight hundred species spread throughout the world. These trees do not bloom in the conventional sense: instead, they have male and female inflorescences that are tightly encased in a succulent-tasting sac called the syconium, and they cannot be pollinated directly because they flower at different times on the same tree. A species of wasp unique to each fig species must carry out this task. The female adult wasp bores through the tip of the syconium, ruining her wings and eventually dying. She lives long enough, however, to deposit her eggs and transfer the pollen from another tree to the female flowers. When the wasp eggs hatch, the wingless male, trapped within the syconium and eventually dying there, impregnates the female and chomps an opening with his powerful jaws for her to escape with another load of eggs. Sustained by sucking alcoholic nectar through her long, strawlike proboscis from the deep corollas of the fig flowers, she goes on to pollinate another fig tree.

While the fig wasps carry on with their secret sex life, air flowing into the hole created by the escaping female causes the syconium to ripen into the fig "fruit." The yeast goes to work and generates the alcoholic fragrances that alert animals to the potential feast. As many as one hundred thousand figs on a large tree can be devoured by birds, bats, monkeys, pigs, and even dragonflies and geckos in a feeding frenzy.

The fig tree illustrates the intricacy and specificity of the web of life. Other plant sugars, such as evergreen saps and flower nectars, have their own stories to tell. A much sought-after and luscious honey in Turkey, for example, is made from pine honeydew. This is a sugar-rich secretion produced by a scale insect, *Marchalina hellenica,* which lives in cracks in the bark of the red pine tree (*Pinus brutia*) and feeds exclusively on the resinous sap. Bees collect the honeydew, and with a specific enzyme, invertase, break down its sugar (sucrose) into simpler glucose and fructose. The final product, honey, is the most concentrated simple sugar source in nature, with the specific plant species from which it derives, red pine in this instance, contributing special flavors and aromas.

Entomologists have exploited insects' taste for fermented beverages by smearing the substances on the bases of trees in order to capture them. Charles Darwin employed a similar tactic: when he set out a bowl of beer at night, a tribe of African baboons were lured in and were easily gathered up as specimens the next morning in their inebriated state. Intemperate slugs—mollusks lacking shells—are less fortunate, as they self-indulgently drown in beer traps. In one carefully constructed set of experiments, it was shown that common fruit flies (*Drosophila melanogaster*) lay their eggs where there are intense odors of ethanol and acetaldehyde, another by-product of alcohol metabolism. The fermenting fruit guarantees that their larvae will be well-fed with sugar and high-protein yeast, as well as alcohol, for which they have highly efficient energy pathways.

Nature's hidden rationale and complex ecological interplay centered on sugar and alcohol resources can have a seriocomic side. Elephants, which consume fifty thousand calories a day, sometimes overindulge in their consumption of fermenting fruit. They can perhaps be excused, as they work hard for their pleasure: they have to remember where to find the trees and travel many miles to reach them at the time of ripening. Unfortunately, they also have a weakness for the human-produced equivalent. In 1985, about 150 elephants forced their way into a moonshine operation in West Bengal, ate all the sweet mash, and then rampaged across the country, trampling five people to death and knocking down seven concrete buildings. This episode highlights problem drinking in higher mammals, including humans.

Birds are also known to gorge themselves on fermenting fruit. Cedar waxwings feasting on hawthorn fruit have suffered ethanol poisoning and even death. Robins fall off their perches. Maturing fruits concentrate sugar, flavor and aroma compounds, and colorants that announce to birds and mammals that they are ripe for eating. As the fruit passes its prime, however, it becomes the target of a host of microorganisms, including yeasts and bacteria, that can threaten the plants. Ominously, the plants defend themselves by generating poisonous compounds. The manufactured plant toxins, including alkaloids and terpenoids, inhibit the growth of virulent microorganisms, as well as fending off noxious insects. A placid-looking apple orchard or idyllic vineyard may not look like a battleground, but a host of creatures are vying for supremacy and defining the balance of power through chemical compounds.

Sometimes, one creature unwittingly steps on a chemical landmine intended for another. If alcohol is dangerous when consumed in excess, plant toxins can be lethal. In one well-documented incident near Walnut Creek, California, thousands of robins and cedar waxwings apparently found the scarlet, mildly sweet berries of holly (*Ilex* spp.) and firethorn bush (*Pyracantha*) too good to pass up. Over a three-week period, the birds overdosed on the berries and their toxins and began crashing into cars and windows. Autopsies revealed that their gullets were bursting with the fruit. (By contrast, the normal, demure courtship behavior of cedar waxwings involves passing a single berry back and forth between the male and female until the gift is finally accepted and the pair copulate.)

As with the West Bengal elephants, the California birds' drunken behavior was due to the excessive consumption of a mind-altering compound. Intriguingly, the compounds in holly berries—caffeine and theobromine—are the same ones humans enjoy today in coffee, tea, and chocolate. Native Americans in the woodlands of the north and the jungles of Amazonia also showed their appreciation for these substances: Spanish colonists observed that they brewed up a bitter but aromatic "black drink" by steeping toasted holly leaves in hot water.

A VERY PECULIAR YEAST

Just as a plant will defend its territory with a chemical arsenal, the invisible world of microorganisms engages in a similar struggle for supremacy and survival. A finely tuned enzymatic system and the production of alcohol are the weapons of choice for *S. cerevisiae,* the principal yeast used by humans in making alcoholic beverages. About the same time that fruit trees were proliferating around the globe, *S. cerevisiae* appears to have acquired an extra copy of its entire genome. Further rearrangements enabled it to proliferate in the absence of oxygen, and the alcohol it produced destroyed much of its competition. Other microorganisms, including many spoilage- and disease-causing yeasts and bacteria, simply cannot tolerate alcohol in concentrations above 5 percent, but *S. cerevisiae* survives in fermenting substances with more than twice this concentration of alcohol.

The yeast pays a cost for its success. In producing more alcohol, it forgoes making more of the compound adenosine triphosphate (ATP), which provides living organisms with the energy for essential biological processes. Pure aerobic metabolism yields thirty-six molecules of ATP from glucose. *S. cerevisiae* makes only two molecules of ATP in air, channeling the rest of the glucose into the production of alcohol to be deployed against its competitors.

S. cerevisiae's apparent loss later becomes its gain. Because of the doubling of its genome, each yeast cell develops two versions of the gene that controls the production of alcohol dehydrogenase (ADH). This enzyme converts acetaldehyde, an end product of glycolysis, into alcohol. One version of the enzyme (ADH1) reliably processes sugar into alcohol in an oxygen-free environment, whereas the other (ADH2) is activated only after most of the sugar has been consumed and oxygen levels start to rise again. For *S. cerevisiae,* this happens after many competing microbes have been destroyed. Then ADH2 springs into action, converting alcohol back into acetaldehyde and ultimately generating more ATP. Of course, other microorganisms, such as acetic acid–producing bacteria, which can tolerate high alcohol levels, wait in the wings. They are ready to turn any remaining alcohol into vinegar unless another hungry organism acts faster or is able, like a human, to improvise a way to preserve the alcohol.

It is still a mystery why varieties of *S. cerevisiae* live on the skins of certain fruits, especially grapes, or in honey, where they are able to tolerate high sugar levels. This yeast is not airborne but can take up residence in special microclimates, like the breweries around Brussels, with their lambic beers, or the rice-wine factories of Shaoxing in China (see chapter 2): both beverages are fermented without intentionally adding yeast. The yeast apparently lives in the rafters of the old buildings, from where it falls into the brew; when the rafters have been covered during renovations, brewers have been unable to start their fermentations. The yeast most likely was carried there by insects, especially bees and wasps, who inadvertently picked it up when they fed on the sweet juice oozing out of damaged fruit, and were drawn to the buildings by the aromas of the sweet worts and juices or musts.

ENTER *HOMO IMBIBENS:* MAN, THE DRINKER

Our world is awash in ethanol. In 2003, some 150 billion liters of beer, 27 billion liters of wine, and 2 billion liters of distilled spirits (mainly vodka) were produced worldwide. This amounts to about 8 billion liters of pure alcohol, representing about 20 percent of the world's total ethanol production of 40 billion liters. Now that alternative energy sources are a priority, fuel ethanol, made mainly from sugar cane and corn, accounts for the lion's share (70 percent in 2003, and more today). The industrial sector of chemicals and pharmaceuticals produces the remaining 10 percent. For the foreseeable future, the fuel sector will probably continue to expand, while the production of alcoholic beverages will show only modest gains to keep pace with the world's population. The world's total annual production of pure alcohol for beverages now exceeds 15 billion liters and is projected to reach 20 billion liters by 2012.

Fifteen billion liters of pure alcohol in naturally fermented and distilled beverages would provide every man, woman, and child on Earth with more than two liters a year. This estimate is likely too low, as illegal production is widespread and traditional home-brewed beverages, consumed globally in great quantities, are not included. Considering that most fermented beverages have an alcohol content of 5 to 10 percent and children generally do not imbibe, there is obviously plenty of alcohol to go around.

How has it come about that humans everywhere drink so much alcohol? Practically speaking, alcoholic beverages supply some of the water that we need to survive. Our bodies are two-thirds water, and the average adult needs to drink about two liters daily to stay hydrated and functioning. Untreated water supplies, however, can be infected with harmful microorganisms and parasites. Alcohol kills many of these pathogens, and humans must have recognized at an early date that those who drank alcohol were generally healthier than others.

Alcoholic beverages have other advantages. Alcohol spurs the appetite, and in liquid form, it also satiates feelings of hunger. The process of fermentation enhances the protein, vitamin, and nutritional content of the natural product, adds flavor and aroma, and contributes to preservation. Fermented foods and beverages cook faster because complex molecules have been broken down, saving time and fuel. Finally, as we have learned from numerous medical studies, moderate consumption of alcohol lowers cardiovascular and cancer risks. People consequently live longer and reproduce more. This was crucially important in antiquity, when life spans were generally short.

Drinking an alcoholic beverage, however, has meant much more to humankind than gains in physical health and longevity. To understand its broader biological and cultural dimensions, we must travel back to the period when *Homo imbibens* first walked the planet. By necessity, our tour guides are archaeologists, DNA researchers, and other detectives of the past, who have patiently excavated and studied the fragmentary remains of our ancestors and the genetic evidence encoded in our bodies today.

By examining the skeletal and dental evidence from early hominid fossils, dating from between about 4.5 to 2 mya, inferences can be drawn about how they lived and what foods they ate as they traversed the African jungle and savannah. Many of the fossils come from the Great Rift Valley of East Africa, including *Australopithecus afarensis,* best represented by the skeleton known as Lucy. Her forty-seven bones show that she could walk on two legs as well as climb trees. These traits would have served her and the rest of her "first family" well, enabling them to stretch tall and clamber through branches to reach sweet fruit.

The smaller molars and canines of early hominids (and the great apes), going as far back as *Proconsul* and other fossils around 24 mya, are also well adapted to consuming soft, fleshy foods like fruit. These dentitions are broadly comparable to those of modern apes, including gibbons, orangutans, and lowland gorillas, who get most of their calories from fruit. Chimpanzees, whose genome is the closest to our own, have a diet consisting of more than 90 percent plants, of which more than 75 percent is fruit. In other words, early hominids and their descendants have favored fresh fruit for millions of years.

If fruit was the food of choice at the beginning of the hominid odyssey, alcoholic beverages were probably not far behind. Especially in warm tropical climates, as the fruit matured, it would have fermented on the tree, bush, and vine. Fruits with broken skins, oozing liquid, would have been attacked by yeast and the sugars converted into alcohol. Such a fruit slurry can reach an alcohol content of 5 percent or more.

Visually oriented creatures that we are, we can imagine that the bright colors of the fermenting fruit, often red or yellow, would have attracted hominid interest. As our early ancestors approached the ripe fruit, other senses would have come into play. The intense aroma of alcohol from the fermenting fruit would have alerted them to the source of nourishment, and tasting it would have brought new and enticing sensations.

We cannot be sure how close to reality such a reconstruction is, since the ancient fossils tell us nothing about the easily degradable sensory-organ tissues. The taste and smell sensitivity of modern humans does not rate particularly high in the animal kingdom, despite the occasional super-taster among us. Early hominids might have had much more acute senses than ours, like the macaque, an Old World monkey, which has exquisite sensitivity to alcohol and other smells.

THE DRUNKEN MONKEY HYPOTHESIS

The biologist Robert Dudley has proposed that alcoholism among humans is rooted in the evolutionary history of primates. This thought-provoking hypothesis, dubbed the drunken monkey hypothesis, draws on the often fragmented and debatable pieces of the archaeological record and what is known about modern primate diets. If we grant that early hominids were primarily fruit eaters, at least up until about 1–2 mya, when they began consuming more tubers and animal fat and protein, then perhaps our early ancestors gained an advantage from imbibing moderate amounts of alcohol, whose benefits have been shown by recent medical research, and adapted biologically to it. On average, both abstainers and bingers have shorter, harsher life spans. The human liver is specially equipped to metabolize alcohol, with about 10 percent of its enzyme machinery, including alcohol dehydrogenase, devoted to generating energy from alcohol. Our organs of smell can pick up wafting alcoholic aromas, and our other senses detect the myriad compounds that permeate ripe fruit.

Among modern humans and other primates, the thirst for alcohol sometimes far exceeds any obvious nutritional or medical benefit (see plate 1). On the remote tropical island of Barro Colorado in Panama, Dudley reports, howler monkeys could not get enough of the ripe fruit of a palm (*Astrocaryum standleyanum*). You might think that monkeys would know better than to binge, in the same way that they avoid unsafe, even poisonous, plants in the natural world, but these monkeys gorged themselves on the bright orange fruit, ingesting the equivalent of about ten standard drinks, or two bottles of 12 percent wine, in twenty minutes. Obviously, there are diminishing returns to life and health if a monkey gets too drunk, misses a leap from one branch to another, and falls or is impaled by a sharp palm spine.

Malaysian tree shrews, who belong to a family dating back more than 55 mya that is believed to be ancestral to all living primates, have a similar penchant for fermented palm nectar. As documented by Frank Wiens and colleagues, they provide elegant testimony in support of Dudley's hypothesis. These small creatures, resembling flying squirrels, often lap up alcohol in excess of the cross-species benchmark for intoxication (1.4 grams pure alcohol per kilogram weight) over the course of a night. That equates to about nine glasses of wine for the average-sized human. Yet the shrews show no signs of intoxication as they make their way deftly through the sharp spines of the palm trees to one oozing flower bud after another. The inflorescences of the bertam palm (*Eugeissona tristis*) are like miniature fermenting vessels where nectar accumulates year-round. In the tropical climate, the resident yeast rapidly converts it to a frothy, strongly scented palm wine with an alcohol content as high as 3.8 percent. The symbiotic relationship between palm and shrew is remarkable: while the animal guzzles, it pollinates the plant. Humans may have lost some of the genetic machinery to metabolize alcohol as efficiently as the tree shrew, but they have emulated its behavior by fermenting the sugar-rich saps and nectars of numerous palm tree species in Africa (chapter 8) and elsewhere.

Ape behavior in the artificial environment of a laboratory cage is equally illuminating. According to Ronald Siegel, chimpanzees given unlimited access to alcohol—an "open bar"—will at first guzzle the equivalent of three or four bottles of wine. Males outdrink the smaller females and get intoxicated twice as often. Over time, their consumption falls into a more restrained pattern, but the chimpanzees still imbibe enough to stay permanently drunk. Such behavior has no apparent evolutionary benefit: intoxication seems to be an end in itself. By experimenting with a range of offerings at the bar, the researchers also noted that their chimpanzees generally favored sweet wines over dry and flavored vodka over pure alcohol.

Rats showed greater restraint than the chimpanzees under comparable experimental conditions. Outfitted with spacious underground quarters and a twenty-four-hour "bar," their drinking patterns assumed a regularity that many of us would immediately recognize. The colony avidly congregated around the drinking hole just before the main feeding time. The predinner cocktail, perhaps to whet the appetite, was followed several hours later by a nightcap before sleep. Every three to four days, the colony drank more than usual, as if they were partying.

DRIVEN BY DRINK

Early hominids and apes had a powerful incentive to overindulge in fermented fruits and other high-sugar resources, such as honey: these foods are only available in season. It might have been possible to store seeds or nuts in a dark, cool cave for a future repast, but tactics had not yet been devised to protect sweet, alcoholic delights from marauders and microorganisms. To tide themselves over the lean seasons, it made sense for our ancestors to eat and drink as much as they could when it could be had.

Gorging on energy-rich sugar and alcohol was an excellent solution for surviving in an often resource-poor and hostile environment. Extra calories could be converted to fat for future use, then gradually burned off in harsher times. For an early hominid, most of this energy was probably channeled into walking considerable distances in search of ripe fruit, nuts and other foods, hunting game, and evading predators. The hominid body, with its powerful leg muscles and generous gluteus maximus behind to balance forward thrust, can achieve relatively high running speeds of up to 48 kilometers an hour. Any overweight individuals were likely quickly weeded out by lions traveling at more than 120 kilometers an hour.

Drunkenness places individual organisms at greater risk of attack by a hostile species, as their reflexes and physical prowess are inhibited. Social animals, including birds and monkeys, have a distinct advantage when engaging in a bout of gluttony. As their muscular coordination and mental acuity decrease, their large numbers help ward off any party crasher in the neighborhood. Before lapsing into oblivion, these animals also usually send up a collective alarm or battle en masse against the intruder. A location safe from attack also facilitates binging, whether by default (if, for example, the inebriating substance is found at the top of a tall tree) or by design, if the fermented food and drink are carried to a mountaintop or into a cave before the festivities begin.

The reasons for alcohol consumption in the animal world are invisible to the observer. Specialists in animal behavior cannot read the "thoughts" of fruit flies or chimpanzees, let alone extinct hominids, to understand what might compel them to eat a batch of fermenting fruit. Although geneticists and neuroscientists have begun to elucidate the molecular mechanisms by which organisms sense, respond to, and metabolize alcohol, any comprehensive explanation of this phenomenon is still a long way off.

THE PALAEOLITHIC HYPOTHESIS

How far back in the mists of archaeological time have humans savored alcohol, and how has it shaped us as a biological species and contributed to our cultures? The drunken monkey hypothesis explores the biological side of the question. The Neolithic period, beginning around 8000 B.C. in the Near East and China (chapters 2 and 3), provides a rich trove of archaeological material to mine for answers to the cultural questions. Humans were then settling down into the first permanent settlements, and they left abundant traces of their architecture, jewelry, painted frescoes, and newly invented pottery filled with fermented beverages. For the Palaeolithic period, beginning hundreds of thousands of years earlier, we are on much shakier ground. Yet this is undoubtedly the time when humans first experimented with alcoholic beverages, as they relished their fermented fruit juices and came to apprehend their ecstasies and dangers.

The evidence from Palaeolithic archaeology is scant, and it is easy to overinterpret and read modern notions into this fragmented past. Archaeologists once thought that early humans were meat eaters on a grand order because their encampments were littered with animal bones. Then it dawned on someone that the remains of any fruits or vegetables simply had not survived, and that the abundance of bones, which were infinitely better preserved, indicated only that meat constituted some portion, possibly minor, of the early human diet.

"I'm getting woolly-mammoth notes."

Figure 1. © The New Yorker Collection 2005, Leo Cullum from cartoonbank.com. All rights reserved.

In *Ancient Wine* I outlined a plausible scenario, which I refer to as the Palaeolithic hypothesis, explaining how Palaeolithic humans might have discovered how to make grape wine. In brief, this hypothesis posits that at some point in early human prehistory, a creature not so different from ourselves—with an eye for brightly colored fruit, a taste for sugar and alcohol, and a brain attuned to alcohol's psychotropic effects (see chapter 9)—would have moved beyond the unconscious craving of a slug or a drunken monkey for fermented fruit to the much more conscious, intentional production and consumption of a fermented beverage.

In an upland climate where the wild Eurasian grape (*Vitis vinifera* ssp. *sylvestris*) has thrived for millions of years, such as eastern Turkey or the Caucasus, we might imagine early humans moving through a luxuriant river bottom. Using roughly hollowed-out wooden containers, gourds, or bags made of leather or woven grasses, they gather up the ripe grapes and carry them back to a nearby cave or temporary shelter. Depending on their ripeness, the skins of some grapes at the bottom of the containers are crushed, rupture, and exude their juice. If the grapes are left in their containers, this juice will begin to froth or even violently bubble up. Owing to natural yeast on the skins, it gradually ferments into a low-alcohol wine—a kind of Stone Age Beaujolais Nouveau.

Eventually, the turbulence subsides, and one of the more daring members of the human clan takes a tentative taste of the concoction. He reports that the final product is noticeably smoother, warmer, and more varied in taste than the starting mass of grapes. The liquid is aromatic and full of flavor. It goes down easily and leaves a lingering sense of tranquility. It frees the mind of the dangers that lurk all around. Feeling happy and carefree, this individual invites the others to partake. Soon everyone's mood is elevated, leading to animated exchanges. Perhaps some people sing and dance. As the day turns into night and the humans keep imbibing, their behavior gets out of hand. Some members of the clan become belligerent, others engage in wild sex, others simply pass out from intoxication.

Once having discovered how to make such a beverage, early humans would likely have returned year after year to the wild grapevines, harvesting the fruit at the peak of ripeness and even devising ways to process it—perhaps stomping the grapes with their feet or encouraging better anaerobic fermentation of the juice and pulp by covering the primitive container with a lid. The actual domestication of the Eurasian grapevine, according to the so-called Noah hypothesis (see chapter 3), as well as the development of a reliable method of preventing the wine from turning swiftly to vinegar (acetic acid), was still far in the future. A tree resin with antioxidant effects might have been discovered accidentally early on, but it would only have delayed the inevitable by a few days. The wiser course was to gorge on the delectable beverage before it went bad.

Similar experiences with alcoholic beverages must have been played out many times, in different places, by our human forebears. Grapes are only one of many fermenting fruits. In sub-Saharan Africa, the heartland of modern humanity (*Homo sapiens*), from where we spread out to populate

---

Map 1 *(overleaf)*. Spread of fermented-beverage experimentation across Eurasia. Fermented beverages were made as early as 100,000 B.P., when humans came "out of Africa" on their way to populating the Earth. Depending upon locally available and introduced domesticated plants, fermented beverages were produced from honey, barley, wheat, grape, date, and many other grains and fruits (e.g., cranberries in northwestern Europe). The earliest beverages were mixed "grogs," probably with added herbs, tree resins, and other "medicinal" ingredients (e.g., ephedra on the Eurasian steppes).

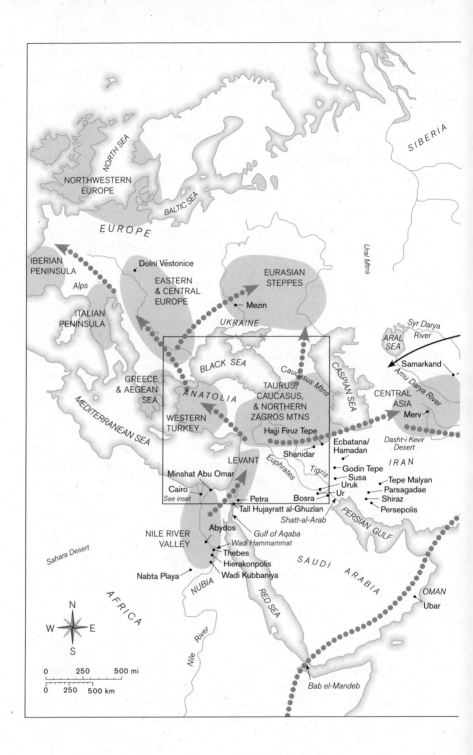

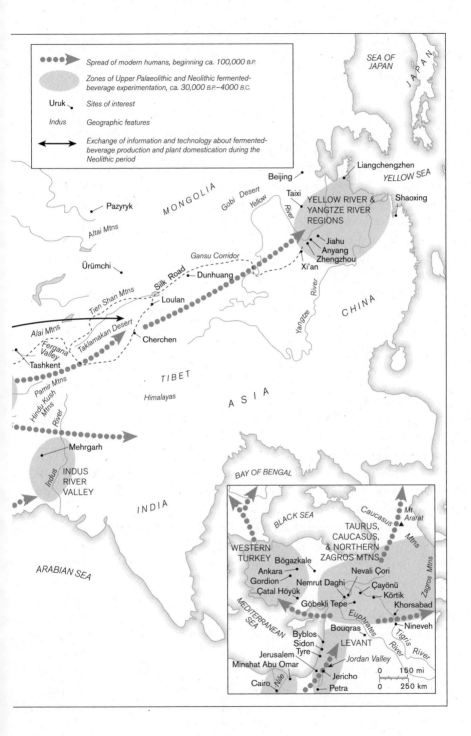

the rest of the world about one hundred thousand years ago, the first fermented beverage might have been made from figs, baobab fruit, or sweet gourds. Honey, composed of 60 to 80 percent simple sugars (fructose and glucose) by weight, would have been highly sought after as an ingredient. Bees in temperate climates have been churning out honey since at least the Cretaceous period, and many animals, including humans, have risked the stings of angry bees to steal the sweet honey from their hives.

Roger Morse, a longtime friend of my family and formerly professor of apiculture at Cornell University, often argued that honey must have been the basis for the world's earliest alcoholic beverage. Imagine a cavity in a dead tree that bees have filled with wax and honey. One day the tree falls to the ground, and the cavity is exposed to a soaking rain. Once the store of honey is diluted to 30 percent honey and 70 percent water, yeasts specially adapted to survive high sugar contents will start the fermentation and produce mead. Along comes our hominid ancestor, who has been watching this hive for a long time. She goes straight to the cavity, has a taste, and if not a selfish sort, calls in her companions to enjoy the alcohol-laced libation.

Many such scenarios can be imagined. Although all are inherently plausible, based on what we know about human societies, the biology of the modern human brain, and personal experience, the main problem with the Palaeolithic hypothesis is that it is unprovable. No containers have yet been recovered from the Palaeolithic period, not even one made from stone. Objects made of wood, grass, leather, and gourds have disintegrated and disappeared. The only real prospect for chemically detecting a fermented beverage from this period is to try to extract what might have been absorbed into a crevice of a rock near a Palaeolithic encampment where the beverage might have been prepared.

Nevertheless, some enticing hints in the archaeological record suggest that the Palaeolithic hypothesis may not be far off the mark. For example, some of the earliest artistic representations of our species depict bare-breasted, large-hipped females, often referred to as Venuses because of their obvious associations with sexuality and childbearing. One particularly provocative Venus (see plate 2) was chiseled into a cliff at Laussel in the Dordogne region of France around twenty thousand years before the present (B.P.), not far from the famous cave of Lascaux, which teems with Palaeolithic frescoes. With one hand on her pregnant belly, the long-haired beauty holds up an object that resembles a drinking horn. Other identifications of this object are possible, including a musical instrument (but then why is the narrow end of the horn pointed away from her mouth?) or a lunar symbol denoting the female (but you could just as easily infer that a bison horn is a sign of complementary maleness or hunting prowess).

A drinking-horn identification is in keeping with the much later predilection of Celtic princes in this region to show off their drinking prowess with magnificent horns. The setting of this Venus in an open-air rock shelter, overlooking a broad valley, would have been ideal for bringing together a large group to enjoy and celebrate life with an alcoholic beverage, perhaps made from wild berries growing nearby (the famous wine-growing area of Bordeaux is only one hundred kilometers away) or a cache of honey. Further accentuating her sexuality and the fecundity of nature, the figure's breasts and belly were strikingly painted with red ocher. In later art, fermented beverages—including wine made from grapes and New World chocolate drinks—were often shown in red and symbolized blood, the fluid of life.

Even if the Laussel Venus is drinking from rather than blowing on her horn, it seems possible that early hominids or humans might have made music while they enjoyed their alcoholic beverage. In a cavern at Geissenklösterle in southern Germany, some fifteen thousand years earlier than Laussel, archaeologists discovered three fragmentary flutes with at least three holes, fashioned from a woolly mammoth's ivory tusk and the wing bones of whooper swans. The holes were beveled, suggesting that the instruments were played, like a modern flute, by blowing across one of the holes with variable lip pressure or embouchure, rather than blowing directly through one end. A range of tones, perhaps even octaves, could have been achieved by fingering, that is, closing off one or more of the holes while blowing.

In China around 7000 B.C., Neolithic people made a very similar instrument from a specific bone of the red-crowned crane (see chapter 2). The choice of the crane and swan bones, although separated by thirty thousand years, might have been quite deliberate, as these birds are known for their intricate mating dances, replete with bows, leaps, wing extensions, and ringing musical notes. The cacophony of hoots and calls can last all night, like a drunken fraternity party.

The high, dramatic flight of these birds over the countryside, especially when large flocks of them moved through during their spring and fall migrations, would also have captured the imagination of early humans. I can remember excavating in Jordan when someone cried out, "Storks!" Their white bodies, accented by black wings, stood out against the blue sky and made us marvel at the world they must inhabit.

The Geissenklösterle flutes do not stand alone. Ten thousand years later, humans were blowing on nearly an orchestra of flutes or pipes at the cave of Isturitz in the foothills of the French Pyrenees. Twenty examples, made from vulture wing bones, have thus far been recovered from what is considered to be the greatest accumulation of art at any site in Ice Age Europe. Four holes had been drilled into each flute, with one pair of holes clearly separated from the other. Because the vulture mating ritual is not very vocal, it might have been the high, languorous, circling flight of a male and female, bonded for life, that impressed early humans.

ENTERING DREAMLAND

Soaring bird flight is a long way from the stupendous art in the prehistoric caves of France and northern Spain. Yet if the skies represented a world beyond the reach of early humans, the bowels of the Earth must have been equally mysterious. Using only the light from animal-fat lamps, the Stone Age artists scaled walls and reached into remote crevices to create a wonderland of black- and red-pigmented animals, mostly bison, lions, mammoths, and other large animals of the hunt, so realistically rendered that they seem to leap out of the stone.

I experienced some of the excitement and awe of this underground world when my wife and I were led by a French guide through the narrow, snaking passageways of Font de Gaume, close to Les Eysies. Stooping down to make our way along, we felt as if we were traveling back in time to the first attempts of humanity to understand the world. As the dim light of our guide's flashlight picked out incised and painted bison, deer, and wolves in the glowering night of the cave, we came away amazed at the skill of the artists in representing the animals of the lush Dordogne Valley.

The naturalistic scenes are accompanied by geometric and figurative motifs—dots, hoofprints, hatched circles and squares, chevrons, and swirling circles—in red ocher. In the cave of Cougnac are the remains of a pile of ocher, apparently used to outline hands by stenciling or to transfer the pigment directly by smearing hands with it and pressing them against the wall.

What was going on in these Ice Age grottoes? They can hardly have been ordinary dwellings, as more convenient, warmer shelters existed closer to the surface. A possible answer can be gleaned from the anthropomorphic faces and figures that occasionally appear in the caves. Heads of humans are shown with horned headdresses or flowing, animal-like manes.

Faces appear to erupt into laughter, and erect penises reach out into the night.

The most wondrous example of anthropomorphizing art was brought to light inside the cave of Les Trois Frères, in an expansive underground chamber called the Sanctuary, which dates from close to the end of the Ice Age, about 13,000 B.P. The Palaeolithic artist had to wriggle out onto a narrow ledge four meters above the floor of the cave to accomplish this masterpiece. The result was a stunning, strange composite of human and animal, nearly a meter tall. A bearded, owl-like face is surmounted by the multipronged antlers of a stag. With paws like those of a rabbit or feline stretched out in front and a horse's tail trailing behind, the figure appears to be stamping out some kind of dance, jumping from one foot to the other. While the lower part of the body is distinctly human, even the exposed genitalia, everything else about the figure boggles the mind. Placed at the highest point in the large artistic composition, the creature appears to oversee the profusion of life below, including stampeding wild animals and even a nocturnal owl, and to reassure us that all is well as "it" stares down at us.

The names used to describe the enigmatic figure in the Trois Frères grotto—Sorcerer, Horned God, and Animal Master—point to the most obvious interpretation. In the jungles of Amazonia, the deserts of southern Africa and Australia, and the frozen tundra of the north, humans have historically assembled into groups dominated by a central religious figure, the shaman or an equivalent. Western observers, with a modern scientific, desacralized perspective, tend to dismiss such individuals as charlatans, witch doctors, or medicine men. But at the dawning of the human race, they would have been the ones who first attempted to understand the forces of nature and the mind.

Even without any written or oral commentary to explain the activities carried out in the Stone Age grottoes, we can appreciate that those orchestrating the proceedings in the caves must have been the most sensitive artists, musicians, dreamers, and likely also the group's principal imbibers of fermented beverages. A woman like the Laussel Venus might have been responsible for making the magic potion that opened up the hidden resources of the human brain, healed disease, and assured a successful hunt. In traditional societies today, women generally take the lead in gathering the fruit, honey, and herbs for alcoholic drinks used to mark burials, deaths, rites of passage, auspicious natural events, and social gatherings; in the Palaeolithic period, perhaps such rituals marked the completion of another cave painting.

Figure 2. The "Sorcerer," the "Horned God," or the "Animal Master" in the so-called Sanctuary of Les Trois Frères grotto in the French Pyrenees, created near the end of the Ice Age, about thirteen thousand years ago. However we describe such shaman-like figures, they were likely the original artistic innovators of humankind, who probably served up the first fermented beverages to their societies. Adapted from drawing by Henri Breuil.

Other elements of a Stone Age ritual can be cautiously inferred from the artworks and their settings in dark caves. The early French explorers of the caves remarked on their extraordinary acoustic properties, especially the resounding echoes produced when they struck the stalagmites and stalactites with bones. A large group of people (their presence recorded for posterity by fingerprints on the walls) could have produced a symphony of sounds. The Sorcerer, wearing a bird-stag mask, might then have tramped out the rhythms of the music, whether choreographed or impromptu. She might dramatize the goings-on by holding up a special symbol, like the bird silhouette shown mounted on a pole next to what may be a bird-headed shaman on the wall of the cave at Lascaux.

Bones might also have been pounded together as musical accompaniment for Palaeolithic ritual. At Mezin on the western plains of Ukraine, a house was discovered that was made entirely of mammoth bones, dated to 20,000 B.P. The excavators argued that the ocher-adorned shoulders, skulls, and other bones of the mammoths that were massed together on the floor of the building, along with two ivory rattles, were percussion instruments. They put their theory into practice by forming a band, the Stone Age Orchestra, whose performance was well received but unlikely to have been as impressive as the music made by hammering sounds out on an "organ" of limestone formations inside a cave.

The red dots, swirling circles, and other designs interspersed with the wild-animal artwork in the caves have also been drawn into the argument for a Palaeolithic shamanistic cult. According to investigators such as David Lewis-Williams, the recurrent motifs represent entoptic phenomena, or optical illusions, of an altered human consciousness. The geometrical interplay of such visual images in our brains can be generated by sensory deprivation, extreme concentration, or repetitive activities like playing music and dancing. But the most direct route to an altered consciousness is a psychoactive drug, and of all the drugs available to early humans, alcohol was far and away the most readily available and best adapted to the human condition. Following its initial stimulatory effects, imbibers would have begun to see visual phenomena and struggled to understand their meaning, possibly culminating in full-scale hallucinations.

One might question the proposition that early humans found these mind-altering properties a compelling reason to consume alcohol. Yet, all of us, not only mystics, engender visual phenomena and hallucinatory experiences every night in our dreams, and nearly a third of our lives is spent in sleep. We can choose to ignore our dreams or pass them off as the detritus of our waking existence. On occasion, however, they rise up and shake us from sleep in terror. They can inspire us, too, and lead to serendipitous juxtapositions of images and ideas that elucidate the world's mysteries. For example, the chemist Friedrich August von Kekulé discovered the ring structure of benzene in a dream: he saw writhing snakes, one of which was biting its own tail and formed a ring. He went to sleep not knowing the answer and woke up with the solution.

The phantasmagoria of our dreams can be extremely fluid and evocative: we might imagine an animal transformed into a human, see ourselves from the outside as if acting in a play, or experience the sensations of flying or falling into an abyss. The Stone Age murals in their dark caverns thus have strong similarities to dream images that well up in our three-dimensional and often vividly colored fantasies in the dark of night. The deep silence of the grotto, intensified by the effects of an alcoholic beverage, might have nourished the imaginations of sensitive individuals, who then represented their inner and outer worlds in two-dimensional art. The shaman and the community could then act out the essential rituals that would guarantee their welfare in this life and the one to come.

The Palaeolithic cave paintings, like so many Sistine Chapels, must have been a monumental task in their day, especially when one considers that they were accomplished with extremely limited technology in pitch-black, nearly inaccessible locations. The motivations for devoting so much time and energy to otherworldly activities were probably similar to those of today. The needs of *Homo sapiens* include social rituals that bring the community together, artwork that symbolizes the workings of the mind and nature, and religious rituals that give human experience meaning and coherence. A fermented beverage or drug can enhance these experiences and stimulate innovative thought. To the people of the Palaeolithic, ceremonial observances, heightened by an alcoholic beverage and other techniques for achieving an altered consciousness, might have been viewed as assuring good health, placating the spirits of invisible ancestors and other spirits, warning of danger, and predicting the future.

SONG AND DANCE

We do not know when humans first became preoccupied with the universal concerns of "wine, women, and song"—to which I would add religion, language, dance, and art. There are faint glimmerings of a new kind of symbolic consciousness at around 100,000 B.P. in sub-Saharan Africa, about the same time that our species began its journeys around the globe. At Border Cave and Klasies River Mouth Cave in South Africa, powdered ocher and a perforated shell, presumably strung as a piece of jewelry, suggest that humans were now interested in making themselves attractive, whether to entice a mate, satisfy vanity, or invoke the help of ancestors or gods. One adolescent skeleton at Border Cave was covered in the pigment, a custom that our ancestors likely carried with them to Mount Carmel in Israel (at the caves of Skhul and Qafzeh) and throughout the Old World. Monkeys and apes may groom one another, but they are not known to engage in intentional beautification. If early humans could adopt the practice of personal adornment, then perhaps they were already using arbitrary sounds and gestures to communicate with one another. Certainly, by the time of the European cave paintings, the quantum leap in cognitive and symbolic ability of our species is on full display.

Early human inventiveness is further reflected in the stone-lined hearths that were used to contain and control fire at Mumbwa Cave in Zambia around 100,000 B.P. This knowledge stood our ancestors in good stead when they spread into the colder regions of the Earth. Intricate bone harpoons from Katanda in the Congo, and carefully wrought microliths—small, sharp flints for specialized use—at Klasies River Mouth Cave were fashioned at a somewhat later period.

Archaeology cannot, however, tell us how the brain was changing and adapting as humans entered new, challenging environments. Endocasts, or plaster casts of the inside of ancient hominid and human skulls, suggest that the human cortex was already distinctly modern by 100,000 B.P. Some researchers have discerned evidence of a region referred to in the modern human brain as Broca's area, the third convolution or gyrus of the inferior frontal lobe on the left side, which is essential for speech and some aspects of music making.

The acquisition of language processing and speech capabilities required a set of interdependent genetic, biological, and social changes. The upright posture on two legs led to the human larynx's being positioned lower in the throat, so that a wider range of sounds could be produced. The tongue acquired a larger supply of nerves, as shown by the larger size of the hypoglossal canal in fossil crania. The canals for the thoracic nerves, controlling the contraction of the diaphragm, were also noticeably enlarged, allowing better control of air flow and sound. New modules in the brain, like Broca's and Wernicke's areas, may have been integrated into or added on to existing brain centers, leading to the development of emotional responsiveness and consciousness. Broca's area, for instance, contains what are called mirror neurons, which, as the phrase implies, may record any action that we observe, and then call it up again, like a photograph, to imitate it. This facility could have been essential in coordinating the facial and tongue movements necessary for speech. The final step that might have tipped the scales toward language in humans could have been a minor change in the so-called FOXP2 gene. A mutation in this gene, which occurs widely in the animal world, resulted in the fine motor control of the tongue and lips that is essential for speech.

Language gave us the ability to articulate our ideas. Many of our thoughts are believed to lie below the level of consciousness, as "logical forms," in the terminology popularized by Noam Chomsky. By bringing these thoughts to the surface—by representing them in a sequence of arbitrary sounds that have been given meaning as words—they are secured in memory and consciousness.

Music, which shares many brain areas with language comprehension and production, might have been the harbinger of language. Like language, music is hierarchical, highly symbolic, and well adapted to our body forms. By changing the intonation, speed, and emphasis of specific sounds, we can communicate emotions. By tapping our feet or joining in a line dance, we can stir our bodies to action and share a sense of community with fellow humans. It's readily apparent today that music is much more than "auditory cheesecake," as the evolutionary biologist Stephen Pinker would have it. From the iPod earplugs sprouting from the heads of commuters to the constant banter about the latest rock star, music is ubiquitous in modern human culture. You might even say that sex, drugs, and rock-and-roll never had it so good.

If we think about how music affects us personally, we begin to see how central it is to our lives and how it might have become part of the cultural package of our forebears. By combining and ordering individual sounds along an arbitrarily defined tonal scale, early humans might have created the first kind of universal language. Although the significance of rhythmic tones is less precise than that of a language using words, it is in some ways more accessible: music made in one culture can be at least partly understood and appreciated by a person in another culture. As we listen to music, we are consciously and unconsciously trying to intuit its emotional significance, including where it is headed and what it means. As when we are trying to figure out where our lives are going or to predict the future, music arouses emotional centers of our primitive brain, the limbic system.

Emotion is as crucial to our survival as rational thought. Being happy, sad, afraid, incensed, or nauseated by some food or beverage, person, or circumstance spurs us to different courses of action, often without thinking. Excitement breeds perseverance—we must be on the right track!—but disappointment or frustration signals that we might be headed in the wrong direction and need to modify our approach or stop altogether. *Star Trek*'s Mr. Spock might have tried to ponder a problem from every angle, but a Palaeolithic hunter or modern homeowner must act more quickly. When a twig cracks in the savannah underbrush, or we hear footsteps close behind us on a dark, deserted street, our emotions mobilize our brains and bodies to evade a perceived danger. It could be a meaningless noise, but by comparing its sound and timbre to others in our memories, we might infer that a lion is ready to leap or a mugger is closing in.

Apes and chimpanzees, the species most similar to us biologically, are also attuned to music. Gibbons in Southeast Asian rain forests put on a musical show of the first order. In ten of the twelve species, a male and female gibbon pair, who mate for life, engage in a duet that seems intended both to defend their territory and to announce their union. The female's "great call," an intricate, rhythmic series of notes, can last between six and eight minutes. It ascends in tempo and pitch as it proceeds. Males do not sing during this monumental performance but follow the female's performance with a kind of recitative or coda. Males also have their own repertoires of shorter songs that round out the program.

We can hypothesize at length about the survival advantages of early human emotions, music, and symbolic systems. Of all the animals that we regularly observe, birds perhaps have the most to tell us about the origins and functions of music. As I woke up this morning, in a dense deciduous forest outside Philadelphia, I listened to the lilt and typewriterlike call of the wood thrushes, recently arrived from Central America. Another neotropical migrant, the black-throated blue warbler, gave out its piercing, ascending trill. The resident tufted titmice, not to be outdone, called insistently and monotonously, "Peter, Peter, Peter." Despite the din, each bird was somehow communicating with others of its own species by using its own kind of music.

My wife, Doris, who is a bird bander, once worked on a project recording the calls of individual prothonotary warblers in the wetlands of southern New Jersey. In this species, only the males sing during the breeding season. The goal was to see whether individual birds had unique songs. Recording the songs and analyzing their frequencies and timing showed that they do, even if the human ear is oblivious to many of the subtle variations. The young birds apparently take elements from the songs of their elders and improvise a distinctive vocabulary of notes and phrases that then becomes fixed for life. Having recorded the songs, my wife did not even have to use her binoculars to confirm that the same birds returned year after year to the same spot in New Jersey. It was a great delight one morning in April, after months of cold weather, to hear the highly distinctive double call of one bird (called Yellow-Yellow because he was banded with two yellow bands).

We cannot know what emotions birds are feeling as they sing. There is little doubt, however, that the main purpose of many of their songs is to attract a mate. When a female hears Yellow-Yellow calling, she can be sure that it is a male of her species. His special call and the brilliance of his yellow plumage are guarantees that he is carrying good genes and can compete with any rival in the neighborhood. The peacock's tail transmits a similar message: in what has been called runaway evolution, a seemingly excessive and burdensome excrescence has become the focus of the mating ritual and is elaborated into an ever more ornate appendage.

Nature is full of other amazing mating rituals based on timed body movements, or what we often call dance. The sexual foreplay of the silverwashed fritillary butterfly might be described as a ballet. While the female fritillary floats languorously through the air, her partner darts seductively all around her, making fleeting contact at specific points in the ritual. The two then land together, make a final check of their specific scents (pheromones), and mate. Seven distinct aerial maneuvers are required for a successful coupling.

A NEW SYNTHESIS

If the emotions and thoughts of early humans in sub-Saharan Africa were likely first conveyed by music and other art forms, then alcoholic beverages can be viewed as nourishing this new symbolic way of life. Indeed, these widely available beverages might well have served as a principal means— another kind of universal language—for accessing the subconscious recesses of the human brain. I have already observed that musical instruments were probably tools of the trade for shamanic figures. These early mystics might also have been the most avid imbibers of fermented beverages, which induced mind-altering visions and enabled them to perform their many other roles. They would have been the doctors who could prescribe the right herb for an ailment, the priests who invoked the ancestors and other unseen presences, and the overseers of the rituals that guaranteed the success and perpetuation of the community. Their Stone Age ceremonies might have been overtly sexual: the humans depicted in cave art, after our species came out of Africa, are invariably naked or have exaggeratedly large sexual organs (note that the human penis, when engorged, is longer and thicker than that of any other primate, both absolutely and relatively when compared by body size).

Perhaps most significant, the Palaeolithic shaman's mantle of office and power had to be passed on to a successor. Because musical and linguistic facility, and even sexual prowess and mystical capacities, often runs in families, the position of the shaman in Palaeolithic society might have been an inherited one. Conscious selection for special traits of musical and artistic ability, mystical absorption, and a capacity for alcoholic beverages would then have been reinforced over time and embedded in our genes.

This book proposes a new framework for interpreting our biocultural past, based on the latest archaeological and scientific findings. As will become increasingly clear in the following chapters as we travel around the world in search of fermented beverages, economic, utilitarian and environmental arguments, which are much in vogue, can only go so far in explaining who we are and how our species has arrived at where it is today. I contend instead that the driving forces in human development from the Palaeolithic period to the present have been the uniquely human traits of self-consciousness, innovation, the arts and religion, all of which can be heightened and encouraged by the consumption of an alcoholic beverage, with its profound effects on the human brain.

TWO

ALONG THE BANKS
OF THE YELLOW RIVER

I NEVER EXPECTED THAT MY search for the origins of fermented alcoholic beverages would take me to China. After all, I had spent more than twenty years directing an excavation in Jordan and working throughout the Middle East. I took the first step on my journey to China when, serendipitously, I attended a session on ancient pottery at the annual meeting of the American Anthropological Association in 1995. There I met Anne Underhill, an archaeologist at the Field Museum in Chicago, who had recently started one of the first American expeditions on the Chinese mainland, after the dry spell of the Cultural Revolution and its aftermath. She was convinced that fermented beverages were an integral part of the earliest Chinese culture, as discoveries by my laboratory had shown for the Near East. In traditional and modern societies around the world today, alcoholic beverages are important in most adults' lives, whether as a reward for a hard day's work or as part of a celebration. Anne believed that as scientific excavation expanded in China, we would learn just how important fermented beverages were to ancient social relations, religious ceremonies, feasts, and festivals there. She proposed that I join her team at the late Neolithic site of Liangchengzhen in Shandong Province and chemically analyze some of the vessels they might uncover.

The opportunity to work in China sounded too good to pass up, even if I knew virtually nothing about ancient Chinese civilization and couldn't read a Chinese character to save myself. I prepared to join Anne's team during the 1999 season. I also began considering other Chinese sites that might shed light on the history and prehistory of fermented beverages.

A colleague at Brookhaven National Laboratory, Garman Harbottle, put me in touch with Changsui Wang, professor of archaeometry at China's prestigious University of Science and Technology. Changsui soon arranged for me to visit leading archaeologists and scientists in Beijing and at sites in the Yellow River basin, where Chinese culture had blossomed. He even accompanied me on overnight train trips, serving as my interpreter and boon companion and introducing me to modern Chinese life and customs—especially its cuisine and alcoholic beverages.

Banquets were a daily occurrence, and it was my formidable task as the guest of honor to take the first bite of the barbecued or baked fish with my chopsticks. If I successfully secured a piece and steered it into my mouth, I was roundly applauded. I soon discovered that toasts with fermented beverages were also an absolute must at these meals, a tradition with roots in the distant past. We raised our glasses repeatedly to good health and the success of our research. To avoid succumbing to the potent distilled beverages, made from sorghum or millet, I usually requested the milder, aromatic rice wine. After all, I was there to study a period before distillation had been discovered.

Six weeks of nonstop travel and banqueting led to tight bonds of collegiality that paved the way for getting archaeological samples approved for loan, through customs, and back to my laboratory at the University of Pennsylvania Museum of Archaeology and Anthropology in Philadelphia. Accomplishing this sort of task in China requires friends in the right places. It also helped to have colleagues who were as enthusiastic as I was in finding out more about ancient Chinese beverages by applying the latest analytical techniques.

Changsui and I eventually made our way to the metropolis of Zhengzhou, strategically situated along the Yellow River (Huang He), among verdant fields. We met Juzhong Zhang at the downtown branch of the Institute of Archaeology, which housed pottery and other artifacts from his excavations at the Neolithic site of Jiahu, located about 250 kilometers southeast of Zhengzhou.

At one time, plant and animal domestication were thought of as having begun in the Near East during the Neolithic period and then spread to the rest of the world. These advances started humankind on the path to "civilization," because food could be provided by a smaller number of people while others were free to pursue other specialized tasks. To be sure, some of the so-called founder plants, including wheat and barley, were brought into cultivation in the Near East, and herd animals, such as sheep and cattle, were first domesticated there.

Turning established wisdom on its head, China's "Neolithic Revolution" has now been shown to precede many of the advances in the Near East. If you think about it, humans probably could not have controlled sheep and goats without dogs, and recent DNA evidence points to East Asia as the place where man's best friend was domesticated, as far back as 14,000 B.P., during the last Ice Age. Domesticated horses, pigs, and chickens probably also trace their ancestry to this part of the world.

Most important for my purposes, the Chinese began making pottery around 15,000 B.P., some five thousand years before this innovation took hold in the Near East. Pottery not only made it possible to prepare, store, and serve fermented beverages, but it also absorbed them into its pores and helped preserve them for analysis. The plasticity of clay enabled the fashioning of a whole range of pottery shapes, which helped in preparing foods to go with the beverages and ultimately in establishing one of the world's great cuisines. One delicacy on the Neolithic menu was long, thin pulled noodles. Excavated at the site of Lajia on the upper Yellow River and dated to around 2000 B.C., the well-preserved yellowish noodles, made from foxtail and broomcorn millet (*Setaria* and *Panicum* spp.), had been piled high in a bowl, just the way the Chinese consume them today.

As Juzhong brought Neolithic pottery vessels down from the shelves for me to examine, I was amazed at their elegant, intricately crafted forms. The jars (see plate 3) had high necks with flaring rims and either smoothly rounded bodies or pronounced, sharply angled shoulders. They would have been ideal for storing or serving fermented beverages. Their handles, made by attaching separate pieces of clay, were as varied as any group of Middle Eastern pottery I had seen and were symmetrically placed to enhance their aesthetic appearance as well as to facilitate transporting, storing, and drinking from the vessels.

The vessels were undoubtedly handmade, constructed by joining and building up coils and slabs of clay. Fine markings along the rims pointed to a final finishing by slow turning, perhaps on a mat. Some jars were covered with a red slip (a thinly applied fine clay fraction), which had been polished to a high sheen. The yellowish and reddish wares were tempered with mineral inclusions, and were well-fired, probably up to around 800°C. The Neolithic jars at Jiahu attested to a high level of technological sophistication and a repertoire of forms that set the pattern in Chinese pottery making for thousands of years to come. Local innovations likely accounted for the manufacturing excellence, as evidenced by eleven pottery kilns thus far excavated at the site.

When I peered into some of the vessels, I had another surprise. Flakes of a reddish residue covered the bases of the jars and continued up the sides, just as one would expect if they had once held a liquid. A dark material filled the extensive, highly unusual grooving on the interior of another vessel, much like that seen in a jar from Iran that provided the earliest chemical attestation for barley beer in the Middle East (see chapter 3). I was entranced by the prospects of analyzing the Jiahu jars.

THE WONDERS THAT WERE JIAHU

Jiahu, in Henan Province of north-central China, is not your ordinary early Neolithic site, which might feature a few scattered hovels, graves, and associated artifacts. At this site in the fertile plains of the Huai River, which merge with the Yellow River basin to the north, three phases of a full-fledged village and adjoining cemetery have so far been uncovered, spanning the period from about 7000 to 5600 B.C.

Not only have the excavations at Jiahu yielded some of the earliest pottery in China, but they have also found some of the country's oldest rice. Surprisingly, it is the short-grain variety (*Oryza sativa* ssp. *japonica*), which was long believed to have been derived from its more tropical long-grain cousin (ssp. *indica*) at sites farther south along the Yangzi River. Recent excavation and archaeobotanical analyses have shown, however, that the subspecies are approximately contemporaneous. We do not yet know in which direction the genetic influence flowed, or even whether the Neolithic rice was domesticated or wild. At Jiahu, the large quantity of rice found implies that it had already been brought into cultivation there. Moreover, to judge from the animal bones recovered at Jiahu, the inhabitants would have had to take precautions to protect their rice stores from domesticated dogs and pigs, who were romping through the streets and splashing in the mud holes.

Figure 3. Early Neolithic "musician/shaman" burial (M282) at Jiahu (Henan Province, China), ca. 6200–5600 B.C., showing flutes at his side (indicated by arrows in this photograph), one of which was carefully repaired in antiquity. Two tortoise shells full of pebbles and pottery jars, which likely contained a mixed fermented beverage, were placed near his head. Photograph courtesy J. Zhang, Z. Zhang, and Henan Institute of Cultural Relics and Archaeology.

The Jiahu inhabitants apparently lived well on the abundant resources of their environment, which also included carp, deer, broad beans, and water chestnuts. They also had a penchant for the symbolic and otherworldly. The site has produced what may be the earliest Chinese written characters ever found: an eye sign, a sticklike figure holding a fork-shaped object, and other designs similar to later glyphs for *window* and the numerals one, two, eight, and ten.

The Jiahu signs were incised on tortoise shells and bones, anticipating a religious practice of some six millennia later at the great Shang dynasty capital of Anyang and associated principalities along the Yellow River. Dating from ca. 1200 to 1050 B.C., the Shang dynasty "oracle bones" and shells, of which more than one hundred thousand have now been found, were used by religious mediums in rituals to predict and assure a good future for the emperor and the royal house. Drilling and heating the cattle bone or shell created a web of cracks that were interpreted by the diviner. The prognostication, along with the name of the medium, was then recorded on the bone or shell for posterity.

It is not known what meaning was attached to the shell and bone signs at Jiahu. From a close examination of the graves where they were found, together with accompanying burial goods, we can infer that they are almost certainly related to ritualistic procedures or religious concepts. The inscribed objects are found only in a handful of male graves, out of nearly four hundred burials that have so far been excavated in the cemetery. In several of these burials, the head of the deceased was carefully removed—whether before or after the flesh had decayed is not known—and replaced by six or eight pairs of whole tortoise shells. The jade "death masks" worn by the upper class during the Zhou and Han dynasties of the first millennium B.C. are a distant echo of this tradition.

In other burials, the tortoise shells are placed alongside the body or near the shoulder, as if they had once been attached to clothing or held in the hand. Many of these shells, including those substituting for the head, contained small, round white and black pebbles, as few as three per shell or stuffed in by the hundreds. The number of stones in each shell might have had some numerological significance. Another possibility is that the shells with their pebbles had been used as rattles by their owners and were subsequently buried with them.

A good reason for thinking that the shells might originally have been percussion instruments is that some of them were accompanied by what have been called the earliest playable musical instruments in the world. In 1986, Juzhong could hardly believe his eyes when his excavation team found a pair of bone flutes in tomb M282. Each had seven holes carefully drilled at precise intervals in a straight line down the shaft of the bone. They looked exactly like the bamboo flutes still used throughout China to play traditional music, based on a five-note (pentatonic) scale. Nothing like these ancient instruments had ever before been found in a Chinese excavation.

As each tomb was excavated, additional flutes were found. To date, two dozen complete specimens have been recovered, along with the fragments of another nine. Such exquisite preservation supports the claim that these flutes are the oldest known playable instruments, as the Palaeolithic flutes from Geissenklösterle and Isturitz are too fragmented to produce reliable

Figure 4. Juzhong Zhang, excavator of Jiahu, playing the early Neolithic flute of the "musician/shaman" from burial M282 at the site. Photograph courtesy J. Zhang, Z. Zhang, and Henan Institute of Cultural Relics and Archaeology.

tones today. The Chinese archaeologists put out a call for an accomplished musician to test the Jiahu flutes. Ning Baosheng, flautist for Beijing's Central Orchestra of Chinese Music, happily volunteered his services. By using a standard side-mouth embouchure and blowing through one end of the artifact, like playing a recorder, Ning immediately produced a deep, sonorous tone that had not been heard for nine thousand years.

The archaeologists and musicians went on to use modern digital recording techniques and computer processing to study a range of flutes from the three archaeological phases. Because no one knows for sure how the instruments were played, and to facilitate matters, simple fingering was used, in which all the holes were closed off simultaneously. That yielded a very precise musical frequency. Then, each hole was uncovered in turn, leaving all the rest covered, and the resulting frequencies recorded. Of course, an expert can produce many more sounds by cross-fingering, varying his or her embouchure, and so forth.

Multiholed instruments became increasingly popular over the 1,200-year span of the site, and they enabled the production of increasingly complex music. Even the earliest example, a five-hole flute, could produce four tones nearly identical to those in our Western twelve-tone scale. The addition of another hole made it possible for even a beginner to play a pentatonic scale. With seven or eight holes, the possibilities for adding and modifying tones increased, until all the tones of a standard eight-tone major scale could be played by simple fingering.

The flutes were obviously highly valued in their day. They were very carefully made by smoothing off the ends and surface and laying out guidelines (also seen on the Geissenklösterle and Isturitz flutes) for drilling the holes. When a flute broke, it was carefully repaired, as a valued Stradivarius violin would be today. In one instance, fourteen tiny holes had been drilled to either side of the break and tied off with string. Most of the flutes were found in pairs, one perhaps having served the owner as a backup instrument.

Amazingly, all the flutes were made exclusively from a specific wing bone, the ulna, of the red-crowned crane (*Grus japonensis*). From a practical standpoint, a hollow bird bone seems an obvious material for a flute, but perhaps this particular crane's behavior also inspired the makers. Adorned with snow-white plumage accented in black and red, this crane performs an intricate mating dance, in which a pair of birds bow to one another, leap in the air, extend their wings, and announce their intentions with intense musical calls. The invention might also have been prompted by hearing the sound made when the marrow is extracted from the bone by sucking, and then blowing back into the cavity.

While it would be fascinating to hear the folk melodies of ancient Jiahu again, possibly evoking the sounds of the red-crowned cranes, the absence of detailed Neolithic writings makes this possibility extremely unlikely. We can, however, be sure that the individuals buried with flutes and rattles played a special role in their community. Their bodies, unlike those of others, were elaborately adorned with imported turquoise and jade jewelry. Yet millstones, awls, and other utilitarian tools also found in their tombs suggest

Figure 5. Red-crowned cranes (*Grus japonensis*) perform their mating dance on the frozen plains of Manchuria. The two dozen flutes from the early Neolithic site of Jiahu were exclusively made from one of the wing bones (the ulna) of this bird. Photograph © by James G. Parker.

that they were not averse to common labor. The mystery deepens when we consider the strange, fork-shaped bone objects among their burial goods. These have multiple perforations; we can surmise that they might have been strung like a harp, or perhaps they symbolized the "new agriculture" or were a kind of tool of the individuals' profession (a point I return to below).

THE WORLD'S EARLIEST ALCOHOLIC BEVERAGE

To end this tale of early Neolithic Jiahu by focusing only on its rice, writing, and music would be to ignore the role that a particular alcoholic beverage played in the developments there.

When Changsui Wang first introduced me to Juzhong Zhang, he put me on the royal road to discovering this beverage and its importance to Neolithic Jiahu society. Juzhong shared his knowledge and his pottery finds, from which we selected sixteen sherds for chemical analysis. They represented a range of jars and jugs that seemed likely to have contained liquids. One large, two-handled jar especially intrigued me; had it been found five thousand years later in the Near East, it could easily have been mistaken for a Canaanite jar, which served as a model for Greek and Roman amphoras used in the vast Mediterranean wine trade (see chapter 6).

The analyses of such important samples could not be undertaken lightly, so I engaged a group of collaborators in China (including the Beijing-based microbiologist Guangsheng Cheng and archaeobotanist Zhijun "Jimmy" Zhao), Europe (Michael Richards, now in Leipzig), and the United States (Robert Moreau and Alberto Nuñez of the Department of Agriculture, and Eric Butrym, now at Firmenich, Inc.). Using a variety of techniques, including liquid chromatography–mass spectrometry (LC-MS), carbon and nitrogen isotope analysis, and infrared spectrometry, we identified the chemical fingerprints of the principal ingredients in the ancient Jiahu beverage. Slowly but surely, we were homing in on what would turn out to be the world's earliest known alcoholic beverage.

In the residues, which were obtained by extracting the pottery with methanol and chloroform, the same chemical compounds kept showing up in one vessel after another. The detection of tartaric acid told us that the likely sources were grapes or hawthorn fruit (*Crataegus pinnatifida* and *cuneata,* or, in Chinese, *shan zha*). Very definitive, so-called fingerprint compounds of beeswax, which is well preserved and almost impossible to completely filter out during processing, revealed the presence of honey. Finally, close chemical matches with other compounds, including specific phytosterols, pointed to rice as the third main ingredient. Analysis of carbon isotopes confirmed that the grain used must have come from a temperate-climate (C_3) plant like rice, not a more tropical (C_4) source like millet or sorghum, which have different mechanisms of photosynthesis and metabolism.

With the help of my colleagues in the Penn Museum laboratory, Gretchen Hall and a native Chinese speaker, Chen-shan ("Ellen") Wang, we then began the arduous task of searching the scientific literature, much of it in Chinese, to identify natural ingredients that would be consistent with our results. Other colleagues at the Museum, Atsuko Hattori and Fumi Karahashi, helped by reading Japanese texts.

If our ancient samples had come from the Middle East, the presence of tartaric acid or tartrate would have definitively signaled a grape product such as wine, because in this region this acid or its salt is found only in grapes. In China, however, tartaric acid occurs in several other fruits—not only hawthorn but also Asiatic cornelian cherry (*Cornus officialis,* or *shan chu yu*) and longyan (*Euphoria longyan, long yan*)—which thus might have been ingredients.

Smaller amounts of tartaric acid can also be derived from other plant sources native to the region, such as the leaves of *Pelargonium* or other flowers in the geranium family. Mold saccharification, the process by which fungi break down rice starches into sugar prior to making Chinese rice wine or Japanese sake (see below), also produces about 0.1–2.0 milligrams of tartaric acid per liter. That, however, is too dilute a concentration to explain the consistently high tartaric acid levels in the ancient samples, and we also know that this method of beverage making probably developed very late in China, perhaps only in the Han dynasty (ca. 202 B.C.–A.D. 220). Only the presence of hawthorn fruit or grape came close to explaining our experimental results.

If we accept that these narrow, splayed-mouth jugs and jars most likely contained liquids, then it is easy to make the case that the vessels contained a mixed fermented beverage. Some wild grapes in China, including *Vitis amurensis* and *V. quinquangularis,* contain up to 19 percent simple sugar by weight, and such high-sugar fruits harbor the yeast (*Saccharomyces cerevisiae*) needed to initiate fermentation. The same species of yeast also lives in honey and becomes active once the thick mass is diluted to about 30 percent sugar and 70 percent water. If the jars contained fruit juices and diluted honey, the mixture would have fermented naturally at moderately high temperatures within days. We may not be able to detect traces of ethanol now, because it is volatile and susceptible to microbial attack, but we can be assured that the end product was originally alcoholic.

A wonderful stroke of scientific corroboration for our chemical results came after we announced that the most likely fruits in the beverage were grape or hawthorn fruit. An archaeobotanical study by Jimmy Zhao identified seeds of those very two fruits and no others at the site. I suspect that both were added to the Jiahu beverage to add flavor and encourage fermentation.

Like grape and hawthorn fruit, the rice in the ancient beverage could have been wild or domesticated. The starches in rice had to be broken down into simple sugars before they could be digested by the yeast living in the fruit or honey. But how was the rice starch converted into sugar at this early date? One possibility is that it was sprouted and malted like barley. Diastase, an enzyme that breaks down the larger carbohydrate molecules of the grains into simple sugars, are released in this process. Another, even more likely possibility is that the rice grains were chewed, so that a related enzyme—ptyalin—in human saliva went to work on converting the starch. In remote areas of Japan and Taiwan, you can still find women sitting around a large bowl, masticating and spitting rice juice into the vessel as they prepare the rice wine for a marriage ceremony. In fact, this method of making an alcoholic beverage from a grain spans the globe, from the corn beers or *chicha*s of the Americas to the sorghum and millet beers of Africa (see chapters 7 and 8).

Whichever process was used, lots of yeast, rice husks, and other matter would have been left floating on the surface of the beverage. Because filtering the debris from a large vessel is cumbersome, the best way around this problem is to submerge a tube beneath the surface and suck up the liquid. Using a straw was a common way to drink a cereal beer in ancient Mesopotamia and most other parts of the ancient world. Today, it is still the way you drink your brew in isolated villages of south China (see plate 4) and among peoples living deep in the jungle of Cambodia at Angkor Wat.

The conclusion of our extensive analyses was that the beverage makers at Jiahu were skilled enough to make a complex beverage consisting of a grape and hawthorn-fruit wine, honey mead, and rice beer. (Throughout the book, I use the term *wine* to refer a relatively potent alcoholic beverage—say 9 to 10 percent alcohol—and usually made from fruit, as distinct from a beer, with an alcohol level of 4 to 5 percent and whose principal component is a grain, such as rice.) You could call this mixed beverage a Chinese extreme beverage or Neolithic grog, which combines several exotic ingredients. Technically, *grog* describes a concoction of rum, water, sugar, and spice that became popular in the British navy beginning in the seventeenth century. The term has taken on a more general meaning, and is especially appropriate for the many mixed fermented beverages consumed in the ancient world.

The greatest surprise from our analyses was the probable inclusion of grape as an ingredient in the Jiahu beverage, representing its earliest use for this purpose anywhere in the world. We might have expected this finding, as upward of fifty species of grape—more than half of the wild species in the world—are found in China. The historical records, however, suggest that the Chinese began to grow and exploit the fruit only much later, when General Zhang Qian traveled to Central Asia as an emissary of the emperor in the late second century B.C. and brought back the domesticated Eurasian grape (*Vitis vinifera* ssp. *vinifera*) to make wine in the capital city of Chang'an, today Xi'an. As far as we know—although further exploration may uncover new evidence—none of the many grape species found in China was ever domesticated.

THE SPIRITS OF THE ANCESTORS

What might at first seem to be unrelated pieces of an archaeological puzzle in the elite musician burials at Jiahu—the flutes and rattles, the fork-shaped objects, the earliest written characters on tortoise shells, the Chinese Neolithic grog—begin to fall into place when we view them as the first glimmerings of a shamanistic cult adapted to the new circumstances of the Chinese Neolithic Revolution. With a more secure economy, the office of "shaman" could have become a full-time profession. For example, music making requires well-developed motor skills, especially hand-eye coordination. By devising more and better musical instruments—the rattles, flutes with impressive tonal ranges, and drums stretched tight with alligator skin—and improving their dexterity, the ritual specialists or shamans of the community could more effectively communicate with the other world, assuring a better life for the villagers, protection from evil forces, and cures for diseases.

Later texts, including the *Book of Records* (*Li ji*) and *Book of Conduct* (*Yi li*), which incorporate rituals and religious ideas going back to the early Western Zhou dynasty around the eighth century B.C., provide clues about what rituals might have been carried out at Jiahu. When a member of the community died, libations of wine and special foods—including steamed millet and roasted mutton—were offered as sacrifices to the clan ancestors and gods. The ceremony was highly formalized, with certain animals killed at specific times and places, and accompanied by music and dance.

The day of the funeral was determined by divination. Then, on the fourth day of a seven-day fast, stalks were cast as lots to select the *shi* ("descendant"), usually a grandson or daughter-in-law of the deceased, who would communicate with the ancestors and perform the burial rites. On this day, the spirit of the deceased was invited, in the person of the *shi,* to "take some refreshment," presumably a drink of a fermented beverage. By consuming the beverage, the *shi* was identified with the deceased and dead ancestors in general.

Physically weakened by fasting for seven days and mentally exhausted, the *shi* was urged to visualize the deceased in as much detail as possible, including his facial expressions, the things he enjoyed most in life, and his voice. At this stage in the ceremony, the *shi* and other participants might well have begun to experience altered states of consciousness and hallucinations.

The coup de grâce came on the seventh day of the fast, when the deceased was buried and the sacrificial meal presented in the temple. The *shi,* who orchestrated the ritual, ate and drank both for himself and for the ancestor world. The *shi* had to drink nine cups of millet or rice wine, served hot in a ceremonial vessel of the *gu* or *zhi* type. These tall goblets, up to thirty centimeters tall, can hold as much as two hundred milliliters. If we assume that the millet or rice wine of the period contained about 10 percent alcohol (see below), the quantity of wine consumed by the *shi* would have amounted to downing more than two bottles of modern grape wine or putting back eight shots of 80-proof whiskey. After the period of fasting, the brain of the *shi* must have been swimming with visions.

Shi ode 209 of the eighth century B.C. captures the mood of the proceedings:

> The rituals are completed;
> The bells and drums have sounded
> The pious descendant [*shi*] goes to his place,
> the officiating invoker makes his announcement:
> "The spirits are all drunk";
> the august representative of the dead then rises,
> the drums and bells escort away the representative
> The divine protectors [the spirits] then return [leave the temple].
> *(Karlgren 1950)*

We can imagine the Neolithic bone flutes and rattles in the tombs of the elite musicians at Jiahu serving a similar purpose to that of the bells and drums of five thousand years later. A mixed fermented beverage made of rice, grapes, hawthorn fruit, and honey would have been used rather than the millet or rice wine. The Jiahu vessels were different in shape but could have held just as much as a Zhou goblet. All the prerequisites of the later ceremony were present in embryonic form at Jiahu.

The roles of the early shamans at Jiahu probably later became separate, specialized functions, such as professional healer, medium, and musician. The Jiahu musicians were probably much more like our concept of the Palaeolithic shamans or their modern Siberian or Amazonian counterparts. Besides being musicians, they would have been the idea men, highly facile with signs and art, technically proficient, and, most important, with a mystical bent, stimulated by a fermented beverage, that brought them into contact with the gods and ancestors.

A later legend about the Yellow Emperor (Huang Di), who is believed to have established kingship in China some four thousand years ago, distills the essence of shamanism. The first emperor sent one of his scholars to the distant mountains of Central Asia to cut and collect bamboo for making flutes to duplicate the call of the mythical phoenix. The music of this special instrument, he believed, would bring his reign into harmony with the universe.

Here again, as for the Jiahu and Palaeolithic flutes, high-flying birds and their songs provide the means of access to invisible, otherworldly realms.

The hypothesis of a shamanistic funeral feast associated with the elite musicians at Jiahu, while extremely plausible, has not been proved by residue analyses of vessels from the tombs. All the pottery I selected for testing came from residences. None of these houses—of which fifty have been excavated to date—stood out as being especially distinctive, so it is surmised that the use of the fermented beverage was widespread throughout the community. Besides being essential to special occasions, it might have been drunk to celebrate good times with neighbors, to sip on when feeling down or sick, or to motivate and reward. Because only 5 percent of the site has been excavated, we should be prepared for future surprises.

BRINGING THE PAST TO LIFE

When our findings from Jiahu first appeared in the *Proceedings of the National Academy of Sciences* toward the end of 2004, we braced for a lot of press coverage. We had discovered the world's earliest alcoholic beverage, and it came from China, not the Middle East as one might have expected. Still, we were not prepared for the extent of the media buzz, which demonstrated that the finding had struck a universal chord.

John Noble Wilford of the *New York Times* was the first reporter to reach me by phone. He had used the term *happy hour* in a previous article about our Near Eastern research, suggesting that he had a penchant for an occasional quaff himself. His story was picked up by the *International Herald Tribune* and went around the world, as did several BBC interviews. The wine writer for the *Philadelphia Inquirer,* Deborah Scoblionkov, was also immediately on the story, and soon a photographer came calling. He captured me on camera doing some nineteenth-century archaeological chemistry—sniffing at the ingredients of one ancient sample—but I did not go so far as to taste it, as one chemist did a century ago. Deborah's story became a Reuters wire story, and soon I had reporters from major European publications—*Focus, Geo,* and many others—wanting their own exclusives. In China, the main government news agency, Xinhua, gave the story prime coverage, and one of my coauthors on the paper, Guangsheng Cheng, wrote to say that "you are now a celebrity of the CCP—the Chinese Communist Party." I had finally arrived!

It was one thing to analyze a 9,000-year-old beverage; but then we started thinking, why not bring it back to life to allow others to enjoy it and feel themselves transported back in time? We had already had some success in re-creating another, more recent ancient beverage, based on residues found in the tomb of King Midas or one of his royal forebears (see chapter 5). I spoke with Sam Calagione, the owner and brewer of Dogfish Head Craft Brewery in Milton, Delaware, who had been the inspiration behind the modern formulation of the beverage we called Midas Touch, and he was game. With his experimental brewer, Mike Gerhart, he conjured up a Neolithic brew.

There were many challenges and lots of false starts in re-creating a Chinese Neolithic beverage, the story of which is amusingly retold by Larry Gallagher in his article "Stone Age Beer," in the November 2005 issue of *Discover* magazine. Should we use only grape, only hawthorn fruit, or both? Because seeds of both fruits had been recovered at Jiahu, I said we should use both. Mike eventually tracked down a Chinese herbalist on the West Coast who could provide us with genuine hawthorn fruit, but we could not procure any genuine Chinese grapes and had to settle for a *V. v. vinifera* cultivar of ancient stock, Muscat. The honey presented a similar problem. One wildflower honey from Central Asia is especially prized, but we had to settle for a more accessible American equivalent.

Chinese rice is readily available in the States. My question to Mike was whether we should use milled rice or brown rice, with the surface bran intact and perhaps even unhulled. The residents of Jiahu had stone mills for processing rice, but it was unlikely that their procedure was very refined. We decided to use a pregelatinized rice, which had already been cooked to a thick, homogeneous paste and dried, with some of the original bran and hulls mixed in.

The next question was how to saccharify the rice. When I told Sam that the earliest way of doing this was likely by chewing, he said, "Okay, let's do it that way to keep it historically accurate." I said that sometimes you could take experimental archaeology too far, and in any case, sprouting rice to make malt might have been discovered at an early date. When Larry Gallagher offered to make his own version of the experimental beverage by chewing rice with his fiancée, we were off the hook. Larry's experiment apparently did not turn out well, as he never sent me a bottle to taste.

At an early stage in the Dogfish Head experiments, Mike tried saccharifying the rice with a traditional Chinese mold concoction (*qu*). My contact in Beijing, Guangsheng Cheng, passed on some of the starting agent, with detailed instructions on its use, through a graduate student, Kai Wang, at Michigan State University. It produced a kind of sour mash. Because it would constitute only a small part of the finished product, we were not worried.

Another critical issue was whether to carry out a natural fermentation, depending entirely on the wild yeast present on the grape skins and in the honey, or to help the process along by adding some cultured yeast. We opted for the latter, but were then left with the problem of what kind of yeast to use. I suggested several strains, but Mike wasn't convinced that they were native to China or had been around for nine thousand years. We compromised and used a dry sake yeast, as the Japanese version of rice wine is a direct descendant of the Chinese beverage.

Our debut re-creation of the beverage was produced using the small-scale setup that had started Sam on his brewing career, some old vats tucked away in a corner of his brewpub in Rehoboth Beach, Delaware. With Larry Gallagher scrutinizing our every move, we started brewing at around nine in the morning. Into the pot went the rice malt, up went the temperatures, and out came the wort (the sweet liquid extracted from the malt). I was most concerned when the powdered hawthorn fruit was dumped into the kettle. I thought there was too much of this rather mouth-puckering, chalky fruit; but Mike had already decided on the proportions, and we kept to those.

We also had two fast-approaching deadlines: one with the U.S. Bureau of Alcohol, Tobacco, and Firearms (ATF) for approval of the beverage, and the other a grand tasting at Manhattan's Waldorf-Astoria Hotel in May 2005, only a few months away. The ATF at first disallowed the use of hawthorn fruit; it was fine as a component of an herbal medicine or tea, but it could not be added to an alcoholic beverage. The distinction, especially since we were using just a small amount, can only be fathomed by a government agency. After endless negotiations, we received the go-ahead.

After some conditioning in a tank, the Neolithic beverage was bottled and ready for its first public appearance. This initial version was well received, with the media, of course, on hand. A lingering concern, however, flitted in the back of my head. The beverage seemed much more sour than any self-respecting Neolithic villager or shaman would have wanted to drink: we know that sugar and sweetness were prized in antiquity.

I broached the problem with Sam and Mike, and over the coming months we made progress. With the help of another brewer at Dogfish Head, Bryan Selders, we tweaked the formula to impart a delectable sweet-and-sour taste, a perfect pairing with Chinese food.

Figure 6. Sam Calagione of Dogfish Head Craft Brewery brought this dream-inspired image to reality when he commissioned artist Tara McPherson to create a label for the "oldest alcoholic beverage in the world" thus far discovered. Chateau Jiahu is named after the Neolithic site in China, which yielded a biomolecular archaeological recipe of rice, honey, and fruit (hawthorn fruit and/or grape), whose residues had been preserved inside jars (see figure 3) from the site. Courtesy of Tara McPherson (original acrylic, 12" × 12") and Dogfish Head Craft Brewery.

While all this was going on, Sam had slipped into shamanistic revelry. He recounted a dream in which a naked Chinese Neolithic girl, with long hair flowing down her back and buttocks, had approached him with the beverage. He commissioned a New York design artist, Tara McPherson, to create a provocative label for our Neolithic grog, named Chateau Jiahu. She placed a seemingly enigmatic tattoo, which had also been part of Sam's dream, on the lower back of the celebrant who graced her label. This tattoo is actually the Chinese sign for *wine* or any other alcoholic beverage. It shows a jar with three drops of liquid falling from its lip. The sign dates back to the Shang dynasty, as early as 1600 B.C., and has been in continuous use ever since.

The latest incarnation of Chateau Jiahu hits all the right notes—an inviting, grapy nose, a Champagne-like effervescence with extremely fine bubbles, a tingling aftertaste that invites you to drink more, and a brooding yellowish color worthy of the Yellow Emperor and the Yellow River. The combination of hawthorn fruit and Muscat grapes, wildflower honey, and unhulled rice malt on a sake yeast yielded a beverage that was exotic but immensely satisfying.

We have since served Chateau Jiahu at special events on the East and West coasts. The East Coast event was at the Cornelia Street Café in New York's Greenwich Village in October 2006. That was an exuberant affair, emceed by my long-time friend and colleague, the Nobel laureate Roald Hoffmann. Intermixing science and art, the tasting was accompanied by music played on wine-filled glasses, a takeoff on Benjamin Franklin's glass harmonica on display at Philadelphia's Franklin Institute. As possessed bacchanals stomped grapes in tubs at the front of the audience, we ducked to avoid being splashed by the dark red must.

In December, two related events were sponsored by the Asian Art Museum in San Francisco. One was held at the home of Farina Wong-Kingsley, a chef and food writer, overlooking the Golden Gate Bridge. Surrounded by the sights and smells of a traditional Chinese garden, Farina made an array of Shanghai delicacies to go with the Chateau Jiahu. The following night, a lecture at the museum concluded with a tasting of the Neolithic beverage against several fine Japanese sakes, courtesy of Beau Timken, owner of True Sake. In my estimation, the more complex Chateau Jiahu won hands down.

AN ERA OF SPECIALIZATION

The Neolithic inhabitants of Jiahu might have developed an exceptional fermented beverage, but humans never seem to be satisfied, as my studies soon revealed. The Neolithic period culminated in the high shamanistic civilizations of the Xia and Shang dynasties, with their capitals north of the Yellow River, about three hundred kilometers from Jiahu. An overnight train ride with Changsui to Anyang brought us to the most extensively excavated ancient city of the time, called Yin, where we were met by the chief archaeologist, Jigen Tang. He gave us a tour of the site, which covered sixty-two square kilometers during its heyday three thousand years ago and has been continuously excavated for eighty years. Mercifully, he showed us only the highlights and then shuffled us off to a grand banquet on a barge in the Yellow River, replete with fine rice wines.

Our descent into the tomb of a consort of one of the Shang rulers captured the splendor of the time. A tall, gently sloping passageway led to the burial chamber, where the queen had been buried in all her gold and jade finery, surrounded by horses and chariots. Chariots were used not just for maneuvering around the empire, but also, as recounted in some of the earliest shamanistic texts (e.g., the *Zhuangzi,* or Book of Master Zhuang, dated to the third century B.C.), for ascending into the heavens. A tomb with chariots also vividly reminded me of the royal tombs of Ur in Mesopotamia (see chapter 3), whose queens were similarly adorned with gold and lapis lazuli jewelry and buried with chariots.

Back at the Anyang dig house, Jigen brought out what was, to my mind, the real treasure—a *liquid* sample from inside one of the magnificent bronze vessels of the period. Until then I had had no idea that liquids had been found in Chinese excavations, preserved for more than three thousand years. I was aghast. Jigen suggested that I smell it, and there was no doubt: it had the characteristic fragrance of fine rice or millet wine made the traditional way, slightly oxidized like sherry, with a perfumed bouquet.

The liquid came from a so-called *he* vessel. Mounted on a tripod base, with a large handle and lid connected by a metal fitting, and with a long spout protruding from one side, it resembles a teapot; but tea had not yet made its appearance in China. The vessel is of a well-known ceremonial type for serving millet and rice wine. The liquid inside had evaporated down to about a third of the full capacity, but because the lid eventually corroded and stuck tightly to the neck, the vessel was hermetically sealed until its excavation thousands of years later.

These days, it seems as though bronze vessels filled with liquids are continually being discovered in Chinese excavations, especially in burials, and excitedly announced in the media. In 2003, for example, in an excavation of an upper-class tomb in Xi'an—also famous for the army of terracotta warriors that accompanied the famous Qin dynasty king, Shihuangdi, to his grave in 210 B.C.—a lidded vessel was found containing twenty-six liters of liquid, which was said to have a "delicious aroma and light flavor." How about a 3,000-year-old vintage? Unfortunately, chemical analysis is yet to be carried out. And drinking royal wine was not necessarily an ethereal

Figure 7. Shang Dynasty "teapot" (*he*) from the upper-class tomb of Liu Jiazhuang at the famous capital city of Anyang along the Yellow River (no. M1046:2, ca. 1250–1000 B.C., height 30.1 cm). It is decorated with the enigmatic *taotie* mask of a bird or dragon and was about a third full when found. The 3,000-year-old liquid still retained a fragrant, sherry-like aroma due to its infusion with elemi tree resin and/or chrysanthemum flower. Illustration courtesy of Jigen Tang/Anyang Field Institute, Institute of Archaeology, Chinese Academy of Social Sciences.

experience. The bronze used in the vessels was alloyed with as much as 20 percent free lead, and as they overindulged, the Shang dynasty emperors were poisoning themselves. That may explain why a number of the dynasty's later kings are said to have gone crazy or committed suicide.

I hand-carried a sample of the Anyang liquid back to Philadelphia, where we subjected it to a battery of scientific tests. We were able to show that the sealed vessel had once contained a very special millet wine. This was not Neolithic grog: it contained no honey and no fruit. Instead, the presence of two aromatic triterpenoid compounds, β-amyrin and oleanolic acid, pointed to the addition of a tree resin, very likely derived from the elemi family (Burseraceae) of fragrant trees. The chrysanthemum flower, which can yield the same compounds, was another candidate. I was reminded of our discoveries of pine and terebinth resins as additives in Near Eastern grape wines (see chapter 3).

Could it be that the Anyang liquid represented one developmental stage in China's long tradition of herbal medicine? Triterpenoids have antioxidant properties, lowering cholesterol and scavenging free radicals that can cause cancer, so a beverage laced with these compounds could definitely have been part of the ancient medical chest. β-amyrin is also an analgesic and has a palatable, citrusy aroma. Recently, I initiated a project ("Archaeological Oncology: Digging for Drug Discovery") with the Abramson Cancer Center of the University of Pennsylvania Medical Center to explore the therapeutic uses of these compounds in ancient medicine. By trial and error, humans might well have discovered natural remedies over the millennia, which lie buried in our archaeological findings.

Returning by train to Zhengzhou with Changsui, we next met with Zhiqing Zhang, an archaeologist at the local Institute of Cultural Relics and Archaeology, which is responsible for all of Henan Province. Zhiqing told us about another upper-class tomb in Changzikou in Luyi County, about 250 kilometers farther east. This tomb yielded more than ninety bronze vessels, and when it was first opened, fifty-two lidded examples amazingly still contained liquid, ranging from a quarter to half full. Zhiqing asked me if I would like a sample of the liquid for analysis. He did not have to ask twice, and soon I held a small vial of liquid from a lidded *you* jar. This tall, elegant vessel was adorned, like the Anyang "teapot," with the enigmatic, ferocious-looking *taotie* motif, a mask of a dragon or birdlike figure, with long horns, penetrating eyes, and a curled upper lip.

To our surprise, the Changzikou *you* contained not a millet wine, like the Anyang teapot, but a specialized beverage made exclusively from rice. Two monoterpenes, camphor and α-cedrene, gave it a fragrant bouquet even after three thousand years. The camphor smell was not as intense as that we usually associate with the pure compound used to repel moths. In fact, the marker compounds in the beverage probably came from a tree resin (China fir, *Cunninghamia lanceolata*, is the most likely candidate), a flower (again, chrysanthemum was at the top of our list), or an herb in the *Artemisia* genus (the same genus that includes wormwood, used in making the very bitter and potent absinthe).

How would a "medicinal" wine with anesthetic and antimicrobial properties be prepared? Tree resins could be collected and added directly to the wine after fermentation, with the high alcohol helping to dissolve the terpenoids.

Figure 8. The author in his laboratory, examining and "sniffing" out a 3,000-year-old millet wine, which was preserved inside a tightly lidded bronze vessel (see figure 7) from an elite tomb at Anyang. Photograph courtesy of Pam Kosty, University of Pennsylvania Museum of Archaeology and Anthropology.

The active compounds in flowers and plant parts might have been isolated by boiling down in water or extracting with an oil, as in a perfumery decoction. The Changzikou tomb itself provided the likely answer. A large bronze bowl had been filled with the leaves of another aromatic tree—*Osmanthus fragrans*—and held a ladle, implying that it had once been filled with a liquid. The leaves of this tree, which have a floral aroma, were apparently steeped in the liquid, as tea is made today. Similarly, the *Artemisia* or chrysanthemum might well have been infused into the rice wine, which was then filtered.

The Shang dynasty oracle-bone inscriptions, the earliest texts from China, distinguish at least three fermented beverages, including herbal wine (*chang*); a sweet, low-alcohol rice or millet "beer" (*li*); and a fully fermented and filtered wine (*jiu*), probably with an alcohol content of 10 to 15 percent, made from the same grains. A whole retinue of high officials and winemakers oversaw the production, made sure that each member of the royal family received their daily allotment, and ensured that enough of each beverage was on hand for the yearly round of ceremonies and special occasions. The king sometimes inspected the beverages to make sure they passed muster.

The succeeding Zhou dynasty may have faulted the last Shang king (paradoxically named Zhou, using slightly different characters) for being a crazed carouser who indulged himself in all-night, naked orgies with a "forest of meat" and a "lake of wine." Nevertheless, the Zhou rulers appear to have liked their wines as much as any other dynasty: the elaborate Shang wine bureaucracy continued to operate and was in fact expanded. At least two more fermented beverages are described in the *Rites of Zhou* (*Zhouli*), one made from a fruit (*luo*) and the other from an unfiltered brew (*lao*) of fermented rice or millet or, perhaps, unfermented wort. A further evolution in winemaking can also be seen in the Chinese word for *physician* (*i*), in which the character for *shaman* was replaced by the wine sign during the Zhou period, succinctly expressing the trend toward more refined beverages.

The number of bronze vessels from the Shang and Zhou dynasties, most of which were filled with one of the official alcoholic beverages, is mind-boggling. Many of them have been found in elite burials at the major urban centers along the Yellow River or its tributaries, including Erlitou, Zhengzhou, Taixi, Tianhu, and Anyang. Their shapes, which include ornate tripod vessels (*jue* and *jia*), stemmed goblets (*gu*), vats (*zun*), and jars (*hu, lei,* and *you*), have much to tell us about how the beverages were prepared, stored, served, ceremonially presented, and ultimately drunk.

For example, according to long-standing Chinese practice, a high tripod vessel, which could be set over a fire, was required to warm wine. A pair of upright posts that projected from the rim—perhaps symbolic of the *taotie* horns—would get in the way of easy drinking, so these vessels were most likely intended for pouring. However, an appreciation for serving the best wines chilled, even thousands of years ago, is expressed in a verse from the *Songs of the South* (*Chuci*), dated to around A.D. 300:

> Jadelike wine, honey-flavored, fills the winged cups;
> Ice-cooled liquor, strained of impurities,
> clear wine, cool and refreshing . . .

"Winged" or "eared" cups suited the wine perfectly, as these shallow bowls with a single ledge handle were often made of jade.
. Many of the magnificent Chinese bronzes probably held *jiu* or its herbal equivalent, *chang*. During Zhou and Han times, *chang* is said to have been made by infusing resinous plant leaves or adding herbs (*yu*) to a fermented beverage. Our chemical results support the textual interpretations and also confirm that these specialized beverages were made by mold saccharification or amylolysis, a uniquely Chinese contribution to alcoholic beverage making. This traditional method exploits molds or fungi—including the genera *Aspergillus, Rhizopus, Monascus,* and others—which are unique to each region of China. The molds break down the carbohydrates in rice and other grains into simple, fermentable sugars. Historically, a special mold-and-yeast starter (*qu*) was first prepared by growing a thick mass of mold on various steamed cereals and pulses. Rice and millet, the principal cereals of prehistoric China, presumably served as early substrates.

Yeast adventitiously enters the process, either brought in by insects or by falling from the rafters of old wooden buildings, as happens in the lambic breweries of the Brussels area. As many as one hundred special herbs, including *Artemisia,* are used today to make *qu,* and some have been shown to increase the yeast activity as much as sevenfold. A congealed white mass inside a jar at Taixi, weighing 8.5 kilograms, was found to be made up entirely of the lees of spent yeast cells, which must have yielded a particularly powerful beverage.

We may never know all the details of how the earliest Neolithic grog of Jiahu, with its complex ingredients, was made, but we can get a glimpse of how a traditional rice wine, comparable to a Shang dynasty beverage, was produced. In the small town of Shaoxing, a short train ride to the southwest of Shanghai, you can watch the steaming of the rice, the double fermentation at high and low temperatures, and the filtering of the brew into jars that are carefully sealed with clay. Before the final closure, the mouth of each vessel is stuffed with bamboo and lotus leaves, and a piece of paper, noting the year of production, is inserted. The exterior of the vessel is often brightly painted with colorful flowers and young women, because traditionally these jars (*nuer hong*, "red daughter") were buried in the ground at the birth of a female child and only recovered, opened, and drunk years later, when the girl married.

According to the oracle bones and other ancient texts, Shaoxing is where Chinese winemaking began. Although our Jiahu analyses have undercut the legend, it is said that the daughter of Da Yu made the first wine around 2000 B.C. Her father, whose name translates as the Mighty Yu, was the founder of the Xia dynasty. According to tradition, he not only survived a great flood, like Noah, but quelled many by building channels and levees and bringing the Yellow and Yangzi rivers under control. He is said to have died at Shaoxing during an inspection tour of the flood controls, and a huge statue of the ruler still stands in imperial splendor in the hall of his mausoleum in the nearby countryside.

I visited Shaoxing in the company of my microbiologist friend and colleague from Beijing, Guangsheng Cheng. We visited the ancient bars of the town, where we tasted the yellow rice wines for which Shaoxing is famous. Most of these wines, which can be aged for more than fifty years, have sherrylike aromas and tastes that reflect the region's unique microflora. We ate "stinky" tofu, another delicacy of the region. We heard the tales about the artists who floated their cups of wine down streams and were obliged to compose a poem and drink the wine where the cup came ashore. But despite the temptations of the present, we remained focused on our goal of gaining insights into ancient winemaking. We went from one large, rambling winery to the next, each clinging to tradition in its own way. We gladly accepted the frequent invitations to test their wines as both an enduring pleasure and an opportunity to learn how the wines were made.

To my mind, the most interesting carryover of ancient technique was the use of *qu* to break down the starches and start the fermentation. Vast rooms in the wineries were stacked high with *qu* cakes, measuring nearly a foot on a side. The use of specialized molds to saccharify the grain and begin fermentation meant that the beverage makers of protohistoric China could forgo chewing or malting the grain and had less need for honey or fruit to supply sugars and yeast than did the makers of Neolithic grog. As Chinese culture advanced, the prehistoric extreme beverage fell out of favor and was replaced by millet and rice wines, like those preserved as liquids inside the Shang and Zhou Dynasty ritual vessels.

Fruits and honey were not totally eliminated from Chinese beverages. Excavations in the Shang dynasty city of Taixi have yielded many funnels and unusually shaped vessels that provide evidence of a lively, diversified local beverage industry. One pottery form, designated the "general's helmet," has a pointed, recessed bottom that would have been ideal for collecting sediments from liquids. Another large jar from the site, in addition to the one containing yeast mentioned above, was filled with peach, plum, and Chinese jujube pits, as well as the seeds of sweet clover, jasmine, and hemp. We can only imagine how delicious and intoxicating this beverage must have been. One of the canonical Shang dynasty wines (*luo*) was fruit-based, and some scholars believe that it was the earliest Chinese fermented beverage, perhaps even the Jiahu grog itself. Today in many parts of China, a popular drink (*shouzhou mi jiu*) consists of rice wine containing fresh fruit pieces.

BRIDGING THE GAP

When did mold saccharification become the sole technique for making fermented beverages? Anne Underhill, who facilitated my entry into Chinese archaeology, also enabled me to begin exploring the six-millennium gap between Jiahu in 7000 B.C. and the Shang dynasty.

As one of the first American archaeologists to resume excavation in China, Anne had begun exploring the potentially very rich area of southeastern Shandong Province, where the Yellow River flows into the Yellow Sea. Her excavations at Liangchengzhen, carried out with colleagues from the Field Museum in Chicago and Shandong University in Jinan, have revealed houses and burials of the Longshan period, dating from about 2600 to 1900 B.C.

Ancient Shandong Province is especially well known for its numerous and elaborate drinking cups, which have been found predominantly in burials and appear to have surged in popularity during the late Dawenkou period (ca. 3000–2600 B.C.). By Longshan times, exquisite, tall-stemmed forms (*gaobing bei*) were being made in a glossy black, eggshell-thin pottery ware. These vessels were accompanied by similarly elegant jars (*lei*), with high shoulders and a pair of loop handles, reminiscent of the Jiahu jars. We wanted to test the absorptive and evaporative properties of modern rice wine in a

container made of this refined ware, so we asked a modern potter to repli-
cate a *lei* jar in the local clay, together with a convex lid. Not surprisingly,
even high-fired pottery is somewhat porous and does not retard evapora-
tion as well as cast bronze. But I hesitated to break the elegant piece to
carry out chemical analyses.

We also chose long-spouted pitchers (*gui*) with high tripod bases, just
like the later Shang Dynasty examples (*jue*) in bronze. By the time we had
completed our selection of pottery types for our study, we had a complete
repertoire of drinking and eating vessels—cups, jars, basins, pitchers, and
even a probable steamer rack and sieve.

Our chemical analyses of twenty-seven samples focused on vessels that
were most likely used to prepare, store, or drink alcoholic beverages. Because
we were not permitted to take our samples back to the United States for
testing, Anne put out feelers around town. In short order, the local middle-
school chemistry teacher, Laoshi Chen, had invited me to use his laboratory when classes were not in session. We procured glassware and solvents
in the city of Rizhao, and I started heating up my sherds in methanol and
chloroform. During breaks, I was challenged to ping-pong by the students, who were shocked when I beat them: I was a high school champion.
When I ran short on distilled water, Mr. Chen improvised a system that
kept it flowing.

Back in the States, we tested the extracts. The results overwhelmingly
pointed to a beverage very similar to the Jiahu grog, which combined a
fruit (grape or hawthorn fruit), rice, and honey. The use of a wild grape in
the Liangchengzhen grog is a distinct possibility, although only three grape
pips have thus far been recovered from Longshan contexts at the site. As
many as ten wild grape species grow in eastern Shandong today, and the
origins of *Vitis* in China have been traced to this region.

Because the Yellow River flows through Shandong, Liangchengzhen
would have been in touch with developments farther upstream, including
advances in producing fermented beverages. A Jiahu-like beverage at
Liangchengzhen indicates that the mold saccharification process had not
yet taken hold in the river basin. Yet our analyses of the Liangchengzhen
beverage did pick up chemical signs that a plant resin or herb had been
added to the grog. Gradually, it would appear, the shamanistic beverage
makers were developing medicinal wines, which led to the Shang dynasty
chang. In the process, they discovered other properties of particular herbs
and molds, which were eventually put to good use in saccharifying rice and
millet and speeding up fermentation.

Our analyses of the extracts also suggested the presence of another, more puzzling ingredient: barley. This staple for making beer and bread hails from the Middle East, where it was domesticated around 8000 B.C. Barley is particularly useful in beverage making because, when malted, it produces a profusion of diastase enzymes that break down starch into sugar. Major American breweries today, like Budweiser and Miller, take advantage of this property of barley by using it to saccharify less expensive rice in their brews. The puzzling aspect of this finding at Liangchengzhen is that no barley kernels or other evidence of the plant has yet been recovered from the site.

On current evidence, barley was a long time coming to East Asia. It is attested as early as the fifth millennium B.C. in Baluchistan, today a western province of Pakistan. It has been recovered from third-millennium B.C. sites in Central Asia. By the second millennium B.C., it had made its way farther east, as shown by occasional botanical finds from other Longshan sites. We also know that by around 1000 B.C. the domesticated plant was present in Japan and Korea, across the Yellow Sea from Shandong Province. I suspect that it is only a matter of time until evidence of barley is found at Liangchengzhen. The wet coastal environment conspires against the preservation of plant remains unless they have been carbonized by burning.

By plotting the findspots of those vessels which contained the Liangchengzhen mixed beverage, the religious significance of the drink begins to emerge. Many of the fine black goblets came from graves, where they might have represented either prized possessions of the deceased in life or burial offerings. Pits crammed with hundreds of whole jars, *gui* tripods, and more goblets were excavated near the burials. But why would serviceable vessels be thrown away? The pits probably hold the leftovers of feasts for the ancestors, as we also believe is the case at Jiahu and is well attested a few centuries later in the major Yellow River urban communities.

Funerary feasts did not seem far-fetched when the temperatures fell below freezing in the late afternoon, and we huddled together in the only warm room in our dig house, the dining room. There, with the moisture from our breath dripping down the inside windows, we feasted on fresh seafood from the Yellow Sea—mussels, gigantic shrimp, and fish of all kinds. It was often washed down with the local beer, Tsingtao, named after the nearby town where Germans established the first European lager production in China.

The Liangchengzhen analyses partly filled in the gap between Jiahu and the Shang dynasty, but we needed to know more, especially about the crucial time at the beginning of the second millennium B.C. before the start of the Shang dynasty. The legend of the Mighty Yu's daughter discovering the first wine in China might contain an element of truth—if this accomplishment were taken to mean the introduction of mold saccharification. I had not gone looking for more samples from the Xia dynasty. Instead, as is often the case in the modern academic world, I received a fortuitous invitation. It took the form of an e-mail message from one of the key researchers of the Xia period, Li Liu, who asked me if I would be interested in analyzing pottery from her site at Huizui and nearby Erlitou. Because Erlitou is believed to have been the capital city for the Xia dynasty, it may give us the evidence we need to fill in the gap between the Longshan period and the Shang Dynasty.

THE WINE POETS OF CHINA

Beginning in about the third century A.D., an exceptional group of Chinese poets celebrated the importance of fermented beverages. With the fall of the Han dynasty, the wisdom and ceremonial formality of Confucianism appear to have failed. Drawing on a long tradition of shamanism and spiritual inspiration aided by alcohol, the poets, known as the Seven Sages of the Bamboo Grove, reinvigorated religious life. Stressing the freedom and naturalism of Daoism, they styled themselves as solitary intellectuals and lovers of nature. In their rustic bamboo grove, they talked philosophy, played music, wrote poetry, and spent much of their time drinking.

When the Tang dynasty rulers ushered in a rare period of internationalism and creativity starting in the seventh century, another generation of wine poets was on hand to document the exuberant times. Wang Ji was the first poet of the group that came to be known as the Eight Immortals of the Wine Cup. His sentiments are summed up in his poem "To the Pupils of the Transcendental Art":

> The Tiered City is too distant for collecting magic herbs
> . . . .
> Where are the music players? . . .
> In spring, pine needles ferment in the wine jugs;
> In autumn, chrysanthemums float in the wine cups.
> When we chance upon one another, we would rather get drunk,
> And definitely will not take up mixing the elixirs.
> *(Warner 2003: 82)*

In this poem, Wang Ji alludes to other worlds, redolent of magic and reverberating with music, at the same time that he captures the immediacy of a good drink made with pine needles and chrysanthemums. Chrysanthemum wine had long been treasured for its special flavor and its yellow color, symbolizing the emperor. There were many other wines to choose from during Tang times: red wines colored by *Monascus* mold, green "bamboo" wine, peppered and honeyed wines. It is no wonder that perhaps the most famous Chinese poet of all time, Li Bo, is said to have drowned when he tried to embrace the reflection of the moon in a river. He had already written:

Among the flowers, a winepot.
I pour alone, friendless.
So, raising my cup, I turn to the moon
And face my shadow, making us three.
(Berger 1985)

Except for the 26,000-year-old pottery figurines from Dolní Věstonice (chapter 9), Japan holds the distinction of having some of the oldest pottery in the world, the Incipient Jomon pottery vessels dating to 12,000 B.P. As I had anticipated, China has now surpassed Japan in this regard: pottery from Yuchanyan Cave in southwestern Hunan Province is reported by the expedition codirector, Ofer Bar-Yosef of Harvard University, to radiocarbon-date to ca. 15,000 B.P. In the development of fermented beverages, China also had a commanding lead. If we view the Jiahu grog as a kind of rice wine, then it predates the rice wine of Japan, sake, by more than seven thousand years. Had it not been for the domestication of rice and development of the mold-saccharification process in China, sake might not even exist. Japan adopted the winemaking tradition from China only in the third century A.D.

Admittedly, no chemical analyses of the Incipient Jomon pottery, many of which are large bowls that might have been used to prepare or drink a fermented beverage in quantity, have been carried out. Even more recent examples of Jomon pottery, dating as late as 400 B.C. and including spouted jugs, high-necked jars, and ornate bowls—all wonderfully adapted for a drinking culture—are yet to be tested.

By the time textual evidence first documents the role of alcoholic beverages in ancient Japanese culture, the debt that Japan owes to China is fully evident. Japan had its own wine poets at about the same time that the Tang dynasty Immortals were holding court. In the eighth century A.D., Ōtomo no Tabito writes in his "Thirteen Songs in Praise of Wine":

Sitting silent and looking wise
Cannot be compared to
Drinking *sake*
And making a racket
(*Berger 1985*)

Sake was served at funeral feasts, as it was in China, and offered up to the gods. The wine god, Ōmiwa no Kami, had shrines set aside in the major sake-producing towns of Nara and Kyoto. Balls of needles taken from the *Cryptomeria* cypress tree are still produced at these shrines and hung in the rafters of the wineries, to announce that sake is being produced. They recall a time when these needles and the resin of the tree were infused into the wine.

When the technology was first transferred to Japan, sake must have been prepared like rice wine in China, using the mold-saccharification process. Because of its relative geographic isolation, however, the range of microflora in Japan was more limited, and a different approach was needed. Removing more and more bran from the outer kernel of the rice ("polishing" the rice) resulted in a more refined product. The rationale for using a single species of *Saccharomyces cerevisiae* to carry out the fermentation follows the same logic. Additives had to be eliminated to keep the wine pure. One must ask, however, in the interests of aesthetics and scientific methodology, whether some of the individual flavors and aromas of a more variable product were not lost.

THREE

THE NEAR EASTERN CHALLENGE

A NEOLITHIC GROG FROM CHINA, dating back to 7000 B.C., challenges the conventional notion that civilization began in the Near East. I had gone to China in 1999 with the same preconception, all the more ingrained because I studied Near Eastern archaeology and history at the University of Pennsylvania and until then had spent most of my career excavating in the Middle East. China is notably absent from all Near Eastern writings until the Roman period. Even the Bible, which purports to give a general perspective of human history and our place in the universe, omits China. The Gospel of Matthew (2:1–12) speaks of the Magi, who followed the star to Jesus' birthplace in Bethlehem, as coming from the east, but this mysterious trio were probably Zoroastrian priests from no farther away than Iran.

I was predisposed to view the Near East as the cradle of civilization for other reasons as well. Our first successes at chemically identifying ancient fermented beverages came with samples from this region. Moreover, according to one theory, the route that modern humans followed when they came out of Africa around 100,000 B.P. led directly to the temperate Middle East, with its range of exploitable plants and animals. (The other possible route would have taken humans across the Bab el-Mandeb, the strait at the southern end of the Red Sea, to the Arabian peninsula.) By the northern route, after crossing the Sinai land bridge, they could have proceeded into the hill country of Israel and Palestine, descended into the lush Jordan

Valley, and followed this extension of East Africa's Great Rift Valley north to the oasis of Damascus and beyond. Our enterprising ancestors certainly would have taken some time to explore the possibilities, even the wonders, of this new land before traveling across the formidable land barriers to the east. Following this line of reasoning, I assumed that the Middle East must have developed fermented beverages before any were discovered in China.

AT THE EDGE OF THE CIVILIZED WORLD

A good shaman might have told me what was coming. In 1988, a phone call from Virginia (Ginny) Badler triggered the start of our investigation into ancient Middle Eastern fermented beverages, which has continued over the past twenty years. She had noted reddish residues inside large jars, which she believed represented wine dregs.

Ginny described an archaeological site, Godin Tepe, located high in the central Zagros Mountains of western Iran. As revealed in excavations by the Royal Ontario Museum of Toronto, some of the first city builders in the lowland Tigris-Euphrates Valley of Mesopotamia, now southern Iraq, had made inroads into the mountains, more than two thousand meters above sea level. At Godin Tepe along the Khorram River, hundreds of kilometers from their home base, they constructed a military-cum-trading base, dated to about 3500–3100 B.C., or what archaeologists of the region call the Late Uruk period.

The Late Uruk period is known for many firsts, including the first code of law, the first irrigation system, and the first bureaucracy, but it is perhaps best known for developing the earliest writing system in the world. Scribes were the backbone of the increasingly complex machinations carried out in the palaces and temples of the great cities of Ur, Uruk, Lagash, and Kish. By incising schematic pictographs onto clay tablets with a stylus, they kept track of economic transactions, offerings, and tribute. They also began to draw together the strands of a history of humankind and the gods, as later encapsulated in the Gilgamesh Epic and the Book of Genesis. This information was recorded in the Sumerian language, which has no known affinities to any other language system. The pictographs, like the incised signs on the Jiahu tortoise shells, denoted the objects or ideas that were being conveyed. But the Mesopotamian scribes carried the process a step further by combining individual signs, or logograms, together into words and even sentences.

In time, the urban development along the Tigris and Euphrates rivers spilled over into the flood plain of the Karun River, to the east in what is now the Shiraz region of Iran and downriver from Godin Tepe. Another people speaking a different language—the proto-Elamites—had already established themselves here in the city-state of Susa. Their material culture could hardly be distinguished from that of their neighbors, and they shared the same writing system, with a similar repertoire of incised signs.

Ginny told me that as many as forty-three tablets with logograms had been recovered from Late Uruk excavation levels at Godin Tepe, which signaled the presence of lowlanders, together with distinctive lowland architecture and imported pottery. The writing on the tablets and the other artifacts were insufficient by themselves to determine whether they were written in proto-Sumerian or proto-Elamite. Because of the direct route from the Susa plain up the Khorram River, the Godin excavators leaned toward the tablets' being written in proto-Elamite.

One tablet particularly caught my attention. It showed the sign for a pottery vessel (*dug* in ancient Sumerian) in the shape of a jar, with a narrow mouth and pointed base. The tablet also bore a group of three circles and a group of three vertical strokes. The circle denotes the numeral 10, and the vertical stroke represents 1. Altogether, then, thirty-three jars were recorded on the tablet. Further details were lacking. I thought our methods of chemical analysis might shed some light on what the vessels had contained.

Whether they were proto-Sumerians or proto-Elamites, the goal of these early settlers in establishing a position in such a remote locale was to exploit the rich resources of the highlands. They sought metals such as gold and copper, semiprecious stones, timber for building, and a host of organic goods that were either unavailable in the lowlands or difficult to produce there. Lush mountain pastures nurtured sheep and goats that produced fine textile fibers and dairy products. Many plants—the domesticated Eurasian grapevine (*Vitis vinifera* ssp. *vinifera*) foremost among them—cannot tolerate the hot, dry climate of lowland Mesopotamia but flourish in upland regions.

Godin Tepe was just one link in an extensive trading network that fueled development in the lowlands, but it exemplifies how the exchange of goods can be a conduit for even farther-reaching changes, often involving fermented beverages. With hindsight, I now see that Godin did not point only westward to the Mesopotamian city-states: it also had contacts eastward in Afghanistan, one of the principal sources of the intense blue mineral lapis lazuli. In fact, the site is located along the High Road or the Great

Khorasan Road of the Assyrian and Persian empires, the route later followed by the famous Silk Road.

The Great Khorasan Road is one of the few routes through the Zagros Mountains up to the high Iranian plateau and points east. It follows a tortuous path through deep ravines and across sheer mountainsides. High up on some of the cliffs, monarchs and generals recorded their successes for posterity. For example, at the imposing pinnacle of Behistun ("the god's place or land"), Darius the Great carved a monumental inscription in Old Persian, Elamite, and Babylonian cuneiform that gave thanks for his victories to the creator god of the Zoroastrian religion, Ahuramazda.

Neolithic humans, and perhaps even Palaeolithic migrants, were likely the original trailblazers of the High Road. They may not have left written records, as their successors did, and the archaeological evidence of their way stations is very thin on the ground, but we can have little doubt that they traveled along this route, largely because there was no better one. Indeed, as I argue below, it is highly probable that during the Neolithic period such travelers, whether inadvertently or intentionally, transmitted ideas about how to domesticate plants and make fermented beverages. As these ideas gradually traversed the vast expanse of Central Asia, in both directions, they had profound effects on the cultures along the way.

The evidence from Godin Tepe, although it dates to several thousand years later, fits with this earlier Neolithic scenario. Throughout the late fourth millennium B.C., the foreigners from the lowlands, who built and maintained the so-called Oval on the Citadel Mound, made the most of their upland circumstances. Ginny Badler's initial surmise about the jars proved correct. The red deposits she had observed on the bases and sidewalls of numerous jars from different areas of the settlement were residues of grape wine: our chemical analyses showed the presence of tartaric acid, the fingerprint compound for grapes in the Middle East.

We began with two jars of unusual design from room 20, each about sixty centimeters tall and thirty liters in capacity. Their narrow mouths and tall necks, which contrast sharply with the shapes of other jars at the site, were well designed for holding and pouring liquids. Although their piriform or pearlike shape occurs elsewhere in Mesopotamia, the application of notched clay coils as rope designs, in the form of two inverted U shapes on opposite sides of each vessel, was unique to Godin. This design seemed meaningless until Ginny suggested that it might have demonstrated how an actual strand of rope could be used to support the jar on its side. Some simple experiments quickly confirmed this as a possibility. With the jars lying on their sides, clay stoppers, found near the jars and having the same diameter as the jar mouths, would have been kept moist by the contents, thus preventing them from drying out, shrinking, and letting in air that would spoil the wine. It also explained why the red deposits were found only on one side of the vessels. In other words, lacking cork, the ancient beverage makers had found a way of preventing "wine disease," the inevitable conversion of wine to vinegar in the presence of oxygen, and improvised the world's first wine rack.

We can imaginatively re-create the ancient scene. Several wine jars were stoppered and stored on their sides in a cellar or dark recess of the Oval. After a year or two, the harsh young wine mellowed, and the solid lees of tartrate crystals and yeast settled out. Then the day arrived when a royal courier or dignitary arrived from the lowlands or a special ceremony was called for, and the jars were brought out. They were set upright, so that some of the lees ran down the sidewalls and collected on the bottoms of the vessels. The mouths of the vessels were carefully chipped away and then lopped off to prevent the stopper and associated debris from falling into the precious liquid. This method of "uncorking" a wine amphora is well attested 1,500 years later in New Kingdom Egypt. It is still used by port aficionados, who clamp the glass bottle neck with hot tongs and then apply a wet towel; the sudden change in temperature produces a smooth break.

One of the wine jars showed evidence of an even more refined unstoppering technique. A small hole was drilled through its sidewall about ten centimeters above the base, opposite the reddish residue on the other side. This would have enabled the wine to be decanted from the jar without disturbing the solids that had accumulated at the bottom. At some stage, however, the drinkers must have become impatient, because the neck of this jar, like that of its partner, had also been cleanly severed from its body. The party or ceremony had begun.

The protohistoric drinking fest, however, appears to have gone too far, because one of the outstanding finds of the excavation, a unique and stunning necklace of more than two hundred black and white stone beads, was lost and buried with the jars. Any excesses of the commandant's wife, who might have been wearing the jewelry, would have gone unseen, as the small room had a curtain wall that shielded it from the courtyard and prying eyes.

The finds from room 18, adjacent to this "party chamber," were equally evocative. This room, the focal point of the citadel, had a large fireplace on its back wall for providing heat during the cold winter months. Two windows looked out onto the courtyard. The room had been left in disarray: carbonized lentils and barley grain littered the floor, and almost two thousand stone spheres, perhaps used as sling stones to defend the Oval, were piled up in a corner. The focus of our biomolecular archaeological research was a number of very large jars, up to sixty liters in volume. When full, these jars would have been too heavy to move, and their contents must have been ladled out.

Room 18 might well have been the central distribution facility for goods needed by the foreign contingent of merchants, soldiers, and administrators. Rations and supplies—a replacement weapon, a clay tablet to write on, barley for bread and beer, or a fine wine for that special occasion—might have been parceled out from here through the two windows.

Directly across the courtyard from rooms 18 and 20, a very large funnel, about a half meter in diameter, and a circular "lid" of somewhat smaller dimensions were excavated in room 2. The funnel strongly suggested that the resinated wine in the jars was produced on site. Similarly large funnels are known from well-attested winemaking installations of the Iron Age and later, and they have also been excavated at other upland Late Uruk sites in eastern Turkey and northern Syria, where the wild Eurasian grape grows today.

Besides being useful in transferring liquids from one container to another, funnels serve admirably as strainers. Lining the funnel with a coarsely woven cloth (which would long since have disintegrated) or simply filling it with a mass of vegetal fibers or hair would have strained out debris from the unrefined grape juice, or must. Grapes might also have been heaped directly into the funnel, and the lid, weighing about a kilogram, used to press out the juice and drain it into a jar.

Sherds of two or possibly three jars with the inverted-U rope appliqué patterns were also recovered from the room, but none had any visible reddish residues on them. It could be that they were empties, waiting to be filled.

The possibility that room 2 served as a winemaking facility was plausible but lacked hard evidence. No grape pips, which are often well preserved, were reported from the room (although the soil had not been screened or floated for archaeobotanical materials), and the funnel might have been used to transfer a liquid other than wine. The "lid" might have been just that—a cover for a wide-mouthed vessel. Only half of room 2 had been excavated when work was brought to a halt by the 1979 Iranian

Revolution. A rectangular bin—perhaps a treading platform?—had begun to emerge, but any further clues about its function must await renewed excavations.

If one went in search of an early wine production center to supply the emergent city-states of lowland Mesopotamia, Godin Tepe would fit the bill. The site is centrally located along a historically important trade route through the Zagros Mountains. Today, luxuriant grapevines cover the area. Perhaps the same was true during the Late Uruk period. The possible winemaking facility in room 2 might have been today's equivalent of an upper-class boutique winery. Larger-scale production would have taken place at facilities closer to the vineyards, which remain to be discovered and excavated. The experimental and entrepreneurial spirit of the period, so clear from the extensive trade, urbanism, and irrigation agriculture and horticulture of the lowlands, might well have found expression in highland winemaking. A Godin cuvée might have been the ancient world's answer to a Ridge Cabernet Sauvignon, which Paul Draper makes from grapes growing on the edge of the San Andreas fault in the Santa Cruz Mountains.

A SECOND BEVERAGE LURKING IN THE REMAINS

There is a further twist to the tale of ancient fermented beverages at Godin Tepe. Any self-respecting lowland proto-Sumerian or proto-Elamite living at Godin would have wanted beer as well as wine. We know from later texts that beer was the drink of the masses in lowland Mesopotamia. Even the upper class would normally have drunk beer, with many varieties to choose from, including light, dark and amber beers, sweet beers, and specially filtered beers.

On the assumption that beer was made and consumed at the site, Ginny went back through the mass of late fourth-millennium B.C. sherds from room 18, the all-purpose general store in the reconstruction of the site. From the jigsaw puzzle of broken vessels, she was able to isolate and reconstruct an excellent candidate for an ancient beer bottle or jug, the common archaeological designation for a jar with handles. The wide mouth of this fifty-liter jug (see plate 5a) set it apart from the wine jars, which had long necks and narrow mouths that could be stoppered. It did have a realistic applied-rope design, like the wine vessels and many others of the period, but this one was of an unusual, still-unexplained type. The artificial rope encircles the top of the vessel and passes through two handles (now missing) placed close together on one side of the jug. Midway between the handles, the rope's realism was accentuated by being tied off as a knot, with loose ends hanging down. Intriguingly, a small hole had been punched below the knot before the vessel was fired.

The interior of this jug was even more strange. It was covered with incised, criss-crossing grooves. Vessels are often decorated with incisions on the outside, but rarely on the inside; usually they are just left rough or somewhat smoothed off. A vessel with interior grooves reminded Ginny of the proto-Sumerian sign for beer: *kaş*. It was written by starting with *dug*—the jar sign on the Godin tablet that so piqued my curiosity—and then adding horizontal, vertical, and oblique markings inside the jar pictograph. Could it be that the jug with the curious interior incisions was related to the beer sign, or, in other words, that *kaş* was a pictorial representation of the curious jug with interior grooves? If so, was the jug originally used to prepare, store, or serve beer?

A yellowish resinous-looking material filling the grooves of the jug turned out to be the linchpin for the argument that the lowlanders at Godin also drank beer. Ginny had first noted the residue as she sorted through the sherds in room 18. Now our laboratory turned to the task of identifying what it was and how it got there.

Our investigation followed the procedures I have already described for the Jiahu grog. My colleague Rudolph (Rudy) H. Michel and I began by searching the literature to learn of any compounds that would unequivocally identify the contents of the vessel as barley beer. Fortunately for us, one particular compound settles out from the liquid during the processing and storing of barley beer. Calcium oxalate, known as beerstone by brewers, is the simplest of organic acid salts, combined with ionic calcium. It's a very bitter, potentially poisonous compound, so it is a good thing to eliminate it from the brew. The pores in the pottery helped do this by removing the calcium oxalate from the brew at the same time that it helped to preserve the compound for our extraction and analysis thousands of years later.

Beerstone can be identified down to the one part per million level using a standard chemical spot test developed by Fritz Feigl. When this test was applied to the ancient residue from the grooves of the Godin Tepe jug, it gave a positive result for oxalate.

The "onerous" task of getting a sample from modern beer for comparison was left to Rudy, who made a trip to the Dock Street Brewery in Philadelphia. Dock Street was one of the first microbreweries to open its doors since the demise of the hundreds of breweries that once made Philadelphia renowned as the greatest brewing city in the Western Hemisphere. The symbolism of the moment was not lost on Rudy when a sample of beerstone from inside a brewing vat was scraped out and presented to him. This sample gave the same test result as the ancient residue.

As a final confirmation, we tested a residue from a New Kingdom Egyptian vessel in the Royal Ontario Museum, which had a high probability of originally containing barley beer. The jar, with its flared rim and rounded base, is referred to as a beerbottle by Egyptologists. It was decorated with lotus petals and mandrake fruit in Egyptian Blue pigment. Based on tomb paintings and reliefs, researchers believe it was used in a special bread-and-beer ritual. Again, it gave a positive result for oxalate.

From these findings, it was safe to say that the unusual jug in room 18 at Godin Tepe once contained barley beer. We could now draw out even more important implications from the evidence. Because carbonized six-row barley of the domesticated species (*Hordeum hexastichum*) was strewn on the floor of the same room and elsewhere in the Oval, it was probably locally grown. It would have been sown and tended in fields around the town, gleaned, the chaff winnowed, and the grain milled with basalt mortars and pestles.

The barley then had to be malted by sprouting (although it might instead have been chewed—see chapter 2). In this process, diastase enzymes become active and convert the grain starches to sugars. The water is drawn off before the sprout grows into a new plant, and the grains are parched and sometimes roasted to make malt. The chemical activity is suspended until water is added back to the malt to make a mash. At this stage, the practical advantages and relative ease of making a fruit wine or honey mead, instead of a cereal beer, emerge. Not only does beer making require the added step of converting the starch into sugar, but grains do not host naturally occurring yeast and thus cannot be directly fermented. To start the fermentation process, the ancient beverage maker had two choices: either wait for naturally occurring yeast to inoculate the brew, as is still done in making Chinese rice wines and Belgian lambic beers, or, more predictably, introduce *Saccharomyces cerevisiae* directly by adding fruit or honey.

The transformation of barley into beer is driven mainly by saccharification and fermentation. Microbreweries today operate in much the same way, if we ignore the stainless-steel vats and thermostatic controls. The ancient process is wonderfully described in a Mesopotamian hymn to the Sumerian goddess of brewing, Ninkasi, dating back to at least 1800 B.C. As the earliest beer "recipe" on record, it contains some untranslatable terms and is highly poetic. For example, the violent fermentation is described thus: "The waves rise, the waves fall . . . [like] the onrush of the Tigris and Euphrates." More practically, however, it observes that malt is prepared by covering the grain with water. The wort (the sugary solution that remains after the spent malt grains are filtered from the mash) is inoculated with both honey and wine, perhaps to assure that enough *S. cerevisiae* is available to start the fermentation. The poem also mentions enticingly that other "sweet aromatics" are part of the mixture. The phrase is ambiguous but might refer to dates or even a more bitter additive, such as radish or skirret, an anise-flavored herb.

In 1989, Fritz Maytag, one of the pioneers of the American microbrewery revolution, and his talented group of brewers at Anchor Steam Brewery in San Francisco took up the challenge of reviving the ancient Sumerian beer. I had the opportunity to taste two versions of the beverage, appropriately named Ninkasi. The first was presented at a tasting with Michael Jackson—the beer and scotch maven, not the performer of dubious reputation—at the Penn Museum. It had an effervescent, champagne-like quality, with a hint of added dates. The second version was unveiled at a special event hosted by *Archaeology* magazine in New York City. This beverage was distinctly different. Its more toasty, caramelly, and yeasty character was due to well-baked bread, also mentioned in the Ninkasi beer hymn, that was added to the brew kettle. In deference to its ancient origins, Fritz decided not to take Ninkasi into commercial production, and we are still awaiting a skirret version.

Turning the clock back again to 3500 B.C. and its more primitive brewing techniques, we are still left wondering why the Godin Tepe jug had interior grooves. Their interpretation as some kind of prototype for the proto-Sumerian beer-sign *kaš* is moot. Because we now know from the chemical evidence that the grooves were filled with beer residues, a practical reason for the grooves springs to mind: they concentrated and collected the bitter beerstone, which would otherwise have spoiled the brew.

Once the beer was ready, it probably was drunk directly from the large jug, like tapping a beer keg. Instead of a tap fitted into the bunghole, the proto-Sumerians and proto-Elamites had another way of accessing the precious brew: they drank it with long drinking tubes or straws, sucking the beverage from below the surface and avoiding the grain hulls and yeast that floated to the top. That this was the way barley beer should be drunk is shown by illustrations on numerous cylinder seals (decorated tubes whose imprints were rolled onto clay to mark personal property), which span thousands of years of Mesopotamian history (see figure 13). Some of the scenes on these seals show an individual dipping his straw into the brew in privacy; others show a man and woman enjoying sips together. The earliest known instance of this motif is a clay sealing (the impression left on clay by a seal) that a Penn excavation recovered from Tepe Gawra in the Zagros Mountains of northern Iraq, which dated to ca. 3850 B.C., several centuries earlier than our Godin Tepe jug. The sealing shows two very schematically rendered figures on either side of a jar that is two-thirds their height. This motif had been impressed at least twice on the shoulder of a jar, perhaps to mark it as a special drinking vessel. The individuals have been interpreted as either holding poles for stirring or drinking through sharply angled tubes. It is also possible that the figures are holding straight straws away from their mouths in between sips, a pose that is well attested on later cylinder seals.

On other seals, large wide-mouthed jars, like the Godin jug, are depicted as sprouting multiple straws and must have been intended for larger social gatherings. Because it does not keep or age well, beer lent itself to fairly rapid drinking, within a day or two, in a communal setting. There are also some practical reasons for drinking beer from the vessel in which it is made. When beer is transferred from one container to another, the nutrients and volatile components bound up in the yeast, the spent grain, and the surface of the container can be lost. As we know only too well from the insipid beers of the world's major breweries, processed beers may sell well, but their taste and aroma profiles are deficient. Moreover, if a vessel is expeditiously emptied and used to make a second batch, yeast that has taken up residence in the pores can be put to work again. Another way to reuse the yeast is to skim off some of the surface detritus, rich in the microorganisms, and set it aside for inoculating a future batch, much as yogurt is still made today throughout the Middle East.

The communal drinking of beer through straws was not just the prerogative of some ancient inhabitants of the Fertile Crescent and environs. It is a worldwide phenomenon—attested in China and the Pacific, the Americas, and Africa and still widely practiced. The custom is so widespread that one suspects that another factor is at work beyond simple utility. Certainly, reeds and stalks are easily come by, and their long, uniform hollowness would have invited blowing and sucking. A solid head of husks and yeast on the surface of a brew keeps out oxygen and preserves the beer longer, so it is worth keeping it intact and using a drinking tube to get at the good stuff below. Even if such practicalities argue for independent invention, one is still left with the question of why drinking through straws and employing the same vessel to both make and consume the beverage are nearly universal practices for cereal beer but generally unattested for fruit wines and mead.

We cannot leave our discussion of the Godin beer jug without posing one further question: What was the purpose of the hole between the handles, beneath the applied-rope knot? It certainly could not have been used to pour out the liquid. It is, however, the right diameter to accommodate a drinking tube. We might imagine that the shamanistic headman of the Godin clan or the leader of the Sumerian trading party was given pride of place at some communal function. Others dipped their straws in through the large mouth of the jug, but he was assigned a special hole of his own.

To date, our Godin Tepe beer jug offers the earliest chemical evidence for beer making and consumption from anywhere in the world, at least for a relatively traditional barley beer. A slight variation on this type of beverage arising at about the same time has been documented far away in the western Mediterranean (see chapter 6). Yet there is a long lapse between the time when barley was first taken into domestication during the ninth millennium B.C. and the manufacture of the Godin jug. This gap raises some crucial issues about what was happening in the interim, as humans went from hunting and gathering to a more settled existence.

WHICH CAME FIRST: BREAD OR BEER?

A major anthropological debate in the 1950s raised another provocative and related question: Did the discovery of bread making pave the way for beer making, or vice versa? In an article in *Scientific American,* Robert Braidwood, the doyen of Middle Eastern prehistoric archaeology at the University of Chicago's Oriental Institute, argued for a direct relationship between humans' settling down in year-round settlements in the Neolithic period and the domestication of wild barley (*Hordeum spontaneum*). Amply supplied with the domesticated grain from their fields and with the knowledge of how to make bread, Neolithic humans would have launched a monoculture food source of enormous potential.

Braidwood's hypothesis was an outgrowth of his extensive surveying of the so-called Hilly Flanks or foothills of the Zagros Mountains. On the assumption that the current climate and range of plants were in place in the immediate aftermath of the last Ice Age, he saw these fertile hills and valleys, extending up into the Taurus Mountains of eastern Turkey, as the literal seedbed for the domestication of barley. A suitable environment, with 250 to 500 millimeters of precipitation per year, would have invited early cultivators to pick out wild plants that held their grains tightly rather than dropping and dispersing them before humans had a chance to gather them up. To release the grains, humans had probably also begun to experiment with threshing and winnowing methods.

In the *Scientific American* article, Braidwood took his theory one step further, arguing that a single processed food—barley bread—was the driving force for the "Neolithic Revolution." Braidwood's approach offered an alternative explanation for the radical shift from hunting and gathering groups to sedentary farming villages. It was a far cry from previous environmental and social deterministic explanations, which stress overpopulation or competition for scarce resources as the motivating forces.

Once Braidwood had laid down the gauntlet, Jonathan Sauer of the University of Wisconsin came back with the reply that beer, rather than bread, would have provided the greater impetus for domestication. Braidwood followed up with a landmark conference titled "Did Man Once Live by Beer Alone?" at which different positions were presented but no resolution reached.

From a pragmatic standpoint, the question is really a no-brainer. If you had to choose today, which would it be: bread or beer? Neolithic people had all the same neural pathways and sensory organs as we have, so their choice would probably not have been much different. For those who require a more scientific argument, barley beer is, in fact, more nutritious than bread, containing more B vitamins and the essential amino acid lysine. But why skate around the compelling reason for favoring beer? With a 4 to 5 percent alcohol content, beer is a potent mind-altering and medicinal substance when consumed in quantity.

The real answer to the anthropological question, however, is that neither bread nor beer came first. Beer was probably not the first fermented beverage, simply because it is more difficult to make. As already noted, barley requires a lot of processing, from sowing and winnowing the grain to milling, malting, and fermenting it. The starches in the grain must be broken down into simple sugars and yeast added to start the fermentation. In other words, wine and honey mead would have readily won the ancient fermented-beverage competition.

EGALITARIAN LIVING AND EASY DRINKING
IN THE NEOLITHIC

My first foray into the world of the Neolithic Middle East and its lineup of fermented beverages came after the seminal 1991 wine conference "The Origins and Ancient History of Wine," at the Robert Mondavi Winery. I returned from that conference fired up with the prospects of finding even earlier evidence of wine. The Neolithic period, from about 8500 to 4000 B.C., seemed to offer the best prospects for discovering more. In this period, humans took control of their food resources by domesticating a variety of plants and animals, leading to the first permanent, year-round settlements in the Near East. The invention of pottery around 6000 B.C. gave impetus to the process of settling down, as it allowed wine and other foods and beverages to be prepared in special vessels and protected from spoilage by storing in stoppered jars. What can be termed a Neolithic cuisine emerged. A variety of food-processing techniques—fermentation, soaking, heating, spicing—were developed, and Neolithic peoples are credited with first producing beer, bread, and an array of meat and cereal entrées, many of which we continue to enjoy today.

The invention of pottery also markedly improved our prospects for detecting residues of ancient foods and beverages. Clays are readily formed into processing, serving, drinking, and storage vessels, which would have been ideal for the production and consumption of wine and other fermented beverages. Once fired to a high temperature, the pottery is virtually indestructible: sherds will survive for millennia even if a vessel is shattered. Most important, liquids and their precipitates readily accumulate in the pores of pottery fabrics, where compounds are preserved from environmental contamination by being sequestered in the chemical matrix of the clay.

The Penn Museum was the ideal place to look for chemical evidence of Neolithic wine, as it has one of the world's best collections of well-documented excavated artifacts. I simply had to ring up and talk with Neolithic archaeologists on staff, or others who had carried out excavations for the Museum, some of whose archaeological materials had been consigned by the host country to its permanent collections. Mary Voigt, now at the College of William and Mary, was my first contact, and, as it turned out, I did not need to look any further.

Mary told me about her 1968 excavations of a small Neolithic village, Hajji Firuz Tepe, in the northern Zagros Mountains southwest of Lake Urmia, at an elevation of more than 1,200 meters above sea level. Its Neolithic inhabitants appear to have enjoyed a very comfortable life. Animal and plant resources were abundant. Their well-made mudbrick homes were approximately square in shape, with a large living room (which may have doubled as a bedroom), a kitchen, and two storage rooms. The buildings are nearly identical to those still seen in the area today and could have accommodated an extended family then as now.

Because the site dated to the Pottery Neolithic, ca. 5400–5000 B.C., my next question to Mary was the obvious one: Had she seen any pottery vessels that might have contained wine (see plate 5b)? Yes, she recalled sherds with a yellowish residue, which were later reconstructed into a complete jar. The residues were confined to the inside lower half of the jar, suggesting that their contents had originally been liquid. Six jars of the same shape, each with a volume of about nine liters, had been set into the floor of a kitchen in one of the Neolithic houses, lined up along one wall. On the other side of the room was a fireplace, and pottery vessels, probably used to prepare and cook foods, were found scattered and broken on the floor. Whatever they originally contained, the six jars were presumably involved in the Neolithic cuisine of the village.

When Mary first noted the residue on the sherds, she had thought they might be from milk, yogurt, or some other dairy product. The vessel was taken apart and scientific analyses carried out to identify them, but the results were negative, probably owing to the poorly developed state of biomolecular archaeology before around 1990.

In 1993, we descended into the storage-room "catacombs" of the Penn Museum and reexcavated the sherds from their modern burial. Chemical analysis enabled my laboratory to solve the enigma of what the jar originally contained. Our identification of tartaric acid confirmed that the jar had been filled with wine. After our finding, reported in *Nature,* became a cause célèbre, I was given access to another, intact jar from the kitchen, on exhibit at the Museum, which had a reddish residue on its inside. Our analysis showed that this, too, came from a resinated wine. Whether this was a red wine, to go with the white (yellowish) wine of the first jar analyzed, can only be determined by identifying the pigment as a red anthocyanin (cyanidin) or a yellowish flavonoid (quercetin), which we have yet to do.

Like the Godin Tepe jars, these much earlier vessels were superbly designed to preserve the precious liquid inside. Their narrow mouths were fitted with tight clay stoppers, recovered in the vicinity, to keep out oxygen and prevent "wine disease."

The chemical analyses of the two Hajji Firuz jars yielded something else of great interest. The presence of characteristic triterpenoid compounds indicated that terebinth tree resin, with known antioxidant and antimicrobial properties, had been added to the grape wine. The terebinth tree (*Pistacia atlantica*, a member of the pistachio family) is widespread and abundant in the Middle East, occurring even in desert areas. A single tree, which can grow to twelve meters in height and two meters in diameter, can yield up to two kilograms of the resin in late summer or fall, just about the same time that grapes are ready to be picked.

Tree resins have a long and noble history of use by humans, extending back into Palaeolithic times. They could be used as glues and were perhaps even chewed to give pain relief, as suggested by lumps of birch resin with tooth marks that were found in a Neolithic Swiss lake dwelling. Early humans appear to have recognized that a tree helps to heal itself by oozing resin after its bark has been cut, thus preventing infection. They made the mental leap to apply resins to human wounds. By the same reasoning, drinking a wine laced with a tree resin should help to treat internal maladies. And the same healing properties might be applied to stave off the dreaded "wine disease" by adding tree resins to the wine.

Resinated wines were greatly appreciated in antiquity, as we have come to see in analyzing wines from all over the Middle East, extending from the Neolithic down to the Byzantine period. Although some wine drinkers today turn up their noses at a resinated wine, now made only in Greece as retsina, the technique is analogous to ageing in oak. The result can actually be quite appealing: the Gaia Estate's Ritinitis has a mildly citrusy flavor, achieved by adding a very slight touch of Aleppo pine resin to a Greek grape variety. Even the Romans added resins such as pine, cedar, terebinth (known as the "queen of resins"), frankincense, and myrrh to all their wine except extremely fine vintages. According to Pliny the Elder, who devoted a good part of book 14 of his *Natural History* to resinated wines, myrrh-laced wine was considered the best and most expensive.

As we have already seen in Neolithic China, the use of tree resins was probably part of the medicinal and plant lore that became widespread at that time, along with many other advances that have stood the test of time. But wine or any other fermented beverage has its own inherent medical benefits, if drunk in moderation. Like the tree-resin constituents, the alcohol and polyphenolic aromatics derived from the plant pigments have measurable antioxidant effects. Resveratrol, which has been touted of late, is only one of a host of these compounds, which counteract highly reactive species in the body, thereby lowering the risk of cardiovascular disease and protecting humans against cancers and other ailments.

Resinated fermented beverages in the Neolithic, whether produced in China or the Middle East, appear to have been shared by the whole community in a fairly egalitarian fashion, perhaps with the occasional special concession to an emergent shamanistic class. There are no marked social divisions at the site: the same pottery types, for example, recur from one house to the next.

If the six jars in the kitchen of one ordinary house are any measure, drinking in the village was not a privilege of only the rich and famous. If all these jars were filled, they held about fifty liters, or forty gallons. If the other households at the site (which has not been excavated fully) followed the same pattern of usage, we are talking about a lot of wine, roughly five thousand liters for one hundred houses.

The availability of such a large quantity of wine implies that the Eurasian grapevine had already come under cultivation at Hajji Firuz. The area was well suited to the growing of grapes. It lies at the easternmost edge of the modern and ancient distribution of the wild vine *V. v. sylvestris* in the hill country bordering northern Mesopotamia, as shown by pollen cores recovered by boring into sediments at nearby Lake Urmia. However, the wild vine would have been less accessible and lower yielding than the domesticated plant. From the amount of wine available in the Hajji Firuz community, we could go a step further and propose that viticulture and winemaking were joint endeavors of the village as a whole. In contrast to its prestige status today, wine might have served as a democratizing element in the Neolithic economy and society.

Hajji Firuz provides our first glimpse of Neolithic wine, but as yet, beer or other fermented beverages have not been confirmed this early. Very much, however, depends on the selection of pottery vessels for analysis, and thus far attention has been directed mainly toward possible wine containers. We need another Ginny Badler to sort through the Neolithic pottery corpus and pick out the potential vessels used to make beer, mead, and other fermented beverages.

The fertile foothills of Iran's Azerbaijan province, where Hajji Firuz is located, merge with the Taurus Mountains, north of the Mesopotamian plain, in eastern Turkey, or Anatolia. Here, in 1983, a tidal shift in Neolithic studies occurred at the site of Nevali Çori, set in the starkly beautiful limestone terrain of the upper Euphrates River valley. To look at the barren hills today, with only a thread of luxuriant vegetation along the river in the distance, it is easy to understand why archaeologists did not venture into the area sooner. The impending construction of the Atatürk Dam changed all that. Teams from the University of Heidelberg's Academy of Sciences, led by Harald Hauptmann, and the Archaeological Museum of Sanliurfa moved in to help in the salvage effort before the lake behind the dam rose to obliterate all signs of ancient human occupation.

The excavators were astounded by the finds uncovered at Nevali Çori, dating to the Early Pre-Pottery Neolithic period from about 8500 to 6000 B.C. Two nearly square buildings, one on top of the other and about sixteen meters on a side, had been carefully constructed by laying out lines of tall, monolithic pillars of limestone formed into a T shape at the top. Stone benches, with pillars built in, lined the walls. In the latest structure, two bent arms with clasped hands had been carved in low relief on the two central pillars. One could almost imagine the pillars as a silent assembly of human onlookers to events in the buildings. The living Neolithic people would have observed from the benches. Never before had monumental architecture on such an elaborate scale been found at an early Neolithic site.

The buildings each had a niche inset into a wall, and in the latest phase, a strange sculpture had been built into or buried in the back wall of the niche: a large fragment of a bald head, with projecting ears and a phallus-like snake slithering up the back of the head. The face was unfortunately broken away, so the figure's sex is uncertain. Although broken at the neck, it appeared to have been part of a larger life-size figure, which Hauptmann conjectured had originally stood on the podium in front of the earlier phase's niche. That niche also yielded a limestone sculpture of a large raptor.

There were no signs that the earlier building had been destroyed and then rebuilt. Rather, the earlier building was filled in intentionally, ceremonially buried as it were, along with eleven more stone sculptures. One of the most remarkable pieces deposited in the fill was a three-dimensional pillar like a totem pole, which shows two figures back to back, arms and legs entwined, each with a large raptor standing on its head. The long, plaited tresses of the heads suggest that the figures are female. The bust of another coiffed statue is held firmly by talons. Two birds face one another on yet another piece. Bird and human appear to have been merged on a fourth example, with arms or wings folded in front of the body; its projecting head and flat facial features are owl-like and eerily reminiscent of a Modigliani painting.

Clearly, the Nevali Çori buildings were no ordinary residences. They are not unique in southeastern Turkey. The nearby site of Göbekli Tepe, from an even earlier phase of the Pre-Pottery Neolithic, has been the focus of Hauptmann's colleague Klaus Schmidt. Located in the so-called Golden Triangle, bordered by the Euphrates, Tigris, and Balikh rivers, the site looks out across the fertile Harran plain from a high hill. The buildings uncovered there have T-shaped pillars that are even more ornately decorated than those at Nevali Çori. Lions leap out from atop the pillars. Snakes undulate up and down. Foxes leap. Boars charge. Ducks flock together. On one pillar, we see an assemblage of three animals—an aurochs (wild ox), fox, and crane—going from top to bottom: the narrow side of the pillar depicts only the horns of the aurochs. Humans are also shown: a sculpture of a female head in the clasp of raptor talons is similar to the one found at Nevali Çori, and an incised slab graphically depicts a naked female, legs spread apart, and penetrated by a penis.

The sculptures at both sites provide the clues to the original functions of the structures in which they were found. We have seen that shamans elsewhere associated their access to otherworldly realms with high-flying birds and their songs and mating dances. Spectacular later Anatolian drinking vessels, with long, beak-shaped spouts, probably perpetuated this tradition. Six millennia following the Neolithic, remnants of some peculiar association between birds and humans (females in this instance) can be seen in depictions of the great mother goddess of the Phrygians, Matar, who is shown holding a raptor or enveloped in its feathers. In short, the structures at Nevali Çori and Göbekli Tepe were cult buildings, representing one of the first glimmerings of an organized religion in the Middle East.

WHAT WERE THEY DRINKING AND SACRIFICING?

If we grant cultic status to the unusual structures at Nevali Çori and Göbekli Tepe, we are still left with questions about whether any fermented beverage figured in the rituals. Two smaller artifacts, a stone goblet and

Figure 9. Extraordinary limestone sculptures adorned the "temples" at Göbekli Tepe, ca. 9000 B.C. This T-shaped pillar realistically portrays a wild ox, fox, and crane. Photograph courtesy of Professor Dr. Klaus Schmidt, Deutsches Archäologisches Institut, Berlin.

Figure 10. Carved bowl or goblet in limestone from Nevali Çori, ca. 8000 B.C., height
13.5 cm. The exuberant dancing scene of two humans and a tortoise on the exterior of this
vessel is unique. Photograph courtesy of Professor Dr. Harald Hauptmann, Euphrates
Archive, Heidelberger Akademie der Wissenschaften.

bowl, from the Nevali Çori excavations suggest that it did. The carved
goblet depicts a male and female dancing with a Euphrates tortoise. A festive
occasion also seems to be represented on the bowl, which depicts three
leaping figures, open-mouthed as if belting out a song. I had seen similar
scenes (minus the tortoise) on Neolithic jars from Georgia in the Caucasus,
and in those instances, the figures appeared to be dancing beneath a grape
arbor. An association with grape wine was strongly implied, as Georgia
was one of the ancient world's great wine cultures. Preliminary chemical results show that Neolithic jars from Shulaveris-Gora and Khramis-Didi-
Gora once held wine.

Stone bowls and goblets similar to those from Nevali Çori have been
found at Göbekli Tepe and other key sites throughout the region, including Çayönü, where researchers have found a long temporal sequence of
monumental cult buildings that were ritually buried by filling them with
soil after they went out of use. The evidence from Körtik and Hallan Çemi,
both situated farther east along tributaries of the Tigris River, is of particular interest because of the quantity and early date of their vessels.

Hallan Çemi, being excavated under the direction of Michael Rosenberg of the University of Delaware, represents an even earlier phase of the Pre-Pottery Neolithic than Göbekli Tepe. Its cult buildings were smaller than those at Göbekli, less well made, and circular. The many fragments of stone bowls and goblets found there are often plain, but when decorated by incising, they feature the same motifs—especially stylized snakes and birds—as at Körtik. Excavation at Körtik, carried out by Vecihi Özkaya of Dicle (Tigris) University, has yielded bowls and goblets only from burials. The vessels number in the hundreds: in addition to the animal motifs, many feature intricate geometric designs. The juxtaposition of birds and snakes, as well as the Nevali Çori dancing tortoise, on many of the vessels also points to a tiered worldview with lower and upper realms, which is characteristic of shamanistic thought. Recently the body of an elderly and disabled woman, who has been identified as a shaman, was found buried with more than fifty complete tortoise shells and the remains of a wild boar, eagle, cow, leopard, and two martens in a cave in the western Galilee region of Israel. Could it be that this special interment, dated to ca. 12,000 B.P. and belonging to the Natufian culture (see chapter 6), is a forerunner of the motifs seen on the vessels and pillars of eastern Turkey or of the incised tortoise shells deposited with the "shamanistic" musicians at Jiahu in China several thousand years later?

The Hallan Çemi and Körtik bowls and goblets were carved from chlorite, a clay mineral with highly adsorbent properties. Such vessels led on to the earliest pottery, beginning around 6000 B.C., which included larger jars and sieves, ideal for processing and storing wine, and which were sometimes decorated with clay appliqués in the form of grape clusters, like the Georgian jars.

On my trip to eastern Turkey in 2004, Vecihi Özkaya made available to me two of the Körtik chlorite vessels for analysis. We were extremely fortunate that copious amounts of ancient organic compounds were retained in pores of the chlorite. Our analyses, still in progress, show very good evidence, based on the infrared results and spot tests for tartaric acid, that the original contents of these vessels were grape wine, not barley beer. More definitive liquid chromatography–mass spectrometry–mass spectrometry (LC–MS–MS) analysis is needed to verify this result.

TO THE HEADWATERS OF THE TIGRIS AND EUPHRATES

Besides securing stone and pottery samples for analysis, my trip to eastern Turkey had another goal. You might say that we were looking for the vinicultural Garden of Eden. The eastern Taurus, Caucasus, and northern Zagros mountains have long been considered the world center of the Eurasian grape: this is the area where the species shows its greatest genetic variation and consequently where it might have been first domesticated. It is also becoming increasingly clear, as we pursue our combined archaeological and chemical investigations, that the world's first wine culture—one in which viniculture, comprising both viticulture and winemaking, came to dominate the economy, religion, and society as a whole—emerged in this upland area by at least 7000 B.C.

Once established, the wine culture gradually radiated across time and space to become a dominant economic and social force throughout the region and later across Europe in the millennia to follow. The end result over the past ten thousand years or so, since the end of the Ice Age, is that the Eurasian grape now accounts for some ten thousand varieties and 99 percent of the world's wine. Even though North America and East Asia have many more native grape species, some with very high sugar contents, there is as yet, amazingly, no evidence that they were domesticated before modern times.

We were interested in finding out whether there was a unique event that precipitated domestication in this core area. This one-time, one-place proposition has been referred to as the Noah hypothesis, an allusion to the biblical tradition that the patriarch's first goal, after his ark came to rest on Mount Ararat, was to plant a vineyard and make wine (Genesis 8:4 and 9:20).

Although eastern Turkey today might not appear to be conducive to viticulture, the recent excavations painted a much different picture during the Neolithic period. Precipitation levels were higher in the period immediately succeeding the Ice Age, and because the Taurus Mountains form part of the Trans-Asiatic orogenic belt, a region of intense geologic activity today and in the past, the soils are rich in all the essential metals, minerals, and other nutrients needed by grapes as well as by numerous other wild fruits, nuts, and cereals.

The calcareous hills and valleys of this upland region are generally characterized by an iron-rich red loam known as terra rossa. This soil is often rocky, encouraging good drainage and root development, and contains enough clay to retain moisture through the dry season. Its slightly alkaline pH and low humus content are also good for grapes. Even if these conditions were ripe for exploitation, the question is whether early humans first domesticated the Eurasian grape somewhere in the Taurus Mountains and began to make wine here.

In collaboration with colleagues in Europe and the United States, we have applied modern DNA analysis to resolve this question. We sequenced specific regions (microsatellites) of the nuclear and chloroplast genome of modern wild and domesticated grape plants from Turkey, Armenia, and Georgia and carefully compared these results with those from European and Mediterranean cultivars. We have already shown that Middle Eastern grapes probably derive from common ancestors and that four Western European varieties—Chasselas, Nebbiolo, Pinot, and Syrah—are closely related to a group of Georgian cultivars and might well have some ancient Georgian ancestors. The extraction of ancient DNA from seeds or other parts of the plant, which should eventually provide more direct evidence, is being pursued.

Our search for wild vines in eastern Turkey turned out to be a high adventure. Together with my associates from the University of Neuchâtel in Switzerland (José Vouillamoz) and the University of Ankara (Gökhan Söylemezoğlu and Ali Ergul), we traveled the dusty highroads and byways in our Department of Agriculture Land Cruiser during the spring of 2004. One dramatic setting for our collecting was in a deeply cut ravine below the famous site of Nemrut Daghi, where the first-century B.C. ruler Antiochus I Epiphanes had statues of himself in the company of the gods hewn out of limestone on a mountaintop 2,150 meters high. Other promising areas were along a river valley cutting through the Taurus Mountains around Bitlis and Siirt, and along the Euphrates River north of Sanliurfa, at Halfeti.

We traveled all the way to the headwaters of the Tigris River, just downstream from Lake Hazar and the city of Elaziğ. Here the river cuts through one of the most metallurgically important areas in the ancient Near East, Maden (Turkish for "mine"), and an area that is still tectonically active. Maden is only about twenty-five kilometers from the important Neolithic site of Çayönü. Fortunately the Earth's crust was quiet, but in my eagerness to reach a particularly enticing grapevine clinging to a bank of the river, I almost fell into the raging torrent of the upper Tigris. But for the sure hands of my colleague Ali, I might not be telling this story.

Our risks paid off when we found a hermaphroditic wild plant which was positioned between a wild male and female vine, exactly the situation that an early viticulturalist would have needed to observe and select for. What makes the domesticated Eurasian grapevine so desirable is that it is hermaphroditic: male stamens and female pistils are located together in the same flowers on the plant, whereas for the wild variety, male and female flowers occur on separate plants. The proximity of the sexual organs on the hermaphroditic plants ensures the production of much more fruit on a predictable basis. This self-fertilizing plant could then be selected for desirable traits, such as sweeter, juicier fruit or thinner skins, and cloned by propagation of branches, buds, or roots.

The hermaphrodites, representing a mutation, account for about 5 to 7 percent of the wild-vine population. Still, it would have taken some pretty sharp eyes to pick out just those plants and domesticate them, as the sexual organs of the flowers are microscopic.

Domestication of the grapevine assumes that humans had discovered how to propagate it artificially, as growing it from seed results in unpredictable characteristics. The natural habit of the wild grapevine also doesn't lend itself to making the best wine grapes or easy harvesting. Left to itself, it grows high up in trees, shading out competing plants and producing fruit appealing to animals, especially birds who spread its seed, but not necessarily to humans, as it can be very sour.

It's not beyond the realm of possibility that Neolithic viticulturalists developed a layering method (*provenage*) to propagate the grapevine from the root and thus train it to grow up a nearby tree. The idea of propping up vines with artificial supports might well have been suggested by vines growing up trees. Early viticulturalists might have also started training the vine's height and shape, which would make gathering the fruit a lot easier.

To date, our DNA studies, based on the samples we collected in eastern Turkey and the Caucasus, appear to support the Noah hypothesis, but more work is needed. Samples are needed from other parts of the Middle East, especially Azerbaijan in modern Iran, and this remains a difficult region to work in. If the hermaphroditic gene itself, a single region of the genome that accounts for the development of both male and female organs in flowers on the same plant, could be isolated, then we could target that gene for analysis in ancient and modern material. Someday soon we will have the answer.

INTO THE BLACK MOUNTAINS

Beer was probably not far behind wine in fueling the Neolithic Revolution. On a tour of Göbekli Tepe with its excavator, Klaus Schmidt, Stephen Mithen of the University of Reading observed that religious ideology might have driven human settlement at the site, more than any economic advantages gained from domesticated plants and animals. Inverting the usual formula invoked to explain the Neolithic, Mithen proposed that the large number of laborers who were needed to construct the cult buildings had to be fed (and, I would add, had to have their thirst quenched), thus creating a need for reliable local sources of food.

In response to Mithen's idea, Schmidt pointed to some mountains about thirty kilometers away: the Karacadağ Range, or Black Mountains. This volcanic area of black basaltic boulders is covered with dense stands of wild einkorn wheat (*Triticum monococcum* ssp. *boeoticum*). Certainly the area is awash in luxuriant grasses in the spring, when our intrepid team of grape explorers went in search of wild vines there and came back empty-handed. Wheat has the upper hand in these hills.

A very persuasive DNA study of the Karacadağ strain of einkorn has shown that compared to other modern wild plants distributed over a wide arc from central Europe to western Iran, the Karacadağ wheat is genetically closer to the modern domesticated cereal (*T. m. monococcum*). The archaeobotanical evidence bears out this finding: the earliest wild and cultivated einkorn has been recovered from early Neolithic sites in this region, including Çayönü and Nevali Çori, as well as from northern Syria. Indeed, the origin of three of the eight "founder plants" that jump-started human agriculture during the Neolithic Revolution—einkorn wheat, chickpea, and bitter vetch in the legume family—have been traced to this area. Another founder plant, emmer wheat (*Triticum dicoccum*), has also been attested in its wild and domesticated forms at Çayönü and Nevali Çori.

Neither Schmidt nor Mithen went on to speculate about whether the local wheats were used to make bread or beer, and no chemical analyses of vessels from the site have yet been carried out. Neither einkorn nor emmer is ideal for making beer, because they yield insufficient diastase enzymes, when the cereals are sprouted, to break down the starches into sugar. Barley accomplishes this objective more effectively: in modern brewing, a wheat beer is made by mixing in some barley malt to promote the saccharification of the wheat polysaccharides. Our inventive ancestors likely fell upon a similar solution by accident.

Especially when the first alcoholic beverages were being concocted, an enterprising Neolithic beverage maker had to be willing to try anything. A pure, refined beverage was probably not the goal. Rather, one envisions energetic experimenters gathered around fermentation vats in Neolithic villages across eastern Turkey. They needed to try different combinations of whatever natural ingredients they could find: fruits, grains, honeys, herbs, and spices. Taste and smell were their main guides. No doubt they received a final verdict on their brew from the rest of the community.

Our beverage maker might well have observed that malted barley tasted sweeter than einkorn or emmer malt. Moreover, because only wild, not cultivated, barley (*Hordeum spontaneum*) has been reported in these early settlements, wheat was probably the more prevalent grain. Addition of wheat would have helped to bulk up a wild barley beer, besides providing its own delightful characteristics.

Domesticated barley (*H. vulgare*), introduced from a nearby area, made its appearance by the late Neolithic. All that was required was a change of two genes to convert a delicate rachis to a tough one that kept the grain from falling to the ground and being lost. Even with enough barley to make a traditional barley beer or a wheat beer, Neolithic beverage makers would have been obliged to add a high-sugar fruit or honey to the vat to get the fermentation going. They might also have reused the same vessel, harboring yeast from past fermentations.

THE CRANE DANCE OF ÇATAL HÖYÜK

Some five hundred kilometers west of the upper Tigris and Euphrates rivers, in the lower foothills of the Taurus Mountains, an extraordinary site, Çatal Höyük, is rich in possibilities for tracing the development of fermented beverages. I say "possibilities" because a biomolecular archaeological investigation remains to be done.

Excavations at Çatal Höyük, in the Konya plain of Cappadocia, by James Mellaart in the 1960s and by Ian Hodder since 1993 have revealed a succession of building levels from about 6500 to 5500 B.C., or the late Pre-Pottery Neolithic. A series of some forty structures, apparently shrines, crowded cheek by jowl within the settlement, was the most awe-inspiring discovery at this site, the largest known Neolithic village in the Near East. The walls of the shrines were adorned with painted and repainted frescoes that evoke Palaeolithic cave art and again point to birds of prey as an important part of ritualistic activity. Direct imprints and negative outlines of hands in red paint, row upon row, take us back to the Ice Age caverns, where a group of humans might have similarly signified their solidarity and communion with the gods.

At Çatal Höyük, vultures (*Gyps fulvus*) are seen feasting on headless humans, and human skulls fill gigantic multiple breasts painted on another wall. Another image shows a group of at least ten hunters with bows and arrows attacking two stags and a fawn. Their efforts appear to be encouraged by a group of dancers, some headless and one perhaps holding a drum.

Actual burials under the floors of the shrines are sometimes headless, and in those instances the person's chest was usually covered by an enigmatic object—a simple wood board, owl pellets, or an animal's penis. Outside the settlement, groups of skulls have been found buried, perhaps the counterparts of the headless torsos.

A strange set of painted interlocking hexagonal cells, whose sides are broken off at the edges, has been interpreted by Mellaart as a honeycomb with bees either encapsulated within their brood cells or emerging above a field of flowers. We should not dismiss this interpretation as reading too much into the geometric imagery. Bees are also likely depicted on a set of unique stone plaques from Körtik, as well as on one of the most elaborately carved pillars in a cult building at Göbekli. Anatolia is renowned for its honey, which includes the delightfully citrusy varieties from the west coast, wildflower types from the central plateau, and those made from honeydew, an insect exudation on red pine trees, in the southwestern forests. Around the highest peak in the Taurus, Mount Ararat, bee hunters still scour the woods for wild hives high in the trees that have not been cleaned out by bears. The great advantage of honey in making a fermented beverage, as I cannot overemphasize, is that it has the highest concentration of simple sugars in nature and, when diluted, will be fermented by its own yeast.

Numerous stone and pottery figurines of a naked, amply proportioned female figure with child, the so-called mother goddess, is also evocative of Palaeolithic Venuses. The Çatal Höyük female is shown sitting regally on a chair or throne with arms resembling leopard's paws. On the frescoes, this "mother goddess" gives birth to aurochs and rams. Vulture beaks protrude through plaster-molded breasts on walls. Although the female is predominant, a bearded male or "god" figure, mounted on aurochs and leopards, is also depicted. The intermingling of human and animal is confounding but at the same time conforms in many respects to later mythological thinking.

We can partly enter into this mystical world of our Neolithic forebears by considering a bird wing that was found deposited in a small, inaccessible cavity, together with an aurochs horn core and two wild goat horn cores. Analysis of the bone identified the bird as a common crane (*Grus grus*), which immediately suggests that something unusual was afoot. As we have seen, wing bones of other crane and swan species were made into flutes in places as far-flung as southern Germany and East Asia. The intricate mating dance of the Chinese red-crowned crane is nearly identical to that

Figure 11. Neolithic "mother goddess" flanked by leopards, from a grain pit at Çatal Höyük, Turkey, ca. 6500 to 5500 B.C. (height 11.8 cm, head restored). It perpetuated a grand tradition of "Venus" figurines, with roots going back into the Palaeolithic period. Photograph courtesy of James Mellaart.

of its Anatolian cousin. Study of the cut marks on the Çatal Höyük wing bones determined that the wing had been perforated by an awl-like tool in a regular fashion. Most likely fibers were strung through the holes so that the wing could be worn on the shoulder of a human as part of the costume for a special dance.

Partial archaeological support for this hypothesis comes from a fresco at the site, which shows a pair of cranes facing each other; on another wall of the same room, five dancing figures wear leopard skins and sport tails made of black feathers, possibly from the common crane. At Bouqras along the Euphrates River in Syria, a painted and incised panel shows seventeen cranes dancing as a group, all posed in the same direction, behavior that has been observed in the wild. And I have already mentioned the crane depicted on one of the Göbekli pillars.

The case for a special crane dance at Neolithic Çatal Höyük gains credibility when we consider that crane dances are found among peoples in Siberia, China, Australia, Japan and other Pacific islands, and southern

Africa. When the Greek hero Theseus escaped the Minotaur on Crete and landed on the island of Delos in the Aegean Sea, the Plutarch legend has it that he danced like a crane.

Although we do not yet have the biomolecular archaeological evidence to show that a fermented beverage might have been associated with a Neolithic crane dance or the geometrical and figural imagery of the frescoes and statuary at Çatal Höyük, other finds are suggestive. The pottery chalices (some made of wood, which had been preserved because of the site's anaerobic, boggy conditions in Neolithic times), funnels which could be used to transfer liquids, and other vessel types suitable for storing and serving beverages—including high, narrow-mouthed storage jars in the shape of a seated "goddess," bird- and boar-shaped forms, and cups—point to a highly developed drinking culture. The recovery of considerable domesticated barley and wheat throughout the site demonstrates that the raw materials for beer were available. Surprisingly, grapes are absent from the archaeobotanical corpus, even though today excellent vineyards flourish only fifty kilometers to the east, at a high elevation. The use of honey is another possibility, based on the artwork, but still unproven. According to Christine Hastorf, an archaeobotanist for the recent expedition to the site, there is one high-sugar fruit—hackberry (*Celtis* sp.)—that might well have been a major ingredient in whatever beverages were concocted at the site. This nutritious fruit has the taste and consistency of a date. Wood fragments of the shrub indicate that the plant grew in the vicinity.

Of one thing we can be certain: the Çatal Höyük inhabitants had some kind of alcoholic beverage. They were situated close to the proposed core area of Neolithic "founder plant" domestication. Grape seeds have been recovered at almost every other Neolithic site in the general area, dating back as early as 9000 B.C. (for example, Çayönü). Other fruits, such as raspberry, blackberry, cornelian cherry, elderberry, and bittersweet, were also being exploited. With such a wealth of fermentable materials to hand, the Çatal Höyük beverage maker probably entered into the spirit of the time and prepared a highly experimental beverage, likely including hackberry fruit and honey.

TRAVERSING THE ASIATIC RIFT VALLEY

The wine culture that was consolidated in the Neolithic core area of southeastern Turkey and northern Syria might better be dubbed a mixed fermented beverage or extreme beverage culture, as it likely made use of a wide assortment of fruits, grains, honey, and various herbs in addition to grapes. As we trace the spread of this beverage revolution to other parts of the Near East, the Jordan Valley is of special interest.

Extending from the Sea of Galilee to the Dead Sea, the lowest point on Earth, the Jordan Valley continues the line of the African Great Rift Valley north into western Asia. Our ancestors coming out of Africa about one hundred thousand years ago probably passed this way before dispersing to other parts of the globe. To judge from the wealth of Palaeolithic encampments throughout the valley, however, many must have been induced by the abundant wildlife and verdant plant life to stay on. It is said that you can hardly take a step without treading on a prehistoric site; but you might get the opposite impression when you initially enter the valley, as I did on my first trip to the Middle East in 1971. Taking the modern highway from Jerusalem to Jericho, which follows an ancient route, feels like descending into hell. As the altitude drops, the moderate, breezy climate of the uplands gives way to a much hotter desert environment. Just when you are about to cry out desperately for a drink, the green oasis of Jericho fills your view. Soon you are enjoying mango juice, eating papaya, and lounging in an open-air cafe.

Ancient Jericho, lying nearly three hundred meters below sea level and close to the Dead Sea, has a sequence of permanent human occupation going back to 10,000 B.C. We have Dame Kathleen Kenyon of Oxford University to thank for carefully peeling back the layers of time in the 1950s and revealing a remarkable early Pre-Pottery Neolithic burial custom similar to what was happening slightly earlier in Anatolia to the north.

Kenyon found groups of plastered human skulls beneath the floors of ancient Jericho buildings, which resemble the human and animal plaster modeling on the walls of Çatal Höyük. All the features were finely delineated. Curiously, the top of the head was left bare and the lower jaw (mandible) removed and replaced with plaster. Cowrie and other shells, which had to be brought hundreds of kilometers from the Red Sea and Mediterranean Sea, were inserted into the eye sockets and gave the eerie appearance of a person sleeping with eyes closed.

It appeared that the plastered skulls were sometimes treated like a community gathering. Three might be grouped together, facing the same direction. In one case, they were arranged in a tight circle, all looking inward. I saw a similar practice in an early Iron Age burial cave with 227 individuals, which I excavated in the Baqʿah Valley, near Amman, less than fifty kilometers away. The skulls, which were not plastered in this instance, had been removed from their bodies in a succession of burials dating from about 1200 to 1050 B.C. and later laid out in a circle around the walls of the cave. At the time, I believed the arrangement represented an ancestral gathering of an extended family in the realm of the dead (Hebrew *Sheol*).

As the pace of excavation in the Jordan Valley and its adjoining highlands quickened in the decades to follow, more plastered skulls were uncovered. One of the most amazing series of finds was discovered by chance. When a new highway was being cut north of Amman on the Transjordanian plateau in 1974, an extensive Pre-Pottery Neolithic village, 'Ain Ghazal, was revealed. A salvage team, headed by Gary Rollefson and Zeidan Khafafi, moved in to preserve what they could. What they discovered were not just plastered skulls, but thirty-two complete statues of human figures. They were found in two pit caches, separated by about two hundred years during the seventh millennium B.C. All the statues had been carefully laid down in an east-west direction.

The 'Ain Ghazal statues were of two general types: one-headed with lower body parts more or less defined, and two-headed, with a shared body or bust. In all cases, the plaster had been molded around reed armatures, not around skulls and other bones. The greatest care had been taken in modeling the heads, which had striking, wide-open eyes and irises outlined in bitumen. The plaster had been polished and given an ocher sheen. Some of the statues were clearly female, since they held their breasts and enlarged bellies with their hands in the way that is so common beginning in the Palaeolithic period and continuing for millennia. The genders of the double figures are less certain, as body parts, even arms and legs, are absent; the heads stick up from solid bases. Measuring about thirty centimeters to one meter tall, the statues could stand on their own and were evidently meant to be displayed.

Another group of finds at 'Ain Ghazal may enable us to see through the eyes of our Neolithic ancestors and begin to understand the complex symbolism behind the plastered skulls and statues. Three plaster masks of a human face, eyes nearly closed in the manner of the dead, were found together. Perhaps these masks covered skulls intended for burial, but another possibility is that they were worn by a cultic representative of the dead ancestors or a shaman. The statues, possibly representing the fertility goddess and her male consort, might also have been paraded in a ceremony. Their wide-eyed, penetrating stares appear to look beyond the grave and to unite living and dead. After the ceremony, they might have continued to exercise

Figure 12. Statue of two Neolithic "ancestors," their bodies
merged, staring out from prominent, bitumen-defined eyes
(height 85 cm). The nearly half life-sized figure was found in
a mid-seventh-millennium B.C. cache of many other plaster
statues at 'Ain Ghazal, Jordan. Courtesy the Department of
Antiquities of Jordan. Photograph by John Tsantes, courtesy
Arthur M. Sackler Gallery, Smithsonian Institution.

their preternatural powers in the confines of a religious structure. The excavators identified a number of circular and rectangular structures, with prominent orthostats or upright stones sometimes demarcating possible altars, hearths, or apsidal recesses as shrines or temples, and the statues might have originally stood in these places.

Two circular shrines provide a further clue to possible cultic activity. A large central hole in the middle of the plaster pavement, which had been replastered over and over again, as might be expected for a repetitive ceremony, fed into subfloor channels. This central feature reminds one of the cult buildings at Çayönü with above-ground and subterranean channels, which the excavators there interpreted as related to ceremonial libations.

As with so much else Neolithic, we have glimpses of the inhabitants' symbolic world but still lack firm evidence about which fermented beverages were integrated into the rituals. No laboratory has yet analyzed the pottery of later phases of the Neolithic period, including jars and slipped and painted cups, which would have been ideal for storing, serving, and ceremonially pouring out a potable. We have no evidence of the domesticated grape on the Transjordanian Plateau or Jordan Valley as early as the Neolithic period. It was not transplanted southward until around 4000 B.C. Domesticated emmer and einkorn wheat, as well as barley, were available for making beer. Honey could have been used.

A recent discovery from another site in the lower Jordan Valley, only twelve kilometers north of Jericho, sheds a new light on the issue. Gilgal I is an early Neolithic village, dating back to 11,400–11,200 B.P. Although excavated more than thirty years ago, its fruit remains were examined in detail only recently, by Mordechai Kislev of Bar-Ilan University. His analysis of nine dried common figs (*Ficus carica*) and hundreds of drupelets, the inner pulp of the fruit, showed that their seeds or embryos had not been fertilized by the symbiotic wasp, *Blastophaga psenes*. He and his colleagues argue that this is presumptive evidence that the fig had already been domesticated. A single mutation enabled the tree to reproduce parthenocarpically (that is, without fertilization by pollen, normally delivered by the wasp) and produce very sweet, edible figs that do not fall to the ground. Because this plant cannot reproduce by seed, however, humans had to step in and propagate the plant by taking and transplanting cuttings of branches. The fig readily adapts to human manipulation because it develops roots more easily than any other fruit tree.

The Gilgal figs were not unique. Kislev went back and looked at the archaeobotanical remains from another site he had worked on, Netif Hagdud,

1.5 kilometers west of Gilgal and of nearly the same date. The nearly five thousand fig drupelets found there showed the same lack of embryos in the fruit, indicating that they came from the same parthenocarpic variety. Figs were also recovered from contemporaneous Jericho and from Gesher, farther north in the valley.

The conclusion that the fig was domesticated by ca. 9500 B.C., a thousand years before any cereal and far in advance of the grape, date, and a variety of nut and other fruit trees, can certainly be challenged. It is possible that the figs at these sites in the Jordan Valley were all taken from female fig trees, which also produce unfertilized, sweet fruit.

Even if we reserve judgment on the domestication issue, the figs from Gilgal and other early Neolithic sites were clearly an important resource: they are well-formed and must have been intentionally dried by humans. When desiccated, figs are the most sugar-rich fruit in nature. Fifty percent of their dry weight consists of simple sugars. In liquid form, figs contain about 15 percent sugar, less than grapes and bananas. Such a sweet fruit would be a natural candidate for a fermented beverage. It is also conceivable that humans had already observed how easily a fig tree could be propagated from a cutting, an observation that was later put to good use in domesticating other plants.

We do have good evidence from about six millennia later that figs played a role in fermented beverages of the Jordan Valley. Our chemical analyses showed that the resinated wine in a royal tomb at Abydos (see chapter 6), hundreds of miles away, had been made in the southern Levant and then exported to Egypt. One peculiarity of this wine remains unique: some of the jars contained a single fig. The fruit had been sliced up and perforated so that it could be suspended in the liquid by a string. Perhaps the fig was a sweetening or fermenting agent or a special flavoring. Cutting it into segments and suspending it on a string would bring more of the wine into contact with the fruit.

It may be proposed, then, that the fig, the earliest known domesticated plant species in the world, was an ingredient of whatever Neolithic fermented beverage was being concocted at Jericho and nearby. This tradition, which was peculiar to the region and not documented elsewhere, was then perpetuated down to the time of the pharaoh Scorpion I, who was buried in the Abydos tomb around 3150 B.C.

From the Neolithic period onward, makers of fermented beverages became increasingly specialized as they moved away from mixed fermented beverages and focused on individual ingredients. Anatolia, within the Neolithic core area, has much to tell us about these developments.

The repertoire of Anatolian wine vessels in pottery, gold, and silver boggles the imagination. At the Museum of Anatolian Civilizations in Ankara, we can see majestic jugs in the red lustrous style, with extremely long spouts, suggestive of birds' beaks, that are sometimes counterbalanced by a raptor-like bird mounted on the handle of the vessel. The spouts of these jugs may be cut away or left open, and some are even stepped, so that as one tilted the jug, the beverage would have cascaded down the spout like a waterfall. Prodigious drinking horns in the shape of birds of prey, bulls, lions, hedgehogs, and other creatures would have satisfied the most ardent upper-class drinker. Waist-high "spindle bottles," whose bodies narrow at the top and bottom, modeled on a smaller version for specialty wines, stand ready to be filled.

We know from texts of the Hittites, who ruled the central Anatolian highlands during the mid- to late second millennium B.C., that most of these vessels once contained grape wine. The Hittites encircled their capital at Boğazkale, ancient Hattusha, with vineyards. They offered up quantities of their wine to their gods, with a considerable amount left over for the living.

Even as beverage making in Anatolia gravitated more and more toward winemaking, ancient traditions died hard. We read in the Hittite texts of olive oil, honey, and tree resins being added to wine. There is even a compound word for the two Sumerian pictograms of beer and wine, *kaš-geštin*, that translates literally as "beer-wine."

At the capital city, any mixed beverage served to the king or enjoyed by his retinue would have been prepared with the utmost care. As exemplified by the Inandık Vase in the Ankara museum, what superficially appears to be a trick vessel had a much more serious purpose. This vase, which sits in regal splendor in the center of the Old Hittite gallery, was outfitted with a hollow ring encircling its mouth into which a liquid could be poured through a large opening on one side. The liquid flowed through the ring and into the interior through bulls' heads whose muzzles were perforated with holes. The vessel has never been sampled and analyzed, but we can surmise from Hittite texts that wine—possibly a raisined variety or an herbal blend, for which the Hittites were renowned and which was used medicinally—was mixed with other ingredients, perhaps some honey, another fruit, or even beer.

What is unique about the Inandık Vase is that the making of the beverage and its ceremonial use are graphically portrayed in four exterior painted panels, which proceed from bottom to top. The lowest panel depicts a vessel like the vase itself being stirred by a man with a long stick, as would be necessary in the making of a mixed beverage. The horizontal metope above shows a figure who can be identified as the king, in standard Near Eastern attire, sitting on a throne resembling a camp stool and being served the beverage in a cup by an attendant, who pours from a beak-spouted jug. Above that is a panel showing musicians, probable sword dancers, and other celebrants in procession. They are headed toward a temple model and an altar, behind which the king and queen sit together on a couch. Although the latter scene has been broken away, it has been convincingly reconstructed as depicting the king pushing back the veil of his spouse. This is the prelude to the topmost panel, in which the king and queen, or sacred prostitute, perform the symbolic sexual act or sacred marriage (referred to as *hieros gamos* in Greek), in which the fertility of all of nature and the well-being of the king and his realm are secured. Musicians again accompany this dramatic reenactment with flutes, harps and cymbals, and dancers leap into the air.

The Inandık Vase, the apotheosis of the Hittite potters' art and expertise, vividly shows how beverage-making had become a carefully controlled royal industry by the second millennium B.C. and how fermented beverages were integrated into religion and the arts. Mixed beverages were never fully displaced by specialization, as the traveler to modern Turkey quickly discovers. Families come out to greet you in the countryside and might even invite you to their house or tent to taste *baqa,* a concoction of fermented figs and dates. More often, you are offered a refreshing glass of *ayran,* a nonalcoholic fermented yogurt beverage. As was the trend during the Hittite period, however, unadulterated wine is the overwhelming favorite in Anatolia today. In the past decade, a boutique wine industry, based on native varieties such as the superb red Öküzgözü ("eye of the ox"), has rekindled the vitality of the ancient industry.

In the lowlands of Mesopotamia, where cereals could be grown in bulk by irrigation agriculture, barley and wheat beers were perfected over the millennia. I have already mentioned the range of ancient "microbrews," which varied in body, taste, and sweetness. An even sweeter beverage came to prominence in the first millennium B.C.: date beer or, more accurately, date wine. Date palms grew in profusion in the lower Tigris-Euphrates Valley, and with twice the sugar content of grapes, their fruit could be fermented to give an alcohol content as high as 15 percent.

All levels of Mesopotamian society, from peasant to king, reveled in these drinks. They helped forge communal ties as people gathered around large-mouthed jars, such as the one we analyzed from Godin Tepe, and drank together through straws. Special jars, sporting two to seven spouts equally spaced around the rim, were made for these occasions. The popularity of communal beer drinking, particularly in the third millennium B.C., is attested by the distribution range of these multispouted jars, found in sites from Lower Mesopotamia, up the Tigris and Euphrates rivers, throughout Turkey, and across the sea in the Aegean islands.

The most extravagant examples of drinking tubes are those recovered by the Penn and British Museum excavations at the Early Dynastic cemetery of Ur, dating to ca. 2600–2500 B.C. The tomb of Queen Puabi had multiple sets of "straws" made from gold, silver, and lapis lazuli. A silver jar, which probably originally held her daily six-liter consignment of beer, was also found in her burial chamber. Common men and women, some of whom went to their deaths when Puabi was buried, did not have it so good. They received only one liter of beer per day in return for contributing to the construction of the early city-state.

Wine belonged to a different social order in lowland Mesopotamia, at least in the south, where grapes could be grown only by irrigation and had to be protected from the intense sun. Only royalty could afford to indulge in this luxury, and, beginning around 3000 B.C., the lower Zagros Mountains in Shiraz were planted with the vine to supply the lowlands. If a king wanted to get his wine from one of the more northerly wineries, shipping it by boat or mule incurred substantial additional charges. The equivalent of a bottle of a California Two-Buck Chuck, coming from Armenia or eastern Turkey down the Euphrates, can be calculated from economic dockets to have cost three to five times as much in Lower Mesopotamia in the early second millennium B.C.

Despite the growing cachet of wine in royal circles, cereal and date beers never lost their allure. Sometimes dates and grapes were mixed together (according to the Greek writer Polyaenus of the second century A.D. in his *Stratagems*). The Sumerian word for *banquet* translates as "the place of beer and bread." Kings boast of lavish feasts, of drinking beer in the temple

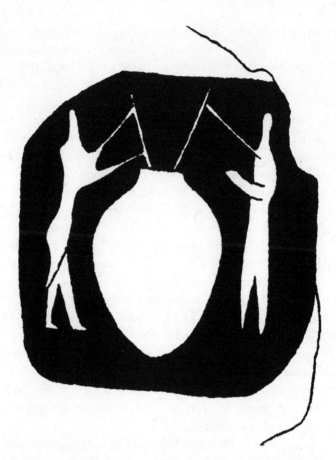

Figure 13. (a, *above*) Mesopotamian barley beer was drunk through straws. In the earliest known depiction of a popular motif, on a clay seal from Tepe Gawra, Iraq, ca. 3850 B.C., two thirsty individuals are thought to be imbibing beer through drinking tubes in this fashion from a gargantuan jar (see also figures 24a–b and plates 4 and 10). Drawing courtesy of University of Pennsylvania Museum of Archaeology and Anthropology; National Museum of Iraq, no. 25408, length 2.9 cm. (b, *opposite*) Drinking at banquets is a recurring theme on Mesopotamian cylinder seals, as exemplified by this impression of a lapis lazuli cylinder seal (length 4.4 cm) from Queen Puabi's tomb in the Royal Cemetery at Ur (British Museum 121545), dated to ca. 2600–2500 B.C. In the upper panel, a couple share a pot of beer. In the lower panel, a wine aficionado, who has already drained one goblet, is being offered a refill from a droop-spouted jar. © The Trustees of the British Museum.

of the high god, and consorting with Inanna (Akkadian Ishtar), the goddess of love. In the sacred marriage ceremony, the king stood in the role of Dumuzi, the deified king of Uruk, one of the Lower Mesopotamian city-states. The celebration was most famously carried out in the goddess's temple at Uruk (the Eanna) for several days at the beginning of the New Year, probably in April or May.

A particularly vivid account of the high status of beer in Near Eastern societies is recorded by the fifth-century B.C. Greek historian Xenophon in his *Anabasis*. After the mercenaries known as the Ten Thousand retreated from Persia on the death of Cyrus the Younger in 401 B.C., they traveled through the threatening terrain of central and eastern Anatolia, where the Tigris and Euphrates begin. Their succor came in the form of a barley "wine," drunk from large jars with straws in a remote village. Barley wine, then as today, likely refers to an unmixed, extremely potent beer made only from barley, so strong in fact that the soldiers had to water it down. It is no wonder that a story took hold in Greece that Dionysos, the wine god, became so angry with the Babylonians that he kept grape wine from them and forced them to drink only beer (according to the third-century A.D. traveler and historian Sextus Julius Africanus in his *Cestus*).

Wine and beer both played central symbolic roles in the sacred-marriage reenactment, which was intended to encourage the fertility of the land and assure the prosperity of the king and his people. In one version of the myth, Dumuzi is holed up in an underworld brewery with his boon companions, a group of sagacious beer-makers. Although this might not sound like such a bad place to be under the circumstances, Dumuzi is rescued by his sister, the wine goddess Geshtinanna (her name includes the Sumerian element *geštin,* signifying "grape," "vineyard," or "wine"). The literal translation of *Geshtinanna* is "leafy grapevine," and she was popularly referred to by the epithet *Ama-Geshtinna* ("root of the grapevine" or "mother of all grapevines"). The outcome of Geshtinanna's efforts is to resurrect Dumuzi to new life on earth. She also eventually finds fulfillment in the world above.

We can plausibly equate Dumuzi with the spring barley and his sister, Geshtinanna, with the fall vintage, as their escape from the underworld took several months. In the real-life reenactment in the temple, the sacral union was probably helped along by the consumption of both types of fermented beverages, or perhaps a mixture, as suggested by the imagery on the Inandık Vase.

Our laboratory has analyzed vessels from the late fourth-millennium B.C. Eanna temple to Ishtar at the site of Uruk, including a jar with a drooping spout and a unique miniature jar, a type known only from Uruk. Both jars contained a resinated wine. The droop-spouted jar is depicted on numerous cylinder seals for serving a beverage that was drunk from a cup or goblet. It seems probable from these results and others from contemporaneous city-states that the beverage in the droop-spouted jars and drinking vessels was wine. On some cylinder seals, a scene showing wine drinking is juxtaposed with another showing beer drinking through straws from a large-mouthed jar. The miniature jar, which was found together with many other examples in a sherd layer under the temple, might have been used in a dedicatory ceremony for the temple.

It appears that in the earliest stages of state formation in the Middle East, the rulers and upper classes increasingly demanded, and got, more specialized beverages. If the climate was unsuitable for establishing local vineyards, wine could be imported as a costly, prestige item, much as it is today when we serve that special bottle of Pétrus, a Super Tuscan Sassicaia, or Ridge Cabernet to our friends. Special brews, perhaps laced with a flavorful or mind-altering herb, served the same purpose. In imitation of this conspicuous consumption, one king after another adopted one kind or another of a fermented-beverage culture wherever we look in the Near East, from ancient Phoenicia and Palestine across the Great Syrian Desert to Iran or south to Egypt (see chapter 6).

Special wine-drinking vessels, sometimes filled with a specialty beverage, were exchanged between Near Eastern rulers. Ceremonies that already stemmed from common Neolithic roots might be transferred, *mutatis mutandis,* from one culture to the next, and the appropriate beverage incorporated into the ritual. Anthropologists call this process elite emulation. Of course, any self-respecting ruler would try to guarantee that his tomb was well stocked with his or her favorite beverages to provide sustenance in the afterlife.

THE BACCHIC POETS

Even when Islam threatened to undermine the foundations of the ancient fermented-beverage traditions of the Middle East in the middle of the first millennium A.D., some hardy souls refused to capitulate. The Koran (5:90) is very explicit in its denunciation: "Wine and gambling and idols and divination by arrows are a defilement of the Devil, so avoid it."

How does one explain the host of Arabic and Persian writers and intellectuals, called the Bacchic poets, who developed a whole genre of love poetry (Arabic *khamriyyāt*) during the height of Arab supremacy in the Middle East, in the sixth to eighth centuries A.D. and continuing until the thirteenth century? These poems, which overflow with eroticism and excessive drinking, seem totally at odds with the tenets of traditional Islam.

'Umar b. Abī Rabī'a, one of the earliest poets in the Umayyad caliphate, who hailed from Mecca, wrote these torrid lines:

> I spent the night being fed wine that had been mixed with honey and
> excellent pure musk.
> I would kiss her and as she reeled she would indulge me with the
> pleasure of her cool [lips].
>
> *(Kennedy 1997: 23)*

Or consider these lines from the same poem:

> She gave me to taste her sweet [saliva] which I imagined to be honey
> mixed with cold limpid water.
> Or a wine aged in Babel, the color of a cock's eye.
>
> *(Kennedy 1997: 24)*

A contemporary of 'Umar, al-A'sā, is worth quoting at greater length:

> Have you not abstained [from love]? Nay, the passion [of love] has
> returned . . .
> I have drunk many a cup of wine, indulging in pleasure, and then
> another to cure the effects of the first . . .

A [pure] red wine that shows up specks of dust in the bottom of
the flask.
We were watched by rose, jasmine and songstresses with their reed
pipes.
Our large drum was constantly played; which of these three [delights]
am I then blamed for?
You see the cymbals answering the [beat of] the drum.

(Kennedy 1997: 253)

The apotheosis of such celebrations of wine, women, and song comes in
the great *Ruba'iyyat* of the Persian poet Omar Khayyam, beautifully translated by Edward Fitzgerald:

A Book of Verses underneath the Bough,
A Jug of Wine, a Loaf of Bread—and Thou
Beside me singing in the Wilderness—
Oh, Wilderness were Paradise enow!
(Aminrazavi 2005: 331, stanza 12)

With the Bacchic poets' blunt affirmation of worldly pleasures, it is no
wonder that they were both praised by hedonists and abjured by prohibitionists from their own time until now. One of the most famous eighth-
century poets, Abu Nuwās, who transformed the earlier, nomadic tone of
the love songs to the more formal *khamriyyāt* genre with the elegant atmosphere of the Persian court, was imprisoned by one caliph and told to write
panegyrics rather than wine verses. Other poets were put to death. For
American prohibitionists as recently as 1890, Omar Khayyam was the epit-
ome of evil, referred to as "the bibulous old Persian."

Muslim scholars and others have tried mightily to reconcile the eroticism
of the Bacchic poets with the tenets of their faith. As with the Song of
Solomon in biblical tradition and hermeneutics, theologians interpret the
love of women, and sometimes of young men in the Arabic and Persian
poems, as an allegory of the love of God. The fullest expression of this
method of interpretation can be found in the many diverse orders of Sufism,
which draw upon Gnostic mysticism—Christian, Jewish, and Zoroastrian—
and esoteric paganism. Sufis sought and still seek to experience God directly
and in all his glory, a state that is referred to as "intoxication." They are not
averse to using physical stimuli to achieve their mystical and ecstatic states,
especially when wine or another fermented beverage for attaining oneness is

forbidden. They spin around in circles, like the whirling dervishes, or repeat Koranic verses and even graphic love and wine lyrics, ad infinitum.

An explicit mystical thread does exists in Omar Khayyam's poetry and has been cited in support of the cause. For example:

> HE IS, and nought but Him exists, I know,
> This truth is what creation's book will show;
> When heart acquired perception with His Light,
> Atheistic darkness changed to faithly glow.
> *(Aminrazavi 2005: 138)*

Abu Nuwās, on the other hand, was unmoved by warnings of the faithful. He wrote: "You are beguiled if you insist on this repentance, tear your garment [for all I care]! I will not repent."

The Arabic and Persian Bacchic poets have much in common with their Chinese counterparts, who served their emperors at about the same time and escaped into mystical revelry in nature with a bottle of wine in hand. The erotic element may be missing from the Chinese verse, but the overwhelming influence on the origin and development of both poetic genres was a fermented beverage—grape wine in western Asia and a cereal wine in the east.

CONCLUSION

The Chinese mixed beverage from Jiahu (chapter 2) may so far be the earliest known alcoholic beverage in the world, but the Middle East was not far behind, and new evidence may reverse the situation. Grape wine was probably being made in the innovative villages of eastern Turkey—the final word from the chemical analyses is still not in—at about the same time that the Jiahu grog was being prepared along the banks of the Yellow River.

As the experimental brewers in both areas played with the many possible variables of ingredients and production, the Neolithic democratizing spirit was increasingly subsumed by hierarchical societies, headed by kings. The more generic role of the shaman was redefined as priest, fortune teller, medicine woman, and beverage maker. Specialized beverages, based on a single ingredient or with just a single additive (such as a tree resin, which helped preserve it), became the rule, and the more traditional mixed beverages were pushed aside.

One is struck by the similar timing of Neolithic experimentation, followed by the refinement of ingredients and processes to make specialized beverages, on either side of Asia. The ingredients differ somewhat in the two areas; only honey and grape, albeit different varieties and species, are common to both areas. It may also be more than coincidence that the ancient Chinese pictogram (*jiu*) for wine or any alcoholic beverage, which shows a jar with a pointed base and three drops falling from its lip, is so similar to the proto-Sumerian pictogram (*kaš*) for beer, which depicts a very similar jar. Perhaps the explanation for this similarity is related to why rice wine is still drunk through straws in Asia, as ancient Mesopotamian peoples consumed their beer thousands of years ago.

Because there is no archaeological evidence of direct contact between the regions in the Neolithic period, I propose instead that the Neolithic Period saw a transfer of *ideas*, very piecemeal, from one group to another across the deserts and mountains of Central Asia. The archaeological picture of cross-fertilization is much clearer when we come to explain how similar wines and love lyrics arose in the Middle East and China during the first millennium B.C. The discovery of our first chemically attested wine vessel, the jar from Godin Tepe, stands as a marker of the possible transmission of ideas and fermented-beverage technology via trade routes across the continent.

FOUR

FOLLOWING THE SILK ROAD

THE SILK ROAD CONJURES UP romantic images of the past. Two grains of opium compelled Samuel Taylor Coleridge in 1797 to write the inspired poem that begins: "In Xanadu did Kubla Khan / A stately pleasure-dome decree." Xanadu, or Shangdu, was the summer palace of the Mongol empire in the thirteenth century A.D. It lay east of the forbidding Gobi Desert, on the high grasslands of the Mongolian plateau. When the Mongol hordes swept into China from the north under Genghis Khan, they took control of northern China and the famed Silk Road. Its eastern terminus was Xi'an, home to the spectacular terracotta army of China's first emperor, Qin Shi Huang.

The intertwining of music, sex, mystical experiences, and exotic beverages in Coleridge's poem evokes the Silk Road's otherworldliness. The poet's vision includes bright gardens, an Abyssinian maid playing music "loud and long" on her dulcimer, and incense-bearing trees that exude enticing scents. Disrupting this idyllic scene are darker elements: a "deep romantic chasm" through which a violent torrent of water runs, and a hint of "ancestral voices prophesying war." The speaker in the poem imagines the intoxicating effects these sensual experiences might have on him if he could relive them:

And all should cry, Beware! Beware!
His flashing eyes, his floating hair!

Weave a circle round him thrice,
And close your eyes with holy dread
For he on honeydew hath fed,
And drunk the milk of Paradise.

These beverages recall the Jiahu grog, which might have inspired its Neolithic shamans, and the resinated wines and beers of the Near East.

According to Marco Polo, whose account is now seriously questioned by some scholars, he and his father, and his uncle even earlier, traveled east from Venice, then slogged across the Gobi and were ushered into the court of the khan. I once had a much more pleasant look at the Gobi when my plane was diverted (by a sandstorm) on a return trip from Dunhuang in Central Asia, another key staging post along the famous trade route. Looking at the Silk Road from above, whether from the window of a plane or the perspective of a satellite hundreds of kilometers above the Earth, underscores the immensity of the journey that traders and adventurers faced along this five-thousand-kilometer stretch of landlocked Central Asia, crossing a host of overland roads, deserts, plateaus, and high mountain passes.

Using data from communication and remote-sensing satellites, archaeologists can learn much about sites in poorly mapped, remote areas of the world. Satellite images can show us the lines of ancient roads down to a one-meter resolution; they were used to locate the fabled city of Ubar in the Saudi Arabian desert. They can discern the huge images of spiders, monkeys, and birds, many kilometers wide, along the desert coast of Peru. Rather than being the creations of extraterrestrial visitors, as Erich von Däniken would have us believe, these strange phenomena were created by the ancient Nazca people (ca. 200 B.C.–A.D. 700) by clearing away the dark, lichen-varnished rocks and exposing the desert sand and lighter-colored stone beneath. In Central Asia, satellite images reveal the lush oases, hundreds of kilometers apart, requiring ten-day treks in the vast Taklamakan Desert of the Tarim Basin. We can look down on the high peaks of the Pamir, Hindu Kush, and Tien Shan mountains, the rolling sands of the Gobi, and the Oxus (Amu Darya) and the Jaxartes (Syr Darya) Rivers flowing thousands of kilometers to the Aral Sea.

Although the route has existed for centuries, the term *Silk Road* was coined only in the late nineteenth century by the German explorer Ferdinand von Richthofen (the brother of Manfred, the Red Baron flying ace of World War I). Von Richthofen's felicitous expression recalls the beautiful, diaphanous silk textiles of China, which entranced the Romans and scandalized the more prudish subjects of the empire. Many goods besides silk traversed the Silk Road by horse, camel, and donkey: Chinese peaches and oranges, fragile and richly decorated porcelain, magnificent bronzes, gunpowder, and paper came west from China in exchange for grapes and wine, gold and silver drinking vessels, and nuts of all kinds, as well as more abstract goods, in the form of religion (including Zorastrianism and Manichaeism from Iran and Buddhism from northern India), art, and music.

The Mogao caves, near the oasis town of Dunhuang, graphically illustrate how religious and artistic ideas were transferred along the Silk Road. In the town's heyday, traders, monks, and scholars crowded its narrow streets. It lies on the edge of the desert at the westernmost end of the Great Wall, which was built over centuries to protect the Chinese empire from the Central Asian nomads. Here, Buddhism penetrated China for the first time in the first century A.D. through the Gansu corridor, running south of the Gobi Desert. Rather than constructing temples of wood, as was typical for the Daoists and Confucianists of the Chinese heartland, converts to Buddhism at Dunhuang decorated the walls and ceilings of nearly five hundred caves in vibrant colors. I stood transfixed gazing at the painted sky-blue bodhisattvas in undulating gowns that grace the high vaults of many of the caves.

Apart from a climb of more than 4,500 meters over one of the Pamir passes, connecting Russian Turkestan with Xinjiang Province in China, the most difficult part of the journey between China and the West was through the Taklamakan Desert at the center of the continent, a thousand kilometers across. The Taklamakan, which has also been called the Desert of Death, is one of the largest bodies of sand on the Earth. *Taklamakan* may derive from an early Turkic expression meaning "unreturnable," which gave rise to the expression "If you go in, you won't come out." It is more likely, however, that the initial element of the name, *takli,* derives from a Uyghur word meaning "vineyard."

Intrepid travelers could skirt the Taklamakan to the north, although this route required a long, difficult trek through shifting sands and barren wilderness. Grasslands occasionally crop up where meltwater from the high snowy peaks of the Tien Shan descends to the plain. The Silk Road leading south around the desert took longer, but the trip was relieved by more oases, fed by waters from the Kunlun Shan range. This was the route taken by most traders, pilgrims, and adventurers, including Marco Polo. A third route crossed the cooler, well-watered grasslands north of the Tien Shan and followed the White Poplar River through the Flaming Mountains down to Loulan on the eastern side of the Tarim Basin, and then continued to Dunhuang and China.

THE FABLED FERGANA VALLEY

Faced with the different options for crossing the Pamirs, most travelers chose a northern route over the high Terek Pass. They needed ample supplies of food and drink, to judge from the famous story of General Zhang Qian, an emissary of the Chinese emperor to the western fringes of the empire in the late second century B.C. Zhang describes a verdant oasis on the western side of the Pamirs—the Fergana Valley—where the wealthy stored away thousands of liters of grape wine, which might be aged for twenty years or more. A century later, the Roman historian Strabo wrote in his *Geography* that enormous quantities of wine were being produced in this distant locale. The vines were enormous, he declared, with huge clusters of grapes. Strabo might have been referring to a unique grape variety of the Central Asian oases—the Mare's Teat, with distinctively shaped, brownish-purple grapes. The wine, which improved with aging for as long as fifty years, was so sublime that it did not require a tree-resin additive, according to Strabo. Modern Chinese winemakers in the Grape Valley of the Flaming Mountains, where the Mare's Teat was transplanted long ago, still revel in its sweetness and succulence.

Like all adventurers, Zhang Qian suffered his share of calamities. He was taken captive by one of the recalcitrant Central Asian peoples, the Xiongnu. Only a short time earlier, this tribal confederacy had defeated the Yuezhi and made their king's skull into a drinking cup. Mercifully, Zhang faced a less dire fate: he was forced to marry a native woman, with whom he had a son, and then he escaped to the Fergana Valley. He had the presence of mind to take cuttings of the domesticated Eurasian grapevine (*Vitis vinifera* ssp. *vinifera*), which grew there in profusion, and bring them back to the capital in Xi'an, ancient Chang'an. They were planted there, and, according to ancient texts, they yielded the first grape wine in China, to the emperor's delight. As we have seen, the Neolithic people at Jiahu were harvesting the native grapes of the Yellow River basin for their mixed beverage much earlier.

The very advanced winemaking industry of the Fergana Valley in the late first millennium B.C. echoes developments that occurred during and after the Neolithic Revolution at both ends of the prehistoric Silk Road. *V. vinifera* still grows wild in Fergana and the other fabled oases of the western Silk Road: Tashkent, Samarkand, and Merv. Although definitive archaeological and chemical research remains to be carried out, we can surmise that the domesticated Eurasian grape was established very early in the Fergana Valley, with the main impetus coming most likely from the ancient Iranian wine culture but possibly also influenced by ideas about fermented-beverage production and plant domestication percolating in from China.

The Fergana Valley lay in the ancient Persian province of Sogdiana, which rose to prominence in the Silk Road trade during the first millennium A.D. Its wine culture is wonderfully captured in two kinds of dances, which likely have very ancient roots. These dances were adopted by the Chinese as early as the Eastern Han Dynasty (ca. A.D. 25–220), and during the seventh and eighth centuries they became all the rage under the Tang rulers, who had a taste for all things Western (that is, from Iran and the Central Asian oasis cultures). In the *hutengwu* dance, as depicted on frescoes, wine vessels, and jade ornaments, a single male dancer was attired in a cone-shaped hat that was sometimes pearl-studded, a silver or brocade belt with grape motifs, a tight jacket or shirt with the sleeves rolled up, and felt boots. As many as ten dancers, each on their own carpet, might perform in turn. With wine cup in hand or a wine gourd strung around the body, each dancer rotated rapidly to the left and right, hands held aloft to clap or beat a small hand drum in time to an accompaniment of waist drums, flutes, cymbals, harps, and lutes. Spinning around on their carpets like whirling dervishes, the dancers culminated their performances with somersaults. A Tang poet described the movements to be like those of a fluttering bird; but after hours of dancing and replenishing their cups from the large wine jar, the dancers staggered around drunkenly and sank to the floor.

The second dance, the *huxuanwu*, was apparently quite similar to the first (*xuan* means "swirling"), although it was less strenuous and performed by women. Limited pictorial evidence, such as the images of solo dancers in the Mogao caves at Dunhuang, suggests that it arrived in China later, perhaps during Tang times, when troupes of dancing women were brought in from Sogdiana.

Travelers in the Middle East and eastern Mediterranean can still experience the thrill of such dances, which are often stimulated by an alcoholic beverage. My wife and I were once treated to the sight of a wild dance late at night on Mykonos, an island in the Aegean. One man danced alone, leaping and twirling to the music, and holding high two live lobsters. Female dances are generally more gentle and sinuous, like the exotic moves of a belly dancer.

During the Tang era the Chinese were enticed by other Western luxuries and customs, including grape wine and fine riding horses. One court official went so far as to have an "ale grotto" built, a gigantic mudbrick edifice fitted with numerous drinking bowls, for his friends to slake their thirst. The most famous Tang ruler, Taizong, signaled his respect for his neighboring Turkic foes by importing their horses; he most desired those from Fergana, the "heavenly horses." Taizong had his six favorite horses immortalized on stone plaques that decorated the burial chamber of his massive tumulus northwest of Xi'an. Each horse is realistically portrayed with a Central Asian riding saddle and stirrups. A groom is shown carefully removing an arrow from the breast of one of the horses, now on display in the Penn Museum.

PERSIA: A PARADISE OF WINE

In light of its present political and religious strictures, it is ironic that Iran, on the western periphery of the prehistoric Silk Road, has yielded our earliest published chemical evidence for unadulterated grape wine. Expatriate Iranians in the United States, however, had no problem reconciling our discovery with their history and culture when the sixth-millennium B.C. Hajji Firuz wine was first announced. I was interviewed by an all-night radio station in Los Angeles with an audience of nearly a half million Iranian emigrés in the Tehrangeles section of the city. Listeners calling in to the show were ecstatic to hear that their homeland might have been the cradle of winemaking. I reminded them that one of their own Bacchic poets (see chapter 3) had said that "whoever seeks the origins of wine must be crazy."

The earliest Iranian winemaking is often traced back to the apocryphal, late story of King Jamshid, whose existence is otherwise unattested in the historical and archaeological records. As a Zoroastrian high priest, it seems, Jamshid not only invented a way to dye silk and make perfume, but also discovered the world's first wine, just as Noah is credited with this advance in the Book of Genesis. Jamshid had a particular fondness for grapes, which were stored en masse in large jars in his palace. Once, when the stock inside one vessel spoiled, it was labeled as poison. A harem woman who suffered severe migraines then tried to cure her woes by eating some of these grapes. She fell into a profound sleep; when she awoke, she was cured. Told of this incident, Jamshid discerned that the liquid was a powerful medicine and ordered more to be made.

The true facts of ancient winemaking in Iran, to the extent that we know them, are no less intriguing. Our biomolecular archaeological research on specific jar types has shown that the domesticated grapevine had been progressively cultivated southward along the spine of the Zagros Mountains. This scenario is supported by a pollen core from Zerabar Lake, near Godin Tepe, that shows that grape did not exist in the area before 5000 B.C. By the late fourth millennium B.C., Susa, one of the early capitals of the Elamites in the Karun River plain, served as a central market or entrepôt for wine shipments from the highlands to the east, such as Godin Tepe, to the lowland city-states of Mesopotamia. The Susan residents were smart enough not to trade away all their wine, reserving some to be drunk or offered to the gods and some to be used in specialty oils and perfumes.

The Susan king very likely initiated and funded the first forays into the mountains of Shiraz to the southeast, 1,800 meters above sea level. This region was the home of the Bacchic poets, including Omar Khayyam, and long before that to the Persian kings, who built their palaces at Ecbatana and, most magnificently, at Persepolis with its soaring columns and sculptured reliefs lining the grand stairway that led to the audience chamber (the Apadana).

In 1974, when my wife and I traveled to Iraq, we hoped to have a first-hand look at these sites. We were told that we could cross the border by ferry at a point along the Shatt-al-Arab, the waterway south of Basra that lies between Iran and Iraq and connects the Tigris and the Euphrates to the Persian Gulf. We sped through the lush jungle, which was a welcome relief from Basra's searing August heat, only to be told that the ferry service had been canceled. We returned to Basra, where we could see the massive spires of flame, like a Zoroastrian fire temple, shooting up from Iranian oilfields a few kilometers away, across the Euphrates. The cool, high plateaus of Shiraz beckoned, but we had already had our share of harrowing travel experiences, punctuated by brushes with the Iraqi secret police. Reluctantly, we set aside our plans for seeing Persepolis and instead made the fifteen-hour trip across the Syrian Desert to Amman the next day.

Other travelers' accounts and archaeological findings can help us to imagine the Persian Achaemenid Empire and enter into its ancient wine culture. Cyrus the Great, who is credited with forging the empire after his defeat of the Medes and the city of Babylon in 539 B.C., hailed from Shiraz.

He began as the ruler of a small kingdom in the region. Its capital was An-shan, known today as Tepe Malyan, an archaeological mound nestled in the oak-covered hills northwest of Shiraz. Excavations by the Penn Museum during the 1970s, under William Sumner, peeled back layers of occupation to reach the Banesh period of the late fourth millennium B.C. At approximately the same time that the Susan king's troops and traders were trudging up the High Road (the protohistoric predecessor of the Silk Road) to Godin Tepe, wine was likely being enjoyed at Tepe Malyan, as implied by grapeseeds recovered in the excavation. Domesticated two- and six-rowed barley, as well as einkorn and emmer wheat, provided the inhabitants with the raw materials to slake their thirst with beer as well as wine.

On current evidence, the grapevine did not originally grow in the uplands of Shiraz but had to be transplanted there from farther north. The Banesh period grapeseeds might therefore have made their way to the site in the unfiltered lees of an imported wine, or even as imported fresh fruit or raisins. The contents of a refuse pit, dated about five hundred years later (the Kaftari period of the mid-third millennium B.C.), however, suggest that the domesticated grapevine was already established, just in time to meet the needs of the growing population of lowland Mesopotamia. The pit was packed full of carbonized and uncarbonized grape pips, along with pieces of grapevine wood. Masses of grapeseeds are unusual in excavations; they generally represent the residue of crushed pomace, the grape pulp left after pressing the grapes to make wine. The mature wood remains are even more telling, as they point to vines growing locally. Presumably, these vines were close relatives of the original transplants and might someday shed light on the true genetic origins of the renowned Shiraz grape. We can conclude that by at least 2500 B.C. and probably much earlier, vineyards had been laid out around the capital and had begun to produce grapes and wine.

Now that foreign expeditions have been allowed back into Iran, new evidence for the transplantation of the domesticated Eurasian grapevine south through the Zagros Mountains to Shiraz has begun to emerge. Unfortunately excavation has not been resumed at Tepe Malyan. Not far away, in the vicinity of Parsagadae, where Cyrus was buried in a monumental tomb, salvage excavation has been spurred on in the Bolahi Valley, where sites are threatened by the rising waters behind the new Sivand Dam. Archaeologists uncovered and located numerous treading vats for stomping grapes in wine production. Most of the installations date to the later Sassanian period (A.D. 224–651), but further exploration should reveal more about the beginnings of winemaking in the area, still festooned with vineyards, and its peak under the Achaemenids.

A glimpse into the early history of Shiraz winemaking is provided by its cylinder seals, which record so much of everyday and royal life in the Near East. One of the earliest known portrayals of a "symposium" (in the original sense of a drinking party) appears on a Kaftari seal. It shows male and female notables or gods, wearing flounced or woven caps and other attire, under an arbor thick with grape clusters. They hold up small cups, which surely must be filled with wine. A nearly identical scene is represented two thousand years later, shortly preceding the rise of Cyrus and the Achaemenids, on an Assyrian relief from Assurbanipal's palace at Nineveh (modern Mosul). While the king reclines on an ornate couch, in what later became the preferred posture of attendees at the classical Greek *symposion* and Roman *convivium,* his queen sits demurely before him on a straight-backed throne. As in the Kaftari seal, both figures hold up wine cups under a bountiful grapevine, with a harpist playing in the background.

This motif of the king raising his wine cup recurs over thousands of years in Near Eastern art. It symbolized the success of a monarch's reign and continuing thanks to his gods. It also appears on a first-century A.D. Sogdian couch, which shows a well-fed patriarch and his wife, wearing rounded and flat caps respectively, like those on the much earlier Kaftari seal. With cups in hand, they enjoy a repast of cakes, entertained by a full orchestra and somersaulting dancers.

During the Persian empire, wine-drinking was taken to new heights in the exercise of statecraft. Herodotus, the Greek historian of the fifth century B.C., reported that "it is also their [the Persians'] general practice to deliberate on weighty affairs when they are drunk; and in the morning when they are sober, the decision which they came to the night before is put before them by the master of the house in which it was made; and if it is then approved of, they act on it; if not, they set it aside." Elsewhere, Herodotus recounts the reverse procedure—deliberate first while sober, then while drunk, to see whether the same decision is reached. Tacitus made the same observation about the bawdy German "barbarians" in the first century A.D. Alcohol, he commented, broke down the inhibitions of the assembled bodies, freeing up usually cautious politicians and producing a bonhomie that led to innovative solutions. Of course, the drinking often got out of hand, hence the need to reconsider the matter with greater clarity of mind when sober.

The Epic of Kings (Persian *Shahnameh*), composed by the renowned Persian poet Ferdousi in the tenth century A.D., recalled this long-standing tradition of deciding matters of war and peace. Like Greek symposiasts or modern statesmen, the "King of Kings" and the heroes of legend discussed weighty matters after dinner, while a cupbearer circulated through the assembly, bearing wine.

We can gain some idea of the quantities of wine drunk by the royal family and their retinue from the Persepolis Fortification Tablets, which were found in a tower of the main platform. Over decades, thousands of texts in the Elamite language recorded that the usual allotment for each member of the royal family was five liters of wine a day. High officials, the royal guard (the Ten Thousand Immortals), and palace functionaries received progressively smaller amounts, but still enough to keep them happy. Excavations of the army barracks yielded enough large pottery jars, pitchers, and drinking bowls to confirm consumption on a staggering scale.

For special occasions, the ruler of the world's largest empire engaged in even more ostentatious drinking of wine. The biblical book of Esther (1:7–10) tells of a week-long feast in Susa where the king, Ahasuerus (probably Xerxes I), serves up "royal wine in abundance" in golden vessels of all kinds. The women indulged in a similar feast, hosted by the queen, Vashti. The merriment continued until the seventh day, when the queen defied the king, and the evil Hamath began to plot his intrigue against Mordechai and the Jews.

Iranian craftsmen throughout the empire, including metalsmiths, stoneworkers, pottery makers, and glass artisans, were among the most skilled in the Near East. They created fabulous wine vessels to grace the emperor's table at feasts and celebrations. Stupendous drinking horns, holding three or four liters and meant to be emptied all at once without setting the vessel down, are especially captivating. The terminals are ornately decorated in three dimensions, usually with lions, rams, birds and bulls, but also with more fanciful sphinxes and griffins. Examples carved out of agate, such as one found in a Sogdian tomb near Xi'an in China (the Hejiacun Treasure), take advantage of the variegated color of the stone to accentuate different features of the animal. Tall ewers, beak-spouted jugs, and multisided cups often show dancing women, musicians, hunting scenes, and heroic tales. One beak-spouted jug type was called a *bolboleh* (derived from the Persian word for a songbird, *bolbol*) because it sang like a bird when wine flowed through its narrow mouth. Floral and geometric designs were also popular. The octagonal gold and silver cups in the Hejiacun

Treasure, which show a different musician in each panel, might have been used by a Sogdian to dance the *hutengwu* or the *huxuanwu* for his or her Chinese admirers.

THE EXOTIC DRUG WORLD OF CENTRAL ASIA

Farther east in Iran along the Silk Road, skirting north of the great salt desert of the Dasht-i Kevir, we can imagine ourselves following in the footsteps of Alexander the Great, Marco Polo, and numerous other adventurers and brigands. The road passes Margiana (centered on the Merv oasis); Bactria, backing up to the Hindu Kush Mountains; Samarkand; and the Fergana Valley of Sogdiana. All these regions were incorporated into the Achaemenid empire and then consigned to Seleucus I after Alexander's death.

For decades, no archaeological evidence from the period before Cyrus and Alexander was found in Central Asia. This situation changed dramatically in the 1970s, when a charismatic and persistent excavator from the Institute of Archaeology in Moscow, Viktor Sarianidi, began to dig in Margiana, in modern Turkmenistan. Over several decades he opened up large-scale exposures at three sites in the well-watered Murgab river basin, near Merv: Gonur Depe, Togolok 1, and Togolok 21. What he found convinced even diehard skeptics that large settlements, based on irrigation agriculture and boasting monumental architecture, had been built in this seemingly remote locale by at least 2000 B.C. However, Sarianidi's more provocative theories, including that of a proto-Zoroastrian cult—spurred on by a sacred beverage called *haoma*—have aroused spirited opposition from other scholars in the field.

Sarianidi believes that he has uncovered proto-Zoroastrian fire temples at the three sites. Fire temples, sacred to Ahura Mazda, the "One Uncreated Creator," had become an integral part of the religion by the time of Herodotus, who describes its adherents as ascending mounds and lighting fires under the open sky to their god. Because Sarianidi's temples precede Herodotus's account, as well as other clear archaeological traces of fire temples, by more than 1,500 years, it is reasonable to insist that his theory meet a higher level of proof.

Sarianidi's primary evidence for the fire temples can be briefly sketched. At Gonur South, the largest Early Bronze Age settlement yet found in Margiana, he marshaled evidence from an elaborately laid-out building constructed in two phases, with multiple open-air courtyards, walls coated with a brilliantly white plaster in places. Clues to the function of the building came from pits filled with whitish ash in the courtyards, heavily carbonized censers scattered here and there, and rooms that showed signs of intensive burning. White ash was essential for purification rites in later Zoroastrianism. To be sure, the more mundane interpretation that the building was a palace or villa could not be ruled out: well-plastered walls are also the norm in such buildings, the ash pits could be simply that or remnants of cooking ovens, the braziers could have served as light fixtures, and the charred chambers could be the result of accidental fires. But Sarianidi had one more argument up his sleeve. In one of the plastered "white rooms" of the building, he found three large plaster-coated bowl or jar bases, one of which held a residue. Archaeobotanical and scanning electron microscopic analysis of the material by palynologists in Moscow revealed that the residue was permeated with the pollen of two mind-altering plants: ephedra (*Ephedra* spp.) and hemp or marijuana (*Cannabis sativa*), together with a large quantity of hemp flowers and seeds, ephedra stem fragments, and other plants (including *Artemisia* spp., a well-known additive in fermented beverages of China and southern Europe). Both ephedra and marijuana have been proposed as constituents in the Zoroastrian *haoma*.

Togolok 1 and Togolok 21, which are close to Gonur South and dated several centuries later, had similarly plastered multiroom complexes around central courtyards. At Togolok 21, Sarianidi again identified circular structures as altars, covered with layers of ash and charcoal, and heavily burned chambers, and theorized that they belonged to fire temples. His Moscow palynologists analyzed the residues inside several very large jars that stood on a mudbrick platform inside a plastered chamber of the Togolok 21 complex. They recovered more ephedra pollen, leaves, and stems up to one centimeter in length, as well as the pollen of another mind-altering plant: poppy (*Papaver somniferum*), from which opium is derived. A bone tube, which had been carved with large eyes, was found on the floor of this white room; it also contained poppy pollen. The tube, which might have been used to suck up *haoma* or to snort a hallucinogen, reminds one of the Neolithic preoccupation with eyes in the Near East, such as those of the plaster-molded skulls found at Jericho and 'Ain Ghazal.

Sarianidi hypothesizes that the sacred beverage was prepared in the white rooms by macerating the plants in the large bowls, grating them, and then straining the juices through funnels filled with wool into the large jars or other, smaller jars mounted on pottery stands. The beverage was fermented in the jars and then poured as libations and served to ritual participants in the public courtyards. He further proposes that a cylinder seal from the To-golok I sanctuary illustrates the prehistoric ritual. Two monkey-headed humans, perhaps wearing masks, hold a pole that a dancer leaps over, while a musician beats out an accompaniment on a large drum. Dancing under the influence of mind-altering substances, as we have seen, was widely practiced in neighboring Sogdiana, and masked ceremonies in which humans assumed animal roles were common in shamanistic cults throughout Asia beginning in the Palaeolithic period.

Sarianidi's interpretation of the residues inside the bowls and jars and the decorated tube does not stand or fall with his theories of fire temples and proto-Zoroastrianism. Unless we totally dismiss the Moscow palynologists' findings, we should take the presence of the ephedra and marijuana, including stems, leaves and seeds, at face value. (However, a reanalysis of the Gonur South sample by Dutch archaeobotanists found evidence only for millet.) Pollen might have been blown into narrow-mouthed pottery vessels from surrounding areas, but the larger-sized plant fragments are unlikely to have been blown or washed in. They are best explained as additives to some kind of beverage contained in the vessels. Moreover, because the same mind-altering additives are found in various combinations in many vessels spanning more than half a millennium at three major sites in the Murgab River valley, presumably this beverage was very important to people in the region.

In light of these considerations, Sarianidi's theory that the vessel and tube residues are related to the later Zoroastrian *haoma* is not as far-fetched as it might at first seem. A Central Asian mixed beverage or grog could well have been developed over millennia of human occupation in the well-watered oases. Such a potent beverage would likely have been endowed with religious overtones and incorporated into rituals. This traditional drink could then have been assimilated by Zoroastrianism, which became the state religion under the Achaemenid kings. Even earlier, about the same time that the monumental buildings near the Merv oasis were being constructed, it could have been carried to India by Indo-European invaders.

Haoma (linguistically equated with *soma* in the Indic *Rig Veda*) is mentioned in the Iranian *Avesta,* the collection of Zoroastrian sacred texts, which were first written down in the sixth century B.C. and received their final redaction in the fourth century A.D. The formulation of *haoma* has challenged many interpreters, who have variously argued that it was made from the urine of a white bull calf, ginseng, Syrian rue (*Peganum harmala*), or the fly agaric mushroom (*Amanita muscaria*), still a favorite hallucinogen among Siberian shamans (chapter 7). Most recently, ergot (*Claviceps* spp.), a fungus that grows on rye and other cereals, has been proposed as the principal ingredient. The alkaloid in this fungus, ergotamine, is closely related to lysergic acid diethylamide (LSD). In various episodes documented since the Middle Ages when ergot has been accidentally ingested on bread made from infected cereal, people have been known to hallucinate, experience burning sensations, and run madly through the streets as they succumbed to what was known as Saint Anthony's fire.

Until the excavations in Turkmenistan, there was no way to decide between the different possibilities. Descriptions in literary sources lacked enough detail to identify the ingredients of the drink. A mushroom might be ruled out by the *Avesta*'s stating that the relevant plant was green, tall, and aromatic, but that still left a lot of room for doubt.

In the *Yasna*, the primary *Avesta* liturgical text, *haoma* is prepared by the priest pounding the plant in a stone mortar, sieving it through bull's hair, dissolving it in water, and adding other, unknown ingredients. When the drink reached India, it was further adapted to use the plants of tropical and temperate regions of the subcontinent.

The most detailed description of how *haoma* entered into Zoroastrian religious thought is found in a very late text, the *Book of Arda Wiraz,* which dates to the ninth century A.D., with some elements possibly belonging to the early part of the millennium. Following the humiliating defeat of the nation by Alexander, Arda Wiraz, the hero of the tale, is commissioned by a grand council of priests and believers to make a journey to heaven to find out whether they are performing the correct rituals. Pious Arda Wiraz consumes three golden cups of a wine laced with an unidentified hallucinogen and is transported to another world. He meets a beautiful woman, crosses a bridge into heaven, and is ushered into the presence of the supreme god, Ahura Mazda. After seeing the souls of the blessed at peace, Arda Wiraz glimpses what awaits those who do not follow the central tenets of the faith: good thoughts, good words, and good deeds. Like Dante descending into Purgatory and the circles of Hell, Arda Wiraz crosses over the river of tears (the equivalent of the Greek River Styx) and sees the sinners in all their agony and despair, suffering eternal punishments to match their transgressions in life. He awakens from his dream after seven days with the assurance from Ahura Mazda that the Zoroastrian faith is the only true faith.

The *haoma* in this tale, strikingly, is administered in wine. By the time this work appeared, however, the influence of both Islam and Buddhism had engendered severe prohibitionist movements in these regions; so by retaining this detail, the *Book of Arda Wiraz* could be harking back to a much earlier tradition. From a chemical standpoint, the advantage of using an alcoholic beverage is that it dissolves the plant alkaloids.

When I first considered wine as the most likely vehicle for *haoma*, it was under the assumption that the Margiana sites were within the sphere of the wine culture that is so well attested in the Fergana Valley, even deeper in Central Asia. Then I received word from Gabriele Rossi-Osmida, of the Ligabue Study and Research Center in Venice, that three grape pips had been recovered at Gonur South. New excavations by Rossi-Osmida in the Adji Kui oasis, to the north of Merv, have even revealed a third- to second-millennium B.C. series of basins containing more grapeseeds, which might have served as a winemaking facility. As I write this in early 2008, Rossi-Osmida is in the field with a cadre of archaeobotanical specialists in hopes of firming up the picture both here and at Sarianidi's contemporaneous sites.

The archaeological and botanical evidence from the Turkmenistan excavations provides new clues for identifying *haoma*, at least in prehistoric Central Asia. If we accept Sarianidi's premise that a special beverage was being prepared in the white rooms and concur with the reading that wine and a hallucinogen were mixed together in the Arda Wiraz story, then the evidence of ephedra, hemp, and poppy pollen in the pottery vessels and tubes begins to make sense. To be sure, hemp and poppy could have been used for other purposes, such as textile production and ornamentation, and for culinary and fuel needs (e.g., cooking with poppyseed oil). Yet these two plants, as well as ephedra, have been well known since antiquity as medicinal and narcotic agents in Central Asia and China.

With more archaeological and chemical investigation, we should eventually be able to re-create the ancient *haoma/soma* or Central Asian grog, which was probably much stronger than modern versions. If Sarianidi's hypothesis holds up, we might envision a kind of brave new world in the Margiana oases, similar to Aldous Huxley's utopia in *Brave New World,* whose inhabitants regularly consume Soma (with "all the advantages of Christianity and alcohol; none of their defects"). The potency of such a mixed drink can be appreciated by examining the psychoactive effects of each additive in turn.

Ephedra's main active alkaloid, ephedrine, a chemical analogue of noradrenalin, stimulates the sympathetic nervous system and induces a mild euphoria. In small amounts, it produces an amphetamine-like high; in larger amounts, it can induce hallucinations and even cardiac arrest. Modern recreational users of herbal ecstasy, made from ephedra, attest to its psychoactive potency. Marijuana contains tetrahydrocannabinol (THC), which is related to anandamide, an endogenous neurotransmitter; it is also euphoric and sometimes stimulates the imagination. The milky latex of poppyseed capsules, which is called opium when congealed, provides a highly concentrated amalgam of some forty powerful mind-altering alkaloids, including codeine, morphine, papaverine, and narcotine. The leaves, which can be smoked, have lesser amounts of these substances.

Combining these plant alkaloids in an alcoholic beverage, which has its own effect on the human nervous system, greatly increases the possibilities for hallucinatory experiences, perhaps culminating in narcosis.

HORSE NOMADS OF THE NORTH

Where did the inhabitants of Gonur South, Togolok, and Adji Kui come from, and how might their predilection for a hallucinatory beverage have affected peoples farther east along the prehistoric Silk Road?

There is quite possibly a very early precedent for the use of ephedra as a hallucinatory agent in the Middle East. A group of intriguing Neanderthal burials, dating back to 40,000–80,000 B.P., were excavated by Ralph Solecki at Shanidar Cave in the northern Zagros Mountains, only about seventy-five kilometers west of Hajji Firuz (see chapter 3). Solecki astounded the archaeological community when he announced that one of the skeletons (Shanidar I, nicknamed Nandy), a forty- to fifty-year-old male who was blind in one eye and had physical disabilities, showed signs of having been empathetically cared for; otherwise, how could this handicapped individual have survived to a relatively advanced age?

Another skeleton, of a thirty- to forty-five-year-old male (Shanidar IV), known as the "flower burial," was adorned with a host of plants with known medicinal value. Besides ephedra, the pollen of yarrow (*Achillea* spp.), grape hyacinth (*Muscari*), hollyhock (*Althea*), ragwort or groundsel (*Senecio*), and Saint Barnaby's thistle (*Centaurea*) were found near the body. Yarrow immediately struck me as highly suggestive of a ritual involving psychoactive plants. It was an ingredient in gruit, a bittering agent in medieval beer making (which also included bog myrtle, wild rosemary, and a variety of other herbs), which was eventually banned in northern Europe—partly because of its aphrodisiac effects—and replaced by hops. Indeed, all of the plants found in the flower burial have known medicinal value as diuretics, stimulants, astringents, or anti-inflammatory agents. It seemed possible that the individual had received some sort of shamanistic send-off into the afterlife or might even have been the community's shaman or healer.

Some scholars disagreed. They argued that the pollen could have been blown into the cave or deposited there by an animal. It seems unlikely, however, that a gust of wind could have propelled clumps of mixed pollen through the entrance of the cave, much less whole flowers, whose presence is indicated by intact clusters in the shape of anthers. A scale from a butterfly wing showed that this insect had been accidentally incorporated into the array of flowers and herbs. If an animal, such as one of the rodents that were burrowing around elsewhere in the cave, were responsible for bringing together this odd assortment of materials, then it must have had a keen instinct in selecting only medicinal plants.

A colleague of mine at Penn, Victor Mair, also stirred the scholarly world when he "uncovered" extremely well-preserved mummies in an all-but-forgotten gallery of the museum at Ürümchi, a town in the mountains north of the Tarim Basin. They dated to about 1000 B.C., and thus were contemporary with the later Togolok palaces or temples. The mummies had been excavated from tombs at Cherchen, on the southeastern side of the Tarim Basin and one of the important way stations along the popular southern route of the Silk Road, bypassing the desert. Males and females wore brightly colored plain and plaited woolen clothes, and rounded and peaked caps of felt and yarn, like those depicted on the Kaftari seal and the Sogdian couch. One man was buried with ten different caps. Such caps became the trademark of the Phrygians, an eastern European people who settled in central Anatolia in the early first millennium B.C., where they enjoyed their own brand of grog (see chapter 5).

Victor was astonished to discover that the facial features of the Ürümchi mummies were vastly different from those of any present-day people of Mongolian origin. The full beards on the men, the high aquiline noses, and tall stature were distinctively Caucasian features. Victor went on to enlist many specialists—geneticists, linguists, and archaeologists—in the task of discovering who these people were and where they originated.

In time, other mummies, dating back to about 2000 B.C., when Gonur South was established, were brought to light and studied. They revealed more fascinating details. Nearly every mummy from the broader Loulan area, where two of the Silk Road routes met on the eastern end of the Tarim Basin, had a bundle of ephedra twigs tied into the edges of the shroud. In life, this small stock of stimulant might have kept a person alert in the demanding desert environment, as coca, khat, tobacco, and coffee punctuate everyday life elsewhere. In death, perhaps it aided the journey into the afterlife.

Victor also pointed out that a series of pottery figurines, which were excavated at key sites extending from Turkmenistan to the Yellow River basin of China, closely resembled the mummies, with many of the same Caucasoid features. They wore high pointed caps and feathered headdresses. Some of the examples dated as far back as 4000 B.C.

An early influx of Indo-European loan words into Chinese gave additional clues to who these people were and where they came from. Victor claimed that the Old Chinese word *$m^y ag$ (the asterisk indicates a hypothetical reconstructed form) derived from the Persian word *maguš*, denoting a Zoroastrian priest. It also gives us our English words *magic* and *magician,* a figure who is often depicted wearing a high conical hat similar to those of the Central Asian mummies and figurines. A class of Zoroastrian priests in Shiraz were known as magi, and three of their number might be those referred to in the New Testament as journeying from the east to see the infant Jesus in the stable in Bethlehem, according to biblical tradition.

Other words in Chinese also derive from Persian roots, including the terms for *chariot* and *mead,* while *silk* was adopted from Chinese in the reverse direction. Even the name for the strategic entrepôt of Dunhuang contains the Persian element for *fire* and supports the idea that languages, technologies, and fermented beverages moved both ways across Central Asia. The capstone to this argument was that a now-extinct branch of the Indo-European language family, Tokharian, once prevailed at sites along the northern Silk Road around the Tarim Basin, extending up into the Mongolian and Siberian steppes.

Another line of early evidence for Indo-European penetration into Central Asia is the proof of domestication of the horse, as attested by horse sacrifices in which the animal was buried with its owner. The earliest ones, dating to 4500–3500 B.C., are found to the west in central Ukraine, but their frequency increases in later periods. Horse sacrifices were practiced to the east in Kazakhstan by at least 2000 B.C., at the same time that other Indo-European groups were moving into Iran and south to India. Spoked-wheel carts, which were much easier for horses to pull than solid wood ones, also appear in Central Asia at this time.

The domestication of the horse gave a huge advantage to peoples living on the grasslands, where agriculture was difficult. On horseback, they could herd sheep and cattle much more effectively. They could live off the secondary products of their animals—milk products, wool, and hair—and carry their possessions on carts drawn by horses or cattle.

The raw materials for a good fermented beverage—fruit, cereal, and honey—were hard to come by on the grasslands. As ever, humans improvised by making a drink (Turkish *kımız;* Kazakh *koumiss*) from mare's milk, which has a higher sugar (lactose) content than goat's or cow's milk and consequently yields a higher alcohol content (up to 2.5 percent). In fact, they probably would not have drunk the milk unfermented, because many Central and East Asian peoples lack the enzymes needed to digest lactose.

A high mortality rate for young foals during the second and first millennium B.C., based on zooarchaeological studies, suggests that the nomadic herdsmen were concerned about producing enough *koumiss* for their needs. Lactation begins when an animal gives birth, and the offspring is then separated from the mother so that humans can collect most of the milk. In Central Asia today, the milking season traditionally runs between May and October, and a typical mare can produce 1,200 liters of milk. When the cold winter arrived, ancient peoples, struggling in the harsh conditions, might well have decided to slaughter the foals, especially by the age of two and a half, when they had put on most of their adult weight, rather than try to keep them alive and use up valuable resources.

A rare discovery of burial mounds frozen into the permafrost layer of the high Altai Mountains at Pazyryk, about eight hundred kilometers north of Cherchen, provides insight into the life of the horse nomads of the northern tundra. A Russian archaeologist, Sergei Rudenko, was called in to excavate burial mounds (*kurgans* in Russian) of fifth-century B.C. Pazyryk nomads, which had been partly looted in antiquity. Like the slightly earlier tumuli at Gordion in central Turkey (see chapter 5), the burial chambers of the five Pazyryk tumuli were made of carefully faced and assembled logs and then covered over with artificial mounds of earth. With hot water, Rudenko freed up and excavated an amazing group of burial goods that had been preserved in the ice. There were intricately carved wooden tables and drinking vessels, multicolored woolen and felted tapestries and rugs, gold and silver ornaments adorning headdresses and belts, a harp and drums, leather pouches and cut-outs of a raptor and deer, a complete chariot with spoked wheels, and accompanying horse burials. Embroidered silk and a mirror came from China. Some of the mummified dead were buried in wooden coffins, like the royal personage interred in the

Figure 14. Nomads of the Siberian steppes were buried with their hallucinogenic smoking and drinking appurtenances under mounds (*kurgans*) at Pazyryk (Russia), ca. 400 B.C. (a, *above*) As in life, so also in death, an individual crawled into his private felt-covered pup tent, supported by a frame of six rods, stoked up a high-footed cauldron or long-handled censer with marijuana (hemp) seeds, and inhaled the fumes in the sauna-like atmosphere. (b and c, *right*) One's thirst could later be quenched using a horn-handled cup to draw a drink from a large jar, here decorated with affixed leather roosters. From S. I. Rudenko, *Frozen Tombs of Siberia: The Pazyryk Burials of Iron Age Horsemen*, trans. M. W. Thompson (Berkeley: University of California Press, 1970). Photographs courtesy Sergei I. Rudenko and Hermitage Museum, St. Petersburg.

Midas tumulus at Gordion, and some bore tattoos of fantastic griffins, winged leopards, and raptors.

Rudenko reported another finding in all the burial chambers, which links the steppe nomads with their more sedentary neighbors in the oases of Turkmenistan and at Cherchen. A group of six rods was found in each tomb—two groups for a double burial—which had originally been fitted together to form a teepeelike frame covered with leather or felt. A high-footed cauldron, filled with pebbles and carbonized hemp seeds, sat in the middle of the tent. Birch bark was wound around the cauldron handles and the rods to disperse the heat.

What was the purpose of the tents and the hemp-filled cauldrons? The answer is provided by Herodotus in his *History* (4.75.1–2). He describes a peculiar custom among a steppe people, the Scythians, who lived farther to the west. Rather than bathe, they climbed under a tent made of felt, threw hemp onto hot stones, and immersed themselves in the intoxicating fumes until they "howled like wolves" in a hallucinogenic version of a Scandinavian sauna.

Presumably some liquid refreshment was needed after this sweltering indulgence. Tall, narrow-mouthed jars stood in each tomb, but whether they held *koumiss,* wine, water, or a milky sort of vodka (distillation was likely unknown), as Rudenko conjectured, is uncertain. The Scythians in the western part of their territory knew about wine from their contacts with the Greeks and perhaps much earlier through peoples to their south in the Caucasus and Iran. As their domain expanded eastward to include Turkmenistan and the oases of Central Asia, they would also have been in touch with other Indo-Europeans there and in the fertile mountain valleys and oases bordering the Tarim Basin, where the domesticated grape thrived. They even enjoyed the occasional beer, according to classical writers.

Today the Xinjiang Uyghur Autonomous Region of China, which encompasses the Tarim Basin and the Tien Shan, has been acclaimed for its table-grape production. It has recently been planted with French varieties, which thrive in the desert climate when properly irrigated. I was treated to a 2002 oak-aged Cabernet Sauvignon made by Suntime Winery in the so-called West Region, one of the rapidly expanding government-owned operations. A French wine merchant, who is now importing bulk Chinese wine into Europe, made the contact, and before long, a bottle arrived by DHL courier on my doorstep from Central Asia. For the Chinese equivalent of a Two-Buck Chuck, however, I was asked to pay customs duties of one hundred dollars. I stood my ground, especially because the wine was only mediocre, and eventually the shipping costs were waived.

Much earlier settlers of the region, coming from the exuberant wine cultures of the Near East, must have recognized the potential of this area for wine grapes and transplanted the Eurasian grape there. Between the second and fourth centuries A.D. this was certainly the case: many "ghost towns," surrounded by abandoned vineyards, dot the southern Silk Road. Now largely covered over by drifting sands from the Taklamakan Desert, they stand as a silent reminder of a once-flourishing industry. Winemaking might have been established even earlier, as a nomadic way of life, powered by horses and other livestock, expanded out on to the Pontic and Caspian steppes by 2000 B.C. Rudenko points out that the dead in the Pazyryk tombs probably belonged to the Yuezhi people, the same group who were humiliated by their king's skull being converted into a wine cup. Even if nomads could not tend vineyards and make wine while on the move, they came in contact with settled communities and could procure wine. They would have had access to some of the ingredients likely used in ancient *haoma/soma*. At Pazyryk, the preferred beverage thus appears to have combined a marijuana high with an alcoholic buzz.

Proto-Indo-European (PIE) historical linguistics, albeit not a precise science, gives another perspective on tracing the ethnic origins of the plains people and their drinking habits. In an important study, Thomas Gamkrelidze and Vjačeslav Ivanov argue that the widespread occurrence of the word for *wine* (PIE *woi-no* or *wei-no*) in many ancient and modern languages (including Latin *vinum*, Old Irish *fín*, Russian *vino*, Early Hebrew *yayin*, Hittite *wijana*, Egyptian *wns*, and so on) makes it an indicator of the movements of the Indo-European peoples. Although still hotly contested, an independent computer-generated study by researchers at the University of Pennsylvania confirmed these reconstructions. Gamkrelidze and Ivanov placed the PIE homeland in the general region of Transcaucasia and eastern Turkey, where the Eurasian grape was probably first domesticated around 7000 B.C. With a generous margin of error, they estimated that the earliest PIE speakers started migrating around 5000 B.C. They envisioned groups, both nomadic and sedentary, spreading out toward Iran and the Central Asian oases, as well as southward to Palestine and Egypt, and westward to Europe.

More definitive human DNA evidence for these migrations is still very limited. The few studies of Central Asian and Chinese populations that have been carried out corroborate the archaeological and linguistic scenarios of more intensive Indo-European influence before 500 B.C., which gave way to a gradually increasing influx of peoples from East Asia.

THE ABIDING MYSTERY OF CENTRAL ASIA

We are still very much in the dark about the dynamics of the transfer of fermented beverages and their mind-altering additives back and forth along the prehistoric Silk Road. The discoveries in Turkmenistan, in the Tarim Basin, and at Pazyryk stand as beacons that begin to illuminate how the earliest fermented beverages—such as the Jiahu grog and the resinated wines of the mountainous Near East—could have appeared at about the same time in the Neolithic period. Yet there are large geographic and temporal gaps in our knowledge. Our evidence from Gonur and Togolok goes back only as far as 2000 B.C. The Fergana Valley, whose luxuriant vines and aged wines were extolled by Strabo and Zhang Qian, remains an archaeological cipher. We are left with two choices, pending new discoveries: either knowledge of how to make a fermented beverage was developed in the Palaeolithic period and came to fruition independently at about the same time on both sides of Asia, or else the key ideas were passed along the pre-historic Silk Road in either or both directions during the "revolutionary" Neolithic period. I am more swayed by the latter hypothesis.

We need some enterprising archaeologist to unveil what was happening at the beginning of the Neolithic period in Central Asia. An inkling of the discoveries that might emerge comes from what is perhaps the most impor-tant Neolithic site on the overland route from Iran to the great sub-continent of India: Mehrgarh in Baluchistan, Pakistan. This village of carefully planned and constructed mudbrick buildings, dating to between 7000 and 5500 B.C., has yielded archaeobotanical evidence for domesticated einkorn and emmer wheat, which must have been introduced from the Near East. Jujube (*Ziziphus jujuba,* also known as Chinese date) and date palm (*Phoenix dactylifera*) seeds were also found. Clearly, the Mehrgarh inhabitants had ac-cess to a wide range of natural products that could have been converted into alcoholic beverages. When pottery first makes its appearance around 4000 B.C., tall goblets, ideal for drinking, dominate the assemblage. The domes-ticated Eurasian grape appears in the archaeological record shortly there-after and had definitely been taken into cultivation by 2500 B.C., as shown by large pieces of grapevine wood found at the site. Without carrying out chemical tests, we cannot be sure whether beers or wines were being con-cocted, but the existing archaeological clues are strong presumptive evi-dence for alcoholic beverages at the site.

More Neolithic sites like Mehrgarh need to be discovered, excavated, and thoroughly studied across Central Asia, including sites on the side routes to India and Russia. Then we might know whether the early Neolithic fer-mented beverages of China and the Near East were independently devel-oped or resulted from the mutual exchange of ideas along the prehistoric Silk Road.

Plate 1. Spider monkey (*Ateles geoffroyi*) feeding on the fruit of the *Astrocaryum* palm tree in the forest of Barro Colorado, Panama. From fruit flies to primates, animals are attracted by plumes of alcohol that lead them to sugar-rich fruits. Howler monkeys have been observed to consume quantities of fermented fruit equivalent to a human's consumption of about two bottles of wine in less than half an hour. Photograph by Christian Ziegler.

Plate 2 (*opposite top*). Could this female figure (height 44 cm), carved about twenty thousand years ago into a cliff face at Laussel on the Dordogne River in France, be holding a drinking horn? Long associated with the Vikings, the tradition of drinking mead from a horn has deep roots in prehistoric European cultures. Photograph by François Hubert, Musée d'Aquitaine, Bordeaux.

Plate 3 (*opposite bottom*). Early Neolithic jars, with high flaring necks and rims, from Jiahu (Henan Province, China), ca. 7000–6600 B.C. Analyses by the author and his colleagues show that such jars contained a mixed fermented beverage of rice, honey, and fruit (hawthorn fruit and/or grape). Photograph courtesy of J. Zhang, Z. Zhang, and Henan Institute of Cultural Relics and Archaeology, nos. M252:1, M482:1, and M253:1 (left to right). The leftmost jar is 20 cm in height.

Plate 4 (*above*). In the matriarchal society of the Qiang of Yunnan Province, China, men and women gather around the rice-wine jar to drink through long reed straws in the traditional fashion. This custom persists in many other places around the world (see figures 13a–b and 24a–b). From M. Chenyuan and Z. Hengang, 1997, *Zhongguo jiu wen hua* (Chinese wine culture, Shanghai: Shanghai ren min mei shu chu ban she, 1997), 213.

Plate 5 (*opposite*). The earliest grape wine and barley beer vessels confirmed by chemical analyses to date, both excavated at sites in the Zagros Mountains of Iran. (a, *top*) Godin Tepe beer jar, ca. 3400–3100 B.C. Contrast the narrow, high neck of the wine vessel below, which was stoppered in antiquity, with the wider mouth of the beer vessel. An applied rope design encircles the beer jar, which is shown knotted, with the two loose ends hanging down. Below the knot, a small hole was made before the vessel was fired. (b, *bottom*) The author "sniffing out" the ancient vintage inside a Hajji Firuz wine jar, ca. 5400–5000 B.C. Photographs courtesy of (a) W. Pratt, with permission of the Royal Ontario Museum, Toronto, © ROM; and (b) David Parker/Science Photo Library and Hasanlu Project, University of Pennsylvania Museum of Archaeology and Anthropology, no. 69-12-15, height 23.5 cm.

Plate 6 (*above*). Winemaking scenes from the Theban tomb of the scribe Nakht, ca. 1400 B.C. The Egyptian pharaohs established a royal winemaking industry in the Nile Delta around 3000 B.C. For thousands of years, tombs contained detailed portrayals of each stage in the process: harvesting and stomping the grapes, collecting the must, and stoppering and inscribing the jars. The Metropolitan Museum of Art, Rogers Fund, 1915 (15.5 19e), image © The Metropolitan Museum of Art.

Plate 7. Roman drinking set, comprising a bucket (*situla*), a ladle and sieve, and several drinking cups, so-called sauce pans, from a cache under the floor of a settlement at Havor, Sweden, in the southern part of the island of Gotland. Analyses by the author's laboratory and colleagues show that the set was used to serve and drink a "Nordic grog" that included grape wine. Photograph by G. Gådefors, from E. Nylén, U. Lund Hansen, and P. Manneke, *The Havor Hoard: the Gold, the Bronzes, the Fort* (Stockholm: Kungl. Vitterhets Historie och Antikvitets Akademien, 2005). Photograph courtesy of KVHAA, Lena Thunmark Nylén, and Statens Historiska Museum, Stockholm.

Plate 8 (*left*). Lock-on lidded jar from a tomb in Río Azul, Guatemala, dated to ca. A.D. 500, used for storing the elite beverage made from cacao beans. Stuccoed and painted, the jar bears the Mayan hieroglyph for *ka-ka-w* ("cacao"). Collection of the Museo Nacional de Arqueología y Etnología, Guatemala City, Guatemala. Photograph courtesy of Bailey Archive, Denver Museum of Nature and Science. All rights reserved.

Plate 9 (*right*). Front-facing god *keros* vessel from the Wari provincial center of Cerro Baúl, southern Peru. Seven sets of four vessels, in graduated sizes, were excavated. The twenty-eight drinking cups were smashed when the brewery at the site was deliberately burned down around A.D. 800. Photograph by Patrick Ryan Williams, The Field Museum.

Plate 10. This magnificent Neolithic rock painting, dating to the third millennium B.C. or earlier, was discovered by the explorer Henri Lhote in the Tassili n'Ajjer Mountains of the central Sahara Desert. Among their herds, nomads appear to engage in a drinking ceremony. A male (kneeling at left), helped by possibly his father or an elder (seated at left), drinks from a large decorated jar using a long straw. From encampment to encampment, cereal beer and its technology made their way from east to west across Africa. Image © Pierre Colombel/CORBIS.

FIVE

EUROPEAN BOGS, GROGS, BURIALS, AND BINGES

THE WORD *EUROPE* FOR ME conjures up a host of fermented beverages: ruby-red clarets, luscious Champagnes, and heavenly Burgundy from France; Riesling and Nebbiolo wines from Germany and Italy; and the wonderful lambic beers, Abbey tripels, and red ales of Belgium. These drinks and many others trace their origins to medieval times.

We owe a debt to the monastic communities of the Middle Ages for most of the European beverages we enjoy today. As well as patiently dedicating themselves to a spiritual life and preparation for the next world, the monks explored, selected, and nurtured the plant life of this world (including hops), concocted new alcoholic drinks, and made beer and wine on a large scale. In Burgundy, the Cistercian monks literally tasted the soils of the Côte d'Or and determined by a centuries-long process of trial and error, beginning in the twelfth century, which cultivars were best suited to grow on specific plots of land (*terroir*). They settled on Chardonnay and Pinot Noir. Farther north, the Trappists, an offshoot of the Cistercians, specialized in beer. Their best-known monastery and brewery, Chimay, still produces an extremely complex and aromatic ale, which can be aged for five years or more. When Tom Peters, the owner of Monk's Café in Philadelphia, served me my first aged Chimay, I was taken aback. Could this be a beer? It had all the sensory richness—the complex aromas and flavors—of a fine wine.

The distinctive Italian and French vermouths, which fall into the general category of mixed fermented beverages, have their roots deeper in the past. Their proprietary formulations involve macerating different tree barks and roots, orange peels, flower extracts, herbs, and spices and infusing them into wine. *Vermouth* derives from the German word (*Wermut*) for wormwood. This herb contains the world's bitterest natural compound, α-thujone, which also has psychotropic effects.

Such compounds, as well as others in digestives and bitters, can have longer-lasting effects, as I learned after a mishap at the Copenhagen airport in 1995. I had brought a gift for my host, John Strange: Fernet-Branca, an Italian bitter made from some forty herbs, plants, and tree resins, including saffron, rhubarb, myrrh, and cardamom. John swears by a draft of the stuff each morning before breakfast, though I can barely swallow a teaspoonful. I had carefully packed the bottle in an aluminum suitcase for protection. At the airport, the suitcase slid off the baggage cart and slammed onto the floor. A pungent brown liquid began oozing out. We quickly removed the broken bottle of Fernet-Branca and tried to clean up the mess. On the other side of customs, John met us and commiserated in the loss. After he delivered us to our accommodations, we hung up the contents of the suitcase (including my lecture notes) to dry. Years later, I can still see the brown stains along the edges of the paper and smell the presence of the bitter. A future archaeological chemist may have a field day with this beverage thousands of years from now.

A MIXED FERMENTED BEVERAGE WITH THE "MIDAS TOUCH"

Although the medieval period was a golden age for the development of alcoholic drinks in Europe, their history goes much further back. The Dardanelles and the Bosporus Strait, which connect the Black Sea with the Mediterranean, mark the boundary between Europe and Asia. Over the millennia, ideas and technologies have flowed constantly from one region to the other. More often, Asia has bestowed its bounty on Europe, beginning at least as early as the Neolithic period, when the Europeans began to adopt its domesticated plants and animals. On occasion, however, the process has been reversed, as when peoples of the northern European steppes penetrated into the southern lands on horseback. Fermented beverages are strongly linked with these phenomena, as they are integral to most religious, funerary, and social customs.

The site of Gordion, near the Turkish capital of Ankara on the central Anatolian plateau, provides an entrée into the world of early European fermented beverages. Following the turbulent transition from the Bronze Age to the Iron Age, around 1200 B.C., the Phrygians crossed from Eastern Europe into Asia. They were filling the vacuum left by the powerful Hittite empire, whose remnants had moved to southeastern Turkey and Syria. The Phrygians established their capital at Gordion.

Gordion, which has been the focus of a Penn Museum excavation for more than fifty years, is renowned for the story of Alexander the Great's neatly chopping through the enigmatic Gordian knot with his sword and fulfilling the prophecy that whoever could undo the knot would rule Asia. Legend has it that the knot firmly tethered an oxcart that had originally transported an impecunious Midas and his father Gordius to the city, thereby inaugurating a golden period of Phrygian rule.

In *Ancient Wine,* I describe the stupendous royal tomb known as the Midas tumulus, dating to around 750–700 B.C. The burial chamber occupied the center of a monumental tumulus or mound, built of soil and stones piled some fifty meters high, that dominates the landscape today as in the past. Constructed of a double wall of juniper logs and cut pine planks, the tomb is the world's oldest intact wooden structure. Located well above the water table and protected under tons of soil, it acted as a hermetically sealed time capsule.

When excavators broke through the wall of the tomb in 1957, they came face to face with an amazing sight, like Howard Carter's first glimpse into Tutankhamun's tomb. They saw the body of a sixty- to sixty-five-year-old male, laid out on a thick pile of blue and purple textiles, the colors of regal splendor. In the background gleamed the largest Iron Age drinking set ever found: 157 bronze vessels, including vats, jugs, and drinking bowls, which were used in a dinner bidding farewell to the tomb's occupant.

Map 2 *(overleaf).* Europe and the Mediterranean. From 30,000 B.P. onward, traditions of fermented-beverage production penetrated into this continent and along the shores of the Earth's largest inland sea. Domesticated plants were introduced from the Middle East during the course of the Neolithic period (beginning ca. 8500 B.C.), continuing until 4000 B.C. The Phoenicians, sailing from the Levant, and the Greeks carried their wine cultures westward across the Mediterranean. The earliest contact dates, as shown by well-attested artifacts and bioarchaeological evidence (including domesticated cereals), are tentatively indicated along the routes traveled.

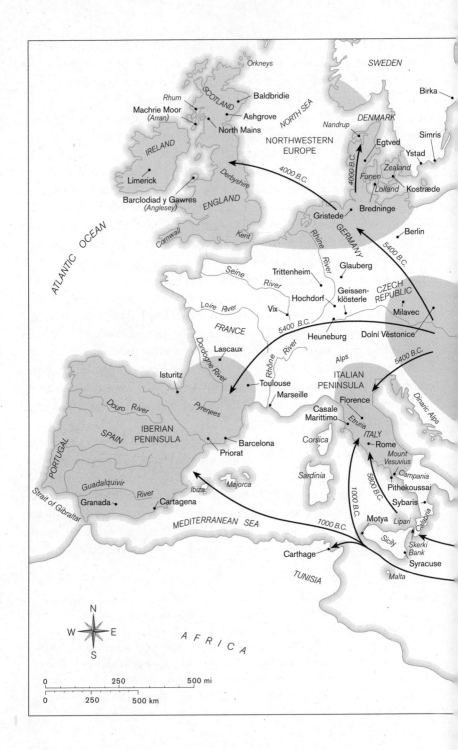

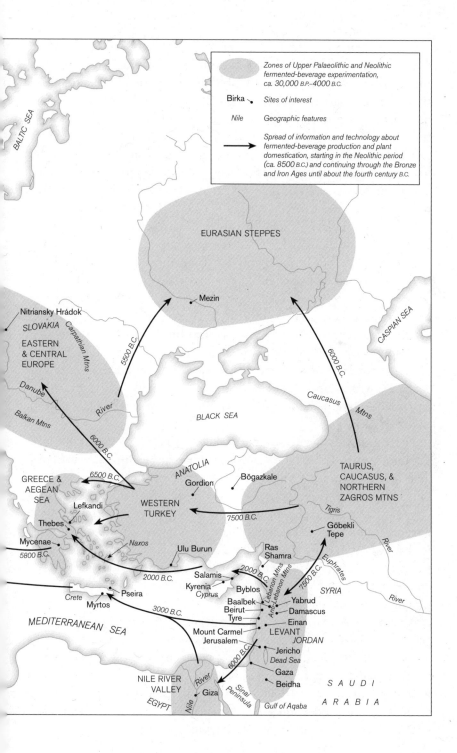

Zones of Upper Palaeolithic and Neolithic fermented-beverage experimentation, ca. 30,000 B.P.–4000 B.C.

Birka — Sites of interest

Nile — Geographic features

Spread of information and technology about fermented-beverage production and plant domestication, starting in the Neolithic period (ca. 8500 B.C.) and continuing through the Bronze and Iron Ages until about the fourth century B.C.

BALTIC SEA

EURASIAN STEPPES

Mezin

CASPIAN SEA

Nitriansky Hrádok
SLOVAKIA
EASTERN & CENTRAL EUROPE

Carpathian Mtns

5500 B.C.

6000 B.C.

Caucasus Mtns

Danube

River

6000 B.C.

BLACK SEA

Balkan Mtns

6500 B.C.

ANATOLIA

GREECE & AEGEAN SEA

Lefkandi

Gordion

Böğazkale

TAURUS, CAUCASUS, & NORTHERN ZAGROS MTNS

Thebes

WESTERN TURKEY

7500 B.C.

Tigris

Mycenae

5800 B.C.

Naxos

Ulu Burun

Ras Shamra

Göbekli Tepe

River

2000 B.C.

Salamis

2000 B.C.

Euphrates

7500 B.C.

Crete

Pseira

Kyrenia
Cyprus

Byblos

Lebanon Mtns

SYRIA

River

Myrtos

3000 B.C.

Baalbek
Beirut
Tyre

Anti-Lebanon Mtns

Yabrud

Damascus

MEDITERRANEAN SEA

Mount Carmel

Einan

Jerusalem

LEVANT

JORDAN

6000 B.C.

Jericho

Dead Sea

NILE RIVER VALLEY

River

Gaza

Beidha

S A U D I

Giza

Sinai Peninsula

A R A B I A

EGYPT

Nile

Gulf of Aqaba

Contemporaneous Assyrian inscriptions suggest that King Midas was not only a legendary figure but really did rule Phrygia, and that he or his father or grandfather, both named Gordius, was buried in this tomb. Although no inscription conveniently proclaims "Here lies Midas," the richness of the tomb furnishings, including some of the finest ancient inlaid furniture ever recovered, assures us that it was a royal burial. The Phrygian king's death prompted much feasting and drinking to honor his popularity and successful reign. The body was then lowered into the tomb, along with any leftovers of the food and drink to sustain him for eternity, or at least the ensuing 2,700 years.

If this is the burial of Midas with the legendary golden touch, where was the gold? The myth, as told in Ovid's *Metamorphoses,* might have promised unlimited riches, but it would also have condemned the king to death by starvation. When he dipped his fingers into a savory stew or sipped some wine, it was transformed into indigestible gold. Perhaps the myth was contrived by some Dark Age wanderer from Greece who caught a glimpse of the spectacular lion-headed and ram-headed bronze buckets, or *situlae,* in the tomb. When they were cleaned of their greenish patina, they glistened just like gold. These vessels were used to transfer a beverage from three large vats, each with a capacity of about 150 liters, to smaller vats, from which it was ladled into more than one hundred drinking bowls holding one or two liters each.

The real gold, as far as I was concerned, was what these vessels contained. Chemical analyses of intense yellowish residues inside the *situlae* and bowls detected the presence of a highly unusual fermented beverage, which combined grape wine, barley beer, and honey mead. Using infrared spectrometry, gas chromatography–mass spectrometry, and other techniques, our research team identified calcium oxalate or beerstone, a marker compound for barley beer; tartaric acid and its salts, which are characteristic of grape wine in the Middle East; and honey or its fermented product, mead, based on the presence of characteristic beeswax compounds, which can never be completely filtered out of honey.

We had discovered a truly distinctive libation that might be called "Phrygian grog." The reader can be pardoned for cringing, as I did, at the thought of drinking such a concoction. I was so taken aback by the notion of mixing wine and beer that I issued a challenge in March 2000 to a group of imaginative microbrewers, following a "Roasting and Toasting" celebration at the Penn Museum in honor of the beer authority Michael Jackson. Their goal: carry out experiments with the ingredients identified in our chemical analyses to prove or disprove the concept of such a drink. Over the ensuing months, they tried many different permutations in the amounts and kinds of ingredients and brewing methods, not always with success. My job was to taste and assess the finished products as they arrived at my front door.

Our chemical analysis could not resolve one crucial issue: we detected no trace of a bittering agent, but one must have been needed to offset the sweetness of the honey, grape sugar, and barley malt. Hops were ruled out, as they did not grow in Turkey at this time and were first used as a beer additive in the Middle Ages in northern Europe. We decided to use saffron, a native Turkish spice gleaned from the female stigmas of the crocus flower and suggestive of the Midas touch in both its golden color and its price. Some five thousand flowers are needed to produce a single ounce of saffron, making it the most expensive spice in the world. It has a wonderful fragrance and a distinctive, slightly bitter taste. It even has an analgesic effect. And it produced a golden color with a hint of the royal color, purple.

Applying his Neolithic beverage-making verve, Sam Calagione of Dogfish Head Craft Brewery emerged triumphant from the microbrewers' challenge. His creation, Midas Touch, has an affinity to Chateau Jiahu (see chapter 2), as both are mixed fermented beverages, but it has a different aromatic and taste profile and is slightly sweeter. The rice in Chateau Jiahu has been replaced in Midas Touch by malted barley, native to the Middle East. Lacking definitive evidence for which grape cultivar might have been used in eighth-century B.C. Anatolia, we used yellow Muscat, which has been shown by DNA analysis to be related to the earliest cultivated grapes in the Middle East. Combined with a delectable wildflower honey and saffron, it produced a golden-hued drink truly fit for a King.

When Midas Touch was introduced to the world in early 2001, we were not sure that it would survive in the highly competitive beer marketplace. Dogfish Head was still struggling to avoid the fate of so many other has-been microbreweries. Midas Touch, with the golden thumbprint of the "king" embellishing its label, was first presented in 750-milliliter corked bottles. Quality was uneven, as could be seen in the variable ullage, or air space, at the top of the bottle and by corks that were often wildly askew. Although the liquid inside the bottles was delicious, Sam had never corked his beer before and needed better equipment. After one of his corkers lost a finger in the machine (which certainly belied the notion of any special touch), he changed the presentation to a four-pack of twelve-ounce bottles, which were crown-capped like most beers. Today, Midas Touch has won more prizes than any other Dogfish Head beverage, having garnered three gold medals and five silvers at major tasting competitions and captured a cult following. Midas himself could not have wished for better.

Although the Phrygian grog is a latecomer as mixed fermented or extreme beverages go, it epitomizes how traditions of beverage making could be passed back and forth between Europe and Asia and harks back to much earlier European traditions. Even before he produced his King Midas golden elixir, Sam Calagione had already dipped unwittingly into this rich heritage of European beverage making when he made a braggot to go with the dessert at the celebratory Michael Jackson dinner in 2000. Though largely forgotten today, medieval braggots combine honey, malt, and often a fruit. Sam's version was a lush but noncloying dessert wine to which plums had been added. By simply exchanging grapes for the plums, he had the basic formula for Midas Touch.

Phrygian grog likely represents the traditional beverage of the Phrygian "homeland," which immigrants brought with them on their journeys to Anatolia. It is believed that this Indo-European people originated from somewhere in the western steppe of the Ukraine and gradually made their way southwest through the Carpathian Basin environs of Hungary and Romania into the Balkans or northern Greece. The Phrygians' ultimate origin on the steppes is borne out by a customary representation: they are shown wearing distinctive peaked hats, often made of felt, of which nearly identical examples have been recovered from the Cherchen tombs in Central Asia. Felt, which formed a thick foundation for the blue and purple textiles on which the royal body was laid out in the Midas tumulus, is a textile widely found among nomadic peoples. The material was made by compacting moistened wool into a tight roll and carrying it on horseback for days on end until the heat and friction bonded the fibers into a fabric.

Long before the arrival of Phrygians and their grog, Anatolia had served as the conduit of cultural and technological influences—including newly domesticated plants and animals, metallurgy, and certainly alcoholic beverages—from western Asia into Europe, going back to the Neolithic period in the sixth millennium B.C. The tradition of a drinking set comprising a bowl, jug, and small beaker or cup had become firmly entrenched by the mid-fourth millennium in the Baden culture (named after a site near Vienna), and examples have been excavated from numerous tombs in the Carpathian

Basin of Hungary and along the Danube River. It has been suggested that the bowl and the jug held different beverages, which were mixed and drunk from the drinking cup. If so, this drinking set may be our first glimpse of what was to become a pan-European phenomenon.

Alcoholic beverages sometimes had a darker side in Baden culture. At the late fourth-millennium B.C. site of Nitriansky Hrádok, in western Slovakia, ten individuals—each kneeling in the same direction with their hands in front of their faces as if in prayer or adoration—had been deposited in a so-called death pit. A single cup and amphora found beneath this gruesome entourage suggested how they had met their fate. Like the servants, women, and horses that accompanied rulers of the "civilized world" in China and Mesopotamia to their graves, this group might have consumed an alcoholic beverage laced with a poisonous herb.

The Baden drinking culture spread out from central Europe to other parts of the continent during the fourth and third millennia B.C. Beautifully burnished and decorated Funnel Beakers (*Trichterbecher*) from sites in Germany and Denmark had extremely long necks, which accentuated the importance of the vessels' contents. Bell Beakers, so named because they are shaped like inverted bells, proliferated at sites in a wide arc from the Czech Republic to Spain, Normandy, and Britain. We are more familiar with the megalithic henge or enclosure monuments of this culture—famously at Stonehenge—that dot the European landscape, but the omnipresent beakers, holding as much as five liters, are another hallmark. A group of ten or more beakers was often deposited in a burial, along with a jug. Again, a final libation and toast to the departed is the most obvious interpretation, even without confirmatory chemical or other evidence.

Once the European drinking culture was established, it was highly resistant to change, as in Asia and the Near East, and as we will see repeatedly elsewhere. But just how did the Phrygian grog reflect broader European beverage-making traditions, and what impact did it have on native Anatolian customs?

ANSWERS FROM THE FAR NORTH

Surprisingly, the earliest evidence of a fermented beverage in Europe north of Greece comes from the islands and mainland of Scotland, more than four thousand kilometers away. Scotland, of course, has always been quite cold, despite its exposure to the Gulf Stream and periodic warming spells since the last Ice Age. This circumstance determined which sugar-rich resources were available to convert into alcoholic beverages. In any case, the Neolithic drink of this region has nothing to do with Scotland's national beverage today. Scotch whisky (from the Gaelic *uisge beatha*, "water of life"), which was introduced in the early Middle Ages, owes its much higher alcoholic content to distillation.

That Scotland has been identified as the earliest site of a fermented beverage in Europe is due to the pioneering efforts of its scientists, in particular palynologists. They were among the first to see the advantages of closely examining residues inside beakers and other beverage containers for pollen and other plant remains. If the same techniques and chemical analysis were applied at sites farther south in Europe, we would likely tap into a treasure trove of fermented beverages to rival those of Scotland.

The Scottish palynologists have probed dark-colored deposits on the inside of complete beakers from tombs at Ashgrove in Fife, north of Edinburgh, and at the henge and barrow (mound) site of North Mains in Strathallan, a short distance farther north. These sites date to ca. 1750–1500 B.C. From a much earlier period, the mid-fourth millennium B.C., large vats with 100-liter capacities have been analyzed from Tayside, also north of Edinburgh, and at the seaside settlement of Barnhouse on Mainland Island in the Orkneys, off the northern tip of Scotland. Lids have been found in the same vicinity at Tayside and Barnhouse, as well as at the famous Neolithic site of Skara Brea on Mainland Island: if they were used to cover the vats, then anaerobic fermentation of sugar-rich liquids in the vats would have been facilitated.

On the west coast, the researchers investigated similar residues adhering to the interiors of vessels from henge sites at Machrie Moor on the island of Arran, along the southwestern coast, and at a site on Rhum, an island in the Inner Hebrides group along the central coast. The former again dates to ca. 1750–1500 B.C., whereas the Rhum site, whose grooved-ware pottery is reminiscent of the large vats at Tayside and in the Orkneys, belongs to the late third millennium B.C.

Very consistent results were obtained from the palynological analyses of the Scottish residues. Honey, deriving mostly from the flowers of the small-leaved lime tree (*Tilia cordata*) and meadowsweet (*Filipendula vulgaris*) or heather (*Calluna vulgaris*), was attested in all the samples. The North Mains beaker and the large vessels from Rhum, Tayside, and the Orkneys also contained cereal pollen. No fruit remains were reported, but because fruits carry minimal pollen compared to nectar from flowers, their presence cannot be excluded. The meadowsweet pollen could have originated directly from the plant rather than from honey. Early herbalists and botanists from the sixteenth century onward describe how the leaves and flowers of medesweete or medewurte (whose name translates as "a pleasing agent or root for mead") were added to wine, beer, and mead to impart the herb's distinctive flavor and aroma. The Tayside residues reportedly contained pollen from henbane (*Hyoscyamus niger*) and deadly nightshade (*Atropa belladonna*), both of which have mind-altering properties, but a follow-up study failed to confirm this finding.

Although some of the pollen evidence is open to interpretation, a good case can be made that the cups and large vessels originally contained a fermented beverage—mead, a sweetened ale, or a more complex "Nordic grog" with added herbs. The honey in the Ashgrove beaker had clearly been diluted, as it had spilled out over the moss and leaves covering the upper body of the man buried there. When watered down, the natural yeasts in honey become active and readily ferment it to mead. Acting on this hypothesis and on the evidence from Rhum, William Grant and Sons, the company that owns the Glenfiddich distillery in Speyside (the heartland of modern Scotch production), made a heather-honey mead. At 8 percent alcohol, this one-time re-creation was described as "quite palatable" by those who tried it.

Taking their cue instead from the North Mains residue, a home brewer, Graham Dineley, and his wife, Merryn, prepared a different re-creation. Their "Strathallan brew" was made from malted barley, with meadowsweet as a flavorant. They used dung-tempered pottery in their experiments, which gave a piquant edge to the beverage. Some who tasted it liked it.

More chemical and botanical work is needed to determine the range and proportions of ingredients in these beverages. Northerners probably already had the means to ferment sugars from cereals and fruit as well as from honey. Cloudberry and lingonberry, which have been recovered from excavated sites, could also have been pressed into service: they make deliciously sweet cordials today.

A STRONGER BREW?

The much-heralded hallucinatory proclivities of Neolithic Europeans are still hypothetical and much in need of confirmatory evidence. As argued by British archaeologists Andrew Sherratt and Richard Rudgley, Nordic grog was often spiked with opium from the latex of poppyseed capsules (*Papaver somniferum*), marijuana from the hemp plant (*Cannabis sativa*), henbane, or deadly nightshade. This hypothesis is attractive because the megalithic passage and chambered tombs, which preceded the great henges, are centered around stelae and large basins carved with entoptic shapes and designs—such as spirals, checkerboards, and nested geometrical figures—that are evocative of an altered human consciousness. David Lewis-Williams and others have interpreted the Neolithic tomb artwork as a re-creation of the deeply mysterious atmosphere of the painted Palaeolithic caves where otherworldly ceremonies were likely carried out (see chapter 1). At Barclodiad y Gawres, on the island of Anglesey in Wales, the central chamber yielded a strange concoction containing the remains of a frog, two species of toad, a snake, a fish, a shrew, and a rabbit, which had been poured over a hearth and intentionally covered with stones, earth, and shells. Could this be the Neolithic equivalent of a magical brew like the one the witches stirred up in their cauldron in *Macbeth,* with the eye of a newt, an adder's tongue, and other delicacies?

We cannot reject this hypothesis out of hand, as we have already seen how opium and marijuana were probably used in preparing a special ceremonial beverage around 2000 B.C. in Turkmenistan, with roots deeper in the past. The incipient Baden drinking culture was in touch with developments on the western Eurasian steppes and might well have ushered into Europe the delights (and dangers) of these drugs. We also know from later literary records that opium was used medicinally to alleviate pain in Egypt, Greece, and Rome.

Poppyseeds are extremely well represented at sites throughout central and southern Europe from the Neolithic period onward. By the Iron Age they had appeared in Britain and Poland. Although the seeds themselves are not hallucinogenic but rather the source of a flammable oil and condiment, they suggest the presence of the more degradable seed capsule, which yields the drug. At Cueva de los Murciélagos (the Bat Cave), in Granada in southern Spain, dated to about 4200 B.C., intact seed capsules were found inside esparto grass bags, reminding one of the ephedra sewn into the hems of the Loulan mummy wrappings (see chapter 4).

Cannabis seeds, too, have been recovered from sites throughout Europe beginning in the Neolithic period. Parts of the plant produce a versatile fiber and seed oil; European peoples might also easily have learned how to infuse the plant's leaves or flowers, rich in the hallucinogenic alkaloid, into an alcoholic beverage. Similarly, so-called vase supports, polypod braziers, and "pipe stems" from sites throughout the continent would have been convenient vehicles for smoking and inhaling the drug, as the ancient Scythians did inside their tents (see chapter 4). Carbonized hemp seeds have been found inside some of these artifacts, probably the detritus left behind after the leaves and flowers had been burned. If marijuana was already an accepted European drug, then the much later acceptance of hops (*Humulus lupulus*), also in the cannabinoid family and an important additive in beer, might be viewed as a natural development.

The hard evidence for the consumption of such mind-altering drugs in an alcoholic potion remains elusive, however. Researchers at the University of Barcelona have made some headway by applying a variety of techniques—archaeobotanical, chemical, and phytolithic (based on microscopic identification of characteristic silica accretions in plants)—to pinpoint additives such as mugwort (*Artemisia vulgaris*) in a barley and emmer-wheat brew, sometimes supplemented with honey or acorn flour. The beverage remains were found inside vats holding 80 to 120 liters, jars, and smaller drinking vessels, including beakers. They come from several sites around Barcelona (the caves of Can Sadurní, Genó, Cova del Calvari, and Loma de la Tejería) and in central Spain (Valle de Ambrona and La Meseta Sur), dating between ca. 5000 B.C. and the beginning of the Christian era.

The Barcelona researchers, Jose Luis Maya, Joan Carles Matamala, and Jordi Juan-Tresserras, went on to re-create the 5,100-year-old Genó beverage with the help of the Spanish-based San Miguel brewery. Emmer wheat, from the last remaining field in Asturias in northern Spain, and barley were brewed with pure water from the Pyrenees in a handmade pottery vessel, like the ancient jar with the residue. Native rosemary, thyme, and mint enhanced the flavor and served as preservatives. A first batch of the thick, dark, gruelly liquid, with an 8 percent alcohol content, was quickly consumed—all four hundred bottles—before it had a chance to go flat. Another batch was prepared by less exacting methods for the first International Congress on Beer in Prehistory and Antiquity, held in Barcelona in 2004. I had the chance to taste the brew at the Bacchanalian-like closing celebration of the conference; unfortunately, its zesty taste was marred by the brew's having turned slightly.

If hard evidence is notably deficient for the proposed hallucinogenic beverages, a recent suggestion from two Irish archaeologists, Billy Quinn and Declan Moore, is even more mind-boggling. They argue that the thousands of curious horseshoe-shaped features (Gaelic *fulacht fiadh*, "wild pit") scattered throughout Ireland were used to produce the earliest Irish beer. They envision that the long central troughs of the *fulachta fiadh*, which date from Neolithic times down to around 500 B.C., were filled with malted grain and water and the resulting mixture heated or mashed with red-hot stones to break down the starches into sugar. Unfortunately, little grain, and none that has been identified as malted or mashed, has ever been recovered from the sites. More common are animal bones, which some archaeologists have taken as signs that the fire-cracked stones were used to boil up meat instead (early corned beef, perhaps?).

As Quinn and Moore explained to me at a bar on the Rambla boulevard of Barcelona, where we were attending the beer congress, they hit on their idea one morning while nursing hangovers from the night before. If other foods were cooked with hot rocks in the Neolithic, why couldn't beer be made the same way? This tradition survives in the modern world: small breweries in Austria and Bavaria (at Marktoberdorf) make their beer with hot rocks and call it *Steinbier*. A New World version was concocted at the Brimstone Brewing Company in Baltimore, where a special Stone Beer was produced until 1998 by dropping heated diabase rocks from a forklift into the wort, generating impressive, billowing clouds of steam. After twenty minutes in the wort kettle, the rocks were removed and put aside in a freezer; they were added back in the secondary fermentation to give a caramelly finish to the beer. Sadly, when the brewery was sold, the new owners decided to drop the labor-intensive brewing method; however, Flaming Stone Beer, made by Boscos brewpubs in Tennessee and Arkansas, carries on the tradition in the United States.

Quinn and Moore were not to be deterred by the absence of spent grain in the *fulachta fiadh* that would have provided confirmation of their idea. They secured a wooden trough of the approximate dimensions of the ancient feature, filled it with water and barley, and dropped in heated stones until they had a sweet wort. A bouquet garni of unidentified herbs was suspended in the liquid as a substitute for hops. After transferring the brew to plastic carboys and adding yeast, they had a "Neolithic" brew within three days. It was a far cry from Guinness, but a group of volunteers concurred that it tasted like a traditional Irish ale.

Archaeologists have long believed that Neolithic Britain stood apart from the revolution in cereal production in continental Europe that led to the building of larger, permanent settlements there. The peoples of Britain seemed content to continue their nomadic ways, with only the occasional construction of a megalithic tomb or henge. A major reassessment of this view occurred when large building, first detected in aerial photographs, was excavated at Balbridie, inland from Aberdeen, on the eastern coast of Scotland and only about 150 kilometers from where the Ashgrove and North

Mains beakers were found. The Balbridie timber building, dating to ca. 3900–3500 B.C., was divided into partitions and yielded masses of barley, emmer and bread wheat, and linseed.

In the last decade, many more such Neolithic "granaries" have been found in England (at Lismore Fields in Derbyshire and White Horse Stone in Kent), Scotland (at Callander in Perthshire), and Ireland (at Tankardstown in Limerick). Because some of these buildings include hearths and open floor spaces, they could have served as combination storage and malting facilities for beer making. The final verdict about their function—theories range from cult installations to simple residential quarters—is still out.

WHERE WAS THE SUGAR?

Compared to their southern neighbors, people in northern Europe had few options for obtaining simple sugars. Honey, which was the most obvious source, was collected wild from the forests during the fall. Marvelous Mesolithic and Neolithic rock drawings in eastern Spain show bee hunters scaling sheer cliffs to procure the precious commodity.

Beekeeping was probably not practiced until relatively late in Europe, as shown by a log hive from Gristede and two beech-tree examples pulled from peat bogs near Oldenburg in northern Germany, dated to the first century A.D. Another tree-trunk hive of about the same date was taken out of the Oder River in Poland. It is quite possible, however, that skeps, woven baskets with a hole for the bees to enter and exit, were used for beekeeping as early as the Neolithic period, especially in less heavily wooded areas of western Europe. Preserved baskets of suitable types have been recovered from Neolithic Swiss lake settlements and other sites in Spain and southwest Germany.

Various cereals, which had originated from the Near East, could be sprouted and their starches converted into sugar. Apples, cherries, cowberries, cranberries, lingonberries, and even cloudberries in the far north, were additional, albeit somewhat limited, sources of sugar. An added bonus of apples was that their skins harbor yeast, which can initiate fermentation.

The burnt-out impressions of wild grape (*Vitis vinifera* ssp. *sylvestris*) occur on Neolithic pottery sherds from sites in southern Sweden, implying that the plant grew locally and was exploited during a warmer period around 2000 B.C. Grape pollen from about the same period has been reported from a site in Denmark, and, most remarkably but probably intrusive, a single pip of the domesticated grape was recovered from a causewayed enclosure in

Dorset in southern England. Although some wild grapes might have made their way into a Nordic grog here and there, no grape remains or pollen have yet been found inside an early pottery vessel from northern Europe.

BINGE DRINKING AND DANCING

Despite the scarcity of sugar, northern Europe's thirst for alcoholic beverages grew dramatically in the millennia following the Neolithic period. The most convincing evidence for a Bronze Age Nordic grog comes from the grave of an eighteen- to twenty-year-old woman who was buried sometime between 1500 and 1300 B.C. in an oak coffin under a tumulus at Egtved, Denmark. An iron-rich clay hardpan had sealed off the burial in central Jutland, so that the organic materials—including the woman's dress, a cowskin wrapped around her, and a textile holding the burnt remains of a child—were preserved. Of greatest interest to a historian of fermented beverages was a birch-bark container, now on exhibit in the National Museum in Copenhagen, placed at the foot of the young woman's coffin. The botanist (not evangelist) Bille Gram examined the container's contents and identified the remains of cowberries (*Vaccinium vitis-idaea*) and cranberries (*Vaccinium oxycoccus*), wheat grains, filaments of bog myrtle (*Myrica gale*), and pollen from the lime tree, meadowsweet, and white clover (*Trifolium repens*). He concluded that the Egtved young woman clearly belonged to the upper class and had been presented with a special mixed fermented drink of mead, beer, and fruit. The bog myrtle (also known as sweet gale or pors) probably gave the brew a special flavor; it is still a popular additive to Scandinavian aquavit.

The Egtved woman was provocatively dressed in a short-bodiced blouse and an open skirt with strings dangling from her hips. Her midriff was accented by a woolen belt, fastened with a large bronze disk that displayed a well-known entoptic design of interlocking spirals. She also sported a wide armband, bracelet, and ring of bronze. Bronze Age figurines from other sites in Denmark wear similar dress and jewelry and are shown dancing with hands on their hips, arching their backs in acrobatic positions, displaying their breasts, and presenting vessels. Dancing under the influence appears to have been as popular in Europe as it was in Asia. Scantily clad or naked dancers, amid spiral designs, are also shown on Scandinavian rock carvings executing backward flips, line dancing, and doing the ancient equivalent of a jig. Rather than being a member of the upper class, the Egtved woman might have been a celebrated dancer, buried with the container of fer-

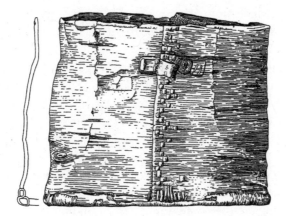

Figure 15. Birch-bark bucket (height 13 cm), filled with a
"Nordic grog"—a combination of mead, barley beer, and
fermented cowberry and cranberry fruit—deposited at the
foot of an oak coffin of a female "dancer" in a tumulus
grave at Egtved, Denmark, ca. 1500–1300 B.C. From
E. Aner and K. Kersten, *Die Funde der älteren Bronzezeit
des nordischen Kreises in Dänemark* (Copenhagen: National
Museum, 1973), plate 15. Drawing courtesy Eva Koch,
National Museum of Copenhagen.

mented beverage that in life she had proffered to others and drunk from to
stimulate her imaginative movements.

From the same period and not far away, male warriors were interred
under barrows at Nandrup on the island of Mors in Jutland and at Breg-
ninge on Zealand. Like the Ashgrove man in Scotland, who carried a beautiful bronze dagger with a hilt of horn and a whale-tooth pommel to his
grave, the men in Denmark were buried with well-crafted long swords and
daggers of bronze. In each Danish tomb, a jar was placed to the side or at
the foot of the body. Abundant lime-tree pollen, together with that of clover
and meadowsweet, was embedded in the black residues inside the vessels,
signs of a rich, spiced mead. My laboratory recently confirmed this finding
using gas chromatography–mass spectrometry: characteristic beeswax hy-
drocarbons and acids mark the presence of honey. The Nandrup jar had
been more than half full at one time, because a crust of material, or the
tideline—solid matter on the surface of a liquid that was left behind after
the liquid evaporated—could be seen just above the middle of the vessel.

We may conclude from these tombs and many others that the macho Bronze Age European male was able to defend his interests and drink with the best of them.

If classical writers are to be believed, binge drinking was the rule by Iron Age times in Europe north of the Alps. The early first-century B.C. historian Diodorus Siculus, for example, wrote that the Gauls (a general Latin term for the Celtic people living in Europe) imbibed beer, "the washings of honeycombs, probably mead," and imported wine (*Library of History* 5.26.2–3). The Gauls were also said to have been repulsed from the gates of Rome by a surprise attack when they lay in a drunken stupor after torching the city in 390 B.C. Celtic beverages were anathema to any cultivated Roman; they were drunk neat or undiluted only by barbarians and mountain folk, through tubes or with their moustaches serving as filters (Diodorus Siculus 5.28.3). Beer in particular was singled out for its foul smell in the late first century B.C. by Dionysius of Halicarnassus (13.11.1), who alleged that Celtic beer was made from barley rotted in water. Even if this was true, who can blame the brewers, with their limited sources of sugar, or their patrons, who had to suffer through a cold, dark winter? People in the north had every reason to prepare and enjoy a mixed fermented beverage when they had the chance: the more, the merrier, you might say.

DOWN INTO THE BOGS

Vessels filled with fermented beverages found their way into places other than tombs. The northern plains of continental Europe and the adjoining islands of Denmark are dotted with bogs. These areas, which were originally lakes or rivers, gradually filled up with moss and other marsh vegetation, which over time was transformed into peat. The peat was exploited as a fuel source, especially during World War II; as it was dug up, many antiquities dating back to the Neolithic period were discovered. The joke was that peat was made up of one-third flammable material, one-third ash, and one-third artifacts. Peat diggers were encouraged to turn over artifacts, sometimes for a small reward, to local museums, and the largest, most comprehensive collection was amassed at Copenhagen's National Museum. Neolithic Funnel Beakers, presumably once filled with Nordic grog, were recovered from scores of bogs, along with axes and weapons, boats, and animal and human remains. Because bog microorganisms consume all the available oxygen, organic remains buried in peat bogs are often well preserved. Residues occur on the interiors of many of the jars but are yet to be analyzed.

In attempting to explain how the bog artifacts ended up where they did, archaeologists have proposed that families or clans made offerings at notable natural features—an open body of water in this instance—which were believed to be imbued with the divine. A strangely shaped boulder or an old, gnarled oak tree might also be the focus of religious fervor or fancy. Based on comparisons with modern societies in parts of Africa, the Pacific, and the Americas at about the same cultural level as that of early northern European peoples, we can speculate that the offerings were made to placate evil spirits or gain the support of more beneficial beings, perhaps ancestral ghosts that dwelt in the vicinity, and ensure the group's well-being. The human condition is a precarious one, and ceremonies involving the presentation of food and drink to the spirits are believed to prevent accidents, cure disease, help women in childbirth, and contribute to the fertility of the earth.

It is doubtful that all the artifacts in the bogs are evidence of ancient sympathetic magic or animistic rites. The body of a man in a boat, for example, could be the result of an accident or a deliberate interment, like the Viking ship burials centuries later. Another human found with a rope around his neck might have been a sacrifice, but his death could just as well have been punishment for a crime. Still, it is difficult to explain the concentrations of numerous jars, particularly on wooden platforms which had collapsed or been deliberately submerged, unless some kind of special activity had taken place that involved Nordic grog. At Lichterfelde near Berlin, nearly one hundred pottery cups were found packed in layers of grass and stones. Pollen analysis of their contents revealed that they very likely once contained a honey and barley-beer mixture, although the excavators interpreted the results as "flower offerings."

Bog drinking vessels dating to later in the first millennium B.C. are more ostentatious than those of Berlin-Lichterfelde, from around 1000 B.C. At Mariesminde Mose, on the island of Funen in Denmark, a large bronze bucket and eleven gold cups were recovered. The cups' handles had horse-head terminals. Each vessel was richly decorated with concentric circles and other geometric motifs characteristic of emergent Celtic art. No ancient residues were found in the bucket or cups, so we cannot be certain what beverage they contained. The bogs, however, have yielded many other buckets, a large percentage of which were imported Greek or Roman wine *situlae,* or cauldrons. One can imagine the odd vessel or two being thrown or falling into a creek or lake. The disposal of such large, valuable vessels made of precious metals—even entire drinking sets—can hardly have been an accident, however, and these finds call for a more compelling explanation.

Sacrificial offerings are undoubtedly part of the explanation. Mead was intimately associated with Odin, the high god of Norse mythology. He is said to have discovered the beverage by a circuitous route. After the gods and the people known as the Vans had made a particularly wise creature named Kvasir by spitting into a large jar, their protégé was murdered by two dwarfs, who then drained his blood into three huge vessels containing honey. The result was a mixed beverage that conferred the gift of wisdom and poetry on the drinker. The intermingling of blood and mead in the Norse tale recalls many ancient Near Eastern, Egyptian, and Greek myths equating wine with blood, and similar claims were made for the renowned chocolate beverages of ancient America (see chapter 7).

Following various machinations in the Norse tale, the drink of blood, spittle, and mead fell into the hands of giants, from whom the gods eventually recovered it by subterfuge. Odin took a job as an ordinary field laborer with the giants and asked that he be paid only by a sip of the special mead. When that was not forthcoming, he took the form of a snake to slip into the cave where the vessels were kept. He prevailed on one of the giants' daughters to give him a portion of the beverage each night that he slept with her. He downed everything from the three vessels, transformed himself into an eagle, and flew back to Valhalla, where he spat out the special beverage into waiting jars. Another Germanic myth describes a well of mead situated next to the "world tree," the connecting link between heaven and earth. Odin drowned by throwing himself into the well and imbibing the beverage—and gaining wisdom, however briefly, in the process.

In the real world, the bog pots probably belonged to members of the society identified as elite, whether socially, religiously, or politically. In many cultures, consuming an alcoholic beverage was a means of exercising authority over others. The highest respect went to those who could afford to drink in the most ostentatious fashion and to throw the biggest parties and feasts. In the American Northwest, this redistribution of fermented beverages, food, and other gifts was known as potlatch; in the anthropological literature and modern America, it is called conspicuous consumption. The Azande people of the Congo have a saying that "a chief must know how to drink; he must get drunk often and thoroughly." Public ceremonies and religious festivals were designed to draw attention to a leader's wealth and gain allegiance from the rank and file in exchange for largesse. At the conclusion of an impressive rite or lavish banquet in northern Europe, the ultimate gesture of a chief might well have been to present the valuable drinking vessels, filled with the Nordic grog, to the gods of the life-giving waters and bogs. We might also imagine that some vessels were thrown into the deep when the feast or celebration got out of hand.

TRULY STUPENDOUS DRINKING

The rulers of the northernmost habitable region of Europe—Proxima Thule to the Greeks—sought to enhance their status in the eyes of their subjects and the gods when they imported drinking sets from south of the Alps. Every skill of the classical artisan was brought to bear in producing these quintessential drinking vessels, which fill the galleries of our modern museums. The northern rulers further set themselves apart, as much as any host of a Greek *symposion* or Roman *convivium,* when they served a more potent and distinctive version of Nordic grog, which might contain more of the valuable honey or imported wine than usual. The competition between Celtic chiefs to purchase only the best food and drink for their feasts and ceremonies was so intense that J. M. de Navarro claimed that Celtic art "owed its existence to Celtic thirst."

The drinking cultures of the wild north and the urbane south were initially worlds apart. The visual signs of wealth and prestige were most readily transferred from south to north as fancy drinking sets and vessels. A shift away from grog to wine, especially wine diluted with water, a trend toward more moderate alcohol consumption, and the adoption of new beliefs and customs came more slowly. The inroads of the wine trade into northern Europe over the centuries can be traced by assessing the number of amphoras that were shipped to Gaul largely for native consumption. More than fifty shipwrecks loaded down with Roman wine have been found along the coasts of Liguria and the French Riviera. According to André Tchernia, a French wine historian and archaeologist, as many as 40 million amphoras were imported in a single century at the end of the Iron Age, culminating with Julius Caesar's subjugation of Gaul in 58 B.C. At 25 liters per amphora, that comes to 10 million liters per year. Combined with the native beverages of mead, barley and wheat beer, and fermented fruit juices, the average barbarian appears to have been well supplied, even if a certain percentage of the inventory was consigned to the bogs.

Figure 16. The tumulus burial of a Celtic prince at Hochdorf, Germany, ca. 525 B.C., is uncannily reminiscent of the Midas tumulus royal burial at Gordion, Turkey, of two centuries earlier. The burial chamber is enclosed in a double wall of logs, and a single male is laid out in his finery, accompanied by a massive "cauldron" and vessels for drinking and eating at a final funerary feast. Instead of "Phrygian grog," the 500-liter cauldron had originally been filled with a beverage dominated by honey mead. Courtesy of J. Biel and Dr. Simone Stork/Keltenmuseum, Hochdorf.

The progress of wine into the hinterlands of Europe took centuries. Sites in southern France, stretching from Marseille to Toulouse, are littered with thousands of Roman and Etruscan amphora sherds as early as the sixth century B.C. The wealthy elite there reputedly traded a slave for a single amphora of wine. By contrast, farther north in Europe—in the so-called Western Hallstatt Zone, the area where Germany, Switzerland, and France come together—finds of amphoras are infrequent, and traditional beverages, including mead, beer and Nordic grog, apparently remained the norm. An especially rich grave at Hochdorf, near Stuttgart, highlights the differences in lifestyles between north and south.

The tomb at Hochdorf, which dates to about 525 B.C., comprised a burial chamber made of a double wall of timbers, with the intervening space filled with stones, which was covered with four layers of logs and a tumulus mound ten meters high. Tumuli to mark and protect burials are widespread across Europe and Asia in many periods. The construction methods of this double-wall burial chamber, however, were like those employed in the Midas tumulus. Once the tomb at Hochdorf was opened and the occupant and his burial goods were brought to light in 1977, archaeologists were astounded by the parallels between the grave in the Baden-Württemburg area of Bavaria and that at the capital city of the Phrygians in central Anatolia.

In the Hochdorf tomb, a forty-year-old male was laid out on a long bronze couch, whose back was decorated with a scene of dancers with swords and a wagon. A full-scale four-wheeled wagon stood opposite, laid out with bronze table settings for nine people, perhaps close associates of the man in life. Rugs covered the floor of the chamber, and finer textiles lined its walls. A peaked birch-bark cap and leather shoes with pointed toes and decorated gold coverings resembled earlier styles in Phrygia. The most remarkable correspondence between the two tombs, however, was in the drinking paraphernalia. A cauldron with a 500-liter capacity lay at the foot of the deceased. It was of mainland Greek design, with three heavy ring handles and three recumbent lions attached to its shoulder. The tide-line inside the vessel showed that it had been three-quarters full when it was placed in the tomb. Mead accounted for most if not all of the 350 liters of liquid in the cauldron, according to a palynological analysis of the black residue by Udelgard Körber-Grohne. The honey contained the pollen of sixty different plants, ranging from wild thyme to field and pasture plants and trees such as linden and willow. A gold bowl with a ring-and-dot motif running around its rim had fallen into the cauldron. Eight bronze-studded drinking horns with gold and bronze fittings and a ninth one of iron, over one meter long and 5.5 liters in capacity, had been hung from the south wall of the chamber. These artifacts, as well as the residue inside the cauldron, were strong indicators that a communal funeral feast had been held in honor of the departed, and that drinking played an important part in the proceedings.

Huge drinking cauldrons appear to have been all the rage in central Europe during the sixth and fifth centuries B.C. At Vix in Burgundy, the largest Greek mixing krater ever found, with a height of 1.6 meters and a capacity of 1,200 liters, was deposited in a tumulus burial for a Celtic woman at approximately the same time as the one at Hochdorf. The stunning piece, which I had the opportunity of seeing close up, has rampant lion figures beneath huge volute handles, and a frieze showing a warrior and chariot procession around its neck. The woman, like the Hochdorf lord, had her own four-wheeled wagon. She was adorned with a stunning massive gold torque or choker whose finials consisted of intricately filigreed and granulated flying horses.

One of the largest European tumuli was excavated at Hohmichele, close to the hilltop fort of Heuneburg, overlooking the Danube River south of Stuttgart. Inside the main chamber, constructed of oak beams, a man and a woman were buried with jewelry, weapons, and a wagon on which a large bronze cauldron had been set. A bronze ladle for serving the beverage it contained—which included honey, according to a palynological study— was found inside the vessel.

During the next century, two burials within another tumulus at Glauberg, northeast of Frankfurt, illustrate how men of different status were treated in death. The first was laid out in a wood chamber in all his gold finery and with an iron lance and sword. A half-meter-tall, four-liter bronze jug was prominent: it was wrapped in a cloth and encircled with a blue ribbon. Again, pollen removed from the substantial residue inside the vessel showed that it was full of a honey mead when it was buried. The second man had been cremated and was buried in a simple grave. He wore no gold jewelry, and apart from his weapons, his only grave good was a jug more than twice the size of that in the first burial. A smaller relative percentage of honey, however, suggested that it contained a mixed beverage, less expensive than pure honey mead, perhaps in keeping with his apparently lower social position.

The many cauldrons from the sixth-century B.C. Western Hallstatt and the fifth-century early La Tène territories of central Europe show how one culture can adopt and adapt the accoutrements of another society. Wine was still a rare commodity in central Europe, and the cauldrons were not used to mix wine and water as was customary in the south. Rather, the vessels, which were produced by Greek and Etruscan craftsmen in the largest size possible specifically for the northern export market, proved ideal for preparing and presenting the Nordic grog at festivals and banquets. Their ostentatiousness made them the consummate burial offerings for rulers and other notables.

Because of the inherent limitations of palynology in recovering evidence for cereals and fruits, we cannot know for certain that the Hochdorf beverage, or those from Scotland and Denmark, was made only from honey. The fermentation of pure honey, however, yields a beverage higher in alcohol, and its flavor is enhanced by the addition of flowers and herbs. As such, mead might have been a higher-status drink than grog, at least during certain periods and in particular parts of northern Europe (for example, Viking Scandinavia during the Middle Ages; see below).

Even if the Hochdorf beverage was a pure mead, we know that some local people were also making and enjoying barley and wheat beer. The archaeobotanist Hans-Peter Stika identified thick layers of a dark malt, covered with charcoal, in eight 6-meter-long ditches at the fortified settlement nearby. (It could well be that the upper-class male in the Hochdorf tomb was the local chieftain of this stronghold.) Stika proposes that the pits were used to sprout the barley and then dry and toast it with an open fire lit from one end to yield a smoky-tasting malt. Pits of this kind have been found only at Hochdorf, and they were evidently intended for mass production, perhaps a thousand liters of beer at a time. Because no brewing vats were found, he suggests that wooden vessels, now disintegrated, were used, heated with fire-cracked stones (as with the beer perhaps prepared in the *fulachta fiadh*). Mugwort and carrot, archaeobotanical remains of which were associated with the malt, would have helped to spice it. Elevated lactic-acid bacteria in the malt suggest that the final brew was sour, like a Belgian red or brown ale.

In order to test the temperatures and times needed to prepare and toast or kiln the malt, the Stuttgarter Hofbräu brewery prepared an experimental batch of "Celtic beer," which was served up at a local festival in period costume to rave reviews. The ancient brewery is prima facie evidence that barley and wheat beer was available at the site and might easily have been added to the Hochdorf beverage. Perhaps some additional fruit juice, herbs, or spices were also mixed into the honey-rich beverage.

Two first-century A.D. drinking horns found close together in a peat bog in the Haderslev region of southern Jutland in Denmark illustrate the challenge of determining the full complement of ingredients in any northern European grog. According to an archaeobotanical analysis carried out by Johannes Grüss in the first half of the twentieth century, now seriously questioned, one horn contained mostly malted emmer wheat and the other primarily honey pollen. Grüss interpreted his evidence straightforwardly: one horn had been filled with wheat beer and the other with mead. But why should two nearly identical horns, found so close together, contain different beverages? It is more likely that both horns originally contained a mixed beverage of beer and mead, and that because of misguided cleaning and restoration efforts when the horns were found, Grüss's analyses were not fully representative of the original contents.

Archaeobotanical analyses of residues from later vessels of the Viking Age (ca. A.D. 800–1100)—especially a large collection of bronze bowls buried individually in graves on the island of Gotland in the Baltic Sea—show that a mixed fermented drink continued to be popular in Scandinavia. As late as the seventeenth century, *mølska,* which combined honey, malt, and a fruit juice, was still being drunk at the Swedish royal court.

My own interest in Nordic grog and the role of wine in northern Europe was piqued by three extended sojourns in Sweden and Denmark. As the pottery specialist of a Scandinavian team investigating a Bronze–Iron Age site in Jordan,.I was invited to study the excavated material that had been brought back to Scandinavia. As a visiting professor first at the University of Uppsala and then at the University of Copenhagen, I found myself ideally situated to learn more about Nordic culture, especially its fermented beverages. In between the periods of study in Uppsala and Copenhagen, I spent another three months in the spring of 1994 at the Archaeological Research Laboratory of the University of Stockholm as a Fulbright scholar. I had the opportunity to meet many scholars, archaeologists, and scientists whose work touched on the fascinating field of ancient fermented beverages. One meeting, one artifact, and one set of research findings must suffice to encapsulate my whole experience.

One weekend, my wife and I traveled by boat to the island of Gotland, a four- to five-hour trip from Stockholm. There we were met by the resident archaeologist and expert on Gotland's history, Erik Nylén. Erik first showed us our room, a restored apartment from medieval times precariously balanced on the old city wall of the capital at Visby. Next he took us on a whirlwind tour of the island, which is about sixty-five kilometers long and thirty kilometers wide. We stopped to see the progress on replicas of Viking ships, which were being built by local farmers and used to follow the trail of the Viking adventurers up the rivers of Germany and Poland, through the mountains of central Europe, and down to Constantinople (modern Istanbul). Besides the sheer amount of labor involved in this expedition, Erik said, a major problem was obtaining enough beer and other potables each day to keep the crew happy. Particularly in Eastern European countries at the time, liquor stores had very short opening hours and had to be sought out early in the day. As we continued our tour of Gotland's archaeological sites, we sampled the local drink, Gotlandsdryka, a spiced barley beer with juniper extract that is still enjoyed at mealtimes in southern Gotland. Locally available sugars, such as honey, are often added to the brew.

We spent the following day examining ancient residues for possible analysis at the museum. The sample we finally settled on was a dark deposit that filled the holes of a long-handled straining cup. This sieve was part of a larger set, dated to the first century A.D., that comprised an imported Roman bucket (*situla*), a ladle, and several "sauce pans" or drinking cups. They had all been found and excavated by Erik in a cache (see plate 7) under the floor at the settlement of Havor in the southern part of the island. The deposit also included a filigreed and granulated gold torque and two bronze bells.

Back in Stockholm, I went to work on the dark residue embedded in the Havor sieve at the archaeometry laboratory, the "Green Villa," nestled in the heart of the university campus and then directed by Birgit Arrhenius. Sven Isaksson, a doctoral candidate who has since published his dissertation, "Food and Rank in Early Medieval Times," joined in the effort. Using gas chromatography, Sven obtained evidence that lipids, including fatty acids and what were likely degradation products of beeswax, made up part of the residue.

I took a sample of the Havor residue back to my laboratory in Philadelphia for further study. The deposit's infrared spectrum was consistent with that of modern beeswax and pointed to the presence of tartaric acid and tartrate salt, marker compounds of grapes and wine. Recent follow-up gas chromatographic–mass spectrometric analyses, using much more sensitive equipment, have shown that the residue is also dominated by birch-resin components (the triterpenoids lupeol and betulin, as well as characteristic long-chain dioic acids).

We have detected birch resin in even earlier beverage containers, including a straining cup from the Danish site of Kostræde, dating to about 800 B.C. (Beeswax components in this sample also marked the presence of honey mead.) Birch resin has been used since at least the Neolithic period for a variety of purposes, including as a mastic to hold haftings onto weapons and tools and as a sealant. Lumps with human tooth impressions from the Swiss lake settlements and a site in Finland suggest that they were chewed as gum. Because some of the compounds in birch resin have analgesic and antibiotic effects, the goal might well have been to alleviate pain or protect against tooth decay. A sugar alcohol derived from birch wood—xylitol—is still used today in Finnish chewing gum as a sweetener and cavity inhibitor. The famous frozen mummy found high in the Italian Ötztal Alps, affectionately known as the Ice Man or Ötzi, carried an extremely well-made copper axe affixed to its yew haft with birch resin. Ötzi also carried birch fungus, which has antibacterial properties and might have been used by the itinerant mountaineer to treat his sores.

Although birch resin is not as sweet as maple sap, it too flows freely in the spring and would have been long ago recognized for its medicinal value, attractive flavor, and potential in making fermented beverages. The common man's drink in Russia today, *kvass* ("leaven"), perpetuates this ancient European tradition; in addition to leavened rye, wheat, or barley bread, which when soaked and fermented produce a mildly (1–1.5 percent) alcoholic drink, birch sap and various fruits are sometimes thrown into the brew.

The upshot of our findings was that the Havor *situla* had contained a Nordic grog in which grape wine was the principal fruit ingredient. The beverage had been ladled out and sieved through the straining cup to remove vegetal and insect matter before it was served in the cups. Subsequently we obtained similar evidence from other samples that I had brought back from Sweden, including the Viking Age bronze bowls from tombs on Gotland mentioned above, which have been carefully studied by Gustaf Trotzig of the National Antiquities Service. Wine continued to be a popular import into northern Europe, according to the ancient organics that we found inside tin-covered liturgical vessels and relief-band jars brought from the Rhineland of central Germany. These vessels had been recovered from what has been called the first city in Sweden, the ninth-century town of Birka, along an estuary south of Stockholm.

Elsewhere in Scandinavia, wine gradually gained in importance, even when it was merely combined with mead or beer to make the traditional Nordic grog. Juellinge, on the Danish island of Lolland in the Baltic Sea, illustrates the pattern, originating in Roman times, that spread out to encompass the rest of Denmark, southern Sweden (Scandia), Gotland, and parts of Norway and Finland. The exceptionally rich burial goods from Juellinge, now on display in the National Museum in Copenhagen, include large, imported *situlae* like the one from Havor, drinking horns, ladles and strainers, and silver drinking cups. Enough space was always left at the head of each burial to deposit the drinking set and other items. Based on his examination of residues in the Juellinge vessels, Bille Gram contended that they had contained both barley beer and a fruit wine. He did not mention mead, but my laboratory has now obtained evidence of the characteristic beeswax compounds from a dark deposit inside one of the second-century A.D. *situlae,* which the National Museum of Denmark allowed me to sample. It remains to be determined whether grapes went into the grog.

The Roman wine set became a fixture in Scandinavian tombs. At Simris in Scandia, for example, the woman in grave 1 held a wine strainer in her hand, while the rest of the drinking set lay at her head, toward the north. European precedents for this practice can be found as early as 1200 B.C. in the Urnfield culture of central Europe, when bronze buckets, handled cups, and strainers were common items in burials. Larger cauldrons were sometimes mounted on wheels, like those from Ystad in Scandia, Milavec in Bohemia, and Skallerup on the island of Zealand in Denmark. The later introduction of Roman drinking vessels into the continent elaborated on this tradition, which eventually encompassed almost all of Europe.

MIDAS *RECIDIVUS*

Turning the clock back again to the sixth century B.C., certain details of the Hochdorf burial preclude direct comparison with the Midas tumulus. The male at Hochdorf, for example, wore the personal jewelry and carried the weapons of a Celtic warrior: a decorated gold armlet, a gold torque around his neck, and an iron dagger in a gold scabbard. The male in the Midas tumulus wore garments fastened only with bronze brooches (*fibulae*) and a belt, and he was not armed. Indeed, none of the artifacts from this tomb were even made of gold. Is it significant that the single Hochdorf cauldron was still almost completely filled with a beverage, whereas the three Midas cauldrons were totally depleted? Probably not. A greater supply of the beverage could have been prepared at Hochdorf, more than enough to satisfy a smaller group of mourners and leave some in the cauldron for the chieftain's journey into the afterlife. At Gordion, the beverage was doled out in more than one hundred bowls to a larger group, so it is not surprising that the cauldrons were empty.

Even so, the similarities between the Hochdorf burial and the Midas tumulus raise an enticing question: Might the origins of the Phrygians be sought in central Europe rather than in northern Greece, the Balkans, or eastern Europe? Perhaps they followed the Danube down to the Black Sea and crossed over the Bosporus into Turkey. In the third century B.C., the Galatians followed this route to Gordion. The earlier Phrygians could have brought a central European tradition of a mixed fermented beverage with them to Anatolia. According to this hypothesis and the cultural conservatism inherent to fermented beverages, during the early Iron Age the Phrygians probably entered a sparsely inhabited region of Anatolia, where they used the plentiful supply of grapes as the main fruit component in their version of the beverage. As they were already familiar with honey and barley, they continued to use them in the Phrygian grog.

As more and more vineyards were planted in the Near East and wine improved during the first millennium B.C., varietal wines from particular regions became a mark of civilized life, marginalizing the more "barbaric" beer and mead. The consumption of grogs was increasingly confined to esoteric religious ceremonies. The occasional *mulsum,* in which grape must and honey were fermented together (according to the Roman agricultural writer Columella), or *omphacomelitis,* a fermented mixture of unripe grapes and honey, might be prepared from time to time. Mead is known to have remained a specialty of the Phrygians until at least the first century A.D., according to Pliny the Elder (*Natural History* 14.113). The Phrygians were also notorious for their beer, which they sometimes drank out of large pots with tubes while engaged in contorted sexual acts like those illustrated in Mesopotamia centuries earlier. As the seventh-century Greek lyric poet Archilochos caustically put it: "[He has intercourse or fellatio with her] . . . just like a Thracian or Phrygian man sucked barley beer through a reed, and she was bent over working hard" (fr. 42 West in Athenaeus, *The Scholars at Dinner* 10.447b). Nevertheless, such tastes were the exception rather than the rule by Roman times.

Wine eventually was accepted by the northern Celts both as a fruit source and a beverage. At first it arrived in a trickle, carried only in amphoras from Marseille (ancient Massalia). That trickle soon became a torrent as the Celts' own technological contributions to the storage and transport of fermented beverages—large wooden barrels—were packed onto oxcarts and boats and made their way inland. After Julius Caesar's conquest of Gaul in the first century B.C., the domesticated grapevine of the Mediterranean and beyond began to be planted up the Rhône River and along the Mosel and the Rhine in Germany.

SIX

SAILING THE WINE-DARK
MEDITERRANEAN

MY WIFE AND I CAUGHT our first glimpse of the azure Mediterranean in 1971, when we traveled south from Germany to Italy, on our way to a kibbutz in Israel and my first archaeological adventures in the Middle East. We had been picking grapes on the Mosel River, and when temperatures dropped in early October, we needed to move to warmer climes. A chill ran up my spine, not from cold but excitement, when we espied the Mediterranean from the high bluff overlooking Monaco. We felt blessed, just as the vineyards of the Mosel were that summer, and we looked forward to leaving Western culture behind and entering the exotic world of the east.

Our journey to the Levant showed us the mercurial nature of the Mediterranean. An all-night ferry across the Adriatic Sea from Bari in Italy to Dubrovnik in the old Yugoslavia shook us to pieces. That crossing was followed by idyllic days and nights on the decks of Greek ferries as we plied Homer's "wine-dark" Aegean. We eventually reached Beirut, then regarded as the Paris of the Middle East with its broad boulevards and luxurious lifestyle.

We could not cross into Israel by land, because the border was closed, as usual. Instead we went down to the Beirut harbor and found a boat that would take us to Cyprus. A small Danish freighter took pity on us, and we were signed on as first mate and assistant cook. We spent the next week luxuriating on the Mediterranean, drinking unlimited quantities of Tuborg beer, enjoying a Christmas dinner with the crew, and using the boat as a hotel to visit nearby Salamis, one of great ancient cities of the Mediterranean, when we arrived in the Cypriot port of Famagusta. Such is the magic of this sea.

PEOPLES OF THE PREHISTORIC SEA

From space, the Mediterranean Sea sits like a shimmering jewel or an alluring woman between Africa and Europe. Some 25 million years ago, this body of water—an ancient remnant of the Tethys Sea—began to form. The basin deepened, waters from ocean and river surged in and out, and gradually it became the planet's largest "inland" sea.

To our earliest ancestors, traveling northward via the Great Rift Valley through Ethiopia or along the Nile River through the Sudan and Egypt, the Mediterranean Sea presented a formidable barrier to progress. Arriving at the Nile delta, they would have surveyed a seemingly endless body of water, with no land in sight. It is more than five hundred kilometers from here to Cyprus or southern Turkey. Without a boat, this might well appear the end of the line. Even migrating birds are intimidated, spending days on shore to build up their caloric reserves before venturing out over the Mediterranean.

The longest north-south crossing of the Mediterranean is about 1,600 kilometers. That compares with only 14 kilometers at the Strait of Gibraltar, the sea's sole natural connection to the world's oceans—still a difficult proposition for a good swimmer. Island hopping is another possibility, especially from Tunisia to Sicily to the toe of Italy. Movement from east to west across the Mediterranean, about 3,900 kilometers, was even more of a challenge. Island hopping and short transits by land or sea along the shore might have been used as strategies by our early ancestors, once they had learned how to make boats.

Before this momentous innovation occurred, however, early hominids and humans had another option. They could bypass the Mediterranean altogether by walking across the Sinai Peninsula, the land bridge between Africa and Asia. This route, later called the Ways of Horus by the Egyptians and the Via Maris by the Romans, takes about fifteen days from the modern Egyptian border to Gaza. For those who blazed the trail it must have seemed an eternity, as they did not know where to find oases to replenish their water supplies. The journey was more predictable once donkeys had been domesticated and settlements were established along the route.

Once they surmounted the Sinai hurdle, the travelers were greeted by a verdant land along the coast and in the inland Jordan Valley. There they might well have stopped and begun exploiting fig and other fruits, cereals, and honey as early as 9500 B.C. The fermented beverages made from these resources were probably presented as offerings to the plaster images of the ancestors and gods at the sites of Jericho and ʿAin Ghazal as early as the seventh millennium B.C.

Early hominids and humans would also have been drawn to the Mediterranean coast north of Mount Carmel, an area that today is shared by northern Israel, Lebanon, and southern Syria. The past half million years have seen a succession of cooler, rainy periods in this region (corresponding to the major advances of glaciers across northern and central Europe), followed by warmer episodes in which elephant, rhinoceros, and hippopotamus roamed the land. Wild grapevines probably already festooned dense forests, and other fruits and nuts were there for the taking.

Although the recent civil war in Lebanon and subsequent troubles have slowed archaeological investigation, prehistorians had discovered by the early twentieth century that the two chains of mountains (the Lebanon and Anti-Lebanon), running parallel to the coast and extending south to Mount Carmel and the nearly 3,000-meter-high Mount Hermon, were riddled with deep caves. Tabun on Mount Carmel in Israel, ʿAdlun in southern Lebanon, Ksar Akil farther up the coast, and Yabrud, looking out onto the Great Syrian Desert from the eastern slopes of the Anti-Lebanon, have come to define an unbroken sequence of Palaeolithic periods and cultures. These and other caves were used by our ancestors for millennia to protect themselves from the elements and marauding animals, to bury their dead, and presumably to celebrate and worship with fermented beverages. Unfortunately, although intricate series of lithic tools and weapons, microlayer on microlayer, have been found, what has been preserved of organic remains gives us only tantalizing hints of what the people ate and drank. A boar's jawbone found in the crook of a male skeleton's arm in one of the Mount Carmel caves suggests that they had a penchant for pork.

The intensity of human settlement is obvious from the depths of the cave deposits, up to twenty meters in places, and from the extensive scatter of hand axes and other lithic tools on the high terraces all along the Mediterranean, where the sea transgressed during drier and warmer spells and then retreated during glacial times. For example, at Ras Beirut, today the chic coastal promontory of the modern capital, the lithics are concentrated on a terrace forty-five meters above the current level of the Mediterranean. Here humans were encamped right along the shore and must have wondered what lay across the sea.

The earliest use of watercraft in the Mediterranean likely dates back to at least 12,000 B.C., when a people known to archaeologists as the Natufians, after the site northwest of Jerusalem where they were first identified, took central stage along the Mediterranean littoral and its mountainous backdrop. (We do know that early humans must have used some kind of primitive boat, probably made by tying logs and reeds together into rafts, to cross from Southeast Asia to Australia around forty thousand years ago.) Rather than relying on hunting the prolific coastal wildlife (fallow deer, bear, and wild oxen) or gathering wild cereals, fruits, and nuts, the Natufians increasingly turned to managed resources that assured a more sedentary existence—grains that could be cultivated and processed and animals that could be herded. They were also beginning to explore the riches of the sea, as revealed by multibarbed harpoons and fishhooks. Their red ocher–colored burials, whose skulls were adorned with hundreds of dentalia and other shell species, testify to their close spiritual kinship to the sea, which reached its fullest expression in the Neolithic period, when the eyes of modeled and plastered skulls were accentuated by cowries and bivalves (see chapter 3).

The only way that the Natufians could have so effectively exploited the riches of the Mediterranean was by boat. Their ability to fashion both incredibly realistic and abstract works of art, often highly erotic, from bone, antler, wood, and stone implies that they had the expertise to make larger constructions, such as the remarkable cluster of circular huts, with storage basins and fireplaces, at Einan, north of the Sea of Galilee. Besides attesting to a sedentary way of life in advance of the Neolithic period, the excavation of this site revealed what has been described as the earliest megalithic burial structure in the world: a pit five meters in diameter was plastered on its interior, the burials positioned within it, and the top of the pit sealed off with stone slabs. A skull on top of the slabs, close to a fireplace, provided a macabre detail: cut marks on the attached vertebrae suggested that the person had been beheaded. More slabs were piled up over this skull and fireplace and a seven-meter circle of stones was built around the pit.

If the Natufians were capable of such monumental feats in stone and plaster, then it seems possible that they also experimented with boat construction. The wooden implements and objets d'art from Natufian excavations, sparse though they may be, attest to their sensitivity and skill in shaping this highly malleable material. They also had a good supply of it right at their doorstep. The mountains of Lebanon were once carpeted with Cedar of Lebanon (*Cedrus libani*), standing forty-five meters tall, together with pines, firs, junipers, oaks and terebinth trees.

We know that the Natufians had sophisticated toothed saws, knives, and other flint tools for cutting and shaping wood. They had discovered the advantages of tree resin as an adhesive and sealant, as can be seen from the abundant use of resin to hold microliths to sickle shafts for cutting grain. They would have had to work out other complex details of boat manufacture, such as bending, joining, and waterproofing long wooden planks. But it could well be only a matter of time until a boat is recovered from a Natufian coastal site. The succeeding Neolithic period shows a similarly close kinship to the sea, especially at the site of Byblos (see below), where pottery was decorated by impressing the edge of a shell into the moist clay, and cowries were imported from as far away as the Red Sea.

SAILING SEA AND SKY

The first definitive evidence for shipping comes from Egypt in the third millennium B.C. David O'Connor, who taught me Egyptology during my graduate days at Penn, was amazed to discover fourteen "boat graves" in the desert near the religious capital of Abydos, which lies along the Nile about 650 kilometers south of where the river empties into the Mediterranean. The boats were part of extensive funerary complexes, surrounded by walls eleven meters high, that belonged to some of the first pharaohs of Egypt of late Dynasty 1 (ca. 2800 B.C.). Although weighing as much as a ton, the twenty-five-meter-long craft had been dragged into place and encased in mudbrick boat-shaped pits, which were covered with gleaming white plaster.

The Abydos boats had been carefully constructed by fitting together variously sized planks, probably made from tamarisk, and tightening them together by running rope through opposing lines of holes. Their hulls were slightly curved, and they had a very shallow draft of sixty centimeters— adequate for navigating the Nile but not enough to weather the violent Mediterranean. The outsides of the ships had been plastered and painted an intense yellow.

The combined effect of seeing a huge armada moored in the desert, shining white and yellow under the intense Egyptian sun, must have been electrifying. These "solar barges" provided a fitting send-off for the king to traverse the heavens with the sun god, Ra; like the sacrificed attendants, animals, food and drink, and other essentials placed in the tomb, they had been buried in anticipation of the pharaoh's every need in the afterlife.

For the next thousand years, Egyptian pharaohs and even high officials were customarily buried with a boat or an entire fleet. The most spectacular example is the ship, one of five, that was buried around 2500 B.C. beside the Great Pyramid of the pharaoh Khufu at Giza. It is 43.6 meters long, nearly twice the size of the Abydos boats and nine meters longer than the *Golden Hind,* with which Sir Francis Drake circumnavigated the globe in the sixteenth century. Khufu's ship for the afterlife was constructed mostly from cedar using the so-called shell-first technique, in which individual hull planks are joined to one another and to the keel by interlocking mortise-and-tenon joints. Although the draft was still shallow, the ship had an impressively high bow and stern, probably intended less for open-water sailing than for ostentatious political and religious displays.

The use of cedar in building Khufu's magnificent funerary barge suggests where we should seek evidence for the earliest shipbuilding. Lebanon was renowned for its cedar forests in the ancient world, and no coastal site was more closely associated with the tree than Byblos, forty kilometers north of Beirut. One of Lebanon's most intensively excavated sites, Byblos provides a detailed sequence of occupation from the early Neolithic period through the end of the Bronze Age. The French scholar Ernst Renan, who wrote the highly controversial book *La vie de Jésus,* initiated exploration here in 1860. More scientific excavations, first under Pierre Montet and then Maurice Dunand, spanned the period from 1925 to 1975.

Byblos, whose name probably meant "mountain city" in Egyptian (*Kpn*) and Phoenician (*Gebal*), was particularly attractive to aspiring sailors for its protected harbor and proximity to the cedar-covered mountains. We learn from third-millennium B.C. Egyptian texts that gangs of woodcutters felled the trees in "God's Land" with copper axes and then transported the logs, most likely by barge, to Byblos. There the cedar timber was used to make the renowned "Byblos ships" (Egyptian *kbnwt*) that made it possible to ferry huge shipments of the wood to Egypt. In one of the earliest accounts, the Palermo Stone Annals of the Old Kingdom, Snefru (the first king of Dynasty 4) claims to have brought forty shiploads of cedar and other conifers to Egypt and built forty-four boats, some of which were one hundred cubits (fifty-five meters) long. The planks intended for the somewhat smaller Khufu ship were numbered for ease of assembly in Egypt.

Regrettably, Byblos has never yielded direct archaeological evidence of shipbuilding. Even the pillars of its temples and palaces, presumably made of cedar, long ago disintegrated in the moist coastal climate, leaving only large stone bases. We can be sure, however, that the Egyptians were there in force in the third millennium B.C. The principal goddess of the city-state, Baalat-Gebal, is represented on a cylinder seal, attired in a long, Egyptian-style tunic and a headdress consisting of a solar disk set between cow's horns, which designates her as the equivalent of the Egyptian goddess of foreign lands, Hathor. Numerous fragments of stone vases also bear the cartouches of Old Kingdom pharaohs who claimed to have journeyed to Byblos for cedar and other woods.

The ancient world's insatiable demand for cedar of Lebanon nearly extirpated the tree. Today it grows only in a restricted area in the upper Qadisha Valley, above Tripoli, and in several small pockets in the mountains. Egypt did not have trees tall enough for seagoing vessels or monumental architecture. According to biblical tradition, Solomon was obliged to import the wood as well as carpenters from Lebanon to build the first temple in Jerusalem.

To secure its hold on cedar and other valuable commodities, Egypt asserted its supremacy over Byblos and Lebanon, as reflected in the stories of its gods. For example, one version of the Osiris resurrection myth recounts how the god of Abydos was murdered by his brother, Seth, and his body laid in a coffin which floated across the open sea to Byblos. It landed near a cedar tree, which grew up around it. When a king of Byblos chopped the tree down to make a pillar for his palace, Osiris's sister and wife, Isis, intervened to return him unharmed to Egypt. Osiris's resurrection was also symbolized by the grapevine, another Levantine plant, that provided Egypt with one of its most significant fermented beverages. Symbolism became reality at the time of the annual flooding of the land by the Nile in late summer, when the land's fertility was renewed and wine flowed in abundance at the Wagy festival in honor of Osiris ("the Lord of wine through / during the inundation").

WINE FROM ACROSS THE SEAS

The truth about how wine first came to Abydos, as revealed by biomolecular archaeological investigation, has little to do with ancient myth. The story begins with archaeologists from the German Institute of Archaeology in Cairo, who were excavating a magnificent "funerary house" in the desert, not far from the later boat graves. This tomb belonged to king Scorpion I of Dynasty 0, around 3150 B.C., and it was fully equipped for the afterlife. Three rooms in the structure were literal wine cellars, stacked high with some seven hundred jars of wine, amounting to about 4,500 liters. The other chambers were crammed with beer jars, bread molds, stone vessels, and cedar boxes full of clothing. The king himself lay in all his splendor on a wooden shrine in the largest room of the structure, with an ivory scepter at his side.

In case the king might have trouble finding what he needed in the afterlife, his undertakers had the foresight to attach incised bone and ivory labels by string to the jars and boxes and to write inked inscriptions on the sides of vessels. In these labels, the earliest hieroglyphic writing from Egypt, it is stunning to see how carefully the figures of plants and animals (including jackals, scorpions, birds, and bulls) are delineated. The labels probably denoted the Egyptian estates where the food and other goods were produced.

As we might have surmised from the very early date, the wine in the tomb did not come from Egypt. The wild grape did not grow in the arid climate of Egypt, and it took some time for the earliest rulers of the country, who were just beginning to consolidate their power, to begin tapping into the resources of the world around them and to develop a taste for wine. Eventually, the kings saw the wisdom of transplanting the domesticated vine to the rich alluvial soil of the Nile River delta. During Dynasties 1 and 2 (ca. 3000–2700 B.C.) they established a royal winemaking industry that assured a steady supply of the beverage. Scorpion I lived a century or two in advance of this development, but he set the stage for what was to come.

Our chemical analyses showed that the wine in Scorpion I's tomb was resinated with pine and possibly terebinth tree resins. Numerous grapeseeds in some of the jars confirmed these results, and although some might interpret this debris as evidence for slovenly winemaking, the finding of whole preserved raisins and carefully sliced figs in some of the jars points to deliberate decision making by the winemaker. Fresh fruits enhanced the wine's sweetness and taste and ensured sufficient yeast to start and sustain the fermentation. If that were not enough to entice the would-be drinker, our most recent analyses revealed other likely additives to the wine, including savory (*Satureja* spp.), balm (*Melissa*), senna (*Cassia*), coriander (*Coriandrum*), germander (*Teucrium*), mint (*Mentha*), sage (*Salvia*), or thyme (*Thymus/Thymbra*).

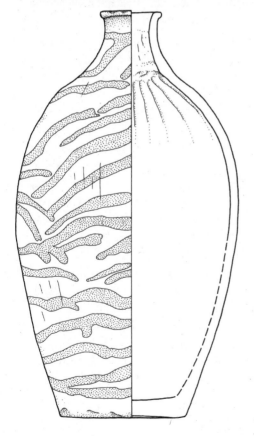

Figure 17. Imported wine in Early
Dynastic Egypt. (a, *above*) Jars
containing resinated wine from
Chamber 10 of Scorpion I's tomb
(denoted U-j) at Abydos, ca. 3150
B.C. The room is one of three that
were filled with layer upon layer of
wine jars—about seven hundred
altogether—that had been
imported from the Jordan Valley
and environs. A single whole,
sliced fig had been suspended into
some of the jars. Photograph
courtesy of German Archaeological Institute, Cairo. (b, *left*)
"Tiger-striped" wine jar (U-j10/33,
catalogue no. 18, height 40.8 cm),
imported from the Levant and
deposited in Scorpion I's tomb.
Drawing courtesy of German
Archaeological Institute, Cairo.

The style of the jars themselves and their labels supplied further clues about where the wine had been made, on the reasonable assumption that the pottery and the wine originated from the same general area. Their decorations of smeared red and white slips, narrow painted bands, or dramatic, swirling tigerlike stripes set them apart from anything made in Egypt. Only one time period and area fit the bill: the first phase of the Early Bronze Age, at sites in the vicinity of Gaza on the southern Levantine coast, in the inland Jezreel and Jordan Valleys, and in the hill country of Transjordan, as far south as the Dead Sea.

Small clay sealings, scattered around the jars, confirmed the foreign origin of the wine. Their backs had been impressed with jar rims and strings, which meant that the clay, when wet, had been applied over a string that tied down a cover, probably of leather, over the mouth of the vessel. When the strings and covers disintegrated, the sealings fell to the ground. The upper surface of the sealings displayed finely cut cylinder-seal impressions of distinctively non-Egyptian types, which combined free-flowing designs of animals (including antelope, fish, birds, and snakes) with geometric patterns. A thorough search of the archaeological literature revealed no exact matches for the cylinder-seal designs, but the closest parallels pointed again to the northern Jordan Valley and the eastern shore of the Dead Sea. Like the hieroglyphs on the bone and ivory labels marking other goods in the tomb, the clay sealings were likely labels for the seven hundred jars: if we could decipher them, they might even tell us the location of the wineries.

Instrumental neutron activation analysis (INAA), another tool of modern molecular archaeology, enabled us to chemically "fingerprint" and trace the wine jars in Scorpion I's tomb to their source. Small amounts of pottery from the jars, on the order of a tenth of a gram, are subjected to a high-energy neutron flux inside a nuclear reactor. This excites individual chemical elements, especially the rare-earth elements which are highly characteristic of specific clay beds around the world, to become radioactive. As each element decays back to its ground state, it emits characteristic gamma rays, allowing the elements to be measured down to parts per million. Extremely powerful statistical methods are then applied to match these results to data from ancient samples and modern clays.

Eleven wine jars, representing all the major pottery fabrics in the Scorpion I corpus, were tested at the University of Missouri Research Reactor in Columbia. Although three of the jars showed no chemical matches with any clay sample or well-defined local group of ancient pottery in our data bank, the other eight were made from clays local to the Gaza area, the Jordan Valley, the southern hill country of the West Bank, and the Transjordanian Plateau to the east. There were no other matches to the more than 5,800 samples in our data bank, and, significantly, Egyptian clays and pottery were not among the possible matches. Surprisingly, several of the Scorpion I jars matched clay beds at the "rose-red city" of Petra in Jordan, renowned for the architecture carved from its red sandstone; it was later a capital of the Nabataeans and a principal caravan stop on the Arabian camel route, one segment of the Silk Road.

The aridity of southern Jordan today would seem to preclude any grape growing or winemaking there. A different picture, however, has begun to emerge from recent surveys and excavations. Early Neolithic sites in the Petra region, such as Beidha and Basta, were some of the largest, most innovative settlements in the Near East. Although grapeseeds are yet to be recovered from these sites, hundreds of winepresses dating from later times attest to a vibrant industry. Recently a temple to Dionysos was uncovered at the Beidha "High Place" by Patricia Bikai of the American Center of Oriental Research in Amman (ACOR). The wine god and his coterie of associated deities (including Pan, Ampelos, and Isis) were stunningly depicted on the capitals of a central courtyard, whose surrounding benches in the style of a Roman *triclinium* might well have been used to celebrate the delights of the beverage. When I was in Jordan in 2006, Patricia and I looked over the pottery in the ACOR storeroom, and our laboratory has since analyzed several jars from the temple. Predictably, they once held resinated wine.

Could any of the wine in Scorpion I's tomb have come from the Petra region, or do the INAA matches simply reflect the chemical similarity of clay deposits in various parts of the southern Transjordanian plateau? The recent discovery of a fourth-millennium B.C. town at Tall Hujayrat al-Ghuzlan on the Gulf of Aqaba, only about one hundred kilometers south of Petra and with clear evidence of Egyptian contacts, suggests that the wine could conceivably have come from this region. From the top of the Gulf of Aqaba across the Red Sea would have been a straight shot by boat to trade routes crossing the Egyptian eastern desert to Thebes and Abydos (for example, via the 150-kilometer traverse of the Wadi Hammamat).

Transshipment of the Scorpion I wine from a Mediterranean port, however, is more plausible. Locations like Byblos, which had access to the necessary raw materials for building ships, were likely integrated into an economic exchange system with inland regions and towns farther south along the coast much earlier than the southern Transjordanian plateau was connected with the Gulf of Aqaba. In either case, the main problem would have been to get the wine from the hill country and the Jordan Valley to the coast without ruining it. Jars were probably strapped to the sides of donkeys, as depicted by figurines of the period, and could have been wetted with water to provide evaporative cooling for the wine under the hot Levantine sun. The nearest ports to the winemaking areas identified by our INAA study were Ashkelon, which has now been shown to have been occupied in the late fourth millennium B.C., and Gaza, still poorly known because it is covered by a modern city.

Travel by boat from Ashkelon or Gaza to the eastern Pelusiac branch of the Nile River would have been the most expeditious and safest way to convey the wine to Egypt. An overland route across the Sinai was also in use at this time, but continued transport by donkeys would have added insult to injury for both wine and animal. On current evidence, the Levantine merchants also controlled the offloading of the wine in Nile delta port areas, such as Minshat Abu Omar on the Pelusiac branch.

Our INAA study bore out the inference of a shipping connection between the southern Levant and Egypt. When we tested one of the distinctive clay sealings of foreign origin in the vicinity of the wine jars, we found it was made of Nile alluvial clay. In other words, when the wine arrived in a Nile delta port, the jar covers must have been replaced, resealed with local clay, and then stamped with the seal of the Levantine merchants. The jars' arduous journey by land and sea meant that any residual fermentation of the wines had already taken place, with the gases escaping through the porous caps. After the jars were brought ashore in Egypt, they could be prepared for their remaining journey upriver to Abydos under Egyptian auspices; some of these eventually found their way into Scorpion I's tomb.

The beverage of a pharaoh deserved only the best treatment, since, according to the Old Kingdom Pyramid Texts, "[the king] shall make his meal from figs and wine which are in the garden of the god." The supply of a wine laced with figs assured the dead king of a fully sanctified meal for the afterlife.

This tomb exhibits another intriguing parallel to the later boat graves. The wine jars are piled in layers inside three rooms of Scorpion I's tomb, much as amphoras were loaded into the hull of a Byblos ship (see below).

In 1997, a U.S. Navy submarine detected a pair of Phoenician shipwrecks sixty-one kilometers offshore from Ashkelon and Gaza, lying two kilometers apart at a depth of four hundred meters. Two years later, Robert Ballard, who famously explored the sunken *Titanic,* deployed a remotely operated vehicle to plot their positions and the cargo debris scattered on the sea floor. It turned out that these ships, dating to the late eighth century B.C., were stuffed from bottom to top with wine amphoras.

The two ships, nicknamed *Tanit* (the principal Phoenician goddess and tutelary deity of the seas) and *Elissa* (the Tyrian princess who, legend claims, founded the important Phoenician colony of Carthage in present-day Tunisia), were sailing westward on a course that could have carried them to Egypt or Carthage. A sudden storm, as sometimes sweeps down from the Sinai Peninsula, probably took them by surprise and plunged them to their watery graves. The ships sank into muddy sediments, and over time their upper wooden sides were exposed and eaten away by wood borers to expose two layers of superimposed amphoras in their hulls. In the hold of the *Tanit,* 385 vessels were visible; inside the *Elissa,* 396 amphoras could be seen. The site has thus far only been imaged and not excavated; many more layers of amphoras might lie unseen below.

The spread of the amphoras on the sea floor marked out the approximate dimensions of each ship, and their size was estimated to have been about 14 meters from stem to stern, with a beam width of 5 to 6 meters. These dimensions were in accord with later classical-period wrecks, such as that of the *Kyrenia,* which went aground off the coast of Cyprus around 300 B.C. Boats of this size weighed about 25 tons when fully loaded. Since an amphora full of wine weighs about 25 kilograms, just the visible amphoras of the *Tanit* and *Elissa* weighed at least 9 tons each. This amounts to about 15,000 liters of wine. But Phoenician ships sometimes carried much more, as recorded in an Egyptian customs docket of 475 B.C. in which one large ship carried 1,460 full amphoras (40 tons), in addition to 4 tons of cedar wood, copper and empty amphoras.

Our laboratory's analysis of the pine-resin lining inside one of the Phoenician amphoras found traces of tartaric acid and its salt, derived from grape wine, absorbed into the lining, so we know that at least one amphora aboard the *Tanit* and *Elissa* contained wine. Of the additional twenty-two amphoras recovered from the wrecks, all had a pine-resin lining, suggesting that most if not all the amphoras contained wine, just as they did in the ship that docked in Egypt in 475 B.C.

The amphoras on the two ships have a distinctive sausage or torpedo shape. A careful study of the style and pottery ware by Lawrence Stager of Harvard University and his students, who accompanied Ballard on his 1999 exploration, showed that the amphoras had most likely been manufactured at a Phoenician city-state along the Lebanese coast. They also retrieved other artifacts from the shipwrecks that clearly pointed to the cultural identity of its sailors. For example, a beautifully red-slipped and highly burnished jug with a flaring mushroomlike lip, in imitation of gold and silver prototypes, was the distinctive calling card of the Phoenicians; it abounds in the Lebanese homeland and at Phoenician colonies and port sites throughout the Mediterranean. Part of the Phoenician "wine set," the decanter was used to serve wine with an ostentatious flourish.

The distinctly Phoenician character of the ships and their crews also emerged from a study of objects found in the sterns of the boats, where their galley or kitchen was located. Here, six cooking pots from the *Tanit* and *Elissa,* probably used to prepare scrumptious fish stews, were familiar eastern Mediterranean types. Prayers to the gods of the sea were also made near the rear of the boat, as seen on fourteenth-century B.C. Egyptian tomb paintings of Canaanite ships. A single adorant is usually shown pouring a liquid offering—most likely wine—from a small vial held in one hand, while incense wafts up from a burner held in the other. An incense burner resembling those in the paintings and of known Phoenician style was recovered from the *Elissa*'s stern. The main deities that the Phoenician sailors would have invoked on their dangerous voyages were the mother goddess Tanit, who was associated with the moon and navigation, and her consort, Reshef or Baal, who controlled the wind and weather.

THE FINE WINES OF CANAAN AND PHOENICIA

The thirty thousand or more liters of wine lost when the *Tanit* and *Elissa* sank represent just a trickle of the huge quantity of wine exported from Phoenician ports such as Tyre, Sidon, Berytus (modern Beirut), and Byblos during the first millennium B.C. Most ships would have arrived safely at their destinations, having loaded and offloaded an impressive array of goods en route. When the biblical prophet Ezekiel excoriated Tyre in the sixth century B.C. and predicted its doom (Ezekiel 27), he compared the

Figure 18. Wall painting from the tomb of Kenamun, the mayor of Thebes during the fourteenth century B.C., depicting a Canaanite ship arriving in port. The captain of the ship holds aloft an incense burner and a cup of wine, which has probably been taken from the amphora in front of him. Illustration adapted by K. Vagliardo for L. E. Stager, "Phoenician Shipwrecks and the Ship Tyre (*Ezekiel* 27)," in *Terra Marique: Studies in Art History and Marine Archaeology in Honor of Anna Marguerite McCann*, ed. J. Pollini (Oxford: Oxbow, 2005), 238–54, fig. 18.12; after N. de G. Davies and R. O. Faulkner, 1947, "A Syrian Trading Venture to Egypt," *Journal of Egyptian Archaeology* 33: pl. 8.

prosperous city-state with a huge seagoing vessel fashioned from the best woods—juniper and cedar from the mountains of Lebanon, oak from Transjordan, and cypress from Cyprus. The metaphorical ship is described as loaded with incense, gold, and camels from Arabia; wheat and olive oil from Israel; tin and silver from Tarshish; horses and slaves from Anatolia, and more—a seemingly endless list of merchandise from the far-flung corners of the known world.

In 1984, George Bass of Texas A&M's Institute of Nautical Archaeology electrified the archaeological world when he announced the discovery of what is still the earliest excavated shipwreck in the Mediterranean, and it has all the international panache of Ezekiel's boat. Found by a sponge diver in 45-meter-deep water along Turkey's desolate southern coast near Uluburun, the ship turned out to be a Canaanite merchantman. It was about the same size as the *Tanit* and the *Elissa,* made entirely of cedar of Lebanon, and built with mortise-and-tenon joints between the planks and the keel (just like the earlier Khufu ship). It was probably headed to Egypt during the fourteenth century B.C., following the counterclockwise currents of the eastern Mediterranean around Cyprus, when a sudden storm drove it against the rocks.

To judge from the astonishing wealth of its cargo, this Byblos ship was likely under royal commission: it contained African blackwood ("ebony") and hippopotamus tusks, ten tons of Cypriot copper ingots in ox-hide and bun shapes, elaborate gold and glass drinking vessels, Canaanite gold pendants, masses of molluscan opercula (the animal's hard footplate, which seals the opening of its shell), a half ton of terebinth tree resin, a double-paneled, hinged "book" for inscribed beeswax tablets (our word *book* derives from Byblos)—the list goes on and on. Canaanite oil lamps and a large set of Levantine animal-shaped stone weights marked its crew, officers, and traders as hailing from a city-state on the Eastern Mediterranean coast.

All that seemed to be missing from the Uluburun wreck was wine. There were about 150 amphoras in the wreck's hull, and some of those were as much as a third full of nodules and chunks of terebinth resin. Others were filled with glass beads and olives. That still left seventy or more empty amphoras, which might originally have carried fine Canaanite wine for the pharaoh or to assuage the thirst of the sailors.

In his prophetic tirade against Tyre, Ezekiel reported that delectable wines from Helbon, near Damascus, and from Izalla on the southeastern Anatolia coast, transported overland in huge jars (*pithoi*) to Damascus, were among the goods transshipped by the Tyrian merchants. Helbon wine, renowned among the Assyrians, came from the small village of Halbun, situated high in the Anti-Lebanon Mountains west of the Damascus oasis. More than five hundred years later, the Roman writer Strabo claimed that its wine was served to the kings of Persia.

The wines of the Phoenicians and of their Bronze Age ancestors, the Canaanites, garner the highest praise in the ancient world. (I am using *Canaan* here in its original, more restrictive sense, as applying solely to the northern Levantine coast; later its meaning expanded to denote more southerly regions of modern Israel, Palestine, and Jordan.) For example, we read in the so-called Rephaim or Rapi'uma texts excavated in the fourteenth- to thirteenth-century B.C. palace of Ugarit (modern Ras Shamra, near Latakia) in Syria, on the northern periphery of Canaan, that "daylong they pour the wine . . . must-wine, fit for rulers. Wine, sweet and abundant, select wine . . . the choice wine of Lebanon, must nurtured by

El [the head of the pantheon]." Later Greek writers, such as Theocritus and Archestratus of Syracuse, single out Bybline wine as "fine and fragrant," the equal of the best Greek wine from Lesbos. Its aroma appears to have been its strong suit, if we are to believe the biblical prophet Hosea, who lauds its scent (14:7).

Where and when did the tradition of making fine Canaanite and Phoenician wines begin? These questions await detailed scientific investigation, but I estimate a sixth-millennium B.C. date for the domesticated Eurasian grapevine's transplantation to the northern Levant and the start of its winemaking industry. Levantine wine later grew into a major economic force. Anatolia, which had contacts with Neolithic Byblos, had already embarked on the same trajectory by 7000 B.C., if not earlier, which led to its all-encompassing wine culture. Gaza, the Jordan Valley, and the southern Levantine hill country had been planted with the domesticated vine by ca. 3500 B.C., to judge from grapeseeds, wood, and even whole dried grapes (raisins) recovered from Jericho and other sites throughout the region. Indeed, the industry had matured to such a degree by the time of Scorpion I (ca. 3150 B.C.) that it supplied all 4,500 liters of his wine for the afterlife. Dating the beginning of the industry in the northern Levant to the sixth millennium B.C. allows enough time for the process to have become established and transferred southward from eastern Turkey to the southern Levant over three to four thousand years.

If the Canaanites and Phoenicians had planted the vine only near their harbor towns, their vineyards would have been confined to a narrow strip of land between sea and mountain. Fortunately, a large, fertile valley between the Lebanon and Anti-Lebanon Mountains—the Beqaa—beckoned inland. Today, the best Lebanese wines come from the Beqaa, even in the midst of sectarian violence and Israeli incursions. It is also where the Romans, around A.D. 150, built temples at Baalbek—the grandest complex of religious structures in the entire empire, dedicated to Bacchus (the wine god), Venus (the goddess of love and fertility), and Jupiter (the king of the gods) who was identified with the Phoenician storm god Baal. Quite appropriately, the Bacchus temple was erected under the aegis of Antoninus Pius, who hailed from the Phoenician (Punic) colony of Carthage in north Africa. The temple astounds the visitor with its well-preserved Corinthian columns, nineteen meters tall, and its richly adorned decoration of entwined grape motifs and reliefs that recount the birth and life of Bacchus. The valley was likely the country's principal wine-producing center in antiquity.

The names of the best-known modern Beqaa wineries, including Château Ksara, Château Musar, and Château Kefraya, reflect the debt that the revival of the industry in the nineteenth and twentieth centuries owes to the French, after more than one thousand years of neglect under Islamic regimes. Bordeaux and Rhône varieties account for most of the six million liters of wine produced annually today. Some Lebanese vintners assert that the original Bybline vine, now called Merweh, is related to the French Semillon, and that the Obedieh vine was carried by the Crusaders back to Europe, where it became known as Chardonnay. Recent DNA analyses, showing that Chardonnay is the result of a cross of native French Pinot with Eastern European Gouais Blanc, disprove the latter claim, but it is still possible that a Lebanese varietal contributed to the genetic heritage of Gouais Blanc or Semillon. If we are ever to recover the true Bybline grape and its relatives, the approximately forty purportedly indigenous cultivars growing in modern Lebanon will need to be genetically fingerprinted.

I have a strong inclination to initiate this research myself. One of my first experiences in archaeology in 1974, before the devastating fifteen-year civil war broke out in Lebanon, was as a pottery specialist for the Penn Museum's last season of excavation at Sarepta (modern Sarafand). Located midway between Tyre and Sidon, Sarepta is one of the few excavated Phoenician city-states in the homeland. As we dug down through the succession of occupations and destructions, the modern version of the ancient struggle between nations and peoples was taking place overhead. Nearly every day, Israeli Phantom jets strafed the Palestinian camp only eight kilometers away, flying in low over the mountains, dropping their bombs, and then fading into the azure blue of the Mediterranean sky and sea. Sometimes rival planes tangled in dogfights, and we saw the loser disappear in a puff of smoke. A boat stood ready for our escape to Cyprus, but luckily we never had to use it.

Our team stayed in the relatively posh facilities of the Trans-Arabian Pipeline Company. Each night at dinner we followed a strict "wine ceremony" devised by the expedition director, James Pritchard. He would first seat himself at the head of the table with an unmarried woman archaeologist to either side. The remaining assembled group of married men (wives were not allowed by the director, because of a bad experience on a previous excavation) and Jesuit priests then arrayed themselves according to status down the table. As a lowly graduate student, I sat at the far end. We were not allowed to drink until the *mudir* (Arabic for "director") had raised his glass to his lips. He had bought up cases of Château Ksara wines, so all could partake of the delicious elixir. After all, excavation is hot, dusty work, and archaeologists need liquid refreshment at the end of the day. (Scotch after dinner was another ritual of Middle Eastern archaeology, not dictated by the *mudir;* we sipped and played bridge overlooking the Mediterranean.)

My interest in the Phoenicians was especially aroused when amphora fragments, covered with an intense purplish coloration on their interiors, started turning up in the thirteenth-century B.C. levels of the excavation. At another site, such sherds might be taken for granted, the staining perhaps attributed to a manganese ore or a strange fungus. But when you find them at a Phoenician site in Lebanon, the homeland of this people, thoughts turn to the celebrated Tyrian purple dye, which was worth more than its weight in gold and the prerogative of priests and kings. Even the names *Canaan* and *Phoenicia* likely derive from roots meaning "red" or "purple," underlining the importance of dyed textiles in these societies. According to Greek legend, repeated by later writers, the dye was discovered by the Tyrian high god and king Melqart, when he and the nymph Tyros went for a stroll on the beach with their dog. The dog ran ahead and bit into one of the mollusk shells that must once have littered the shore. It came back with its muzzle dripping with a purple substance. The discovery was not lost on Melqart, who immediately dyed a gown with the dye and presented it to his consort.

The first foray of our laboratory into biomolecular archaeology was to put the Melqart legend to a scientific test. A battery of analyses conclusively showed that the purple color inside the Sarepta amphoras was true molluscan purple, or dibromoindigo. This compound is produced in nature only by three Mediterranean species of *Murex* and *Thais,* along with related mollusks around the world. When a purple-dye factory, with piles of shells, special processing vats, and heating facilities, was found in the same area at Sarepta where the purple-stained sherds were excavated, we had an open-and-shut case for the earliest evidence of royal purple production; and, just as the legend claimed, it was from Phoenicia. Other piles of the same mollusks have been found elsewhere in the Mediterranean, but so far earlier evidence for a dye factory (as opposed to discarding the shells after eating the animals or stockpiling them for pottery or plaster manufacture) has not emerged.

What remains to be done on the biomolecular archaeological front in Lebanon is to analyze more vessels for wine, as much a luxury good as the purple dye. We should cast our nets as widely as possible, including material from Sarepta and other coastal and inland sites (for instance, from the new excavations at Sidon and from Kamid el-Loz, a rich Bronze and Iron Age city-state in the southern Beqaa Valley), to determine the starting date and dimensions of the wine industry.

THE CANAANITE AND PHOENICIAN WINE CULTURE

As with so much else Phoenician and Canaanite, our knowledge of this wine culture is severely limited by the scarcity of archaeological and textual evidence. Yet some understanding of its allure is needed to explain how this hardy maritime people propelled viticulture across the Mediterranean during the second and first millennia B.C. In its wake, native fermented beverages, including grogs and beers, were marginalized, modified, and displaced.

The extensive literary corpus of Ugarit is our most reliable source for second-millennium B.C. Canaanite society, and it portrays a people, with its gods and revered ancestors, focused on grape wine. Here and there, honey is mentioned; beer is noticeably absent. This might be expected in a region where grapes did well, gave a better return on investment, and used up less arable land than cereal production. Even today, wild Eurasian grapevines survive along the coast of Lebanon, at the southernmost extent of their distribution. More important than these considerations, however, wine was probably preferred simply because it contains twice as much alcohol as beer.

We read in the Baal Cycle, a group of tales about the trials and exploits of the storm god and other Canaanite gods, of Baal's grand feast after he defeats the sea god, Yamm. He celebrates by taking a large goblet in both hands—"a large vessel great to behold, a container for mighty men"—which is filled by a "thousand pitchers . . . [of] wine." He "mixes a myriad in his mixture," which may be a reference to various tree resins or herbal additives. Like the Sogdian *hutengwu* dancer who is spurred on by drink (see chapter 4), Baal then breaks out in song, accompanying himself on cymbals. The story continues with the construction of Baal's palace, made from the choicest cedar of Lebanon and adorned with silver and gold. In celebration, Baal brings out jars of wine for the gods, who sit on their chairs and enjoy goblets and gold cups filled with the elixir. Sometimes the divine party goes to extremes, as best illustrated by El, the supreme god, who gets so drunk that he staggers home and collapses in his own excrement.

The available archaeological depictions of the gods and kings are not nearly as graphic as these literary descriptions. One of the best known stelae from thirteenth-century B.C. Ugarit shows El in the standard regal pose, sitting on a chair and holding a wine cup in salutation. Three centuries later, even though the Near East had passed through a turbulent period of foreign invasion and economic collapse, the early tenth-century B.C. ruler of Byblos, Ahiram or Hiram I, appears in a similar pose on his sarcophagus. He sits upright on his cherub-sided throne, one hand grasping a cup and the other a lotus flower (a common wine additive in ancient Egypt), with a feast laid before him. Solomon commissioned this same Hiram to build the first temple in Jerusalem, made of cedar of Lebanon like Baal's palace, glistening in gold and decorated with statues of cherubim and purple hangings.

The ancestors—likely the best understanding of the Rapi'uma in the Ugaritic texts—had been an essential part of Levantine religion since the Neolithic period (see chapter 3). The Canaanites and Phoenicians maintained this tradition by their institution of the *marzeah*. At regular intervals, the dead were honored at elaborate funeral banquets. The most highly placed and privileged members of the community, men and women alike, would gather in a *bet marzeah* (Semitic "house of the *marzeah*"). There, a feast, liberally accompanied with wine, would be overseen by a *rb marzeah* ("prince of the *marzeah*"), a forerunner of the Greek symposiarch, who served as host and toastmaster. All celebrants were expected to provide food and wine from their own estates. As in Burgundy today, the Ugaritic countryside was a patchwork of family-owned vineyards; according to a fifteenth-century B.C. tablet, the vineyards of one small village in the realm were carved up among eighty-one owners.

Proper homage to one's ancestors meant drinking and eating in excess, according to the divine standard set by Baal, El, and other gods. We can imagine that music, dance, and the recital of Canaanite myths accompanied the merriment, along with bouts of sexual intercourse to match any Roman bacchanal. It can be inferred from the prophetic warnings and abjurations in the Bible that a *marzeah* in Phoenician Byblos, Sidon, or Tyre was just as dissolute as any Canaanite ceremonial feast.

THE WINE CULTURE TAKES TO THE SEA

The Byblos ships of the Canaanite and Phoenician seafarers carried much more than huge shipments of wine, purple textiles, and other exotic goods.

They also conveyed a new way of life, based on wine, which gradually permeated the societies, religions, and economies of those they came in touch with. We can see much the same thing happening today in New World locales. Whether in Australia, South Africa, Argentina, or frigid North Dakota (the last state in the United States to acquire a winery), a sea change in wine production has occurred over the past forty years. When I was growing up in Ithaca, New York, cloying Niagara or Manischewitz wine was the norm, served only on special occasions. Now, for many, a meal is not complete without wine or another fermented beverage, and a vast media enterprise has grown up around the art of matching food and wine.

The most dramatic example in antiquity of a wine culture "captivating" another people came in Egypt. We have seen how Scorpion I began importing large quantities of this previously unknown beverage into the country around 3150 B.C., and how he felt compelled to store wines for eternity (the ultimate in cellaring and aging). A century and a half later, at the beginning of Dynasty 1, the pharaohs of a united Egypt went further. Rather than rely on the foreign suppliers to import enough fine wine, and perhaps in order to tailor the wines to their tastes, they established the first royal wine industry in the Nile delta.

Soon, extensive tracts of the delta were planted with the domesticated grapevine, a feat that could have been accomplished only by employing specialists from the northern or southern Levant. It served as a kind of dress rehearsal for building the pyramids, when the pharaohs called on their own people to accomplish this grand enterprise. For the wine industry to succeed, foreign traders had to supply the grapevines, which would have been brought in most conveniently by ship. Grapevines embedded in soil have been noted among the dunnage used to cushion the wine amphoras of later shipwrecks (see below); the hull of the Uluburun merchantman was also packed with branches and leaves that have yet to be identified. Embedding the vine roots, branches, or buds in soil was essential to keep them moist and alive. Once the grapevines reached the delta, other Canaanite experts stepped in. Farmers and horticulturalists had to lay out the vineyards, train the vines on trellises, and dig irrigation canals. Architects and craftsmen were needed to construct winemaking facilities, especially winepresses, and to make specialty vessels for processing and storing the wine. Above all, vintners were required to oversee the operations. It can take up to seven years before grapevines begin to produce fruit. Vines had to be tended and fermentation and aging of the wines carefully managed. Thousands of years later, the imprint of the Canaanites in setting up this industry was still evident in the Semitic names of many ancient vintners (for example, those recorded on the inscriptions of New Kingdom wine amphoras).

Local inhabitants must have provided most of the manual labor at first and later shared in the day-to-day activities of winegrowing. Slowly but surely, they too were being absorbed into the Canaanite wine culture. Except for drinking, treading the grapes at harvest is probably the most visceral, sensual experience in viticulture. The later colorful depictions of winemaking in Egyptian tombs show lively bands of stompers, who hold tightly to grapevines to keep from slipping into the pomace as they sing to the snake goddess (see plate 6). In 2003, I had the opportunity to appreciate this way of making wine on a trip to the upper Douro River in Portugal, where fine port is produced. After a memorable dinner at Dirk van der Niepoort's Quinta do Passadouro—enhanced by German Rieslings, a Burgundy Richebourg, and a 1955 Passadouro vintage port—we put on swimming trunks, climbed into the *lagar* or winepress, and began sloshing through the knee-high mass of skins and juice. I am told that the best port is made by this labor-intensive method: the human foot, it seems, is ideally configured to extract the juice without breaking the seeds that introduce bitter tannins, which instead float to the surface.

Especially striking about the new Egyptian industry was its level of sophistication from the outset. Of course, the Canaanite specialists had many millennia of tradition behind them when they brought grapevines to the Nile delta. Even the Egyptian hieroglyph meaning *grape, vineyard,* or *wine* is a telling piece of evidence for viticultural expertise. As the earliest written character referring to the domesticated grapevine and wine from anywhere in the world, the hieroglyph graphically depicts a well-trained vine growing up onto a trellis of vertical poles, forked at their upper ends to hold the vine. The plant is rooted in a container, probably for ease of watering. One could say that the best practices of modern vineyard management, including a drip system, were on display at the inception of the ancient Egyptian industry.

The Canaanite winemakers also had to think outside the box. Levantine vineyards, generally sited in hilly terrain with good drainage during the rainy winter, had a terroir much different from the flat, alluvial Nile delta. With the blistering summer heat and much lower precipitation, Egyptian crops, especially water-sensitive grapes, had to be irrigated. A pergola system minimized direct exposure of the grapes to intense sunlight.

Fortunately, the rich alluvium of the delta, washed down from the upper Nile during the annual inundation, was well drained and salt-free. The conglomerate of sands, clays, and diverse minerals was a calcareous soil, not so different from parts of Bordeaux.

The Levantine winemakers succeeded beyond the wildest expectations in transferring their wine culture to Egypt. Until the Islamic invasions of the seventh century A.D., the delta domains supplied the temples of Egypt and its kings with millions of amphoras of wine. Wine, which was specifically identified in hieroglyphs by its place of origin in the delta—the ancient equivalent of today's vineyard-specific wine labels—had achieved the status of an essential funerary offering by Dynasty 6, around 2200 B.C. In time, nearly every major religious festival, including the all-important *heb-sed* to guarantee the continued welfare of the pharaoh and the fruitfulness of the land, called for wine offerings and prolific drinking, often lasting for weeks.

Despite the significant inroads of wine into Egyptian society, however, it never supplanted beer, the drink of the masses. Beer always preceded wine in the offering lists and was the focal point of many Egyptian festivals and myths, such as the Drunkenness of Hathor. Large public projects, exemplified by the pyramids, depended on the workers' getting their daily provision of beer and bread. Like wine, beer was likely introduced from the Near East. Barley and wheat seeds grew in profusion all along the Nile and in the oases. Millet, introduced from central Africa, was also grown and made into beer (see chapter 8).

One advantage of a beverage fermented from cereals was that, unlike fruits, the grain could be stored long-term for conversion to beer as needed. This circumstance, as well as the need to feed a burgeoning population, may explain why other native Egyptian beverages—in particular, date wine and honey mead—barely receive a passing mention in the literary sources and are as yet unattested in the archaeological record.

ESTABLISHING A BEACHHEAD ON CRETE

With the Egyptian winemaking success behind them, the Canaanites on their Byblos ships ventured farther and farther out into the Mediterranean. They applied a similar strategy wherever they went: import wine and other luxury goods, befriend the rulers by presenting them with specialty wine sets, and then wait until they were asked to help in establishing native industries. Besides offering expertise in winemaking, the Canaanites and later the Phoenicians could also instruct their trading partners in the production of purple dye (the requisite mollusks were found throughout the Mediterranean), shipbuilding (assuming that wood was available), and other crafts (especially metalworking and pottery-making). Once they had established a foothold in the foreign land, other, less tangible expressions of their wine culture—perhaps an artistic style or a mythological motif— might be adopted or merged with indigenous customs.

According to our biomolecular archaeological evidence, one of the first stops in the island-hopping jaunts of the Canaanites across the Mediterranean was Crete. Nearly one thousand kilometers from the port city-states of Lebanon, this large island at the entry to the Aegean Sea lies on the threshold of the Greek world. Although modern scholars are understandably skeptical about the often contradictory and fantastic tales of classical writers, a recurring element running through many accounts has Dionysos, the Greek manifestation of the Near Eastern wine god (known to the Romans as Bacchus), voyaging from Phoenicia to Crete as a daring seafarer. One beautifully painted drinking cup (*kylix*), made by the master potter Exekias in the sixth century B.C., shows the god single-handedly manning a small sailboat, its mast festooned with a luxuriant grapevine. Apparently when attacked by pirates, Dionysos fought back by miraculously growing the vine and dousing his attackers with wine; they were transformed into frolicking dolphins, who are seen circling around the boat. Could this tale have been inspired by an actual voyage that carried the domesticated grapevine to Crete aboard a Byblos ship?

Numerous Greek legends tie Crete to Phoenicia. Europa, a daughter or sister of the king of Phoenicia, is said to have been ravished by Zeus (the Semitic El or Baal) in the form of a bull and carried off to Crete. As if looking forward to the day when most of Crete and the rest of Greece would be planted with grapevines, she is often shown draped with dense vine leaves and grape clusters. In yet another story, Dionysos marries Ariadne, the daughter of King Minos, after she has been abandoned by Theseus, the slayer of the half-bull, half-man Minotaur, on the Aegean island of Naxos. Perhaps this tale reflected other journeys of Canaanite ships deeper into Greek waters, following the same route as the Uluburun ship along the southern coast of Turkey into the Aegean. Or could it be that the Bronze Age Minoans (Minos being their eponymous founder) transferred the Near Eastern wine culture to their neighbors?

Dionysos himself is represented as being just as fun-loving and ebullient as any Canaanite deity or shamanistic reveler in Central Asia or northern Europe. Popular winter and spring festivals, called Dionysia, took drinking, singing, dancing, and ribaldry to new heights. As in a Latin American carnival today, people paraded in costumes and played games, such as trying to balance on a greased wineskin. The frivolity eventually led, in the sixth century B.C., to the earliest public theater in the world: the Theater of Dionysos at the foot of the Acropolis in Athens.

Yet there was a darker side to this revelry: the "Bacchic rage," in which the emotions unleashed by the god and his beverage knew no bounds. Euripides' fifth-century B.C drama *The Bacchae* illustrates the serious tensions that Dionysiac worship introduced into Greek life. By transforming himself into a bull, Dionysos incites the women of Boeotian Orchomenos, northwest of Athens, to flee into the hills, where they dance and sing praises to the wine god. They sacrifice a child, tear animals apart, and eat them raw. In the tragic finale, the prince regent Pentheus of Thebes, who appears in the guise of a lion, is dismembered by the women, including his sisters and mother. They proudly carry his head back to his father and king, Theseus, who recoils in shock and disgust. This orgy of wild abandon and violence is too much for the Theban monarch (who also traced his ancestry to Sidon or Tyre, according to Greek mythology).

Peter Warren of the University of Bristol has taken some of the tantalizing hints embedded in the classical literature and set them on firmer ground. He excavated a small, late third-millennium B.C. farming community at Myrtos-Phournou Koryphe, along the rugged southern coast of Crete. Belying their seemingly unpretentious character, the storerooms and kitchens of ordinary houses throughout the site yielded up numerous large jars (*pithoi*), each with a capacity of about ninety liters.

Even before Peter Warren sent samples to us for analysis, we might have anticipated that the jars had once contained wine. They had peculiar exterior dark red splotches and drips that were reminiscent of the Egyptian Scorpion I jars. And like the latter, many of the Myrtos vessels had reddish interior residues. Some even contained grapeseeds, stems, and skins. Horizontal rope appliqués running below loop handles under the wide mouths of the jars suggested, again like the Egyptian jars, that leather or cloth covers had originally been secured by rope. Another peculiarity that the Myrtos jars shared with some of their Near Eastern counterparts from Godin Tepe and other sites in the Caucasus and Anatolia (see chapter 3) was a small hole near the base, deliberately made before firing the pottery, for decanting a liquid.

Our analyses of four of the Myrtos jars confirmed that they had held a resinated wine. Indeed, this is the earliest evidence to date of retsina from

Greece itself, the only country in the world that has perpetuated this ancient tradition until the present. Granted that retsina is an acquired taste (easily come by when traveling in Greece, as I discovered), it is essentially a variation on ageing in oak. As already mentioned in chapter 3, modern Greek winemakers have begun toning down their retsinas by adding small amounts of pine resin to their native varietals.

Peter Warren excavated numerous circular vats, often called bathtubs, and *pithoi* at Myrtos. Such finds, also well attested in ancient Egypt, are most often associated with industrial winemaking. The bathtubs, outfitted with spouts for draining the grape juice into the large jars, allowed a succession of workers to stomp the grapes: as one tired, the next one could step into the vat and take over. Large-scale production was also marked by a massive funnel, the stock in trade of the Near Eastern winemaker; and impressions of grape leaves on the pottery pointed to vineyards in the vicinity.

The wineries were overseen by a tutelary deity (the "goddess of Myrtos"), who was honored by a figurine in a small shrine on the southwest side of the excavation. She is shown in frontal view, with her breasts exposed and pubic triangle indicated, like the earlier Neolithic figurines. She is clearly on her way to becoming the awe-inspiring mother goddess of the Minoans, whose breasts protrude from a tight bodice above a flounced dress. The Myrtos deity holds a jug with a cutaway spout, a type of vessel with numerous parallels in Near Eastern wine cultures, in the crook of one arm. She was mounted on a low stand (or altar), with offering vessels laid out at her feet. Her association with winemaking activities at the site was unmistakable, as her shrine adjoined a room filled with spouted jugs, *pithoi,* a stomping tub, and a spouted bowl containing grape pomace.

Much like the royal winemaking industry in Egypt, the Myrtos enterprise appears to have suddenly sprung up. It is possible that winemaking had already reached the island from other parts of Greece, especially Macedonia, where squashed grape skins were found at fifth-millennium B.C. Dikili Tash, and some of the Aegean islands (Syros, Amorgos, and Naxos), where domesticated grapes and grapevine leaf impressions on pottery are reported from the third millennium. Then there is the notable finding of domesticated grape pips inside a *pithos* from House I at Aghios Kosmas in Attica, about twenty kilometers south of Athens near the coast. The large jar had a hole near its base, just like the Myrtos vessels. This is prima facie evidence that winemaking, perhaps on the same scale as at Myrtos, was known on the mainland at about the same time.

Did the impetus to make wine at Myrtos come from elsewhere in Greece, or was it brought to this island by the Canaanites? On balance, the latter position is better supported. Myrtos lay on a landfall of a well-traveled route for ships from Egypt and the Levant, and the distinctly Near Eastern character of its winemaking industry bespeaks influence from this quarter. The Canaanites were looking to spread their wine culture, and they saw a wide-open opportunity in Greece to work with the local Cretan people in advancing their interests.

The debt of Greek winemaking to the Canaanites, as well as their Egyptian trading partners, is also reflected in the later signs for *grape, vineyard,* and *wine* in the earliest Greek scripts, including Cretan Hieroglyphic and Linear A. The characters are unquestionably derived from the Egyptian hieroglyph, which shows a well-trained vine growing on a horizontal trellis.

Even after the Greeks had become seafaring merchants in their own right and began competing with the Phoenicians for control of the Mediterranean, they expressed their ultimate debt to the eastern Mediterranean wine culture in a profound way. They adopted the Phoenician alphabet, which is the ancestor of our own. They used this revolutionary writing system not merely to inventory goods or log their sea journeys, but rather to express their sentiments about wine. The earliest archaic Greek inscription, incised on a wine jug (*oinochoe*) in the eighth century B.C., reads: "Whoever of all dancers performs most nimbly will win this *oinochoe* as prize." Later in the same century, another amazing inscription is recorded on a Rhodian wine cup (*kotyle*) from the tomb of a young boy at Pithekoussai, an early Greek colony established on the island of Ischia in the Bay of Naples. It states in elegant dactylic hexameter, the poetry of the Homeric epics, that "Nestor's cup was good to drink from, but anyone who drinks from this cup will soon be struck with desire for fair-crowned Aphrodite." The Dionysiac interweaving of wine, women, and dance jumps out at us from across the centuries.

Another piece of evidence for the Canaanite introduction of winemaking to Crete via Egypt is more controversial. If this was the direction of influence, then we might expect to see evidence of the simultaneous introduction of barley beer, which was the preferred beverage in Egypt. Without intending to confirm this idea one way or the other, our analyses of two of the Myrtos *pithoi* showed the presence of calcium oxalate or beerstone, a byproduct of barley-beer production. Peter Warren was more than willing to take up the banner for barley beer at Myrtos, as he noted that one of the jars with the beerstone had been found in a room with barley chaff and other evidence of grain preparation. Yet ever since Sir Arthur Evans, the excavator of the famous Minoan site of Knossos, claimed that Minoans had made and drunk beer, this point has been hotly contested among Greek archaeologists.

THE LAST GASP OF A NATIVE GREEK BEVERAGE

Oddly, the two possible beer jars at Myrtos also once contained resinated wine. Maybe the vessels were reused, but a more likely explanation is that beer and wine were already being mixed together to make a "Greek grog."

The grog at Myrtos might well have been the forerunner of a phenomenon that engulfed all of Greece beginning around 1600 B.C., at the start of the Late Minoan IA period. A truly mixed beverage of barley beer, grape wine, and honey mead from that time (according to the analyses of our laboratory and that of Curt Beck at Vassar College) appears at many sites throughout Crete and the Greek mainland. It was served in a new type of vessel, the so-called conical cup, which has been recovered in incredibly large numbers in what are believed to be cultic contexts. By Mycenaean and Late Minoan times (ca. 1400–1130 B.C.), the unusual beverage is attested in elaborately decorated vessels—high chalices (*kylikes*), so-called beer mugs, stirrup jars, and stupendous spouted drinking horns (*rhyta*) that could take the form of bulls' heads or be decorated with swirling octopi. Such vessels occupied a central position in Greek social and religious life.

Where this Greek grog ultimately came from remains uncertain. The earlier beer and wine combination from Myrtos is probably a blip in the panorama of Greek fermented beverages, recalling the Near Eastern *kaš-geštin* or "beer-wine" (chapter 3). The more usual formulation of such a beverage would have included honey mead, well attested in Europe and consistent with the formula for Phrygian grog. According to a hypothesis prevalent among Greek scholars, new peoples moving into Greece from Europe shifted the balance of power from Crete to the Mycenaean mainland during the second millennium B.C. If this hypothesis is correct, these people might have brought the new Greek grog, a variation on the Nordic grog, with them.

The discovery of the so-called Nestor's gold cup from a sixteenth-century B.C. royal grave (Grave IV in Grave Circle A) close to the Citadel at Mycenae, usually identified as the palace of Agamemnon in the Homeric epics, adds a special twist to this story. Just such an elaborate gold cup, with figures of doves mounted on top of its widely splaying handles, is described in the *Iliad* (11.628–43), which is believed to have been written down around 700 B.C. and to reflect earlier traditions. There, we read that Nestor's mistress, Hecamede, tended a wounded soldier in the battle of Troy by serving him *kykeon* from the gold cup. The *kykeon* was a "grog" of Pramnian wine, barley meal, and probably honey, with goat cheese grated on top.

Kykeon, which can be translated as "mixture," fits the general chemical profile of the Phrygian, Nordic, and Greek mixed beverages: a combination of wine, beer, and mead. Although the cheese has yet to be identified chemically, cheese graters retrieved from warrior tombs in Greece and Italy corroborate the Homeric recipe. Our laboratory and Curt Beck's at Vassar College could not analyze any residue from the celebrated golden cup of Nestor from Mycenae—which had long since been cleaned out for conservation purposes—but we were fortunate to test a pottery beer mug of the same type from the site. It contained vestiges of the Greek grog.

Kykeon was more than an odd assortment of ingredients with the potential to produce an alcoholic high. According to the *Odyssey* (10.229–43), when Odysseus and his companions were making their circuitous route by sea back to their home island of Ithaca, they encountered the treacherous sorceress Circe. She transformed Odysseus's crew into pigs by tempting and stupefying them with a *kykeon,* which was strengthened with a *pharmakon* (Greek "drug"). It might be that the added psychoactive punch came from the Pramnian wine, which some scholars argue was an herbal wine. More likely, Circe used a specific spice or herb to gain her advantage. Rue, a narcotic and stimulant, is a possible candidate, as Curt Beck has detected compounds of this plant in cooking vessels from Mycenae and Pseira, a Minoan port town on a small island off the north coast of Crete. Saffron is another excellent possibility because of its analgesic effects. Some of the most delightful Minoan frescoes show women passing through fields of crocus and collecting the flowers, from which saffron could have been gleaned. Poppy and its derivative, opium, are strongly implied by a female figurine, dated to the period after 1400 B.C. when the grand palaces had been destroyed: she is shown with poppyseed capsules sprouting from her head. As yet, however, no definitive biomolecular archaeological evidence has been obtained for the drug in *kykeon.*

The Greek grog finally lost out to the Phoenician wine culture in the centuries following Homer, as the Greeks fought for control of foreign markets in the Mediterranean and consigned their beer and other mixed drinks to the barbarous European hinterland. *Kykeon* was never totally forgotten, because it was incorporated into the Eleusinian Mysteries. The little we know of this mystical religion of the Hellenistic and Roman eras suggests that the initiatory rites involved drinking a mixed beverage that promised expiation for one's sins, along with otherworldly delights. Some investigators surmise that a hallucinogenic mushroom or the fungus ergot, which infects rye and wheat, might be involved; this also remains to be proved.

Although I was never as adventuresome as the priests of the Temple of Demeter at Eleusis or its sister temple near the Acropolis in Athens, I did carry out some experiments in re-creating a modern-day *kykeon*. With the help of Takis Miliarakis, owner of the Minos winery in the beautiful Archanes hill country south of Herakleion on Crete, we gathered local herbs, including diktamon (*Origanum dictamnus*, which has a taste like oregano) and saffron. We found the best mountain honey, for which the island is well known, and negotiated for fine Cretan barley malt. The plan was to make a "Bull's Blood" concoction for the 2004 summer Olympics in Athens. The name alluded to the close association of Dionysos and bull sacrifices in Minoan religion. The frescoes on a sarcophagus from the palace or villa at Ayia Triada during its heyday, from about 1600 to 1400 B.C., were among our inspirations: they show the blood of the bull, symbolizing Dionysos, being collected in a jug, while a figure believed to represent a priestess presents another beak-spouted jug, presumably containing Greek grog, before a horned altar. We thought the blood should be reflected by a grog in which dark red wine predominated. The project, unfortunately, ground to a halt when the winemakers tasted the result and were repulsed (they never sent me a sample to try). Either they did not have the experimental fortitude of a beermaker like Sam Calagione of Dogfish Head, or they still harbored some prejudice for a purer wine, even a retsina.

REACHING OUT TO ITALY

The Homeric period of the eighth century B.C. saw the climax of Phoenician and Greek competition for the hearts, minds, and palates of native peoples throughout the Mediterranean. Many islands—Cyprus, Malta, Sicily, Sardinia, and Ibiza—were parceled up by the two seafaring nations.

The evidence from the trading colony of Pithekoussai on the island of Ischia, which had been established by immigrants from Euboea, an island in the Aegean not far from Athens, illustrates how carefully one must disentangle the overlapping Greek and Phoenician wine cultures to understand how they influenced the peoples of Italy and the Western Mediterranean. A series of elite warrior tombs at Pithekoussai, as well as at their home base of Lefkandi on Euboea and elsewhere in Campania and Etruria, yielded very similar assemblages: large metal cauldrons of Near Eastern style, and sets of kraters, filters, and ladles for serving wine, and cheese graters.

The sources for the metal cauldrons can be debated, but we know that the initial inspiration for the vessels' designs came from the eastern Mediterranean. Cauldrons of the same type are illustrated in the Assyrian reliefs decorating the royal palace of Sargon II at Khorsabad, dating to 714 B.C., and these were likely made by Phoenician or Syrian craftsmen for the Assyrians. One of the richest burials on Cyprus, tomb 79 at Salamis, yielded similar cauldrons with griffins, sphinxes, and other protomes or busts attached to the rim. A particularly spectacular cauldron from Salamis was filled with tin-plated, mushroom-lipped juglets, which pointed to Phoenician involvement.

Most of the cauldrons shown on the walls of Sargon's palace very likely held only wine, as the Assyrians are known to have had extensive vineyards, and wine is frequently mentioned in their texts. However, our analyses of the residues from the Midas tumulus (see chapter 5) indicate that these cauldrons were filled with Phrygian grog, not wine, and a similar pattern might well hold elsewhere outside Assyria proper.

Could it be that the cauldrons in the Italian warrior tombs also held a grog rather than wine? This hypothesis is ripe for biomolecular archaeological investigation. The presence of the cheese graters in these graves is a very strong signal that these vessels held a mixed fermented beverage. These heroic warriors had little need for a cheese grater in this life or the next, except to prepare the ceremonial Greek *kykeon,* which was garnished with cheese. The females, who accompanied the warriors to their graves, also wore clothes that were held together by fibulae with attached miniature cheese-grater pendants. Like Hecamede and Circe in the Homeric epics, these women probably prepared the *kykeon* for their fallen heroes, following in the long tradition of women serving as beverage makers in the ancient world. Moreover, the early Greek inscription on the Rhodian *kotyle* from Pithekoussai implies that it contained a stronger version of the *kykeon* beverage in Nestor's cup.

Archaebotanical and other archaeological evidence can be cited in support of the hypothesis that a Greek-style mixed beverage was known in the West. For example, a cauldron containing a piece of honeycomb was found in the courtyard building at Murlo in Tuscany, dated before 575 B.C. *Phiales* (handleless drinking cups of eastern Mediterranean type) and pilgrim flasks found at Casale Marittimo appear to have contained a resinated mixed beverage flavored with hazelnuts and pomegranates, and more honeycomb was found inside a strange cylindrical vessel, possibly used for fermentation, at this site. Biconical kraters from eighth- to seventh-century B.C. tombs at Verucchio yielded both grape pollen and cereal grains, suggesting that something more than pure grape wine was being produced.

I am proposing that the Etruscans, like peoples in other parts of Europe, already had a tradition of making a mixed fermented beverage before the Phoenicians and Greeks arrived on their shores. The traders lured them into the eastern Mediterranean wine culture by presenting them with cauldrons, kraters, and other drinking vessels. At first, the Etruscans simply adapted the vessels to their existing customs, using them for their native mixed beverage, as the Celtic princes and their coteries did farther to the north (chapter 5). They went on to make their own versions of the vessels—"mixing bowls" with high pedestals and silver and gilded drinking bowls of Phoenician style—and in time were won over to the eastern Mediterranean wine culture. Of course, only extensive chemical analysis of a range of native and foreign vessel types dating from before, during, and after the Etruscans' contact with the traders will show whether my hypothesis is correct.

Either wild or domesticated grapes might also have gone into the Etruscan grog, as numerous grape pips were recovered from a Middle Bronze Age subterranean room at San Lorenzo a Greve at the gates to Florence. But we have to wait until the beginning of the Iron Age in the ninth century B.C., when the traders began to arrive in force, to see large-scale wine production take off, steadily gaining momentum in the following centuries until it displaced the Etruscan grog. Just as the Canaanites tutored the Egyptians and probably later the Minoans in viticulture, the Phoenicians likely passed along their knowledge, as well as transplanted grapevines from their homeland, to the Etruscans. The transfer of the Semitic alphabet followed, and like Greek, the first Etruscan and Roman inscriptions were inscribed on wine vessels. Presumably many other accoutrements of the eastern Mediterranean wine culture were also enthusiastically embraced. From these small beginnings, Italian winemaking grew to be the enormous enterprise that it is today. .

I believe that the Phoenicians were mainly responsible for bringing Etruria into the wine-culture fold, at least during the initial stages of foreign contact, as the Greeks were still largely wedded to their *kykeon*. The Etruscan amphora is modeled after the Phoenician amphora, and similarity of form often implies similarity of function and contents. The answers will come only from more intensive excavation of early Etruscan coastal sites, where amphoras predominate, and the discovery and investigation of more Mediterranean shipwrecks holding wine-related pottery. The Phoenician settlements most likely to have had a role in bringing viniculture to Etruria are Motya, an offshore island at the western tip of Sicily, and the Lipari islands in the Tyrrhenian Sea. Motya later became known for its exquisite Marsala wine.

Grapevines embedded in soil found among the substantial cargo of the fourth-century B.C. El Sec wreck, off the coast of Majorca, suggest that they were being transported for transplantation. This ship also carried numerous amphoras from throughout the Mediterranean and the Black Sea, drinking bowls (*skyphoi*) of the Athenian Fat Boy type, and cauldrons and buckets in styles well documented elsewhere in Europe for making a mixed fermented beverage.

Several grapevine fragments in soil aboard a single ship, however, may be insufficient evidence of intended transplantation. The recently excavated Grand Ribaud shipwreck off the coast of southern France, dated to about 600 B.C., also contained numerous grapevines, but they are believed to have served to cushion the seven to eight hundred amphoras the ship was carrying. Perhaps grapevines were also used as cushioning on the El Sec ship, but it is strange that so much soil was preserved on the example illustrated in the published report, unless the goal was to keep the vines alive and ready to replant.

A profusion of Iron Age shipwrecks have now been located and excavated along the Italian and French coasts. They were so heavily loaded with wine-related vessels that one could say that the transfer of Phoenician and Greek culture to the western Mediterranean was mediated by their wine cultures.

Whether the Etruscans learned to make wine from the Phoenicians or from the Lydians of western Anatolia, as implied by Herodotus, they went on to become the principal exporters of wine to southern France by 600 B.C. The Romans followed in their footsteps, and as they say, the rest is history: wine continued northward to trans-Alpine Burgundy and the Mosel, displacing the native beverages, until it reached the northern limit of the domesticated vine. The Nordic grog still prevailed in the regions beyond.

COLONIZING IN THE WEST

The Phoenicians and the Greeks had much to gain by founding permanent colonies in the western Mediterranean, closer to their prospective clients. Rather than ship wine thousands of kilometers from the east, they could plant vineyards on foreign soil and begin producing wine for local consumption.

The Greek success in following this formula can be seen in the coastal cities of Oenotria ("the land of trained vines"), now Calabria in the toe of Italy. Their efforts here show how serious they were about promoting the culture of the vine and wine. One city, Sybaris, flourished to such an extent that its name became synonymous with a luxurious and dissolute lifestyle.

In 2005, I had a chance to see how these Greek and Phoenician efforts had paid off in Italy when I was invited to travel there at the invitation of the Associated Winegrowers of Italy (Associazione Nazionale Città del Vino). Apparently, the translation of my book *Ancient Wine* (*L'archeologo e l'uva*) had struck a chord in the wine-loving Italian soul. After giving a lecture at an Etruscan wine conference in Tuscany, I embarked on a journey southward in the company of Paolo Benvenuti, director of Città del Vino, and Andrea Zifferero, an Etruscan archaeologist from the University of Siena. We set our sights on experimental vineyards throughout Italy. At Pompeii at the base of Mount Vesuvius, we visited the project of the Mastroberardino Winery. Its vintners are growing what they consider to be Roman cultivars here (e.g., Greco di Tufo, Coda di Volpe or Foxtail, and Vitis Apiana/Fianco/Muscat) on the site of an ancient excavated vineyard, using Roman trellis methods. These include training the cordons or branches to grow on a single support, on more elaborate arbors and pergolas, or up a tree. The most common Roman method, as today, was to train the vines to grow vertically upward so as to open the grapes to air flow and sunlight to ripen them and to facilitate care and harvesting. This experiment has led to the release of a high-end wine named after the famed Villa of Mysteries (Villa dei Misteri).

We then traveled on to ancient Oenotria, where we examined the association's project at Locri, devoted to growing the numerous Italian varieties (upward of one thousand) and preserving this wealth of grape genetic or germplasm diversity. Much remains to be learned about the modern varieties and their ancient roots, figuratively and literally. For example, my geneticist colleague José Vouillamoz recently identified the immediate forebears of Sangiovese, the famous Tuscan cultivar, as Ciliegiolo and Calabrese Montenuovo. Although Ciliegiolo is a well-known variety in Tuscany, Calabrese Montenuovo is almost extinct in Campania and Calabria (conjectured to be its home). Earlier ancestors of the vine could have come from Greece, but this theory is yet to be confirmed. Preserving the varieties now growing in the country will enable their ancestry to be ascertained and contribute to new varieties with desirable characteristics.

But to return to the larger picture of Phoenician colonization in the West, their largest colony was Carthage, on the North African coast in what is now Tunisia. According to classical sources, the city was founded in the late ninth century B.C., when the Assyrians threatened the Phoenician city of Tyre, and Elissa (Dido), a Tyrian princess, fled by ship. Archaeological evidence roughly supports this chronology. Dido and her band of Tyrian patricians settled in an ideal, strategic spot at the end of a peninsula across from Motya. The main settlement occupied a high promontory with a port at its base and large lagoons to the north and south. A vast hinterland of rich soils, very similar to those of their homeland, invited the Phoenicians to plant cereals and, above all, the domesticated grapevine.

The north African coast was much less densely populated than other regions of the Mediterranean, so the Phoenicians could adopt a different strategy with the native Berbers, who were pastoral nomads. Rather than keeping a low profile and offering aid in setting up industries to promote trade, the Phoenicians became true colonialists. In the following centuries, as Carthage grew and sprouted satellite settlements along the coast, it became the capital of the Punic empire and a supplier of goods to the Roman empire. Its prosperity has recently been revealed by Robert Ballard and his fellow deep-sea explorers. Using a submarine and a remotely operated vehicle, they have documented numerous trading ships and long lines of amphoras spread out on the sea floor at a depth of one thousand meters: these fall on a direct line from Carthage through the Tyrrhenian Sea's

Skerki Bank and on to the Roman port at Ostia. Those ships and their cargoes may have gone down, but many more made the journey safely.

Wine was the beverage of choice in ancient Carthage. One of the first treatises on viniculture and other forms of agriculture was composed by a third- to second-century B.C. Carthaginian named Mago, who is quoted extensively by later Roman writers (Varro, Columella, and Pliny the Elder). Presumably he drew on Phoenician traditions dating from the founding of the colony. To date, however, the earliest excavated evidence for the domesticated grape at Carthage is pips from the fourth century B.C.

Although the wild grape grows in Tunisia, special measures had to be taken to enable the domesticated vine to survive in the hot climate. Mago advised on how to aerate the soil and plant vineyards to compensate for the low rainfall. His recipe for raisined wine involved picking the grapes at peak ripeness, rejecting damaged berries, drying the grapes in the sun for several days under a reed shelter (taking care to cover them at night so that they were not dampened by the dew), resaturating the fruit with fresh juice, and then treading it out. A second batch was prepared in the same way, and then the two lots were combined and fermented for about a month, finally being strained into vessels with leather covers. Mago's raisined wine can be compared in taste and production methods to a luscious Tuscan Vin Santo or an Amarone from the Valpolicella region of northern Italy. To make an Amarone, harvested grapes are first dried on racks in barns and then trodden, pressed, and fermented on their lees in sealed jars for a month. After filtering, Amarone is further aged in well-sealed jars. Even nearer at hand, however, are the delicious Muscat wines of the island of Pantelleria, less than one hundred kilometers offshore from Carthage.

Carthage's influence eventually extended across the Mediterranean to Spain's Costa del Sol and as far west as the Pillars of Hercules at Gibraltar. The Carthaginians aimed to exploit the rich tin, lead, and silver ores of the Iberian Peninsula's inland Guadalquivir River. But once again they discovered that the rich maritime plains were ideal locales for colonizing and transplanting their wine culture. Another recent discovery of two seventh-century B.C. shipwrecks in the Bay of Mazarrón, near Cartagena, shows the importance of ship transport in expanding the Punic empire. These two ships, which were excavated by Spain's National Museum for Maritime Archaeology, are only one-third the length of a standard Byblos ship but would have served admirably for short hauls along the coast.

Before the arrival of the Phoenicians and Carthaginians, the native peoples of the southern Spanish coast enjoyed a liberally spiced mixed beverage of barley, emmer wheat, honey, and acorn flour (see chapter 5). Whether under duress or voluntarily, they were soon won over to the wine culture, and today we can enjoy the fruits of the ancient labor that went into laying out the first Spanish vineyards and establishing excellent cultivars.

When I attended the Barcelona conference on ancient beer in 2004, my colleague at the University of Barcelona, Rosa M. Lamuela-Raventós, invited me on a very special tour of the coastal and mountain wine regions. Rosa and her student Maria Rosa Guasch were responsible for detecting a red pigment in some of the amphoras in Tutankhamun's tomb and developing a more precise method using liquid chromatography–mass spectrometry–mass spectrometry to identify tartaric acid in ancient samples. We now know that the nineteen-year-old pharaoh drank red wine, but a later study by the Barcelona group showed that at least three of the twenty-six amphoras in his tomb contained white.

Rosa's family, Raventós, is a long-established producer of Cava sparkling wine (sold under the Codorníu label), and also owns still-wine estates. After days spent tasting wines and visiting their state-of-the-art vineyards and wineries, followed by nights feasting on thick steaks and Catalan specialties in castles, the high point of the trip came with a visit to Priorat, a remote area away from the coast and at a high altitude. The Raventós winery here, Scala Dei, is named after a twelfth-century Carthusian monastery, which is built into a sheer rock face and whose name recalls Jacob's stairway to heaven, described in Genesis 28. Low-yield vines provide grapes for the Scala Dei wine, a very intense blend of the native Garnacha with Cabernet Sauvignon and Syrah. Its alcohol content of 14 percent is high, but other Priorat wines are even more potent, at 16 to 17 percent, near the limit of what an unfortified grape wine can achieve. Descriptions of their deep red colors and layered aromas and tastes cannot suffice; these wines must be experienced firsthand to be appreciated. I later tracked down some of the last bottles of the 2000 Scala Dei in the United States, tucked away on the topmost shelf of Manhattan's Soho Wines and Spirits. When I open one after aging for ten years or more, it will evoke memories of my trip and the much earlier adventures of the Phoenicians.

The Phoenicians ventured ever farther afield. They went beyond Gibraltar out into the Atlantic. They traveled to Cornwall in England, where it is believed they exploited the tin ores. They traveled down the west coast of Africa, and if Herodotus is to be believed, they circumnavigated the African continent. Some scholars argue that they even made it to the New

World, on the basis of Phoenician inscriptions found in Brazil and eastern North America, but the latter are likely forgeries. So far, no sign of their wine culture has been discovered there; we must look in a different direction to discover where the peoples of the Americas came from and what fermented beverages they produced and enjoyed.

SEVEN

THE SWEET, THE BITTER, AND
THE AROMATIC IN THE NEW WORLD

WHEN THE ARCHAEOLOGIST THOMAS DILLEHAY of Vanderbilt University began excavating in 1977 at the small prehistoric settlement of Monte Verde in Chile, he could hardly have imagined the scholarly furor he would arouse. He and his colleagues discovered that the site, located fifty-five kilometers inland from the Pacific Ocean and once home to about thirty people, was one of the earliest human settlements in the Americas, dated to around 13,000 B.P. If humans had crossed from Siberia to Alaska on a land bridge (Beringia) created at the end of the Ice Age, as available genetic evidence suggested, how had they reached the tip of South America, nearly fifteen thousand kilometers away, so quickly? To many scholars, this discovery flew in the face of conventional wisdom and could not possibly be correct.

HUNTERS, FISHERMEN, OR FRUIT EATERS?

It had long been believed that the first humans who arrived in the Americas were highly aggressive and successful hunters who wielded carefully flaked stone spearheads, called Clovis points. With their weapons, they had brought down woolly mammoths, saber-toothed tigers, and other extraordinary Ice Age creatures, a practice that contributed to the wholesale extinction of these animals. This picture is now thought to be overdrawn, and the extinctions are attributed to additional factors, such as abrupt shifts in climate, disease, and competition with other mammals (such as the moose and brown bear) coming from Asia.

The "Clovis First" theory fails on other counts, not least of which is the very early date of Monte Verde. The earliest known site with Clovis points dates to ca. 11,500 B.P., a millennium and a half later than Monte Verde, and is located in northern South America. Moreover, not a single Clovis site has yet been found on either side of the Bering Strait in Alaska or Siberia, where the land crossing began and ended. Another assumption of the Clovis First theory—that the earliest human explorers of the New World traveled inland after the crossing through an ice-free passage between the two massive Laurentide and Cordilleran glaciers covering North America—has been undermined by recent geological data. It is now widely believed that our ancestors, after their trek across Beringia, followed a coastal route southward.

When the sea level dropped 120 meters and exposed Beringia in glacial times, it did not remain barren tundra for long. Within centuries, if not decades, it was carpeted in heath meadows and swathed in birch forests, teeming with animal life, that invited human migration and exploitation. But movement farther south was blocked by massive ice packs along the northwest coast and inland. It would take another thousand years before a passage through the interior was freed up. Even today, the inland route can be formidable, as my wife discovered when she drove our Volkswagen camper nearly seven hundred kilometers along the Dempster Highway, north from Dawson City in the Yukon Territory to Inuvik on the Arctic Ocean. She was greeted by spectacular birdlife and the occasional grizzly bear, but the open tundra, punctuated with numerous marshes and moraines, is virtually impassible in warmer weather, except by following the elevated, two-lane gravel "highway."

Rather than slog across wide expanses of ice or boggy tundra, early humans likely saw another opportunity. By following the Inside Passage along the northwest coast by boat, they could have leapfrogged from one secluded bay to the next, following a strategy similar to the one we believe humans followed in hopping from oasis to oasis in Central Asia or from island to island in the Mediterranean. When the ice packs along the coast began to melt, between about 17,000 and 15,000 B.P., ice-free refuges were formed in estuaries, which would have been a fisherman's and fruit gatherer's paradise.

Anyone who has traveled the Inside Passage today can attest to its rich marine and plant resources. Meandering in and out of fjords, bordered by densely forested mountains, early peoples could have feasted on wild straw-berries, soapberries, elderberries, fruits of the manzanita (whose name in Spanish means "little apple"), thimbleberries, and salmonberries. By throw-ing a line or net over the side of a boat or by wading through shallow waters with digging sticks, they could have landed a huge king salmon or halibut, or collected tasty clams and mussels.

American archaeologists have not been as fortunate as their Mediter-ranean counterparts in discovering the boats that the early Americans used to make their maiden voyages. *Homo sapiens* had already crossed open water to reach Australia by 40,000 B.P., so we can infer that the peoples in-habiting Siberia had their own kinds of watercraft, whether log rafts, leather kayaks, or reed boats. Thor Heyerdahl, the Norwegian adventurer, proved the basic concept of Ice Age sea travel when he sailed his balsa-wood raft *Kon-Tiki* (an older name for the Incan sun god) nearly seven thousand kilometers across the Pacific Ocean to Polynesia from Peru.

The early coastal settlements that served as the stopovers for the boats, however, have yet to be discovered. These sites and boats must have disap-peared beneath the sea as the glaciers melted and the sea level rose. Some innovative underwater archaeology along the lines of Robert Ballard's (see chapter 6) will be needed to uncover the evidence. Negative arguments leave a lot to be desired, as much as they spur new exploration. But if the land route was blocked by ice, there can be only one explanation for the very early founding of a site like Monte Verde in southern South America: the first wave of human settlers during the glacial period must have trav-eled by boat.

A MARITIME PEOPLE WITH A PENCHANT
FOR UNUSUAL BEVERAGES

Monte Verde did more than pound a nail into the coffin of the Clovis First theory. It had other surprises in store. The site was situated on a tributary

---

Map 3. The Americas. Humans crossed over the Bering land bridge (Beringia) by around 20,000 B.P. Many fermentable natural products were discovered and converted into beverages over the coming millennia, including honey, maize (corn), cacao pod, and probably many other fruits (e.g., Peruvian pepper tree), root crops (such as manioc or cassava), and grasses. These drinks were often mixed together with "medicinal" herbs, tree resins, and other additives (including chili, vanilla, and blood).

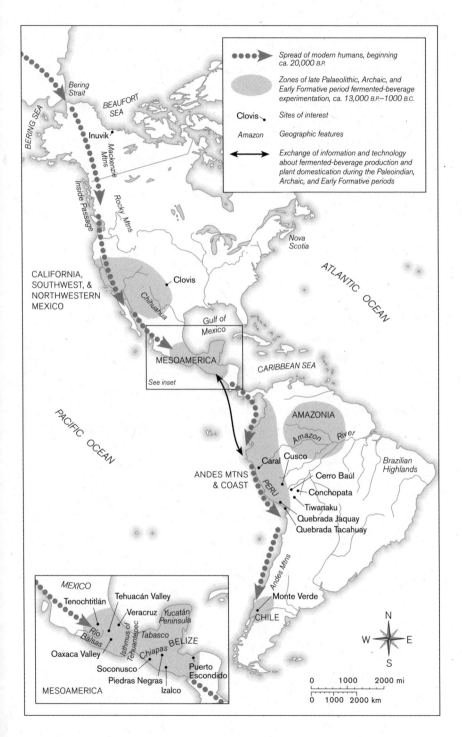

Bering Sea

Bering Strait

BEAUFORT SEA

Inuvik

Mackenzie Mtns

Inside Passage

Rocky Mtns

CALIFORNIA, SOUTHWEST, & NORTHWESTERN MEXICO

Chihuahua

Clovis

Nova Scotia

Gulf of Mexico

ATLANTIC OCEAN

MESOAMERICA

See inset

CARIBBEAN SEA

PACIFIC OCEAN

AMAZONIA

Amazon River

Brazilian Highlands

Caral

Cusco

Cerro Baúl

ANDES MTNS & COAST

PERU

Conchopata

Tiwanaku

Quebrada Jaquay

Quebrada Tacahuay

Andes Mtns

Monte Verde

CHILE

N
W — E
S

0   1000   2000 mi

0   1000   2000 km

MEXICO

Tenochtitlán

Tehuacán Valley

Veracruz

Yucatán Peninsula

Río Balsas

Isthmus of Tehuantepec

Tabasco

Chiapas

BELIZE

Oaxaca Valley

Soconusco

Piedras Negras

Izalco

Puerto Escondido

MESOAMERICA

of the Maullín River, in a cool, moist birch forest. The rising waters of the stream eventually submerged the settlement and encased it in a peat bog. The result was some of the most remarkable preservation of organic materials at any Palaeolithic site in the Old or New World.

The excavators uncovered two structures made of log and plank foundations, secured by wooden stakes, and walls made of animal hides tied by reed ropes to poles. One building, probably the living quarters for the community, was twenty meters long and subdivided into individual chambers by interior log-plank and pelt walls. Each chamber had a small fire pit, from around which was recovered the detritus of meals. Together with remains of mastodon, paleo-llama, and freshwater mollusks, the food debris included quantities of seeds, nuts, tubers (including wild potato), mushrooms, and berries. A second, similar building was devoted to butchering mastodons and preparing their hides, to judge from the congealed animal fat that covered its floor.

The range of plants that the community exploited reads like a pharmacological and nutritional cornucopia. The rich forest and bog environs of the site provided more than enough supplies to tide the inhabitants over the winter. Indeed, based on the plant and animal remains, the excavators believe that these first Americans inhabited their settlement year-round, a phenomenon generally associated with the beginnings of the Neolithic Revolution elsewhere in the world several thousand years later.

The Monte Verdeans also ranged up into the high forest, two hundred kilometers north of the site, to collect the leaves and fruits of the *boldo* tree (*Peumus boldus*), which have marked medicinal and hallucinogenic effects. They made up quids for chewing by combining the *boldo* with local *junco* reed, which produces delicious young shoots, and, most intriguingly, no fewer than seven species of seaweed from the Chilean coast. The presence of seaweed at an inland site betrays the people's close connection to the ocean and quite possibly their original migration route. Seaweeds, of course, are extremely nutritious: they provide a full complement of trace elements, some protein, and vitamins A and B_{12}, in addition to aiding the body's immune system and contributing to beneficial calcium and cholesterol metabolism.

A host of other saltwater marsh and dune plants were exploited for food and medicine, in particular foxtail (*Polygonum sanguinaria*), which acts as an analgesic, diuretic, and fever reducer. The salt content of these plants also filled a nutritional gap in the diet that was not met by the local flora.

One plant, club moss (*Lycopodium* sp.), came from the Andean grasslands fifty kilometers away. Whether gathered by the inhabitants themselves or obtained from exchanges with others, club moss constituted the most prevalent archaeobotanical material recovered from Monte Verde, with seventeen thousand spores found distributed over thirty-three locations. The highly flammable spores could have served as a fire starter or been used as a talcumlike skin powder to offset the high humidity, still a common practice among the local Mapuche Indians.

For me, it was particularly exciting to learn that the Monte Verde diet included many edible berries and the abundant bulrush (*Scirpus* and *Carex* spp.), which are eminently fermentable. Even today, the Mapuche use at least two fruits found at the site—*Aristotelia chilensis* (a deciduous shrub, also known as the *maqui*) and *Amomyrtus luma* (a fragrant evergreen)—to make fermented beverages (*chichas*). Sweet bulrush stalks, leaves, and rhizomes are known to have been chewed by Paleoindian and Archaic Americans as early as about 10,000 B.P. in caves in the southwestern United States, where quids were found. Wild potato tubers (*Solanum magalia*) might also have been masticated at Monte Verde; an especially powerful potato *chicha* is made today by the Mapuche and Huilliche peoples, albeit by saccharifying the potato starch with barley malt. Enzymes in human saliva break down starches into sugars, so chewing a plant to enhance its sweetness was likely one of the first ways that humans discovered how to make a fermentable mash. East Asians and Pacific Islanders still practice this ancient technique in making rice wine (see chapter 2).

But did the early Monte Verdeans make an alcoholic beverage from a fruit, or by chewing and spitting out the sweet juice of a bulrush or some other starchy plant? It is reasonable to assume that they collected the berries in some kind of container, as the abundant fruit ripens quickly during late summer and fall and must be gathered before it spoils. Once fruit has been piled into a container in a boggy climate, rife with microorganisms, fermentation cannot be far behind. Unfortunately, the excavators have not yet recovered any containers that might have held a fermented beverage and could be tested. Woven reeds, which are known to have been made into rope, might have been made into containers. Wooden containers are another good possibility, especially as wooden grinding mortars were preserved and found at the site. The latter even had traces of *junco*, bulrush, and wild potato embedded in their surfaces from grinding the starch-rich plants, perhaps as a first step in preparing a fermented beverage. No quids of these plant remains, however, have yet been recovered at the site.

The Monte Verdeans obviously possessed deep knowledge of the region's natural resources. They knew which plants and animals could meet their needs for food, fuel, shelter, and drugs. Long before the intricate mythologies and religions of later peoples, they had probably begun to explore the mind-altering effects of alcoholic beverages and hallucinogens. Such finely tuned information must have been generations in the making, which once again underscores the likelihood that humans did not dawdle in the Arctic but speedily made their way southward by boat. By moving inland, the Monte Verdeans could enjoy the natural bounty and diversity of ocean, marsh, river, and mountains. People at Quebrada Tacahuay and Quebrada Jaquay in southern Peru, by contrast, inhabited shoreline settlements between about 11,000 and 10,000 B.P.; they enjoyed a satisfying diet of anchovies, cormorants, mollusks, and crustaceans, but not much else.

CHEWING THE CUD

In the past decade, a wealth of new information about the first American domesticated plants has been revealed by archaeobotany, phytolith and pollen study, starch-grain identification, and stable isotope and DNA analyses. Many of the staples or "founder crops" of American cuisine can now be traced back to a period shortly after 10,000 B.P.

Findings from Guilá Naquitz cave in Oaxaca, Mexico, and from villages in the lower Peruvian Andes suggest that squash (*Cucurbita* sp.) was the earliest domesticate. Peanut (*Arachis* sp.), long dismissed as a latecomer, has been dated as early as 8,500 B.P., according to wild-looking specimens found at Andean sites; these are distant from the peanut's presumed area of origin in the Amazon Basin, suggesting earlier cultivation. Quinoa (*Chenopodium* sp.) seeds have an equally long ancestry. Domesticated peppers (*Capsicum* sp.) from two sites in Ecuador come in somewhat later, around 6000 B.P., where they were associated with corn (maize), manioc or cassava, squash, beans, and palm root as part of a broader agricultural complex. Cotton (*Gossypium* sp.), again from the Peruvian sites, is similarly dated to ca. 6000 B.P. The organic remains from Monte Verde also indicate that coca, potato, and many other plants were also likely manipulated, cultivated, and eventually domesticated by humans at a very early date. So it seems that the first immigrants to the New World were as agriculturally innovative as their Old World counterparts.

The shift from hunting and gathering and the increasing reliance on domesticated plants is especially intriguing because it is a worldwide phenomenon. Northern South America, the Andes and Amazonia, and south-ern Mexico are at the forefront of the Neolithic Revolution in the Ameri-cas, whereas East Asia and the Near East paved the way in Asia. Theories of economic and climatic determinism argue that the impetus for domes-tication in these "centers of origin" came from the warming trend at the end of the Ice Age. Plants thrived in an atmosphere much richer in carbon dioxide, and human populations grew in response. Then a global cold snap called the Younger Dryas, around 13,000 B.P., threw these burgeoning com-munities back on their own resources. Forced to focus on high-carbohydrate plants to survive, over time and by trial and error they domesticated these plants for their ease in harvesting, nutritional value, and other desirable traits.

By contrast, the Palaeolithic and drunken monkey hypotheses (see chap-ter 1) contend that humans were motivated by more than economic neces-sity. Because they were "driven to drink," they intensively explored and exploited their surroundings for sugar-rich resources which could be made into fermented beverages. If the early Americans came from East Asia, where we have the earliest chemical evidence for a fermented beverage, they probably already had some knowledge of how to make such a bever-age. As they traveled through the Inside Passage, explored the coast of South America, and began moving into the interior, they would have been on the lookout for these potential sugar resources. Berries and honey, when available, entered into alcoholic beverages that were central to social and religious life. In many parts of the New World, however, humans faced environments that were too dry, too cold or too hot, or too high to support sugar-rich fruits or wild bees.

Then came what must be the most far-fetched human experiment in domestication ever attempted—the cultivation of maize (genus *Zea*). The seeming impossibility of this endeavor was likely overcome by an over-powering desire of humans to alter their consciousness by alcohol.

A series of careful DNA studies identified teosinte (genus *Tripsacum*) as the wild ancestor of maize. This mountain grass grows in the Río Balsas drainage of southwestern Mexico. One cannot imagine a less inspiring plant to domesticate. The ears of this primitive corn, which are barely three cen-timeters long and contain only five to twelve kernels, are trapped in a tough casing. Even if you manage to free up the kernels, their nutrient value is es-sentially nil. Eating just one of the five hundred or more large, juicy kernels in a modern ear of corn provides the nutritional equivalent of an entire teosinte ear. But there was a logic to the early Americans' seeming madness.

As teosinte was domesticated, starting around 6000 B.P., it lost its many thin stalks in favor of a single stem, and the number of kernels and ear size increased. At the same time, it became one of those rare domesticates whose propagation depends solely on humans' extracting the kernels from the husk and replanting them. Such a monumental effort had its rewards. The resulting maize was soon transported to other parts of the Americas, and wherever it went, it became imbued with supernatural significance, especially when it was transformed into *chicha,* a generic Spanish term for any American fermented beverage but most often equated with corn beer.

Chicha's importance in the social and religious world of ancient South America can best be appreciated by focusing on the drink's central role in the much later Incan empire of Peru. Spanish chroniclers in the fifteenth century A.D., including F. Guaman Poma de Ayala, Bernabé Cobo, Girolamo Banzoni and others, describe and illustrate how *chicha* was prepared, distributed to work parties, drunk in massive amounts at feasts, offered to gods and ancestors, and shared according to strict protocols. For example, at the Incan capital of Cusco, the king poured *chicha* into a gold bowl incorporated into the navel of the Incan universe, an ornamental stone dais with throne and pillar in the central plaza. The *chicha* cascaded down this "gullet of the Sun God" to the Temple of the Sun as awestruck spectators watched. At most festivals, ordinary people participated in days of prodigious drinking after the main feast, and the Spanish looked on aghast at the drunkenness. Human sacrifices first had to be rubbed in the dregs of *chicha* and then tube-fed with more *chicha* for days while lying buried alive in tombs. Special sacred places, scattered throughout the empire, and mummies of previous kings and ancestors were ritually bathed in maize flour and presented with *chicha* offerings to the accompaniment of dancing and pan-pipe music. Even today, Peruvians sprinkle some *chicha* on Mother Earth from the communal cup when they sit down together to drink; the cup then proceeds around the group according to social status as an unending succession of toasts are offered.

The Spanish chroniclers recorded that the making and serving of *chicha* was a woman's activity, as it often has been elsewhere. The Incan rulers isolated groups of beautiful women (*mamakona*) to remain chaste for life and to make the *chicha* for the festivals and palace life. Special sites (e.g., Huánuco Pampa along the Inca Trail), together with elaborately constructed terraces and irrigation systems, were devoted to growing maize and making *chicha* on a vast scale. The women of a village or royal facility rolled balls of maize flour in their mouths until their saliva broke the starches down into sugars. This mash was heated and diluted, and the resulting liquid was fermented in a container for two to three days, usually reaching an alcohol content of about 5 percent. At modern social gatherings and festivals, women still sit apart with their jars of *chicha* and serve the men engaged in their drinking rituals.

The Andean archaeological record is replete with vessels for making, serving, and drinking *chicha*. These include cups (*keros*), high-necked decanters (*aribalos*), jars (*tinajas* and *upus*) of various sizes, and intricate trick drinking vessels (*pacchas*) in which the beverage is directed through a maze of channels from an upper container. These pottery containers can take various shapes, such as corncobs, llama heads, and reed boats mounted on long handles. *Pacchas* were even made from enemy skulls, which were sometimes outfitted with intercommunicating gold bowls and silver drinking tubes through the top of the skull and the mouth. When you walk through a museum gallery of pre-Columbian South American antiquities, you are probably looking at the accumulated debris of numerous drinking fests, similar to the elaborate bronze vessels of Shang Dynasty China or the drinking sets of the classical Greek symposiasts. The Incas not only drank copious amounts of their fermented beverages, but they also devised intricate artistic creations for the conspicuous display and enjoyment of their drinks.

Many types of vessels that are known to have been used for *chicha* in Incan times have their counterparts in much earlier periods. The earliest pottery in South America, dating back to ca. 5000 B.P., seems to have been predominantly intended for fermented beverages. As yet, no chemical analyses of these vessels have been carried out, but this supposition is plausible given what we know about the difficulty of domesticating maize and the pivotal place of *chicha* in the mythology and social life of communities throughout the ancient Americas.

Another tool of modern scientific archaeology—stable isotope analysis of ancient human bones—has helped determine whether corn *chicha* was being drunk by early Americans. The foods we eat leave telltale chemical signatures in our bones in the form of different isotopes of carbon, nitrogen, and other prevalent elements. Some very interesting results emerged when human bones from sites throughout the New World were examined. Because maize had been domesticated by about 6000 B.P., one would have expected to see a specific carbon-isotope composition that reflected the increased consumption of maize, but it was strangely missing.

Some scientists have proposed an explanation for this anomaly. Because the analyses measured only the collagen in bone, its main proteinaceous connective tissue, they were biased toward detecting high-protein foods. Solid foods made from maize, including gruel or bread (e.g., tortillas), fit this requirement, but not fermented beverages like maize *chicha,* largely composed of sugar and water. Consequently, if people between 6000 and 3000 B.P. were consuming their maize as *chicha,* very little protein would have been incorporated into the collagen of their bones. The researchers speculated that humans began using maize as a solid food only after its ear had been substantially enlarged by selective breeding, around 3000 B.P. After this point, the carbon isotope compositions of bones dramatically changed.

The isotopic results raise the American version of the Near Eastern query: Which came first, bread or beer, and which product spurred the domestication of barley in the Middle East and teosinte/maize in the New World?

According to a recent proposal by John Smalley and Michael Blake, it was corn beer, or more precisely, a corn wine, that came first and provided the impetus for domesticating the plant. When a beverage is broadly dispersed, it is likely to be of deep antiquity. One of the most widely distributed fermented beverages in the Americas today is a wine fermented directly from the ultrasweet juice of pressed maize stalks. It does not go through a saccharification step, as is typical of beer. Smalley and Blake noted that modern cornstalk wine is made by pressing or chewing stalks of teosinte. Teosinte and maize both concentrate high levels of sugar in the stems of young plants. As the plants mature, the sugar moves to the kernels and is converted into starch. Collecting the stalks and ears early in their growing cycle guarantees a high-sugar resource (as much as 16 percent sugar by weight), ideal for making an alcoholic beverage. The same kind of reasoning lies behind the growing use of corn as a biofuel, which now accounts for most of the world's production of alcohol.

Conspicuous signs of prehistoric American interest in fermenting the sweet essence of maize show up in the form of chewed stalks, leaves, husks and ears left behind in caves of the Tehuacán Valley of Mexico, not far from the center of teosinte domestication in the Río Balsas. From about 7000 to 3500 B.P., the number of chewed maize quids declined. Over the same period, teosinte was being domesticated, and corn was coming into its own as both a liquid and a solid dietary staple.

If teosinte and corn were exploited initially more for their sugar and wine potential, that could explain the gradual decrease in quids. This reasoning is consistent with the isotopic bone evidence implying that maize was first made and consumed as a beverage and the rapid dispersal of maize to other parts of the Americas only after it had been transformed into the larger-eared domesticate.

As maize developed into some five thousand varieties of diverse colors, sizes, and degrees of sweetness, early Americans discovered more efficient ways to produce cornstalk wine. For example, the Tarahumara of Chihuahua in northern Mexico developed a process using ingenious nets woven of yucca fibers that replaced the chewing of the maize "cud." By placing the cornstalks in the nets and twisting the nets between two poles, they could wring out nearly every drop of the nectar-like juice. The method is almost identical to the way ancient Egyptians carried out their final pressing of grapes.

Other refinements followed. Perhaps as early as 3000 B.P., it was found that the tough hull surrounding each kernel could be removed by soaking and heating the milled corn in a dilute alkali solution, made from lime, wood ashes, or crushed shell. This procedure, called *nixtamalization* after the Aztec Nahuatl word for dough, also enhanced the amino-acid content and nutrient value of the corn.

Ultimately, cornstalk wine slid in popularity when early Americans discovered that they could mass-produce a beer or *chicha* from the larger maize kernels and ears. By sprouting the maize kernels, they could activate enzymes, related to those in human saliva, that break down starches into sugar. The resulting sweet malt could be toasted, dried, and stored for future use, or diluted and fermented immediately into corn *chicha*.

What the early Americans did not understand was how to start the fermentation. Unwittingly, insects probably transferred *Saccharomyces cerevisiae* to the sweet concoctions, whether cornstalk wine or *chicha,* and the yeast culture was perpetuated by using the same fermentation vessels repeatedly. Or possibly a tradition of mixing fruit and grain beverages accompanied human emigrants from Asia or became established in the Americas in the wake of experimentation with the new plants. Adding a high-sugar fruit, which has already been inoculated with yeast by insects, to a malt is a more assured way to initiate fermentation. A potent version of such a beverage from central Mexico, called the "bone breaker," is recorded by the Spanish chroniclers: it combined cornstalk juice, toasted corn, and seeds of the Peruvian pepper tree (*Schinus molle*), another popular South American plant that could have provided yeast (see below).

The domestication of the cacao tree (*Theobroma cacao*) represents another signal achievement by early Americans. As with maize, the impetus for domesticating cacao was likely the production of a wine from its sweet fruit pulp. Cacao occurs naturally in the tropics, especially along the Pacific and Caribbean coasts of Central and South America and in Amazonia. It requires year-round water, temperatures that do not fall below 16°C (60°F), and dense understory debris to provide habitat for the midges that pollinate the cacao flowers.

The fertilized flowers grow into football-sized pods that jut from the trunk and larger branches of the tree. Inside the pod is a juicy pulp surrounding thirty to forty almond-shaped seeds, known as beans. The beans, which contain concentrated bitter and aromatic alkaloids and other compounds, provide us with the wondrous "food of the gods" (the translation of the plant's Latin genus name, *Theobroma*) that we know as chocolate. The same compounds, including the methylxanthines theobromine and caffeine, serotonin (a neurotransmitter—see chapter 9) and phenylethylamine (which has a structure closely related to dopamine and amphetamine, two other neurotransmitters), impart a similar chocolaty taste and aroma to the fruit. Ripe cacao fruits attract monkeys, birds, and other animals who are hungry for their abundant sugar (as much as 15 percent), fat (cacao butter), and protein. But animals eschew the intensely bitter beans and scatter them on the ground, where some take root as new trees.

If a ripe pod strikes the ground and splits open, the pulp becomes liquid and begins to ferment. The Spanish chroniclers observed that native peoples along the Pacific coast of Guatemala delighted in a mildly alcoholic beverage derived from fermented cacao pulp, which they made by piling the fruit into their dugout canoes and letting it ferment there. "An abundant liquor of the smoothest taste, between sour and sweet, which is of the most refreshing coolness" (a long way from the sweet, hot cocoa to which we in the West are accustomed) accumulated at the bottom of the boat. A similar beverage is still enjoyed in the Chontalpa region of Tabasco in Mexico and elsewhere in Central and South America where the tree grows wild or is cultivated.

Fermentation of the pulp produces a liquid containing 5 to 7 percent alcohol. This is the first step in making modern chocolate: a mass of pulp is piled up at the cacao plantation, and after the pulp has fermented, it disintegrates and can be removed to collect the beans. As the pulp ferments

Figure 19. Mesoamerican *criollo* cacao pod, full of almond-shaped seeds or "beans," in a juicy, sugary pulp. The initial impetus to domesticate the plant probably came from converting the pulp into a fermented beverage, still made in Central and South America. Photograph courtesy of Dr. Nicholas M. Hellmuth, FLAAR Photo Archive. Photograph by Edgar E. Sacayón. *Theobroma cacao,* Arroyo Petexbatún, Sayaxché, El Petén, Guatemala.

and heats up, the beans start to germinate, until the internal temperatures rise to 50°C (122°F), which stops most biological processes. After five or six days' fermenting, the beans' astringency has given way to a more familiar chocolate flavor. The beans are laid out to dry in the sun for one to two weeks and then roasted for about an hour at temperatures approaching 120°C (240°F) to enhance aromas, colors, and tastes. Finally, the beans are shipped to chocolatiers round the world, who refine and blend them to create an array of culinary delights.

Before the early Americans learned how to make the chocolate beans into chocolate bars, sauces (*moles*), and beverages, they were captivated by the wine that came from the cacao fruit. Once again, biomolecular archaeology has provided the key data about this beverage. Fortuitously, in the fall of 2001, the lead story in the newsletter of my alma mater, Cornell University's College of Arts and Sciences, was "The Birth of Chocolate" by the archaeologist John Henderson. He described how he and his colleague, Rosemary Joyce of the University of California at Berkeley, had excavated very early pottery vessels from the site of Puerto Escondido, on the Ulúa River in northern Honduras. He thought it likely that these vessels had once contained a chocolate beverage and concluded the article by stating what was really needed was chemical analysis of vessel residues to provide hard evidence for his hypothesis. It was as though a fellow Cornellian (John graduated a year after I did) was reaching out across the decades and asking for help. Although our paths had never crossed in Ithaca, I wrote to him to say that such an investigation was right up my team's scientific alley and to propose a collaboration. Although we had previously devoted our efforts to unlocking the secrets of Old World fermented beverages, the same techniques could be applied in the New World. I soon heard back from John, who negotiated to bring some of the pottery back to the United States, and we were off and running on our scientific quest.

The pottery samples from Puerto Escondido were some of the earliest yet found anywhere in Mesoamerica, dating back to around 1400 B.C. The site preceded the first urban communities of the Olmecs, centered on the Gulf Coast of what are now the Veracruz and Tabasco provinces of Mexico. Archaeologists had long surmised that the Olmecs, along with carving monumental stone heads and fashioning exquisite jade jewelry for their revered ancestors and gods, were the first to domesticate the cacao tree. This might explain why the best cacao in later Mayan and Aztec times came from the Chontalpa zone of western Tabasco, a dense, swampy area from which seafaring peoples carried their precious cargoes by canoe to Honduras. The ancient Mayan word for chocolate, *kakawa* or *kakaw*, derives from the Mixe-Zoquean family of languages, the same one to which Olmec belongs.

Other regions of Mesoamerica well known for their cacao included the Aztecs' prize area of Soconusco (Xoconochco) on the Pacific coast of southwest Mexico, the Ulúa Valley where John Henderson was working, and Izalco on the Pacific side of the narrow Isthmus of Tenuantepec. Some debate still exists among geneticists about where *T. cacao* was first taken into cultivation within its broad natural range. Truly wild plants are difficult to differentiate from feral descendants of cultivated plants, and sampling for wild and domesticated varieties in the historically important regions has been uneven. Yet all the archaeological and historical evidence points to Mesoamerica as the region where beverages and foods made from cacao were taken to their most sublime level. The particular cacao variety which is found there—*criollo*—also has an unsurpassed flavor and aroma profile, despite the more warty-looking appearance of the pod compared to the smoother and rounder *forastero* fruit of South America. It would be surprising if Mesoamerica, where so much effort was expended to make the best chocolate possible, was not also the area the tree was first domesticated.

The Ulúa Valley would have been an excellent locale from which to disseminate this valuable product to other parts of Mesoamerica. The cacao tree thrives in the valley's rich alluvial soil and tropical climate. Transport is facilitated by interconnecting waterways—mangrove lagoons, marshes, and lakes—which lead out to the river and the Caribbean. It is no wonder that when the Spanish invaded in the sixteenth century A.D., a king of Chetumal in the Yucatán, more than three hundred kilometers away, sent out a fleet of war canoes to defend the Ulúa Valley against the interlopers. The Spanish, of course, eventually won, but the fame of the valley's cacao plantations spread to the Old World.

To test whether the Ulúa Valley was indeed one of the earliest areas for cacao development in the New World, John chose jars and bowls from the earliest phases of the Puerto Escondido excavation, in which residences, defined by postholes, ranged from about 1400 to 200 B.C. During the first millennium B.C., the Maya civilization emerged in the lowland jungles of Guatemala and the Yucatán. Because these vessels had similarities to later spouted jars and drinking cups that the Maya reserved for their spiced, frothy chocolate drink, John surmised that the people of Puerto Escondido might have prepared a similar beverage for feasts and ceremonies.

Either John had an eye for picking out chocolate vessels or Puerto Escondido was awash in cacao. Eleven of the thirteen pottery sherds tested positive for the fingerprint compound of cacao, theobromine. Theobromine occurs in other American plants, especially *Ilex paraguariensis,* a South American relative of holly whose leaves and twigs make the stimulating beverage maté or yerba-maté. This beverage is still consumed throughout South America, sometimes from a silver-accented gourd through a silver drinking tube. But among plants native to Mesoamerica, only cacao yields theobromine.

In collaboration with the chemist Jeffrey Hurst of Hershey Foods, we demonstrated by gas and liquid chromatography, coupled to mass spectrometry, that theobromine was present in the eleven vessels and could only have been deposited there by a cacao product. Two of the jars tested were clearly intended for liquids (see figure 21). One that dated from the site's earliest phase (the Ocotillo, from about 1400 to 1100 B.C.) had a tall neck and was strikingly shaped like a cacao pod, as if it were an ancient advertisement for its contents. The second jar dated to the most recent occupation (the Playa phase from 900 to 200 B.C.), and belonged to the well-known "teapot" type. Jeff had already shown that the teapots of the Middle Preclassic period (ca. 600–400 B.C.) at the Mayan site of Colha in Belize contained a chocolate beverage. This type of vessel is widely dispersed from Middle Preclassic times until the Late Formative period (ca. 200 B.C.–A.D. 200) in the main areas of cacao production, from southern Mexico to El Salvador along the Pacific coast, and from Belize to Honduras along the Gulf of Mexico. It has also been found at many inland sites, including Veracruz, highland Chiapas, the Valley of Oaxaca, and central Mexico. The finest examples have been recovered from elite burials, such as those from a tomb at Monte Albán in Oaxaca in which nearly half the vessels were bridge-spouted teapots. Several were adorned with human "effigy" figures, with one wearing a macaw mask.

Until Jeff's analyses, it was pure speculation that the teapots might have once held a chocolate beverage. They are not illustrated on any of the later Maya frescoes and painted vessels. They appear to have first been associated with chocolate by the early twentieth century archaeologist Thomas Gann, who recovered several from a Mayan tomb at Santa Rita Corozal in Belize and noted their resemblance to the typical serving decanter for chocolate used in Europe since the sixteenth century.

Curiously, the spouts of some of the early American teapots were attached near the base and curved backward, so that it would have been nearly impossible to pour a liquid from them. This odd spout placement is quite likely an important clue to their function. Later Mayan depictions of the

Figure 20. Painting from a Late Classic Mayan vase, showing a ruler about to partake of a foaming cacao beverage. Probable tamales covered with a cacao-mole sauce are heaped inside a serving bowl under the ruler's platform. Photograph K6418 © Justin Kerr.

cacao drink preparation show the beverage being poured at a substantial height from one cylindrical vessel into another in order to create a thick head of foam. Thousands of years later, the Spanish chroniclers describe how the Yucatán Indians, descendants of the Maya, made a "foaming drink [from cacao and maize] which is very savory, and with which they celebrate their feasts." Conceivably, the awkward-looking teapots might have been used in an earlier period to create a foam by blowing air through the spout or stirring the beverage vigorously through the main opening. As the foam rose through the spout, one had the option to inhale the foam or drink directly from the mouth of the vessel.

The earliest chocolate aficionados during the Ocotillo phase at Puerto Escondido lacked such vessels to prepare their drink. They did have cacao-shaped serving jars and elegant high-fired and burnished cups, decorated with carved and molded designs of stars, diamonds, and human faces. Yet we have no evidence that they frothed this beverage, and our biomolecular archaeological results indicate that the primary attraction of this first cacao drink was its alcohol content.

The later adoption of the teapot probably signals a shift to making a frothed beverage from the bitter, more chocolate-flavored beans. This change is consistent with the expanding use of the seeds of other plants—including sapote, ceiba, and palm—which were ground and roasted for nutritional, culinary, and medicinal uses.

Figure 21. Vessels for serving and consuming the elite cacao beverages of the Americas.
(a, *above*) High-necked jar in the shape of a cacao pod, corresponding to a type produced and probably used for serving an alcoholic beverage made from cacao pulp between 1400 and 1100 B.C. at Puerto Escondido, Honduras. Chemical analyses by the author's laboratory and colleagues support this conclusion, which would make these vessels among the earliest known evidence for an alcoholic beverage from cacao. Drawing by Yolanda Tovar, courtesy of John S. Henderson and Yolanda Tovar; Collection of the Instituto Hondureño de Antropología e Historia, Museo de San Pedro Sula, Honduras. (b, *right*) "Teapot" from an unidentified site in northern Honduras, corresponding to a type produced between 900 and 200 B.C. at Puerto Escondido. Photograph courtesy John S. Henderson, Cornell University; Collection of the Instituto Hondureño de Antropología e Historia, Museo de San Pedro Sula, Honduras.

A MIXED CACAO BEVERAGE

By the time the frothed beverage took hold in later Mesoamerican societies, hieroglyphic writings had begun to refer to a host of additives to the cacao beverage made from beans. A monumental Mayan lintel stone, spanning a doorway at Piedras Negras in the jungle of northwestern Guatemala, has an inscription that reads "chili cacao." At nearby Río Azul, a stupendous screw-on stirrup-lidded jar (see plate 8) was found in a fifth-century A.D. tomb, where a ruler had been laid out on a ceiba and cotton mattress and surrounded in Midas-like fashion by a drinking set of tripod cylindrical vessels (see chapter 5). The surface of the unusual container was stuccoed and painted with six large hieroglyphs, which read, "A drinking vessel for *witik* cacao, for *kox* cacao." The italicized terms are yet to be translated, but they may refer to other ingredients in the cacao beverage. Chemical analysis by Jeff Hurst has confirmed that the jar held cacao. Another reference on a polychrome vase mentions *k'ab kakawa,* literally "honey-cacao," a delicious-sounding drink.

An opulent tradition of mixing chocolate with other flavorings is revealed in the Spanish accounts of the Aztecs. In Fray Bernardino de Sahagún's anthropologically astute *General History of the Things of New Spain,* we read that the ruler was served chocolate in the privacy of his home: "Green cacao-pods, honeyed chocolate, flowered chocolate, flavored with green vanilla, bright red chocolate, *huitztecolli*-flower chocolate, flower-colored chocolate, black chocolate, white chocolate" (Coe and Coe 1996: 89–90). *Huitztecolli* is the ear-shaped flower of *Cymbopetalum penduliflorum,* a plant in the custard-apple family, whose peppery, resinous flavor was highly valued; it had to be imported from the lowland tropics. The chronicles also mention the "black flower," our vanilla plant (*Vanilla planifolia*), an orchid fertilized only by the stingless American bee (*Melipona* spp.) to yield aromatic black seed pods. Other flowers and spices include the "string flower," a member of the *Piper* genus and similarly peppery; magnolia flowers; the "popcorn flower," with a rose scent; ceiba seeds; sapote seeds, with a bitter almond flavor; chilis of all kinds; allspice (*Pimenta officianalis*), which contributes pumpkin accents; and achiote or annatto (*Bixa orellana*), which colors the beverage an intense red. Because cane and beet sugars had not yet been introduced into the Americas, honey from the native bee was used to offset the bitterness of the chocolate and other additives. The Spanish, who attempted to stamp out most native customs, were intrigued enough by the beverage to carry a version of it back to the Old World. Today, the traditional beverage is perpetuated among a small population of the Lacandón Maya in eastern Chiapas, who still consider the chocolate foam the "most desirable" part of the drink. Similar ingredients are combined to create an array of chocolate drinks elsewhere in Mexico and Guatemala.

Many of these additives, which we specifically targeted in our chemical tests, were missing from the earliest vessels at Puerto Escondido. This result implies that a different beverage was consumed at Puerto Escondido, apparently an unadulterated alcoholic beverage made only from the sweet cacao pulp. This tradition was probably never totally lost, as some Mayan painted jars refer to "tree-fresh" cacao, and a passage in Sahagún's account describes the effect of the king's "green cacao": "[It] makes one drunk, takes effect on one, makes one dizzy, confuses one, makes one sick, deranges one. When an ordinary amount is drunk, it gladdens one, refreshes one, consoles one, invigorates one. Thus it is said: 'I take cacao. I wet my lips. I refresh myself'" (Henderson and Joyce 2006: 144). Can there be any doubt that Sahagún is describing an alcoholic beverage?

The Aztecs had a mixed view of fermented beverages. On the one hand, they allowed the elderly to drink four cups a day of *octli* (pulque), a beverage with 4 to 5 percent alcohol made by collecting and fermenting the sugar-rich sap of the agave, or century plant. At grand feasts they encouraged public drunkenness, even among children. The king frequently indulged as well. Bernal Díaz del Castillo personally observed "50 great jars of prepared good cacao with its foam" being served by women attendants to Motcuhzoma Xocoyotzin ("Montezuma") throughout an epic banquet of three hundred courses.

Such extravagances, however, flew in the face of the Aztecs' need to maintain military discipline and public order. They strictly regulated who could drink what and when, as they viewed themselves as rulers of an empire and guarantors of the cosmic order in the epoch of the Fifth Sun (albeit from humble origins). Drunkenness was punishable by death, and Aztec literature warns of the evils of drink as severely as do the puritanical tracts that led to prohibition in the United States. The Zhou Dynasty's negative reaction to the excesses and self-destructiveness of the Shang monarchs is an apt parallel from ancient China (see chapter 2).

Like the Muslim invaders from Saudi Arabia into the Middle East, Aztec tradition recalled a glorious past of relative deprivation and struggle in the deserts of northwestern Mexico before they conquered the central part of the country in the fourteenth century. According to their foundation legend, they established their capital at Tenochtitlán, a group of islands in the middle of the Lake of the Moon, which then filled the Valley of Mexico, when they saw an eagle with a snake in its beak perched on a prickly-pear cactus (*Opuntia* spp.). This myth alluded to the primary drink of the Aztecs in their homeland, which was made from the fruits of the prickly pear and the giant saguaro and pitahaya cacti, as well as from the pulp of mesquite pods and the flower stalks of agave and yucca. By baking these plants in pits or boiling down their juice, the extract could be preserved as a high-sugar concentrate until it was needed.

Because these beverages quickly turned into vinegar in the hot climate, the native peoples had to drink them fast. They had developed a reputation for being "drunkards in the highest degree" by the time the Spanish arrived. The women stoked the flames of this addiction by preparing a wine every third day, when, one observer noted, "the men drink so much that they lose their senses." One observer of the Guasave Indians wrote: "They are much given to wine, for they have many fruits of which it is made. During the three months when they are in season drunkenness is almost continuous, and dancing so frequent and long continued that it seems that those who engage in it must have superhuman forces" (Bruman 2000: 10).

Northwestern Mexico was also the epicenter of a hallucinogenic cult in which peyote (*Lophophora williamsii*) was consumed by decocting the exposed part of the cactus, the so-called mescal button, as a tea. The active alkaloid in peyote is mescaline, derived from phenylethylamine, one of the compounds also found in cacao. It is not known when the peoples of this region began exploiting peyote. Quite possibly they discovered the mind-altering properties of various plants in the Paleoindian or Archaic period, when they first began chewing, pounding, pressing and cooking up whatever they found in the desert. Peyote might also have been dispensed in an alcoholic beverage to intensify its effects: the Spanish chroniclers noted this use of corn *chicha* and pulque.

Whatever the origins of peyote, the Aztecs left it behind when they migrated and replaced it with substitutes available in central Mexico, including members of the mushroom genus *Psilocybe*. The principal active alkaloids of these fungi are psilocybine and psilocine, which are indoxyl derivatives related to serotonin (see chapter 9). The Aztecs referred to the mushrooms as *teonanacatl* ("flesh of the gods"). Sahagún says that they were eaten with honey before dawn and washed down with a cacao beverage, and they induced hallucinations, dancing, singing, and weeping.

When the Aztecs conquered Soconusco, one of the prime cacao-producing areas, they were introduced to yet another plant from which to make a beverage. They soon made special cacao beverages the sole prerogative of the elite, just as the ancient Maya had. The only people permitted to drink them were the king, his entourage, highly placed soldiers, and a merchant class, the *pochteca*, who were charged with transporting the cacao and other luxury goods (jaguar skins, amber, and the sublimely beautiful feathers of the quetzal bird) from the Pacific lowlands through enemy territory to Tenochtitlán. Except for the king, who could drink his fill, the cacao drinks were reserved for the end of a meal or feast, when they were enjoyed with a tobacco pipe, animated discussion, and entertainment, in keeping with the customs of male societies around the world. Sahagún tells us that in the competitive world of the *pochteca*, the custom was to grasp a gourd containing the drink in one's right hand, while the left hand held the stick for frothing the beverage and a holder for laying down the gourd between quaffs.

Perhaps because the cacao tree was so alien to the Aztecs, they gave it and its beverages an extraordinary place in their culture. For instance, cacao beans were the currency by which all goods and services were valued. Montezuma had a veritable Fort Knox of cacao in his storerooms at Tenochtitlán, which, according to one Spanish chronicler, held nearly a billion beans.

Aztec mythology divided the universe into the four cardinal directions, supported by "world trees." Their unique folding-screen bark codices represented the trees as radiating out, like a mandala, from the sun god, Huitzilopochtli. The cacao tree grew in the south, appropriately enough as cacao came from that direction, and was associated with the ancestors and the color of blood. The cacao pod itself, which is shaped like a human heart, reinforced this symbolism. When a slave or prisoner was sacrificed at the Great Temple to Huitzilopochtli in Tenochtitlán, the priests tore out the still-beating heart of the victim and held it high toward the sun. The severed heads of the sacrifices were displayed on racks. In one annual ceremony to Quetzalcoatl (the Feathered Serpent), a perfect specimen of humanity was identified with and regaled in the dress and jewels of the god and expected to do a celebratory dance before his demise. If he faltered, he was given a gourd of chocolate, mixed with caked blood from the obsidian knives of earlier sacrifices. This drink was said to provide the courage and joy needed to complete the dance and keep the universe from imploding.

Hundreds of years earlier, the Maya were similarly obsessed with cacao's place in the universe. In the images that adorn their beautiful polychrome cylindrical drinking vessels, the head of the Maize God, who was slain by lords of the underworld, is often depicted hanging amid the pods of cacao trees. According to the *Popol Vuh* (Book of Counsel) of the Quiché Maya of Guatemala, which was partly transcribed by the Spanish from lost hieroglyphic originals dating back millennia, the Maize God was resuscitated when his head was displayed to the daughter of a Mayan ruler. She gave birth to the Hero Twins, Hunahpú and Xbalanqué, who brought the Maize God back to life and were established forever in glory as the sun and moon. Later in the epic, humans were created from maize, sweet fruits, and cacao.

Like the Aztecs, the Maya equated cacao with blood, and in the illustrations on some chocolate vases, gods puncture their necks and spray blood onto cacao pods. In another scene, a blowgunner, who probably represents one of the Hero Twins, hunts a quetzal. As in later Aztec tombs, effigy jars in Maya burials are adorned with cacao pods. Even the later *pochteca* merchants find their match in the Mayan Merchant God, Ek Chuah or God L, who is shown on chocolate vessels approaching a cacao tree surmounted by a quetzal, with another quetzal perched on his backpack. Repeatedly, Mesoamerican societies reveal the intimate connection between maize and cacao, blood and fertility, fantastic birds, dreams and hallucinations, music, and dance.

THEOBROMA FOR THE MASSES

Our discovery of the earliest cacao beverage naturally made me start to think about how such a beverage might have tasted and whether we could re-create it. I again enlisted the help of the adventuresome Sam Calagione and his fellow brewer, Bryan Selders, at Dogfish Head Brewery.

We debated how best to carry off this new venture into the wilds of ancient America. If the first cacao beverages were made from the pulp of the tree's fruit, should we try to import pods from Central America, preferably Honduras, the source of the pottery we had analyzed? Unfortunately, because the fruit is so perishable, this was impossible, barring our traveling there and doing our experiment on site. We had another idea: why not make an alcoholic beverage based on corn and honey, well-known ingredients in the later Mayan and Aztec drinks, and then go a step further and include some additives based on the accounts of the Spanish chroniclers? Although we couldn't get the cacao fruit, we tracked down a purveyor of dark chocolate (Askinosie Chocolate in Missouri) that could provide us with cacao nibs and powder from the premier area of Aztec chocolate production, Soconusco. Its bitterness would be offset by the honey and corn. The herb achiote would provide a special touch of intense red, recalling the Aztecs' preoccupation with human sacrifice. Finally, some chilis would add zest to the concoction, but rather than fiery-hot habañero, we settled on the milder ancho. We might also have tossed in peppery "ear flower" or a hallucinogenic mushroom if they had been available. The fermentation was carried out with a German ale yeast, which is not obtrusive and brings out the flavors of the other ingredients.

We went through several trial runs—closely watched over and filmed by California video companies—and then asked volunteers to taste the results at brewpubs in New York, Philadelphia, and Rehoboth Beach, Delaware.

After some more tweaking, we produced Theobroma, a truly innovative beverage that captures the spirit of the New World, at 9 percent alcohol. In tasting it, one first detects the distinct aroma of dark chocolate; then come the flavors of paprika from the ancho chili, smokiness and earthiness from the achiote, and the aromatic accents of the honey. My only complaint is that the beverage isn't frothy enough to be inhaled, as a Mayan king might have done.

BURNING DOWN THE BREWERY

A remote stronghold in the Andes foothills, only about seventy-five kilometers from the Pacific Ocean in southern Peru, has shed new light on how early American peoples must have searched their environments for sugar-rich resources to make fermented beverages. Cerro Baúl, where the Wari state built a colonial outpost and palace-temple complex on a 2,590-meter summit around A.D. 600, has been dubbed the Masada of the Andes. Native Peruvians are said to have escaped to Cerro Baúl during the Incan conquest, and held out against their enemy, like the Jews in their mountain stronghold resisting the Romans, until their food and water ran out. The Wari survived, unlike the Jews, but around A.D. 1000 the site was abandoned. Whether they had become tired of lugging water up the steep slopes, dealing with the logistical problems of being six hundred kilometers away from their capital, or negotiating with the rival Tiwanaku state, which had insinuated itself into the border area, we do not know: the Wari simply picked up and left. Before leaving, however, they held a grand feast, lubricated by copious amounts of their state beverage, after which their drinking vessels were ceremonially broken and the whole complex put to the torch.

The Wari beverage was made from the fruit or drupes of *Schinus molle*, the Peruvian pepper tree, an ingredient in the Mesoamerican bone-breaker drink. The tree, which grows to fifteen meters in height, is widely dispersed in Peru, along the coast and up to an elevation of 3,600 meters. When its fruit ripens in the summer (January and February), the branches of the tree are bowed down by the weight of the berries. Early humans were probably first attracted to it by the intense red color of the fruit.

The Spanish chroniclers and modern informants describe how a wine was and still is made from the fruit. The berries were heated and soaked in water to release a sugary mash from the pulp, and especially from fleshy pockets on the seed. The mash has a distinct taste of fennel and pepper; the seeds and outer skin are bitter and resinous and need to be strained out. Fermentation proceeded in large, covered jars for several days, the yeast probably being resident on some of the broken berries. Garcilaso de la Vega reported that the beverage "is very good to drink, very tasty, and very healthful"; indeed, the name for the pepper tree in the Peruvian Quechua language translates as "tree of life." In areas where there was already an appreciation of the value of mixing different ingredients in a fermented beverage, such as Mexico, the fruit of the pepper tree was soon being combined with cornstalk and cactus juices and maize malt.

Although the Spanish friars denigrated native beverages as the work of the devil, they were so enthusiastic about *Schinus molle* that they transplanted it throughout the Pacific rim. Their goal was to produce a competitor to black pepper (*Piper nigrum*), produced in the Dutch East Indies and highly prized, and to use the tree's resinous oils for warding off insects, treating disease, producing gums and dyes, and yielding a decay-resistant lumber.

At Cerro Baúl, the Wari established the largest known production facility in the Americas for making a fermented beverage. The intended product was *Schinus molle* wine, not corn *chicha* or an elite chocolate beverage. In a trapezoid building, adjacent to the palace, a series of rooms were devoted to milling tubers and chili peppers, perhaps additives to the beverage; heating the mash in twelve large vats; and fermenting the beverage in gourd containers. Thousands of pepper-tree seeds and stems were found around the hearths for heating the vats, suggesting that the berries were cleaned and sieved from the mash here. Each vat had a capacity of 150 liters; altogether some 1,800 liters of the wine could be prepared at one time. Based on field experiments by David J. Goldstein and Robin Coleman, about four thousand berries, or the fruit from several trees, are needed for twenty liters of the wine, so more than a hundred trees would have had to be harvested for the final celebration. Special shawl pins (*tupu*), worn only by women, were found scattered through the facility, implying once again that the preparation of the beverage was a woman's job.

And drink they did. In the patio in front of the large industrial complex, twenty-eight high-status *kero*s (see plate 9) were found. There were seven sets of four vessels each, decorated with elite white-and-black designs or displaying the supreme Front-Facing God of the Wari, with pronounced eyes and a high headdress. The *kero*s were graduated in size from thirty milliliters to more than a liter, probably reflecting the social status of the drinkers; the "King Midas feast" celebrants were also distinguished by the size of their drinking vessels (see chapter 5). When the brewery or beer hall, according to the excavators' terminology, had been set ablaze, the twenty-eight Wari lords apparently threw their *keros,* in a final act of dedication, into the fire. Six shell and stone necklaces were thrown on to the smoldering heap for good measure.

The Wari fermented beverage was conspicuously unlike the preeminent beverage of ancient Peru, corn *chicha.* If any maize was added to the *S. molle* wine, the quantity was trivial: the cereal constituted less than 1 percent of the total archaeobotanical materials recovered from the site, including the winemaking facility.

The final rites for the colony atop Cerro Baúl were repeated in the palace. In an interior patio, food remains suggest that the inhabitants enjoyed an extraordinary "last supper": vizcacha (Andean hare), venison, llama or alpaca, and no fewer than ten species of fish (including anchovy, sardine, herring, silverside, flying fish, and tuna). The site was, of course, not far from the Pacific, but these leftovers suggest that the inhabitants of the site, like those of Monte Verde, traced their origins to the sea. Other bones from the palace—of the Andean condor, a flycatcher, and a pygmy owl—need not have been part of the repast: these are very rare birds and might instead have conveyed some ritual significance. More than thirty serving vessels, but no *keros,* were smashed on the floor of the patio before the building was burned down.

Another ceremony by fire was carried out in an annex to one of the temples, close to the palace. Together with burials of an infant and adolescent below its floor, one room produced a most unusual artifact: the body of a drum painted with stylized birds and naked dancers, whose frontal positions and high headdresses were reminiscent of the Front-Facing God. Drums, along with percussion instruments, pan pipes, flutes, and trumpets, were an essential part of shamanistic ceremonies throughout the Americas from an early date. For example, at the late Archaic city-state of Caral on the Pacific coast of Peru, dated between 3000 and 1800 B.C., thirty-two flutes of pelican wing bones were found hidden in a crevice of the main temple, probably an offering after a particularly auspicious ceremony.

The *S. molle* wine must have been a cultural and ethnic marker of great importance among the Wari. Recently, a winemaking facility similar to the one at Cerro Baúl was uncovered in the heartland of the Wari at Conchopata, several hundred kilometers to the north. A nonelite household winery was also found a short distance downriver from Conchopata at La

Yaral, inhabited by the Chiribaya, who continued the Wari tradition. In both buildings, archaeobotanical remains of *S. molle* were strewn in the vicinity of hearths and heating vats.

Making a peppery wine, transforming a minuscule mountain grass into the world's most prolific source of alcohol, and fashioning elaborate drinks from cacao pods and beans are just a few examples of early Americans' ingenuity in crafting fermented beverages—a foretaste of the future, you might say. In other parts of the Americas, a range of other ingredients were used, some of them still popular today.

In Amazonia, manioc or cassava (*Manihot esculenta,* also known as yuca and arrowroot) has been a favorite ingredient for at least six thousand years. A beer can be prepared from the thick roots of the plant by chewing them and releasing their sweet juices or converting their starch to sugar (as with maize stalks and kernels). Saliva was believed to have a magical power that was conveyed to the brew, causing it to bubble wildly and turn into a potent beverage. The drink was essential to feasts of all kinds—for accessing the ancestral realm, celebrating a victory, marking rites of passage, and observing astronomical cycles.

Humans elsewhere in South America—in the mountains and pampas and along the coasts—had many other fermentable and mind-altering natural products to choose from. Sugar-rich fruits, which could be easily plucked from a tree, were probably exploited first. The peach palm (*Bactris gasipaes*) is one example: its sap and pinkish fruit pulp make a delicious, mildly alcoholic drink. Chonta and coyol palms, wild pineapple (*Ananas bracteatus*), the plumlike *Gourliea decorticans,* cacti (including *Opuntia tuna* and the saguaro), and *Tizyphus mistol,* which looks like a luscious grape, were among a host of other possibilities. The drinks could be mixed with more powerful herbs, such as ground tobacco or coca leaves; the seeds of angel's trumpet (*Brugmansia* spp.); a decoction of San Pedro cactus or seed pods of the yopo or cebil tree (*Anadenanthera* spp.), rich in indoxyl compounds; or a tea made from ayahuasca (literally "vine of the soul"; *Banisteriopsis* spp.), which produces visual hallucinations and today is the focus of a rapidly expanding shamanistic New Age religion.

Farther north in Central America and southern Mexico, hog plums (*Spondias* spp.), cherrylike *Prunus capuli,* the prickly custard apple or guanabana

(*Annona muricata*), pineapples, coyol and corozo palms, cashew, and wild banana are some of the many fruits that were made into wine. Sweet potatoes and manioc were chewed to make beer. In the Yucatán and the Chiapas highlands, a mead was fermented from the native honey. The Lacandón Maya of Chiapas prepared theirs in quantity in hollowed-out logs shaped like canoes, to which the bark of one particular tree, the balché (*Lonchocarpus longistylus*), was added. A Spanish informant described it as "milk white, sour to the smell, and at first very disagreeable to the taste." Of course, an alcoholic beverage could also be spiked with a hallucinogenic drug derived from the seeds of morning glory (*Ipomoea* and *Turbina* spp.) or the psilocybin mushroom.

Ingredients for fermented beverages become scarcer as one moves up into the cactus regions of northern Mexico and the southwestern United States. There is some evidence for the use of elderberry, manzanita, and wild grape to make wine in the more temperate regions along the Pacific coast; in the interior, fermented beverages made from the fruits of agave, prickly pear, organ-pipe and other cacti, and especially mesquite pods, with 25 to 30 percent glucose in their pulp, were well entrenched from an early date. Rainmaking ceremonies centered on wine made from the giant saguaro were the most important festivals of the year for the Tohono O'odham people of the Sonoran Desert. Women matured the wine underground and encouraged it by repeating the refrain: "Do you ferment and let us be beautifully drunk." Two nights of singing, dancing, and carousing were intended to encourage rain clouds to form and drop their life-engendering liquid.

North and east of central Arizona, however, alcoholic beverages are mysteriously absent from the archaeological and ethnographic record. As a seventeenth-century French missionary, Gabriel Sagard, observed: "Our savages, in their feasts, are, thank God, free from such misfortune, for they use neither wine, beer nor cider; if any one among them asks for a drink, which very rarely happens, he is offered fresh water" (Havard 1896: 33).

When the Vikings first visited North America a thousand years ago, they marveled at the grapevines festooning the trees, so much so that they called the new land "Vinland." The sobriquet was appropriate: except for China, more species of wild grape (twenty to twenty-five) are found in North America than anywhere else in the world, and some have a high sugar content. Nevertheless, except for the occasional grapeseed find, no decisive archaeological or chemical evidence has yet been discovered to demonstrate that any native peoples collected the wild grape for food, let alone domesticated the plant or made wine from its fruit. Even when extensive tracts of forests were cleared around A.D. 800 to grow maize in the American heartland and eventually all the way to the eastern seaboard, it was not used to make corn *chicha.*

What accounts for this absence of alcohol, so much at odds with the rest of the Americas? Perhaps the Aztec aversion to excessive drinking of alcoholic beverages (at least among the general populace), already evident in their aboriginal home in northwestern Mexico, was shared by some of their neighbors. The Pueblo people, for example, grew maize and were surrounded by groups who drank corn *chicha,* but they eschewed the beverage (unless ongoing analyses from Chaco Canyon in New Mexico are borne out). Except for tobacco, they also avoided other drugs, including the omnipresent mescal beans (*Sophora secundiflora*) and roots of *Datura stramonium* (also known as jimsonweed or thorn apple).

Yet the Pueblo people did play flutes and drums at Pecos Pueblo, just east of Santa Fe, and we know such instruments are often tied to celebrations with alcoholic beverages in other parts of the world. In the period between about A.D. 1200 and 1600, what are described as "ceremonial caches" of as many as twelve bird-bone flutes were deposited in rooms and burials of the large complex. Like the many flutes from the Old World, dating as far back as 35,000 B.P., most of those from Pecos were made from a specific bone: the forewing (ulna) of the whooping crane, golden eagle, and red-tailed hawk (and in one case a turkey leg bone). The four or five holes of the Pecos flutes had been carefully drilled, using guidelines, as elsewhere. Could these flutes, so similar to those from Jiahu (see chapter 2), hark back to the time that the first Americans crossed over from East Asia?

It could be that tobacco (*Nicotiana* spp.), which grows everywhere in the Americas and which Native Americans used from an early date as their principal means of communicating with the gods and as a social lubricant, filled the niche that alcoholic beverages occupied in other cultures. Tobacco was chewed and sucked, given as an enema, smoked from long pipes in the shapes of eagles and condors and decorated with their feathers, and snorted through bird bones or from trays from which the animal totem stared back at the reveler. Tobacco smoke was viewed as the "proper food of the gods," and as it ascended to the heavens, like a bird, a shamanistic priest or medicine man was transported into an ecstatic state by flooding his body and brain with nicotine.

Grapes and maize were only part of the natural bounty that North Americans could have exploited for making a fermented beverage if they had been so inclined. Many species of trees—maple, box elder, white walnut, and birch—produce a sugary sap in the spring, which can be tapped by piercing the outer bark. The Indians concentrated the resulting liquid by dropping red-hot stones into a bark or wood vessel full of the sap, or by repeatedly freezing it and removing the ice. The syrup would have been an ideal starting material for an alcoholic beverage, but the Native Americans apparently used it only as a sweetener and medicine.

The question of why the North American natives lived such a teetotaling existence, when other New World peoples quaffed quantities of alcoholic beverages, can be approached in another way. If the first Americans all trace their ancestry back to northern and central Siberia, then a fermented-beverage tradition might well have been brought across Beringia, down the coast, and into the interior. But Siberia, being singularly short on high-sugar resources, appears to have lacked such a tradition.

In place of any alcoholic beverage, the Siberian peoples engaged in shamanistic practices based on the hallucinogenic fly agaric mushroom (*Amanita muscaria*). When European explorers finally braved the frigid tundra of Siberia, beginning in the mid-seventeenth century, they recorded how the shaman often dressed in a deer costume with antlers, like the Palaeolithic creature depicted in Les Trois Frères cave (see chapter 1). After consuming the mushroom, he would beat on a large drum, whose monotonous repetition reinforced the effects of the active hallucinogenic compounds (ibotenic acid and muscimole) and took him into the ancestral dreamtime. The mushroom was administered in various ways. Women might roll dried and diced pieces around in their mouths to make quids that were presented to the shaman. The fungus might be decocted and mixed with berry juice. The shaman might even consume the mushroom secondhand by drinking the urine of a deer or human who had already ingested it. The active agents, which are not metabolized by the mammalian body, can be recycled, as it were.

Fortunately for the early human migrants from Siberia, *A. muscaria* also grows in North America. In the Mackenzie Mountains of northwestern Canada and along the shores of Lake Superior in Michigan, Athabascan and Ojibwa (Ahnishinaubeg) people still use the mushroom in ceremonies very similar to those of the Siberian shamanistic cults. Could these be the remnants of Ice Age traditions, passed down from generation to generation since humans first entered the New World? If so, then as they traveled farther south, out of the range of this hallucinogenic mushroom, they had all the more reason to begin experimenting with plants never before encountered—teosinte, cacti, and fruits like cacao—and converting them into alternative mind-bending fermented beverages.

EIGHT

AFRICA SERVES UP ITS MEADS, WINES, AND BEERS

OUR EXPLORATION OF FERMENTED BEVERAGES on planet Earth brings us full circle back to Africa. This is where our forebears of one hundred thousand years ago first spread out from the Great Rift Valley to other parts of the continent and then across the Sinai land bridge or the Bab el-Mandeb to Asia, eventually opening themselves up to the whole world.

Many Westerners imagine Africa as a continent of impenetrable jungles, lush grasslands, rolling sand dunes, and the occasional snow-capped mountain like Kilimanjaro. Its peoples present a bewildering picture of diverse cultures and languages. My initial impression of Africa was little different: I was struck by its awesomeness, even dread, especially after reading Joseph Conrad's *Heart of Darkness*. His novella, inspired by a steamboat trip up the Congo River in his early youth, is saturated with the darkest images of man and nature. The river is likened to a huge, sinister snake, which takes the narrator into an unfathomable world of vegetation and humanity gone wild, with the incessant pounding of drums, accentuated periodically by hideous screams in the night. It creates an impression of traveling back to a prehistoric Earth, to a primeval forest inhabited by the earliest humans. Savage hunters, clad only in leopard skins or sporting antelope horns on their heads, and equally magnificent women, adorned in glittering metal jewelry and vivid attire, face the wilderness with unbridled pride and mystery. Shriveled human heads, hanging from poles, are no less terrifying than the moral abyss of the Western ivory hunters. This existential and natural quagmire of Conrad's Africa, to which T. S. Eliot fittingly refers in the epigraph of his poem "The Hollow Men," seems to swallow up everything in its wake.

Many of us still harbor similar sentiments about Africa today, which are reinforced when we hear of the scourges of AIDS and other diseases, families on the edge of starvation, and Tutsis and Hutus killing one another in Rwanda and Burundi. Closer examination, however, reveals another Africa. Ebullient strains can be heard in its uplifting music and detected in its mesmerizing dances and colorful ceremonies. Its people show a facility for language, as might be expected for the continent that gave rise to our species: some two thousand distinct languages are spoken, according to a recent estimate. Pottery was likely independently invented here around 6000 B.C., at about the same time as in the Near East. Native cereals (e.g., finger and bulrush millets, fonio, and teff) and tubers (yam and nut grass) were cultivated about the same time and eventually domesticated. Many of these advances were probably fueled by a desire for alcoholic beverages. Yet our "first home" in sub-Saharan Africa, which displays so much human ingenuity, was ironically cut off from the outside world for millennia by geographic barriers.

YELLOW GOLD

Until the domestication of the camel made it possible for humans to cross large tracts of desert, the main route in and out of Africa was along the Nile River, the longest river in the world, which traverses 6,700 kilometers, half the length of the continent. Bordered by vast stretches of desert today, the verdant ribbons of the White and the Blue Nile wend their way from their headwaters in the Great Rift Valley and the highlands of

---

Map 4. Africa. The basic ingredients of fermented beverages in the "homeland" of humanity included honey (especially in the Great Rift Valley), barley and wheat (especially in the Nile River Valley), sorghum and millet (especially in the Sahel and Sahara Desert), palm sap, and many other fruits (e.g., *Ziziphus*), root crops, and grasses. These drinks were often mixed with "medicinal" herbs, tree resins, and other additives (including the incense tree and iboga shrub). Some indigenous cereals were probably domesticated as early as the Neolithic period. Ideas and technology about making fermented beverages (e.g., mashing installations for grains in Egypt and Burkina Faso) flowed between the Nile River and West Africa.

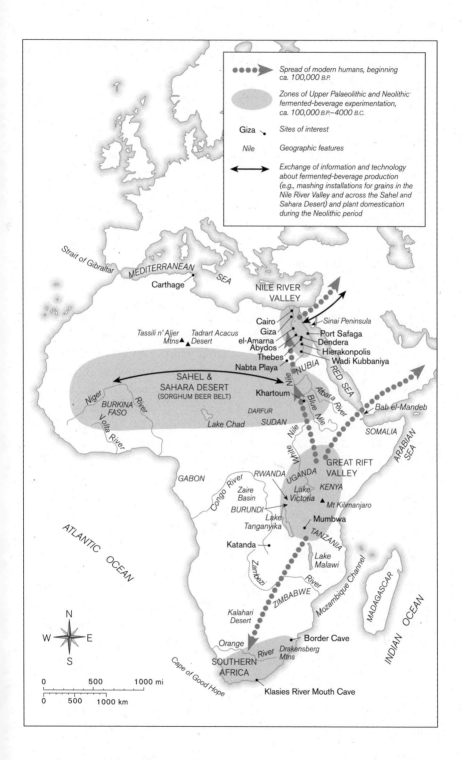

Spread of modern humans, beginning ca. 100,000 B.P.

Zones of Upper Palaeolithic and Neolithic fermented-beverage experimentation, ca. 100,000 B.P.–4000 B.C.

Giza — Sites of interest

Nile — Geographic features

Exchange of information and technology about fermented-beverage production (e.g., mashing installations for grains in the Nile River Valley and across the Sahel and Sahara Desert) and plant domestication during the Neolithic period

Strait of Gibraltar

MEDITERRANEAN SEA

Carthage

NILE RIVER VALLEY

Sinai Peninsula

Cairo
Giza
el-Amarna
Abydos
Thebes
Nabta Playa

Port Safaga
Dendera
Hierakonpolis
Wadi Kubbaniya

Tassili n' Ajjer Mtns

Tadrart Acacus Desert

NUBIA

RED SEA

SAHEL & SAHARA DESERT (SORGHUM BEER BELT)

Khartoum

Atbara River

Bab el-Mandeb

Niger River

BURKINA FASO

Volta River

Blue Nile

DARFUR

Lake Chad

SUDAN

SOMALIA

ARABIAN SEA

GABON

Congo River

RWANDA

UGANDA

Zaire Basin

BURUNDI

Lake Tanganyika

Lake Victoria

KENYA

Mt Kilimanjaro

GREAT RIFT VALLEY

Mumbwa

Katanda

TANZANIA

White Nile

Nile

ATLANTIC OCEAN

Zambezi

Lake Malawi

River

ZIMBABWE

Mozambique Channel

MADAGASCAR

INDIAN OCEAN

Kalahari Desert

Border Cave

Orange River

Drakensberg Mtns

Cape of Good Hope

SOUTHERN AFRICA

Klasies River Mouth Cave

N
W   E
S

0   500   1000 mi

0   500   1000 km

Ethiopia, with their high concentrations of hominid and early human fossil remains, to Khartoum, where the rivers meet. From here, the Nile River proper flows through Egypt to the Mediterranean Sea.

Ethiopia's national fermented beverage, *tej* or *t'edj*, is a kind of liquid gold and a fitting counterpart to the solid metal that was exploited here in antiquity. According to the Roman geographer Strabo in his *Geography* (16.4.17), this drink of the nomadic peoples then inhabiting the land, the Troglodytes ("cave dwellers"), was made from honey and consumed exclusively by the ruler and his retinue. Very likely the honey beverage, which Europeans first encountered when they began exploring Ethiopia and was still being served to Emperor Haile Selassie in the early twentieth century, followed a recipe going back thousands of years. By mixing five or six parts water with one part honey, a perfect acidic medium is established for the activation of *Saccharomyces cerevisiae* yeast, already present in honey. As the liquid ferments for two or three weeks in a gourd or pottery jar, much of the sugar is consumed and excreted as alcohol and carbon dioxide by the microorganisms, to yield a beverage with 8–13 percent alcohol.

This fermented honey beverage or mead was not restricted to Ethiopia. Many African peoples have been drinking some variation of a fermented honey beverage for a very long time throughout the continent. The strongest versions have been reported from the Rift Valley, where added fruit (e.g., of the sausage tree, *Kigellia africana,* and tamarind), with additional yeast to spur an extended fermentation, boosted the alcohol concentration.

Sub-Saharan Africa is a honey-eater's and mead-drinker's paradise. The familiar European honeybee (*Apis mellifera*) makes its home here, but some of the subspecies are more aggressive than their European relatives, which accounts for the sensational name "killer bees" for Africanized crosses between the two populations. Native peoples seem to have been undeterred by the bees' reputation for ferocity. For example, the Mbuti pygmy peoples of central Africa would set aside everything else to collect honey from a beehive. They scaled high trees with improvised liana ropes to reach the hive; once at the nest, they would plunge their arms deep within it and immediately cram as much as they could of the comb, dripping with honey, into their mouths. The pleasure they derived from this indulgence apparently made up for the hundreds of bee stings they sustained. In southern Sudan, the Bviri honey hunters go naked, as the bees can get caught in clothing and sting later.

Even with the obvious deterrent, many animals readily raid beehives. The honey badger or ratel, which inhabits sub-Saharan Africa, at certain times eats nothing but honey. Its sharp eyesight enables it to follow airborne bees back to their hive. The ratel then simply tears the hive apart to devour its contents; sometimes it first drives out or asphyxiates the bees by rubbing an anal secretion around the hive's entrance.

Among African hominids, the chimpanzee, which shares 99 percent of our genome, most ingeniously hunts and exploits beehives. Chimpanzees have been observed cooperating at the task, with one chimp prying open a hive with a stick while another pulls out the honeycomb. An eleven-year-old female chimp in Zaire was extraordinarily enterprising in her use of tools: she used two thick, chisel-like branches to ream a hole into the hive, then pierced the wax layer protecting the honey storage compartment with a sharp-ended stick, and finally swished a long, flexible vine around inside the nest for ten minutes, collecting as much honey as possible. Simian bystanders threw screaming fits while the female gathered her feast, but she treated them to an occasional piece of comb, still oozing honey, which she tossed to the ground. The Belanda-Biri tribe of southern Sudan described the chimpanzees in their district as "great honey thieves."

Humans undoubtedly took some cues from animals to perfect their beehive-raiding techniques. They also immortalized the activity in spectacular depictions of honey hunting, such as those engraved and painted on rock faces and boulders in South Africa and Zimbabwe over millennia. Although difficult to date precisely, they represent the enduring record of native peoples, including the San (Bushmen). A typical scene shows someone climbing a flimsy-looking liana ladder to a single enormous hive or cluster of hives suspended under cliff ledges. Swarms of enraged bees encircle the hives and the plundering humans.

One evocative painting in the Matopo Hills of Zimbabwe, which reputedly dates from as early as 8000 B.C., shows the hunter perched on one knee on a ledge, as he or she (the person has long hair pinned at the back, perhaps with a bird's feather) holds out what looks like a mass of smoking vegetation to a cluster of hives. Bees are seen leaving the hives. Smoking out the bees was (and remains) a technique for subduing a bee colony before removing the honey. In Zimbabwe and other parts of sub-Saharan Africa more recently, the use of specific plants and fungi with narcotic properties for this purpose has been documented (e.g., *Spirostachys africana,* a tree that exudes a toxic latex, and the giant puffball fungus). Some of the hives targeted by the ancient Matopo Hills hunter have darker rear sections behind lighter areas marked with small dots, likely a depiction of brood cells at the front of the hive, separated from the darker honeycombs that provide their food.

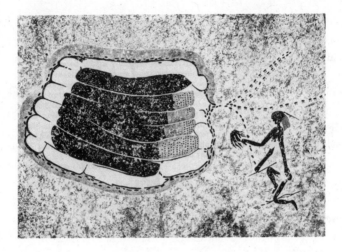

Figure 22. A rock painting in the Matopo Hills of Zimbabwe, dating possibly as early as 8000 B.C., showing a befeathered, long-haired honey hunter smoking out a hive of bees on a ledge. The hairstyle is similar to that of the central Saharan sorghum-beer drinkers (see plate 10). After H. Pager, 1973, "Rock Paintings in Southern Africa Showing Bees and Honey Gathering," *Bee World* 54(2): Register ZW-001.

The Matopo paintings include numerous concentric arcs, which have been interpreted as a view of a beehive from below, its honeycombs stacked one upon another, hanging from a cliff cavity. A rock painting in the Drakensberg area of South Africa shows a swarm of bees moving in and around a set of five such curves. This geometric figure has been described as an entoptic phenomenon (see chapter 1) that the brain generates in the first stage of a mind-altering experience, such as a shamanistic trance state. As common motifs of rock art around the world, such phenomena could have been inspired by consuming an alcoholic beverage or plant hallucinogen or by sensory deprivation or overload.

A closer look at African rock art has convinced investigators that their meaning extends beyond aesthetic enjoyment to address spiritual and religious concerns. As in the Stone Age caves of Europe, handprints are common, as are strange animal-headed figures and fantastic creatures (see chapter 1). Among the latter, images that may represent mother goddesses or rainmaking animals in San mythology are sometimes shown mobbed by bees: blood streams from the noses of the animals, and dancers leap and somersault. Figures that merge into crevices and cracks in the rock suggest that the artwork paralleled the changes occurring in the mind, aiding the shaman's access to another realm.

According to the San, bees provide power for taming the animal world and ensuring rain. When honey is in season—major flows occur once or twice a year—men go out on week-long expeditions. They collect as many as ten nests in a day, which can yield five to thirty kilograms of honey. The hives are often located by following bees from a watering hole back to their nests and observing their minute droppings as they fly. An amazing symbiotic relationship also developed between the hunters and the honeyguide bird (*Indicator indicator*). As its name implies, the bird can locate a beehive and steer a human or other mammal to it by attracting attention to itself: it lands on a nearby, conspicuous perch, performs a distinctive song, and flies a short distance while displaying its outer white tail feathers. Step by step, the bird leads its "partner in crime" on a beeline for the hive. The bird cannot open up the hive without the partner's help, and the partner reaches the sweet reward much sooner with the bird's assistance. By imitating the honeyguide's call and luring the bird, a human can save several hours of honey hunting. Shamanistic "spiritual flight" might well have taken a cue from the honeyguide's close association with the bees.

Today, a hunting party's return to the camp or village with honey is a cause for great celebration. Perhaps, in Palaeolithic times, the hunters brought back not only honey but also on occasion an animal skin or gourd full of mead. Rainwater might have filled the nest of a fallen tree and fermented the honey, as envisioned by the Palaeolithic hypothesis (see chapter 1). One of the crucial requirements in making mead is a relatively airtight container, and the hive itself, lined with propolis gums and resins by the bees, met this need. Eventually, an enterprising human might have thought of making mead in a more controlled fashion in a leather bag, gourd, or bark container. The honey-hunting scenes of eastern Spain, which closely resemble the African depictions and are approximately contemporaneous (ca. 8000–2000 B.C.), sometimes show the hunter holding such a vessel, precariously balanced on a rope ladder beside a hive and reaching inside to fill the vessel.

The probable importance of mead among early hominids is reflected in its central role in many religious and social ceremonies throughout sub-Saharan Africa. Today among the Kikuyu people of Kenya, for example, a prospective suitor is expected to offer twenty liters of mead to his future father-in-law as a bride price. Generally made by men (contrary to the general rule that beverage making was a woman's job), mead was regularly drunk by very old men: it was seen as one of the benefits of growing old and a recognition of the closeness of the elderly to the ancestors. Another group in Kenya with different origins and leading a pastoral way of life, the Masai, celebrate the circumcision of young boys with a feast among adult near relatives and neighbors at which mead and meat are served; the young males, however, are expected to drink only cow's blood and milk. When the young teenagers are ready to live in separate households, the older family members are plied with mead to keep them in good humor and secure their blessings. The teenagers are then allowed to drink a horn of blood and mead. When it comes time to marry, not only are the elders satiated with mead, but a sacrificial ox is first made drunk, then slaughtered. The goodwill of the elders is conveyed by their spraying mead onto the assembled group. There is hardly any Masai ceremony—whether an inheritance, funeral, impending crisis, removal of a curse, expiation for a sin, or marriage—that cannot be enhanced by pouring out or sprinkling mead on the ground or formally presenting it to the aggrieved or petitioned party.

We must be cautious, however, in too easily transposing current practice to a period in the distant past. Honey was the most concentrated source of sugar available to early humankind; when eaten as honeycomb filled with brood, its protein and nutritional content exceed those of meat. As other fermented beverages made from grains and roots became popular, honey, which had always been in short supply, might have been used more as a sweetener than as a source of mead. Similar developments can be traced in the Near East and China. Even in Europe north of the Alps, which trailed Asia in technological development, mead gradually lost its grip on the popular imagination as the supreme beverage of gods and kings and was eventually displaced by wine, beer, and, later yet, distilled beverages.

Ancient Egypt serves as a case study for tracing how honey and mead could shift in symbolic and social value. Located in the northeastern part of the continent and serving as the gateway to western Asia, Egypt is the source of our earliest depictions of beekeeping and the processing of honey from anywhere in the world. The grandiose sun temple of Pharaoh Neuserre of Dynasty 5, ca. 2400 B.C., at Abu Ghurab, just upriver from Cairo and the Great Pyramids, sets the pattern for the next two thousand years. A long, covered corridor, lined with finely painted reliefs of the flora and fauna that the sun god Re had bestowed on the land of the Nile, led from the king's pyramid to his funerary temple close to the river. There, in a courtyard open to the sky and marked by an obelisk to the radiant sun orb, his death was commemorated with offerings of oxen and other royal fare. Before the priests emerged into daylight from the corridor, they would have seen the careful rendering of the hieroglyph for the honeybee, showing the Egyptian subspecies (*larmarckii*) in profile. They would also have gazed on an elaborate scene that showed very sophisticated beekeeping. One worker in the scene apparently blows smoke from a container into the ends of nine sun-baked clay beehives to drive the bees out. Other workers transfer the honey to large basins and tall jars, which are then sealed shut.

Later scenes, especially from the New Kingdom and the Late Dynastic period, follow a similar pattern. In the tomb of the vizier Rekhmire at Thebes, which is also well known for its winemaking fresco, the hives are constructed like those shown in the tomb of Neuserre. Wisps of smoke leap from bowls in the direction of the hives, and round cakes of honeycomb are being removed and stacked. Other workers pour honey into jars and containers, made by placing two large bowls mouth to mouth, and seal them with clay.

It is not known how early the ancient Egyptians adopted this method of beekeeping, nor whether they were influenced by practices in the Levant or areas to the south of Egypt, where wild beehives are abundant. Evidence for gigantic stacks of artificial hives have thus far been discovered at only one site in the Middle East—Tel Rehov in the northern Jordan Valley—but its relatively late date, around 900 B.C., does not help us to decide whether this mode of beekeeping was an Egyptian innovation. Ancient beehive complexes have not been discovered in Egypt itself or elsewhere in Africa. Much later, sub-Saharan African peoples did make long cylinders, similar in shape to those of ancient Egypt, out of bark, plant leaves, woven reeds, gourds, and sometimes clay; these hives, however, were not stacked up but hoisted high into trees and dispersed widely. One thing is clear: the symbol of the bee was supremely important in ancient Egypt from the dawn of its dynastic history, ca. 3100 B.C., when Narmer or Menes, the first pharaoh of the united country, chose the honeybee (Egyptian *hit*) hieroglyph to represent his conquest of Lower Egypt and the unification of the country. This hieroglyph preceded the pharaoh's name in the royal titulary, a practice that continued until the demise of the Late Kingdom at the hands of Alexander the Great in 332 B.C. The close and enduring association of bee and pharaoh points to even earlier prehistoric developments, which would account for the precociousness of the industry.

The quantities of honey produced by ancient Egyptian beekeepers are staggering. If we take one of the New Kingdom pharaohs, Ramesses III, at his word, he offered fifteen tons of honey to the god of the Nile. Inscriptions describe different grades of honey: for example, a light-colored "pure" variety and a darker, reddish blend from the desert. Pollen analyses of ancient samples have shown that the honey came from a variety of domesticated and wild flowers and trees, including cloverlike lucerne and other desert plants, the persea or Egyptian avocado tree (*Mimusops schimperi*), the fragrant balanos oil tree, clover, currant, flax, marjoram, rose, and many more. Among the analyzed samples, a New Kingdom bowl, similar to those illustrated in frescoes of the period, is especially noteworthy: it contained a large piece of well-preserved honeycomb.

One issue that likely challenged early Egyptian beekeepers was how to keep their bees busy throughout the flowering season, which began earlier in the hotter climes of the south and progressed to the more temperate north. A river that flowed in the same direction provided a ready solution. As a French traveler reported in the eighteenth century, the hives were placed on boats, which were moored at one locale after another. The bees were not choosy about their pollen sources, and by the end of the trip, the honey could be sold in Cairo. Because the Nile was the principal means of transport in antiquity (see chapter 6)—whether the cargo was granite columns for temples or the exotic goods coming from Punt, thought to be located in Somalia or Ethiopia—this solution probably dawned on an entrepreneurial beekeeper who had nautical contacts. Moving bees by boat would have been a much more efficient method than that used today by my uncle, a beekeeper in South Dakota, who has to move his hives overland in trucks from field to field and as far as Texas or California for overwintering.

The great antiquity of honey production in Egypt raises the question of whether mead was made from all this honey. My thorough search of the voluminous ancient Egyptian literature, as well as artistic and archaeological materials of all kinds, came up empty. The ancient Egyptians had many other uses for honey, among them as a bactericide and salve for wounds, an internal medicine, a sweetener, an ingredient in cosmetics, and a component of offerings. So why was it not made into mead, one of the easiest beverages to produce and likely one of the first beverages enjoyed by our ancestors millennia ago?

The most likely explanation for the notable absence of mead in ancient Egypt is that other alcoholic beverages were already predominant there by ca. 3000 B.C. and captured the imagination, palates, and pocketbooks of kings and peasants. We have already seen how a Dynasty 0 pharaoh, Scorpion I, was captivated by grape wine (see chapter 6). Beers could be made in quantity from wheat and barley, which flourished in the Nile floodplains and were much cheaper and easier to obtain than precious honey. Perhaps ancient Egyptian tastes had shifted from sweet to sour, just as Americans moved away from the ultrasweet jug wines and pink Zinfandels of the 1970s and '80s to today's drier varieties. Whatever the explanation, honey went to making specialty items and for ceremonial use during historical times in Egypt.

A GRUELLISH BEVERAGE

Egypt launched its royal winemaking industry around 3000 B.C. Because wild wheat, barley, and sorghum grew in the Nile Valley, beer making could have begun even earlier. Excavation of a transitional Early to Late Predynastic site in Upper Egypt at Hierakonpolis, where the famous Narmer palette commemorating the union of the country was discovered, suggests that the brewing of beer was underway by at least 3500 to 3400 B.C. Where the Wadi Abul Suffian opens onto the Nile alluvium at Hierakonpolis, archaeological excavation during the 1970s and 1980s by a team from the University of South Carolina revealed a curious complex of structures. On a built-up platform three to four meters in diameter, Jeremy Geller uncovered six "firing pits," which he interpreted as parts of a large oven for baking bread. Six large, wide-mouthed, conical vats were found on another platform nearby, apparently freestanding and surrounded by carbonized debris. A thick black residue coated their interiors, gradually tapering off and disappearing toward the bottom of the nearly meter-high vessels. Quite possibly the residue ended where a bowl had once been inserted at the bottom of the jar, as suggested by comparisons to similar facilities at other sites.

Analyses of the Hierakonpolis vat residue by Yordan Popov of the Ferrosilicon factory in Edfu on the upper Nile and by the Archaeobotany Laboratory of Cairo University yielded intriguing results. Popov claimed to have detected a very high-sugar, caramelized product smelling like burnt brandy. The Cairo laboratory reported that more than a quarter of the residue was composed of preserved sugars, organic acids (including malic, succinic, lactic, and tartaric) and amino acids; the remainder was sand and pottery debris. The laboratory also noted intact grains and other remnants of domesticated emmer wheat and barley, fragments of date-fruit endocarp (*Phoenix dactylifera*), and domesticated grape pips embedded in the residue. A colleague of mine at the Penn Museum, the archaeobotanist Naomi Miller, confirmed the presence of emmer wheat, but did not observe any domesticated grape in the limited material that she examined. If the Cairo University's finding holds up, it would push the earliest grape remains from Egypt, which must have been imported from the Levant, back another two hundred years. Geller himself expressed some doubts about the finding: he wrote that "due to deflation and disturbance from burrowing insects, their [the dates' and, by inference, also the grapeseeds'] association with the vats cannot yet be asserted beyond doubt."

Geller went on to make some telling comparisons with similar vat installations at other Predynastic sites in Upper Egypt, which were excavated at the end of the nineteenth century and the beginning of the twentieth century. At Abydos, which eventually became the religious capital of the country, T. Eric Peet and W. L. S. Loat found eight complexes, of which the largest had thirty-five vats in two parallel lines of seventeen and eighteen vessels, each supported by long, upright firebricks around the outside. The staggered arrangement of the vats enabled alternating stoking holes for fuel to be built into the sidewalls that connected the vats. A roof and end walls enclosed the firing chamber surrounding the vessels, leaving the vats open to the air. A bowl, probably used to collect yeasty sediments, had been placed at the bottom of each jar, where lumps of black material similar to the Hierakonpolis residues were recovered. This residue, which had probably spalled off the inside of the vats, was described as carbonized, with whole grains of wheat in its matrix. At nearby Mahasna, John Garstang discovered a single vat; its features are nearly identical to those of the other installations, except that short clay bars were also used to buttress the bottom of the vessel. J. E. Quibell reported another badly damaged vat at Ballas, just a short distance farther downstream from Mahasna.

The excavators at each site ruled out the possibility that the vats were used in the Predynastic preparation of beer, as the pottery wares were too porous. However, a thin layer of clay had been applied to the vessels' interiors, and the buildup of a thick deposit on their interiors is suggestive of heating some kind of sugar-rich liquid. If the vessels were used to parch grain, as the renowned archaeologist W. M. Flinders Petrie proposed, then how had such a uniform residue formed?

Geller at first argued that the Hierakonpolis vat installation was used for preparing a malt. This suggestion was in keeping with Petrie's proposal because malt often goes through a final roasting. Later Geller revised his view and thought it more likely that the vats were used to mash the malt. In mashing, low heat (66–68°C) is applied to the liquefied malt (for approximately one hour in a modern microbrewing facility, but up to three days by traditional African methods), to speed up the conversion of starches to sugars. If the temperature exceeds 70°C, the diastase enzymes may be destroyed. Because the installations clearly seem to have been intended to achieve a moderate heat, and both wheat and barley grains have been found in the congealed interior residues, this interpretation is in accord with the facts and beer making practice. If the vessels were used over and over again, one might expect a caramelized deposit to build up, which would in fact help in moderating the heat.

What remains a mystery is where and how other stages in the beer making process were carried out at any of these sites. For example, where were the malting facilities if the vats were used for mashing? How was the liquid wort separated from the spent grain? If separate vessels were used to ferment the wort after it had cooled, can they be identified in the excavation corpus? Most important, the telltale chemical evidence of barley-beer fermentation—beerstone, or calcium oxalate, as was detected inside the Godin Tepe beer jug (see chapter 3)—has not yet been confirmed from any vessel at these Egyptian sites.

Then there is the mystery of why grape and dates would have been added to the mash. Mixing barley and wheat malt together makes sense, because barley is a much richer source of diastase enzymes than wheat. Perhaps the fruit was also mixed in to provide yeast and an immediate dose of sugar that encouraged an initial fermentation, which marginally elevated the alcohol level and limited the growth of harmful microorganisms. The higher temperatures of mashing, however, would have killed the yeast, which cannot tolerate temperatures above 40°C. Another possibility, consistent with the way sorghum beer is made in the West African nation of Burkina Faso today (see below), is that the primary fermentation was carried out in the same jar as the mashing. After the wort had cooled down, fruit was added to jump-start the main fermentation, contribute flavors, and increase the alcohol content.

Lacking chemical confirmation for beer making, we cannot exclude the possibility that the vats were used to make a hearty, nonalcoholic cereal gruel. Nevertheless, Geller's proposal that a gruelly beer "with a kick" was being produced at these Upper Egyptian sites, thus making them the earliest breweries in the world, makes excellent sense in the long view of Egyptian history. Later Egyptian texts, art, and archaeological remains show the

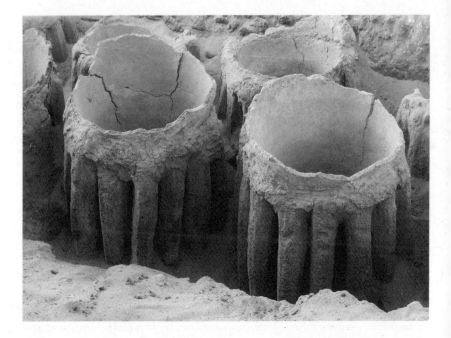

Figure 23. (a, *above*) The mashing of grains for beer in Predynastic Egypt was carried out in large vats, with capacities up to 500 liters each, as at this installation near the temple of Seti I at Abydos, ca. 3500–3100 B.C. Note that each vat was supported by firebricks and was open to the air. Originally a wall with stokeholes for fueling enclosed the double line of vats. From T. E. Peet and W. L. S. Loat, *The Cemeteries of Abydos,* part 3 (London: Egypt Exploration Society, 1913), pl. I.2. Courtesy Egypt Exploration Society. (b, *right*) A modern mashing installation in Burkina Faso whose construction is remarkably similar to the facilities of Predynastic Egypt five thousand years earlier. Photograph courtesy Michel Voltz, Université de Ougadougou, Burkina Faso.

importance of a gruelly, sour wheat beer, which is still known as the national beverage. Along with bread, beer was a staple for commoner and king alike. Unfiltered beer has even a higher nutritional content than leavened bread, with a higher protein content (mainly from the yeast), more B vitamins, and fewer phytates (polyphenols that bind essential minerals, such as calcium, and prevent them from being absorbed in the intestines). It is doubtful that the Great Pyramids and the other grand monuments of Egypt would have been built without beer. The workers who supplied the back-breaking labor for these endeavors received a daily allotment of two or three loaves of bread and two bottles, or about four to five liters, of beer. Michael Chazan, a former student of mine and now a professor at the

University of Toronto, had the privilege of excavating the bakeries and breweries at Giza, which supplied the pyramid workers around 2500 B.C. Here, vats like those at Hierakonpolis could have been used to make bread or beer, and the area was strewn with a vast number of the standard Egyptian beerbottles.

Beer was the quintessential funeral offering, surpassing the canonical set of five wines. Even Scorpion I had a chamber full of beer bottles in his tomb at Abydos, along with his amply stocked wine cellar (see chapter 6). The goddess Hathor, "the mistress of drunkenness," was the Egyptian equivalent of the Sumerian beer goddess, Ninkasi (see chapter 3). She was closely associated with a lesser goddess "who makes beer," Menqet. One festival to honor Hathor, appropriately designated "the Drunkenness of Hathor," at her temple in Dendera, recalled the story of how the goddess had gone on a rampage to destroy a rebellious humanity in one of her alternative forms as the lioness goddess, Sekhmet. Just in time, Re diverted her from her mission by filling the inundated fields with red beer, which Hathor interpreted as a sign that she had accomplished her task. She then overindulged and forgot to carry out the devastation of mankind. The yearly celebration at Dendera coincided with the inundation of the Nile during the summer, when reddish, iron-rich soils were washed down from the Atbara River in the Sudan, giving the waters the appearance of red beer. By drinking both wine and beer at the festival and celebrating with music and dance, humanity shared in Hathor's transformation into her more benign form, the cat Bastet.

Beer making is illustrated over and over again, from the Old Kingdom through the New Kingdom, on tomb walls and by small-scale models of breweries, which were intended to keep the deceased supplied with beer in the afterlife. Although subject to different interpretations, the depictions and models show both men and women grinding and pounding grain, which is then made up into flat and variously shaped breads, cut into pieces, and mashed in large open-mouthed jars by stirring. The mash is filtered through open-weave baskets and the liquid transferred to preheated bowls. The wort is finally transferred by spouted pitchers to the fermentation jars, which are sometimes shown being inoculated with a starter (likely date or grape juice, or possibly a yeasty concoction from an old batch of beer), and sealed with clay stoppers. Papyri and inscriptions refer to many different kinds of ancient Egyptian beer, including dark beer, sweet beer, iron beer (perhaps distinctively colored red?), "beer that does not sour," enema beers, beers imbibed with celery for healthy gums, "beer for eternity," date beer, and *hes* or garnished beer (perhaps specially flavored with an herb, fruit, or tree resin).

A very similar process for making a wheat beer is known in Egypt today, especially among peasants and boatmen along the Nile. Especially popular in Nubia, it is called *bouza* in Arabic (no relation to the English word "booze"). First, cereal—generally wheat, but also barley, millet, and sorghum—is ground and lightly baked as leavened bread, with a moist, yeasty center. The bread is broken, diluted with water, and combined with malt. The resulting mash is moderately heated for several hours and more water added, and, sometimes after a filtration step, the beverage is primed with some old *bouza* and set aside to ferment for several days. Essentially the same process was used to make beer in Egypt 1,500 years earlier, as detailed by the Greek alchemist Zosimus.

Chemical and taste tests of *bouza* have been carried out. One investigator, Sabry Morcos, reported that *bouza* purchased in the 1970s in the Cairo souk, which had been fermented for a single day, had an alcohol content of 3.8 percent; after three days, it had risen to 4.5 percent. Alfred Lucas, who also collected samples from the souk in the 1920s, found that those beers were more powerful (6.2–8.1 percent). He described the unfiltered beverages as having the consistency of "thin gruel: they contained much yeast, were in an active state of fermentation and had been made from coarsely ground wheat." Morcos's beers, which had been filtered, were "a thick, pale yellow beverage with a yeasty or alcoholic odor and agreeable taste." J. L. Burckhardt, the illustrious early nineteenth-century explorer of Nubia, noted the same differences between filtered and unfiltered *bouza*. One high-quality variety, strained through a cloth, was named the "mother of the nightingale" (Arabic, *om belbel*), because "it makes the drunkard sing."

Unfiltered *bouza* is usually drunk with a straw to screen out solids, as is customary throughout modern Africa. Pottery drinking tubes, set at a right angle and fitted with strainers, have been recovered from ancient Egyptian sites. One funerary stela from el-Amarna, the capital of the New Kingdom under Pharaoh Akhenaten (ca. 1350 B.C.), shows an Egyptian man, sporting a Semitic-style beard, quaffing his brew through a drinking tube, aided by a servant boy. The cup in the latter's hand might have been used to dispense a special ingredient or hallucinogen, such as essence of blue lotus. Another wonderfully rendered scene in the New Kingdom Theban tomb of Ipuy shows a moored ship and its sailors coming ashore to barter grain for fish, baked goods, vegetables, and drink. One quayside booth is well supplied with beverage amphoras. A prominent drinking tube projects from one of the vessels, so that the beer can be tested first.

Even with such a long, highly conservative history of beer making in ancient Egypt, one might still harbor doubts about whether the installations at late Prehistoric Hierakonpolis, Abydos, and the other Upper Egyptian sites were containers for mashing grain (mash tuns). I did, but my skepticism was finally assuaged by a photograph of a very similar modern-day facility: a sorghum-mashing facility in Burkina Faso. There were the large (80- to 100-liter) wide-mouthed jars clustered together, supported by firebricks,

Figure 24. Drinking beer through a long straw is an ancient tradition that continues today throughout Africa. (a, *above*) Funerary stela from el-Amarna (ca. 1350 B.C.) showing an Egyptian man, sporting a Semitic-style beard, quaffing his brew through a drinking tube, aided by a servant boy. The cup in the latter's hand might have been used to dispense a special ingredient or hallucinogen, such as essence of blue lotus. Photograph courtesy of J. Liepe, Ägyptisches Museum, Staatliche Museen zu Berlin, Bildarchiv Preussischer Kulturbesitz/Art Resource NY #14,122. (b, *right*) Tiriki men of western Kenya still drink millet and sorghum beers through long drinking tubes. From J. L. Gibbs, ed., *Peoples of Africa* (New York: Holt, Rinehart, and Winston, 1978), 74. Used by permission of Holt McDougal, a division of Houghton Mifflin Harcourt Publishing Company.

and a firing chamber enclosed by packing mud up to and around the vessel mouths. Although this site was nearly three thousand kilometers from the border of Egypt, seeing that photograph was like peering back 5,500 years to a time when the first large population and ceremonial centers, likely governed by the forerunners of the pharaohs, were developing. The late Prehistoric rulers-cum-priests probably realized that to consolidate their power and to build their towns and outfit their tombs, they needed lots of beer to slake the thirst of and motivate their people.

The one malting facility at Hierakonpolis—more are likely to be found at the site when excavation is resumed—had a capacity of 390 liters (65 liters per vat). If the vats were repeatedly used, perhaps as many as six times per day for two-hour periods, and the liquid transferred to fermentation jars, then nearly 2,500 liters of beer could have been produced daily. The output might have been considerably less—possibly only 130 liters per day—if mashing times were lengthened and fermentation carried out in the same jars. The eight malting complexes at Abydos, the largest of which numbered 35 vats, could have produced much more. In close proximity to the tombs of the Predynastic kings, including Scorpion I, mash tuns testified to the innovative, large-scale developments that were to launch Egypt on an era of unrivaled growth, prosperity, and influence.

Such massive prehistoric mashing facilities, however, were short-lived and have been found only at late Prehistoric sites (unless Old Kingdom Giza represents a continuation of the tradition). Freestanding jars and relatively small, preheated bowls replaced them, to judge from later tomb artistic depictions and models. The modern Burkina Faso facilities for sorghum mashing thus stand as anomalies to be explained (see below). The basic concept of the Upper Egyptian Prehistoric mash tuns is comprehensible and practical. The heat-absorptive and heat-conductive properties of the firebricks supporting the vats and enclosed in a firing chamber would conserve fuel and yield a moderate, long-lasting, and well-controlled heat source ideal for mashing.

When the father of Tutankhamun, the heretic pharaoh Akhenaten, built his capital city at el-Amarna on the middle Nile River around 1350 B.C., he included what were likely a bakery and brewery in the sun temple of his wife, Nefertiti. Excavation of the site by Barry Kemp of the University of Cambridge and palaeobotanical analyses by Delwen Samuel of the McDonald Institute for Archaeological Research led to a re-creation of ancient Egyptian beer by Scottish & Newcastle, which went under the name Tutankhamun's Tipple or Nefertiti's Nip and quickly sold out at $100 per bottle. According to Samuel's findings, emmer wheat and barley malt and gelatinized grains were brewed together; she found no evidence that bread was part of the recipe. The end result was a cloudy, golden liquid at 6 percent alcohol, somewhat sweet, with a fruity nose.

A CONTINENT OBSESSED WITH BEER

Beer is a fact of life over all of sub-Saharan Africa. One eighteenth-century traveler claimed that there were "a hundred and a hundred sorts," but African beers are remarkably consistent in style, production technique, and their role in society.

For the Kofyar, sedentary farmers in northern Nigeria, nearly every facet of their existence revolves around millet beer, a thick, cloudy brew containing up to 5 percent alcohol. According to an anthropological observer in the 1960s, Kofyar elder males, in particular, "make, drink, talk, and think about" beer all the time. The brewery occupies the village center, both geographically and metaphorically. The six days of the Kofyar week are denoted by stages of the brewing schedule; our Friday is their *jim,* the second day for grinding malt. Most of the Kofyar harvest goes to making beer, consumed in a constant round of community "drinks," at which gourds of beer are passed around, the mood lightens, disagreements are resolved, lovers sidle up to one another, and singing and dancing ensue. Harvest laborers expect and get payment in beer, like the Old Kingdom pyramid workers.

The Kofyar's spirit world is just as beer-centered as their social, economic, and political lives. Medicine men and shamanistic diviners receive beer without asking. Families honor their ancestors, who must be continually placated by pouring and blowing beer on to their graves and breaking beer jars over their stone markers. Religious festivals, such as the great flute chorus and dance, are liberally lubricated with beer. Finally, beer saturates Kofyar mythology. Its "culture hero" is said to have founded certain villages by stopping to brew beer there, and he purposely left a huge beer jar at the highest point of the tribal territory. In one of many Kofyar legends, a black-crowned crane (*Balearica pavonina*) finds a jar of beer inside the ancestral stone in an African version of the Ali Baba story, where the hero gains magical access to a cave full of treasure.

Similar beer-laden stories and ceremonies recur across sub-Saharan Africa. At the southern tip of the continent, the king of the Zulus claimed in 1883 that "[millet] beer is the food of the Zulus; they drink it as the English drink coffee." It was also the "food of the gods," and, as noted by a seventeenth-century explorer, it was essential to feasts and honoring royal ancestors. Men of the Tsonga tribe, who were conquered by the Zulus, could spend a week away from home going from one beer-drinking session or "drink" to another.

The pastoralist Xhosas, the second largest indigenous group in South Africa (of which Nelson Mandela is a member), have much the same relationship with Bantu beer. It is made from millet or sometimes maize, which was introduced from the Americas. They drank it in such quantity and so incessantly that the British provincial administration in the early 1900s passed measures—ultimately unsuccessful—to control what were described as "nocturnal jollifications." A frequent topic of conversation among the Xhosas was where the next beer was coming from and how good it might be. Beer also is imbued with powerful ritualistic and symbolic significance: the ancestors delighted in it when they were alive and expected their descendants to keep brewing and offering it to them "in spirit."

Village women in Malawi make beer from sorghum, which provided the population with 35 percent of their caloric intake in the 1930s. The average consumption for men has held steady at five liters per day, though some of it is now commercially brewed. As Benjamin Platt, a nutrition scientist, stressed, "Records from several parts of Africa show that men will rarely drink anything but beer." The Pondo, another Zulu people in the Eastern Cape of South Africa, rank beer feasts above meat feasts because beer lends a party atmosphere to the work involved in organizing the feasts. And the Suri of southern Ethiopia say, "Where there is no beer, there is no work."

In Kenya, a Masai informant of Justin Willis, then director of the British Institute in Eastern Africa, insisted that "if there is no beer, it's not a ritual." The Masai sometimes used other sacred fluids in their rituals—mixing mead and blood, sprinkling fermented milk, and spitting saliva—but only beer was versatile enough for every occasion and, as the "drink of the country," was enjoyed by both the living and the dead.

A related group, the Iteso of Kenya and Uganda, believe that the ancestors are greedy for finger-millet beer. The dead must be placated by five funerals spread out over many years. For a child to be named and achieve personhood, the maternal grandmother must first dip her finger in beer and let the child suck on it. If the child swallows, the "sucking name" is accepted. Frequent beer drinking is governed by a specific protocol. In the hut of the hosts (husband and wife), the sexes are separated into two concentric circles around the communal beer jar; parents and children of the hosts sit to the right as one enters, and grandparents, grandchildren, and siblings, together with the hosts, to the left. Individuals on each side generally share drinking tubes, and drinking from a communal jar emphasizes familial bonds.

Many other rules apply, some of which have obvious rationales, such as removing the straw from the jar when sneezing, and not blowing air through it and bubbling the beer. Less obvious guidelines include not holding the straw in one's left hand and not looking directly into the beer vessel. It is also forbidden for a husband and wife to share drinking tubes with their respective parents-in-law. This stricture can be rescinded only if the wife prepares a special brew for her father-in-law at the beginning of the drink and then presents him with the drinking tube and takes a drink herself at his request. An even more intimate exchange occurs between the husband and his mother-in-law: while standing in the thatched portico of the wife's sleeping hut, each takes a mouthful of beer and sprays it on the other. Elders among the Iteso are least hemmed in by custom, perhaps because age is equated with wisdom and they are only a step away from becoming ancestors themselves. They spend afternoons wandering the village paths, toting long reed straws in special carriers like so many billiard cues, in search of the next serving of beer.

In eastern Uganda, fifty or more men might gather around the central beer pot to share a single drinking tube, each being allowed three minutes to draw from the pot. When modern culture intruded to suggest that more than beer might be shared by this practice—for example, a communicable disease—the men rented sterilized straws or brought their own specially decorated and labeled straws. The men probably should have held their ground, as the alcohol content of the brew makes it more hygienic than the local water.

From the highlands of Ethiopia, where mead is highly regarded as the "good one," the Blue Nile flows through the Sudan and into Nubia. Here, in the eastern Sahel, the semiarid scrub grasslands south of the Sahara Desert, sorghum has been king for thousands of years. It remains the most important crop for all of sub-Saharan Africa, feeding hundreds of millions of people and providing three-quarters of the caloric intake, mostly as beer, in many areas. How did it become such a staple?

The greatest genetic diversity of sorghum—some 450 local strains—occurs in the Sudan, and it has been proposed that *Sorghum bicolor,* which is closest to the wild progenitor *Sorghum verticilliflorum,* was domesticated here around 6000 B.C. and spread westward to the Atlantic coast. The key site is Nabta Playa in southern Egypt, deep in the eastern Sahara. Excavations here by Fred Wendorf of Southern Methodist University uncovered a series of hut floors, replete with fireplaces, numerous large storage pits, wells, and pottery. The settlement, dating back to 6000 B.C., then lay on the edge of a lake surrounded by relatively dry terrain and received much higher rainfall than today.

From tens of thousands of carefully collected archaeobotanical specimens, it became clear that the inhabitants of Nabta Playa had an intimate knowledge of the plant resources in their environs. They also fished and hunted hare and gazelle, but plants were their forte. Their storage pits held a plethora of wild seeds, fruits, tubers, and grains of some forty plants, which could have sustained them throughout the year. In addition to sorghum, there were several varieties of millet, bulrush, *Rumex* (an herb genus in the buckwheat family), legumes, *Setaria* (bristlegrass), mustard, caper, fruits and seeds of *Ziziphus* (a tree genus in the buckthorn family, which includes Chinese jujube), and various unidentified tubers. Such exuberant plant exploitation strikes one as remarkably like what was happening at Monte Verde in Chile at 13,000 B.P. (see chapter 7) and, no doubt, in many other parts of the world as the last Ice Age gave way to moister, milder climatic conditions.

The finding of bulrush (a related species was documented at Monte Verde), tubers, sorghum and millet, and very sweet *Ziziphus* fruit at Nabta Playa raises the intriguing possibility that one or more of these plants was made into a fermented beverage. No mortars for crushing the grains or rhizomes were found, but that does not preclude the possibility that they existed. The much earlier site of Wadi Kubbaniya near Aswan, also excavated by Wendorf, yielded numerous grinding stones, which have been radiocarbon dated to 16,000 B.C. Starch grains embedded in the stones' surfaces show that more tubers were pulverized than other plants, just as at Monte Verde. Could it be that, in both areas, the people had happened on a particularly effective way of preparing wild roots for saccharification by crushing them first, to make them easier to chew and then ferment? Alternatively, a fermented beverage could easily have been made from the *Ziziphus* fruit at Nabta Playa.

Such hypotheses, however, need more direct evidence. In 1996, Fred Wendorf sent me some Nabta Playa pottery, recovered from several storage pits, for chemical analysis. They likely represented vessels that had been emptied of their contents and discarded into the pits. Because we had not worked out the chemical fingerprint compounds for any of the plants that we might likely detect, in particular sorghum and millet, I decided to delay any analysis. A scholarly furor over the dating of supposed domesticated plants at the two sites, including barley, lentils, and chickpeas, later shown to be intrusive and not good evidence for extremely early domestication, further dampened my enthusiasm. As I was writing this chapter, my curiosity was once again aroused, and we tested the sherds. Unfortunately, they yielded no ancient organics, only calcium carbonate from the desert sands.

Although tubers might well have been ground and processed into fermented beverages during the Palaeolithic period, cereals took central stage during the Neolithic. Sorghum emerged as the most likely ingredient along the upper Nile and its tributaries. This grain, along with several others and *Ziziphus* seeds, was accidentally imprinted onto pottery jars at many Neolithic sites because of its abundance. The many thousands of grinding stones found at Kadero, Um Direiwa, and Khartoum in the Sudan are believed to have been used in processing sorghum.

At Nabta Playa, we can already see the pendulum swinging toward sorghum, whose grains have been directly radiocarbon dated to ca. 6000 B.C. and are unquestionably contemporary with the settlement. This cereal, unlike others at the site, was concentrated in large amounts in some huts and not intermixed with other grains or grasses. In other words, it was being processed en masse for a specific purpose—and that objective might well have been to make a fermented beverage.

Chemical analyses also suggest that the sorghum seeds at Nabta Playa, although they externally resemble the wild type, have some traits in common with the domesticated *bicolor* subspecies. Whether sorghum was domesticated this early, or not until the first millennium A.D., as some argue, is not of critical importance. The wild species, which would have been abundant across the moister Sahara and the Sahel in the early Holocene, can be harvested simply by beating or shaking the grain from the heads into baskets. Unlike wild barley and wheat, whose brittle stems cause their seeds to be dispersed on the ground before they can be collected, wild sorghum was gathered for millennia. Its popularity was evident even in the heyday of the cosmopolitan Egyptian New Kingdom, when quantities were buried with Tutankhamun, perhaps to feed his animals in the afterlife.

Sorghum beer is certainly a great favorite in the eastern Sahel today. The grain is sometimes saccharified by women chewing and spitting it out, a technique unattested in ancient Egypt but widely used in the Americas in making corn beer and still found on some Pacific islands in making rice beer. More typically, the grain was made into a fermented dough, which can be further processed into a heavy porridge or dumplings but mainly goes into beer. Because sorghum lacks gluten, it is not made into bread; it thus distinguished the diet of sub-Saharan Africa from that of the Middle East until barley and wheat were introduced into Africa during Islamic times in the seventh century. Before then, the peoples of the eastern Sahel were apparently content with their gruels and beers. To judge from the distinctive tall-necked, globular jars that were deposited in Nubian tombs for millennia, sorghum and millet beers were also considered essential for the dead. Ethnographic studies of the Nuba, Nuer, and other Sudanic peoples show that ceremonial, social, and other uses of beer in this area closely resemble those elsewhere in Africa. Festivals to assure enough rain, initiations, work parties, beer drinks, and the installation of priests all require quantities of the brew.

Sorghum beer making probably progressed rapidly across the Sahel from east to west after 6000 B.C., because of the generally mild, humid climate that continued through the sixth millennium. At this time, a huge delta system extended inland more than 3,500 kilometers from the Atlantic Ocean to Lake Chad. Fishing was a major source of livelihood, dramatically illustrated when an eight-meter-long mahogany dugout canoe was found intact at Dufuna near Lake Chad. In the eastern Sahel, thousands of fish bones, representing some thirty species and including deep-water perch more than two meters in length, have been recovered from sites along the Nile and its tributaries.

Wherever one looks in the expanse of the Sahel and Sahara during the early Neolithic period, one is struck not only by the very similar lithics and pottery but above all by the prevalence of bone harpoons and fishhooks. Fishers were also joined by pastoralists, who had begun to move their flocks of Barbary sheep and unhumped cattle freely through the region. Both groups probably had a role in transmitting new cultural and technological ideas.

In the upper Volta River region, where I was taken aback to discover that brewers were still mashing and fermenting sorghum in facilities that resembled those of 5,500 years ago at Hierakonpolis and other Upper Egyptian sites, beer manufacturing likely arrived at a very early date. In Burkina Faso today, only red sorghum goes into the brew, and it generally yields a light, brownish-red beer with about 4 percent alcohol. Rarely, the alcohol is elevated by mixing in white sorghum, which contains more sugar, or boiling down the wort to half its volume before fermenting.

According to tradition, only women make sorghum beer, which accounts for half of the caloric intake in Burkina Faso. In 1981, 700 million liters of beer were made, equivalent to 236 liters per person. As women and children consume much less than men, each male likely drinks an average of a liter or two every day.

Rather than use a fermented dough as a starter, Burkina Faso beer makers first sprout the sorghum and make a malt. This procedure takes seven or eight days: the grain is submerged in water in large jars for two days, then allowed to sprout for another two or three days, and finally sun dried for several days, depending on the season. Mashing takes place over two or three days in the large jars of the special mashing facility. The resulting unfermented sweet wort is clarified by adding the bark of raisin bush (*Grewia flavescens*) and okra (*Abelmoschus esculentus*), and it is sometimes served to children, women, and Muslims before fermentation. The remainder of the wort is cooled in the mashing jars, and yeast gleaned from the jar bottoms of an earlier fermentation is added, recalling the bowls that were probably used to collect yeast from the Prehistoric Egyptian mashing vats. An initially pasty and milky substance is dried in the air and sun, yielding grayish crumbs of yeast.

Fermentation takes place during a single night. Individual brewers have secret formulas of special ingredients, which might include bark of the whitethorn tree (*Acacia campylacantha*), the fruit of the soapberry tree (*Balanites aegyptica*), or grains of hallucinogenic jimson (*Datura stramonium*). Some groups add honey to the beer presented at funerals to bring the alcohol content up to 10 percent.

Secular and sacred uses of sorghum beer permeate traditional West African societies. The creator god is said to have told women how to make sorghum beer and porridge. When consumed, these staples caused humans to lose their tails and fur and become truly human, a motif that recalls the Mesopotamian Gilgamesh epic.

The memorial funeral for adult men ("lords of the earth"), which elevates them to the status of ancestors, exemplifies the centrality of beer in these societies. It takes place months or years after death because of the huge expense involved. On average, every adult at the funeral, which can encompass hundreds of people in a village, drinks ten to twenty liters of beer per day in the course of a week-long celebration. After the ceremony, gourds of beer, plates of porridge, and the personal effects of the deceased are placed on the grave. Then, as in an Irish wake, the music, dancing, and games begin. Without the drink, it is difficult to imagine where the energy and enthusiasm for this nonstop activity would come from.

As if the year-round cycle of celebrations and special ceremonies were not enough, everyone is guaranteed some fun on Thursday, the "day of the ancestors." A sacrificial chicken is presented, along with a gourd of beer, and then rich and poor alike are proffered quantities of the beverage and encouraged to join in the festivities. Beer "drinks" in which the beer gourd is passed around are also very popular, and as women brewers are accustomed to open their huts early, patrons can start their day off with a liquid breakfast.

How the Upper Egyptian mashing techniques of 3500 B.C. reached the upper Volta region (Burkina Faso) is still an enigma. The technology had gone out of use in Egypt by the early Old Kingdom, so the transfer must have occurred earlier. Perhaps it made its way along the upper Nile into Nubia and Ethiopia. As the exploitation of sorghum spread across the Sahel, it might have been transmitted from one settlement to the next, eventually reaching West Africa. This scenario counters the widely held notion of very early independent domestication and cultural development in sub-Saharan Africa, divorced from any Afro-Asiatic migration or influence from Egypt. It does fit with a more nuanced version of diffusion in which the Neolithic period of the eastern Sahel was a hotbed of experimentalism, which had far-reaching consequences for the rest of Africa.

One clue that this reconstruction is not contrived comes from a rock shelter at 1,500 meters above sea level deep in the Tassili n'Ajjer Mountains in the Algerian Sahara, an area that teemed with life from the end of the last Ice Age until about 3000 B.C. According to its discoverer, Henri Lhote, the paintings on the walls of so-called Dr. Khen shelter are the "most accomplished" of the many thousands that his expedition located and recorded throughout the Sahara, and represent the "masterpiece of the Neolithic naturalist school." Radiocarbon dates from encampments and nearby paintings suggest that the rock shelter was painted around 3000–2500 B.C. or earlier.

One painting in the shelter stands out for its sheer size (4.5 meters long by 3 meters high, covering an entire wall), its vivid colors, and its dramatic depiction of a drinking ceremony (see plate 10). We see a small encampment of tents, set amid sheep and cattle herds and surrounded by wild giraffes, antelopes, and ostriches. A woman sits at the entrance to each tent, her hair carefully coiffed and accented by a high barrette, dressed in a beautifully woven and flounced dress and shawl, and with a dark animal skin tied around her waist. Each woman looks every bit the Minoan "mother goddess" (see chapter 5). At one tent, which is somewhat set apart from the others, the woman drinks from a large, decorated jar through a long straw. She leans intently over the jar, one hand on the drinking tube and the other on what has been interpreted as an ostrich-egg stopper which is punctured by the tube, and sucks up the beverage. A male, carrying a similarly decorated and stoppered jar, exits to the left of the imbibing woman. He is preceded by three other men, each wearing leather breeches and shirts and with one or two feathers stuck in their long, loosely strung hair. They approach another male, who is kneeling and drinking from a decorated and stoppered jar in the same fashion as the imbibing woman. The male imbiber is assisted in holding his long straw by a second figure, whose fuller beard, prominent animal-hide vest, and a large pendant suspended from his neck torque mark him as older and of higher status.

The overall composition of this painting suggests that it shows a marriage ceremony or the rapprochement between a husband and wife and their respective parents-in-law, reminiscent of the Iteso sorghum beer ceremonies (above). According to the traditions of this East African tribe, the woman should make the beverage, which is then served at the entrance to her hut or carried to in-laws by near relatives. The close correspondence between such traditional ceremonies and an ancient "Neolithic" depiction, all within the hypothesized sorghum-beer belt extending across the center of Africa, cannot be accidental. To my mind, the painting at Tassili n'Ajjer, about halfway between Hierakonpolis and the upper Volta region, provides compelling evidence that Neolithic traditions of sorghum beer manufacturing were indeed carried one step at a time across the Sahel and Sahara to Burkina Faso, where their influence persists thousands of years later.

PALM WINE AND OTHER LIBATIONS

Converting cereals into alcoholic beverages, assuming one had the expertise to process, saccharify, and ferment the grains, had distinct advantages over making drinks from honey, fruits, and other natural products. Most high-sugar resources were available only at certain times of the year and could not be kept for long. Honey was the exception, as its high sugar content gave it a long shelf life; but it was in limited supply and quickly used up. Africa, however, had no shortage of wild cereals, which could be kept in sealed storage bins for months until needed to make the next batch of beer.

Beer never totally displaced other fermented beverages, which had their own special flavor profiles and potentially higher alcohol content and could be effectively mixed with a cereal beverage. Generally, archaeo-botanical research in Africa shows that fermentable fruits figured prominently, as might be expected for a fruit-loving species such as ours (chapter 1). Sweet and luscious *Ziziphus* fruit is recorded not only at early Neolithic Nabta Playa but also at contemporaneous sites on the upper Nile in Sudan and at late Neolithic Naqada, close to Hierakonpolis along the middle Nile. Hackberry (*Celtis* spp.), which we have already surmised might have been used to make a fermented beverage at Neolithic Çatal Höyük in Turkey, is attested at the same Sudanese sites and at fourth-millennium B.C. Kadero, north of Khartoum; it shows up in Mauritania, in the western Sahel, between 1500 and 500 B.C. Dried fruits of the fig, soapberry tree, and other plants were recovered from caves in the remote Tadrart Acacus mountains of the Libyan Sahara. Moreover, many of these fermentable fruits were associated with traditional medicinal additives to wine and beer—for example, caper, *Rumex,* and borage—or could themselves have been used as principal ingredients. The date palm (*Phoenix dactylifera*), a later source of fruit for making a potent wine, is also in evidence in the Tadrart Acacus around 6000 B.C. and is the basis for beer drinks in modern Darfur.

Of all the potentially fermentable substances in Africa, the enormous variety of palm tree species, adapted to semiarid and rain-forest conditions, stand out. Many produce fruits that are turned into wine, but an even more intriguing alcoholic beverage is made from their sap or resin. The most important species for making palm wine are the oil palm (*Elaeis guineensis*), the ron or palmyra palm (*Borassus aethiopum*), and the raphia palm (*Raphia vinifera*), which are concentrated along the humid east and west coasts as well as in the dense jungles of the interior.

Today, adroit "tappers" clamber up the rugged bark to the towering fronds by tying a vine or rope around their waists and hoisting themselves up step by step. Our inherited primate propensity for climbing trees to get fruit (chapter 1) is a distinct asset. At the top of the tree, the tappers skewer male and female flowers, bind them up so that there is a steady flow of sap, and attach a gourd or other container to collect the sap. A healthy tree can produce nine or ten liters a day and about 750 liters over half a year. A more brutal approach is to fell the tree, thus killing it, and collect the sap all at once.

Because the sap has already been inoculated with yeast by insects eager to consume the milky, sweet exudate, the fermentation process is self-starting. Within two hours, palm wine ferments to about a 4 percent alcohol content; give it a day, and the alcohol level goes up to 7 or 8 percent. The end result is an aromatic and slightly carbonated elixir: the paleontologist Pierre Teilhard de Chardin described it as a *pétillant* French Champagne, and another early European explorer likened it to a fine Rhine white wine.

The long pedigree of palm wine in Africa is provocatively intimated by the 18,000-year-old botanical finds at the Upper Palaeolithic site of Wadi Kubbaniya. In addition to wild grains, tubers, chamomile, and water lily (*Nymphaea* spp.), which might have been made into beverages or used as additives, this important site yielded fruits of the dom palm (*Hyphaene thebaïca*), which is eminently tappable. This tree thrives in the blistering temperatures of the Horn of Africa, today the nations of Somalia and Dji-bouti, where the local peoples still skewer the flowers and collect the resin in tightly woven palm-frond baskets to make a mildly alcoholic wine. Be-cause fermentation proceeds so quickly in the hot climate, a tapper can enjoy a taste almost immediately and pass along the bounty to helpers on the ground. When humans chop into its flowers and stems, the tree grows luxuriant foliage along its trunk.

Farther west in the Sahel, tropical palms proliferate. Beginning by at least 2000 B.C. and continuing into the first millennium B.C., a mixed for-aging and horticultural society, centered on the oil palm, had spread out across the region that is now Burkina Faso, Ghana, Cameroon, Gabon, and the Congo Basin. Numerous sites, even in the poorly explored inte-rior jungles, are littered with ground stone axes and hoes, which could have been used to tend and thin out competing trees or, less likely, to chop down palm trees for their resin. A sharp rise in oil-palm remains during the second half of the second millennium B.C. strongly suggests that tap-ping techniques had been refined. Because the tree propagates itself by dropping its fruit or through dissemination by humans and other animals, it does not need to be domesticated; only careful management is required. Intriguingly, the oil-palm remains are very often associated with fruits of the incense tree (*Canarium schweinfurthii*). Today the aromatic, resinous bark of this tree is employed in the treatment of numerous illnesses and infections, from eczema to gastrointestinal complaints, coughs, and gonor-rhea. One way that it is administered is by preparing a decoction in palm wine.

African jungles, like those of South America, teem with potential me-dicinal plants, which innovative humans had probably already begun to explore for their healing properties when they were first encountered; the centrality and persistence in religious traditions of some of these plants im-ply as much. For instance, peoples throughout the region where the oil palm was exploited practice the Bwiti religion, whose main beliefs re-volve around the iboga shrub (*Tabernanthe iboga*). According to one found-ing legend, a pygmy fell out of a tree while collecting fruit. A creator god picked him up, cut off his fingers and toes, and planted them; they grew up as the iboga.

The roots of the iboga are rich in indoxyl compounds with powerful hallucinogenic properties. Among the Bonga of the lower Sangha River, a tributary of the Congo, palm wine laced with these hallucinogens lubri-cates all-night ceremonies overseen by a shaman and accompanied by drum and harp music and exuberant dancing. The initiates say that iboga, the "generic ancestor," transports them into the kingdom of the ancestors, who lead them along dazzlingly colored roads and rivers to the gods.

Throughout Africa, drinking palm wine is a practice with intimate ties to the ancestors. Social drinking only proceeds after flicking some of the beverage onto the ground to honor the deceased, much as Mother Earth first needs to be moistened with *chicha* in the Andes. The funerary ceremonies of the Giryama people in coastal Kenya, whose livelihood once depended exclusively on their palm-tree holdings, illustrate how an alcoholic beverage mediates between this world and the next and effectively integrates the social, spiritual, and natural orders. When a respected plantation head dies, the first funeral lasts seven days and nights for a man, and six days and nights for a woman. Hundreds of wailing mourners gather around the grave. After the mourning period comes feasting and dancing. By plying themselves with palm wine, the celebrants assuage the grief of the dead ancestor, whose spirit looks on with pleasure and recalls how he or she enjoyed the same beverage in life. After another one to four months, the festivities are repeated for three days and nights at a second funeral, at which the new plantation head is named. The enormous cost of these funerals must be justified by the way they serve to bind the community together, but shrewd plantation owners plan ahead by expanding their palm estates through astute negotiations for additional wives.

Contrary to the view that sees our "ancestors" in sub-Saharan Africa as totally benighted and resistant to new technologies and ideas, peoples there made pottery as early as the supposedly more advanced Near Easterners. They herded animals and cultivated a huge range of plants from at least around 6000 B.C. and likely much earlier. They also developed their own fermented beverages, like palm wine, or were ready to try new ones with some help from the outside, as is likely the case with making sorghum beer. Although most African fermented beverages were improvised from locally occurring plants, sometimes a cultivar that could provide special delights was introduced from a distant locale. The domesticated grape from the Levant was transplanted up the Nile and out to the desert oases over the course of Egyptian dynastic history. Vineyards were planted in Nubia and Ethiopia by around 2000 B.C. so that the peoples there could make their own wine. Recently, grapes and wine have seen a resurgence throughout the continent, so that virtually every country, just like every state in the United States, now produces wine. The modern colonial period opened up Africa to American crops, including cassava or manioc, which can be made into beer in the same way that the native yam can be transformed into an alcoholic beverage.

One imported foodstuff from Southeast Asia highlights the need for much more intensive archaeological research in Africa. Scientists have long believed that the banana (*Musa* spp.), which was domesticated in New Guinea in the fifth millennium B.C., reached Africa only in the mid-first millennium A.D. Then, in 2000, came the astounding announcement that a banana phytolith, a characteristic microscopic silica accretion that forms in its leaves, had been found embedded in a first-millennium B.C. sherd of what was undoubtedly locally made pottery at Nkang, Cameroon. This site belongs to the far-flung West African societies that had begun exploiting the oil palm and other plant resources. This archaeological bombshell was followed by another in 2006: the bottom layer of a sediment core from a swamp at Bunyoro, Uganda, radiocarbon-dated to the mid-fourth millennium B.C., contained fourteen *Musa*-type phytoliths. At one fell swoop, the date for the earliest banana in Africa was moved back three thousand years.

Because the phytoliths were recovered only in a single layer, and thousands of years separate them from specimens of the past five hundred years, one wonders whether the phytoliths are intrusive. It's wise not to make too much out of a unique find, such as the domesticated wheat and barley from Wadi Kubbaniya and Nabta Playa (above) or the domesticated fig at Gilgal I in the Jordan Valley (chapter 3). We might be assured that a cluster of phytoliths were found and that all the radiocarbon dates are consistent, but how can we be confident that a single banana-leaf fragment did not somehow contaminate the sample, perhaps by groundwater percolation or an animal's moving it there from an upper level of the core? The radiocarbon dates of the core could be genuine but the banana evidence intrusive.

Whatever the date of its arrival, the banana had made serious inroads into Africa before the beginning of the Christian era, possibly brought to the east coast by proto-Malaysians who traversed the Indian Ocean in outrigger canoes. The ripe fruit, with 20 percent or more fermentable sugars, had enormous potential for making an alcoholic beverage, and where the plant took root, especially around the lakes in the Great Rift Valley, the resulting drink acquired all the significance and accoutrements of a native beverage.

The Rift Valley peoples had other fermentable materials available to them—millet, sorghum, honey, and palm sap—but during the past two millennia, banana wine came to the fore in both east and west Africa. Starches in bananas naturally break down into sugars as the fruit ripens, leaving a sweet pulp inside the darkening skin. That makes it challenging to peel and eat an overripe banana but facilitates the production of a fermented alcoholic beverage.

Among the Haya people of Tanzania, it is a man's job (contrary to the more common practice of women being responsible for beverage making) to extract this sugary liquid from the fruit and keep the village well supplied with banana wine. Ripe bananas, peeled or unpeeled, are piled into a wooden vat or hollowed-out log, mixed with fine dried grass, and then stomped by foot, just like grapes. In the past, women of each household probably made the wine by a less labor-intensive method, squeezing out the juice of the bananas by hand. Once collected, the mush is kneaded and pressed through the grass, to which the peels adhere, until a thick creamy mass has formed. After filtering through a grass sieve, the fruit pulp is topped up with water; additional cereal malt might be added; and the trough or vat is covered with banana leaves to keep the liquid warm. Fermentation commences quickly, especially if the same vat or log is used repeatedly, and continues for at least a day, yielding a beverage with about 5 percent alcohol. Longer fermentation yields more potent beverages but makes the wine more prone to spoilage.

The Haya have very specific rules governing the consumption of banana wine. A man sips his through a reed drinking tube from a gourd with a long, narrow neck. Women can drink either from a banana-leaf cup or a short-necked gourd but must not use a straw. Before anyone of either sex imbibes, a gourd of banana wine is offered to the ancestors at the household altar. The king, who traditionally received sixteen or more liters of wine from large-scale consignments, propitiated the ancestors with banana wine in grander style: he donned his ceremonial cow and leopard skins and, in the company of priests and to the sound of drumming, presented gourds of wine at their graves and shrines. The new moon was a critical time for these ceremonies, as it was believed that the ancestors roamed the land then and could cause disaster unless they were placated with the banana wine that they had enjoyed while alive.

Placating the dead was clearly a widespread preoccupation in Africa. The prayer of the Tiriki of northwestern Kenya, as they sprinkle a cereal beer onto the ancestral shrine and drink it with straws from a jar set among the stones of the monument, captures the spirit of the diverse, exciting world of fermented beverages on the continent where our species began:

> Our forefathers, drink up the beer!
> May we dwell in peace!
> Everyone is gathering; be pleased, oh ancestral spirits.
> And may we be well; may we remain well.
>
> *(Sangree 1962: 11)*

NINE

ALCOHOLIC BEVERAGES

Whence and Whither?

TO UNDERSTAND THE MODERN FASCINATION with alcoholic beverages of all kinds, as well as the reasons why they are also targets of condemnation, we need to step back and take a longer view. Alcohol occurs in nature, from the depths of space to the primordial "soup" that may have generated the first life on Earth. Of all known naturally addictive substances, only alcohol is consumed by all fruit-eating animals. It forms part of an intricate web of interrelationships between yeasts, plants, and animals as diverse as the fruit fly, elephant, and human, for their mutual benefit and propagation. According to the drunken monkey hypothesis, most primates are physiologically "driven to drink," and humans, with bodies and metabolisms adapted to the consumption of alcohol, are no exception. Like water, a fermented beverage refreshes and fills us up, but it does much more. Apart from the peoples in the Arctic and those at the southern tip of South America in Tierra del Fuego—dwelling in climates too harsh to support any sugar-rich plants—almost every known culture has produced its own alcoholic beverage. Signs of indigenous fermented drinks are also so far noticeably absent from Australia, perhaps owing to limited excavation there. The use of the hallucinogen pituri by Aborigines may be a later substitution for alcohol, as tobacco might have been for native North Americans.

Beyond the physiological imperative, the universality of fermented beverages in human societies cries out for even farther-reaching explanations.

Certainly, the natural occurrence of fermentation, one of the key processes that humans harnessed during their Neolithic revolutions, provides part of the answer. As Benjamin Franklin said in a letter to André Morellet in the late 1780s, "Wine [or any fermented beverage, for that matter] is continual proof that God loves us and that he likes to see us happy." Fermentation contributes nutrients, flavors, and aromas to food and drink—whether a lambic beer, Champagne, cheese, or tofu. It removes potentially harmful alkaloids, helps to preserve them because alcohol kills spoilage microorganisms, and decreases food-preparation time and hence fuel needs by breaking down complex constituents.

Moreover, alcoholic beverages within human cultures effectively transcend the natural process of fermentation. They have a long and widespread history as superb social lubricators. The great monuments of the human civilization—for example, the Egyptian pyramids and the Incan royal centers and irrigation works—were built by rewarding the workers with vast quantities of alcoholic refreshment. Today, fund-raising and political success can hardly be imagined without a liberal supply of drink. On any night in any part of the world you will find people gathered in bars, pubs, and drinking halls, conversing animatedly and relieving the stresses of the day.

Before modern medicines, alcoholic beverages were the universal palliative. The pharmacopeias of ancient Egypt, Mesopotamia, China, Greece, and Rome depended on fermented beverages for treating every kind of ailment. They were also used as vehicles for dissolving and dispensing medicinal herbs, resins and spices. Past peoples didn't need science to tell them about alcohol's antiseptic and antioxidant properties or other benefits that prolonged life and increased reproductive rates. They experienced or observed some of the beneficial effects firsthand.

The psychotropic effects of alcoholic beverages stoked our religious propensities worldwide. Sub-Saharan Africa, where the human odyssey began, is today awash in alcoholic beverages made from honey, sorghum, and millet. Virtually every important religious festival, celebration, or rite of passage—above all, those honoring ancestors—is marked by the presentation and drinking of a fermented beverage. Even in secular Western culture, where drinking alcohol is more of a recreational diversion than a religious passion, people follow distinct protocols in their consumption of the beverages, whether partaking of a favorite beverage at cocktail hour or carefully managing an intake of stimulants to prolong the frenzy of an all-night binge. Every culture has its own formula and terminology for coping with a hangover the morning after, perhaps by drinking more alcohol (the hair of the dog), downing a witch's concoction of vitamins, herbs and other exotic ingredients, or simply taking in lots of water (alcohol dehydrates the body) and food.

The close association between religious practices and alcohol attests to either firmly entrenched biological tendencies or long-established cultural traditions. In other words, investigating the consumption of alcoholic beverages highlights the classic dilemma in studying human society: are certain behaviors more the result of nature or of nurture? Around the world, the available archaeological, chemical, and botanical evidence attests to the close association between alcoholic beverages and religion. Except where alcohol has been proscribed or access to the divine has been achieved in other ways (e.g., through meditation, as in Hinduism and Buddhism), important religious ceremonies often center on an alcoholic beverage. In the West, the wine of the Eucharist is at the heart of Christian religious observances, and every important Jewish ceremony is marked by the drinking of a specific number of glasses of wine.

Other common cultural threads connecting alcoholic beverages and human culture run through my narrative. Some of these strands likely reflect the fact that our species arose in sub-Saharan Africa and then spread out to the rest of the world only about one hundred thousand years ago. Humans everywhere sought sugar-rich, naturally fermenting fruits, honey, grasses, tubers, and other ingredients for fermented beverages. These resources were often combined to make a stronger grog or a drink with more potent medical or psychotropic effects. The earliest inhabited sites in the Middle East, central Asia, China, Europe, Africa, and the Americas are replete with fermentable natural products. Where artwork and artifacts have survived, they support the idea that the preparation and use of fermented beverages during the Palaeolithic period was focused on an authority figure, the "shaman," who oversaw a community's religious and social needs. Even in this early period, tight bonds must have existed between fermented beverages, religion, music, dance, and sex. Ocher pigmentation of burials and bones, probably symbolizing blood and sometimes the fermented beverage itself, is widespread. Musical instruments were made from specific bird bones, probably because of the associations with their mating calls, dances, and other unusual and seemingly otherworldly behaviors. People donned the costume of birds such as the crane and danced to the music.

By the Neolithic period, humans around the globe had developed very similar methods of saccharifying the starches in cereals to sugars by chewing or sprouting. All the most widely planted cereals in the world today—

wheat, rice, corn, barley, and sorghum—were processed by these methods, and the available evidence suggests that the initial domestication of these grains in the Middle East, Asia, Mexico, and the Sahel of Africa was motivated by a desire to increase alcoholic-beverage production. The extraordinary transformation of the minuscule teosinte into maize is difficult to explain unless humans were initially attracted to the plant's sweet stalks, ripe for fermentation, and then, over millennia, bred it selectively for larger and sweeter kernels. The methods for making and drinking cereal brews—including early Mesopotamian barley beer, Chinese rice wine, and American corn *chicha*—were also broadly similar around the world and remain so in many places: ferment a wort in a large, open-mouthed jar, and then drink from the same vessel with a long straw, usually sharing the brew with a group of family or friends. Alcoholic beverages made from sweet fruits, including grape, fig, date and cacao, probably also prompted the domestication of these plants.

One particularly surprising result from our biomolecular archaeological investigations was the discovery that the earliest-known alcoholic beverages came onto the world scene at about the same time—the early Neolithic period, ca. 7000–5000 B.C.—on either side of Asia. In the west, we find the resinated wines of the northern mountainous region of the Near East; five thousand kilometers away, we find the Jiahu grog of China, made by combining rice, hawthorn fruit, grapes, and honey. I have proposed that ideas and traditions of plant domestication and beverage making must have traveled piecemeal, with other aspects of culture, across the expanses of Central Asia, following a prehistoric predecessor of the Silk Road. But an equally compelling hypothesis that would explain these facts, as well as the emergence of new beverages at so many times and places across the planet, is that humans are by nature both innovative and attracted to fermented drinks. In short, if alcoholic beverages are such an integral part of human life, perhaps we are "programmed" with the urge to make and drink them, without needing to invoke any cultural traditions.

IS DRINKING IN OUR GENES?

It may help to look inside ourselves before tackling the more difficult scientific issues. People's reactions to alcohol run the gamut of emotions, from euphoria to belligerence and nihilism. Fortunately, most of my own experiences have been benign. I cannot remember ever having an aversion to alcohol, but this may be the Irish in me speaking. When the McGoverns settled in Mitchell, South Dakota, they set up the town's first bar. The Norwegian side of my ancestry, at least going back several generations, took the opposite tack, railing against the evils of drink. Perhaps one set of genes balanced out the other, but I have been able to maintain a fairly balanced approach to my alcohol intake—more so than many people, including a number of my Irish relatives.

My first excessive experimentation with alcohol came rather late in life, at the age of sixteen. I had, of course, sneaked a few nips of a martini or Manhattan at my parents' cocktail parties or wangled some crème de menthe in a parfait on the weekend, which seemed vaguely reprobate but adult. It was the flavors of the herbs in these liqueurs that enticed me more than any consciousness-altering effects of the alcohol. All that changed on a two-month cycling trip to the German Alps in 1965.

Before embarking on our adventure, my fellow cyclists and I stopped by the famous Hofbräuhaus in Munich, where the barmaids' arms were lined with liter-sized beer mugs. Although I joined in the drinking songs, at first, as a good American, I stuck with Coca-Cola. About three weeks into the tour, however, it dawned on me that beer was actually less expensive than Coke, so it made sense to stretch my budget by quaffing a brew, or two, at dinner. The problem was that beer was served by the liter, and by the time our *Schweinbraten* or *Knockwurst* was served, the first glass was empty, and it was time for a second. This set me up for the challenge at the end of the meal, when I had to recount to the waiter exactly what I had had, so the bill could be tallied. Being three sheets to the wind, I felt great but dreaded a memory lapse. With some prompting, I usually managed to remember. Stumbling out the door and back onto our bikes—speeding through the night while avoiding pedestrians and cars—was equally challenging.

Back home, I returned to my previous abstemious lifestyle. I still felt the occasional hankerings for a beer, but it was never all-compelling. On a lark, while still underage, I once dressed up in my Tyrolean alpine outfit of *Lederhosen* and suspenders, along with a green peaked hat adorned with a feather and jewelry, and paid a visit to the neighborhood bar. A few carefully turned German phrases convinced the bartender I deserved a beer.

Most of us have our own vivid memories of our first taste of alcohol and drinking derring-do. Yet we are generally ignorant of the mechanisms by which this drug unleashes such powerful emotions and whether its effects are due more to nature or to nurture. Brain research, molecular biology, and epidemiological studies have begun to provide some answers.

Controlled scientific studies of large families (e.g., the Collaborative Study on the Genetics of Alcoholism), twins, and adopted children show that more than half of an individual's susceptibility to excessive drinking has a genetic basis. The other half is due to our environment, like the opposing principles that were conveyed to me by my parents or the influence of my fellow bicyclists exerted on me as we frequented the beer halls and restaurants of Germany.

Scientists have also made considerable progress in unraveling the neurological and genetic bases of the effects of alcohol on the brain, especially with respect to addiction, a major medical and social problem. This is no simple matter, in part because of alcohol's pervasiveness from the beginning of life on Earth, but also because it involves the human brain—the most complex known biological structure, with more than 10 billion interconnected and interacting cells.

Medical ethics prohibits inserting probes into the human brain to measure the effects of alcohol. (Monkeys and rats, as I learned to my chagrin while sharing an office with a fellow grad student at the University of Rochester's Brain Research Center, are less fortunate.) In lieu of probes, neuroscientists have devised innovative indirect measurement techniques. Electroencephalographs can record the overall activity of brain waves. Radioactive markers can be injected into volunteers under the influence to trace the physical path of alcohol as it courses through the body and crosses the blood-brain barrier into the brain. Using f-MRI (functional magnetic resonance imaging), PET (positron emission tomography), or SPECT (single photon emission computed tomography), researchers can observe real-time changes as chemical signals activate and deactivate different brain regions. An individual's cellular and molecular peculiarities can be defined through biopsies of cadaver tissue samples.

The major neural pathways affected by alcohol are the emotional centers, in particular the brain stem and the limbic system deep within our brains, comprising the hypothalamus, thalamus, amygdala, hippocampus, and other structures. These areas are connected by pathways of nerve cells, or neurons. The brain stem and limbic system are often referred to as the "primitive brain," as similar structures are present in animals which appeared earlier on the Earth. In humans, this primitive brain is encased within a large cortex of gray matter, the locus of our peculiarly human traits of language acquisition, music making, religious symbolism, and consciousness of self. Dense neural connectivity with the limbic system assures that no thought or sense memory, perhaps the taste of the legendary 1982

Pétrus or the award-winning Midas Touch, goes unrecorded: it may arouse powerful emotions and be remembered years later.

Other organisms attracted to sugar and alcohol, including the slug and the fruit fly, lack cortices and must have an entirely different experience. Nevertheless, in keeping with the continuity of all life on this planet, the genes that determine the structures of their more primitive nerve centers and account for their responsiveness to alcohol (which scientists have identified by such evocative names as *barfly, tipsy, cheapdate,* and *amnesiac*) are essentially the same as those of humans. The responses of a roundworm (*Caenorhabditis elegans*) or fruit fly (*Drosophila melanogaster*) as it consumes progressively more alcohol are familiar to anyone who can recall having had too much to drink—agitated movement, followed by incoordination, lethargy, sedation, and finally paralysis. And, like humans, these lower animals, whatever they "think" about the experience, can become habituated or addicted to alcohol.

The neurons in our brains communicate via chemical messengers, or neurotransmitters. Alcohol coursing through the blood prompts the release of these compounds into the synapse, or the gap between the neurons. The neurotransmitters travel across the synapses and attach to receptors on the next neuron, triggering an electrical impulse. As we sip that drink, neurons fire at high speed seemingly ad infinitum. Different types and quantities of neurotransmitters activate specific pathways of neurons in our emotional and higher-thought centers. More alcohol leads to more activation, which we experience as the conscious or not-so-conscious feelings of elation or sadness, dizziness, and eventually stupor.

Among the neurotransmitters responsible for our varied responses to alcohol, the most important compounds are dopamine, serotonin, the opioids, acetylcholine, γ-aminobutyric acid (GABA), and glutamate. In particular, many neuroscientists have focused on dopamine, which initiates a "reward cascade" in our brains when we drink. The gene DRD2, on chromosome 11, appears to regulate the dopamine receptor and the availability of this so-called pleasure compound. It is believed that dopamine helps to mellow us out by relieving anxiety and depression. By reducing risky behavior, it causes us to cut back on the amount of alcohol we need to get "high," and curtails our impulse to drink. Although the verdict on the role of dopamine is still out, it is clearly one of the main compounds that controls our impulse to drink.

Of the other neurotransmitters, I have a special interest in serotonin, because my laboratory analyzed the earliest sample of royal or Tyrian purple, the famous dye of the Phoenicians (see chapter 6). The core of this molecule, which occurs naturally only in certain mollusks, is shared by serotonin. It has been hypothesized that the purple molecule serves to anaesthetize potential predators, much as cuttlefish chase off their enemies with their ink. When our articles on purple started appearing, I unexpectedly began receiving inquiries from drug companies. I had never considered that the dye might have a mind-altering effect or other medicinal benefit. Now I am much more open to the possibility that ancient peoples over thousands of years might have accidentally stumbled upon unique natural resources in their environments that turned out to have medicinal effects. We plan to put purple to the test in our drug-discovery project (see chapter 2). Who knows—we may discover another drug, like aspirin (from willow bark) or the anticancer drug taxol (from yew bark).

Serotonin resides in the nervous system, where it is released when we take a sip of an alcoholic beverage. Like dopamine, it calms the frayed emotions of depression, anger, and mood disorders. It and other related compounds also occur naturally in a wide range of plants, animal venoms, and fungi, such as the psychedelic psilocybin mushroom that played an important role in the religious and social life of some early Mexican groups. As we have seen, ancient peoples often administered these additives in fermented beverages, thus making for a double whammy. Monoamine oxidase (MAO) inhibitors to treat depression and designer drugs are the latest in a long line of concoctions that have been used to boost our natural stores of serotonin. Drinking alcohol, like sexual activity, a long-distance run, or a nasty cut, also releases opioids (including the β-endorphins and enkephalins) in our brains. These compounds can elate us or give us temporary relief from pain. In nature, they are most famously found in poppies (*Papaver somniferum*), the source of opium. By administering this drug in a fermented beverage, ancient peoples of central Asia and Europe probably were able to mimic and accentuate the effects of our own neurotransmitters.

Acetylcholine bears mentioning because one variant of its receptor (M_2), traced to the gene on chromosome 7, is also sensitive to a related compound found in the fly agaric mushroom. The mushroom has been proposed, probably incorrectly, as the basis for Zoroastrian *haoma* and Vedic *soma* and is still a popular drug among Siberian shamans. Carriers of the CHRM2 gene, which directs the production of the M_2 receptor, appear to be more subject to depression in adolescence and therefore more prone to self-medicating with alcohol later in life.

Many other genes, unrelated to the neurotransmitters and their receptors, play roles in our decision to drink alcohol. Pure visual delight, perhaps induced by a deep red or translucent yellow color or bright, effervescent bubbles, might draw us to take a sip of a fermented beverage, but if the liquid tastes or smells repugnant, we recoil. When a bad smell is not enough to send us running, our taste buds—bundles of receptors on our tongues and other mouth parts for sweet and sour, bitter and salt, fat, and the meaty-cheesy umami taste—take over. Bitterness especially signals a potentially dangerous substance, and we are a thousand times more sensitive to compounds triggering this receptor than those of much-preferred sugary substances. Researchers have found that one variant of the bitter taste receptor (hTAS2R16), traced back to a gene on chromosome 7, causes decreased sensitivity to bitter tastes in nearly half the African-American population. This genetic predisposition makes the hops in a beer or the tannins of a grape wine less of a turnoff and possibly more of a turn-on.

Understanding the full dimensions of alcohol's impact on mammalian and primate genetics, brains, and emotional and mental states is a work in progress. For example, in 2004 researchers reported that lower levels of CREB (cyclic AMP responsive element binding) protein and neuropeptide Y—crucial compounds for learning, emotional stability, and feeding in mice—were linked to having only one copy of the CREB gene rather than the normal two. The deficient mice, possibly because they were less able to control their appetites, were driven to drink: they preferred alcohol to water and lapped up half again as much alcohol as their littermates.

One gene in humans, ALDH1 (aldehyde dehydrogenase 1), shows that genetics really do matter for understanding alcohol consumption. Overindulging in alcohol can destroy liver cells and increase susceptibility to various cancers, especially of the upper gastrointestinal tract. Our metabolic systems are prepared for the assault up to a point. Alcohol dehydrogenase enzymes transform any alcohol that enters the body into acetaldehyde. But because acetaldehyde is more toxic than alcohol, the ALDH gene produces another enzyme, aldehyde dehydrogenase, that converts the acetaldehyde into relatively harmless acetate. A variant of this gene (ALDH1), however, throws a molecular monkey wrench into the works and in so doing demonstrates how our genetic constitutions can significantly impact our intakes of alcohol.

The ALDH1 variant rids the body of acetaldehyde less efficiently than the normal gene. Virtually nonexistent among people in the West, the mutation occurs in about 40 percent of Asians and causes unpleasant symptoms for carriers who drink alcohol. Their skin flushes to a bright red, and they experience nausea and dizziness.

Why should such an anomalous gene, which subjects the body to a perilously high level of acetaldehyde, persist in the human genome? The probable explanation is that it protects these individuals from the even more damaging effects of excessive alcohol consumption. The implication is that some time during the course of human evolution in Asia, one solution to problem drinking was a genetic mutation. Of course, humans, being naturally innovative, will try to find a way around even a genetic roadblock. In China, one determined ALDH1 carrier simply drank minute amounts of alcohol throughout his waking hours, thus staving off the worst effects of acetaldehyde poisoning while maintaining a perpetual state of inebriation.

Scientists have already articulated many of the key elements in a neural and genetic explanation of how the modern human brain behaves under the influence. These processes are largely beyond our conscious awareness. Each person's response to alcohol is unique. For example, a person prone to depression or risk taking is more apt to overdrink to relieve negative feelings or get a thrill. For an artist or poet, an alcoholic beverage may liberate the imagination.

The emerging picture of how the intoxicated human brain reacts may seem daunting, with hundreds of genes and a vast array of interconnecting neurons, neurotransmitters and their receptors, and enzymes to catalyze and coordinate the complex chemical symphony. Inject some alcohol into the system, and it's off and running. You can be excused for crying out for a drink, as your head swims with the complexity.

When you take that next drink, beware of the neuroscientist who may be watching. As an example of the power of the new, noninvasive techniques in monitoring the brain's activity under the influence, Alessandro Castriota-Scanderberg of the Functional Neuroimaging Laboratory of the Santa Lucia Foundation in Rome used f-MRI in 2002 to test the tasting abilities of seven wine sommeliers and seven novice drinkers. Enclosed within the claustrophobic confines of the MRI cylinder, the subjects were given wines through plastic tubes while Castriota-Scanderberg scanned the parts of the brain that lit up in response. Predictably, every subject's orbitofrontal cortex and insula (part of the limbic system), which process olfactory sensations, became active. The sommeliers, however, showed activity in some brain areas that were quiescent in the novices' brains. The amygdala and hippocampus of the sommeliers' brains suggested they were extremely motivated, perhaps racking their memories for clues in discerning the wine's taste.

Their prefrontal cortices also went on high alert, probably as they sought to describe in words what they were experiencing. But if you thought that the professional tasters were totally objective in their assessments, you would be sadly mistaken. Other f-MRI studies have shown that tasters are much more strongly influenced by the color of liquid and the label on the bottle than by its actual taste. In one deceptive experiment, the tasters thought they were drinking a red wine, but it was actually a white wine colored with a red dye.

THE CULTURAL PART OF THE EQUATION

Once our species started down the road of drinking alcoholic beverages, there was no turning back. At the same time that the human body and brain adapted themselves to the drug, those unique symbolic constructions of humankind—its languages, music, dress, art, religion, and technology—were emerging and even reinforcing the phenomenon. How else can we explain the near-universal prevalence of fermented-beverage cultures in which alcoholic beverages (whether wine, beer, mead, or mixed grog) came to dominate entire economies, religions, and societies over time? In such cultures, everyday meals, as well as social events and special celebrations from birth to death are marked by the drinking or offering of an alcoholic beverage. Many examples might be cited from the Old World; in the New World, the wine and beer cultures of California and Australia might be viewed as among the latest entries.

The connection between alcoholic beverages, religion, and the arts is especially pronounced in the archaeology and history of our species. Music, for example, is wonderfully adapted to conveying a range of information—from matters as specific as territoriality and sexuality to the more nebulous realm of emotions, which alcoholic beverages also impinge on. When we talk to infants or pets, we tend to fall into a primitive language of fragmentary song, simplified words, and exaggerated facial and body gestures, almost as if this behavior were programmed into us and the creatures that we are trying to influence. If we accept the premise and ever-accumulating evidence for a modular human brain, with a vocabulary of logical forms underlying our acquisition of music and language, then the newly born child is like a computer operating system, ready to take in, cull, organize, and improvise on the stimuli bombarding it. As the child ages and brain matures, its baby talk is transformed into one of the many culturally defined human languages and specific musical genres. As a conduit for human emotions and accumulated collective wisdom before written language, music would have been the ideal medium. We can imagine that powerful lyrics set to music were already being performed by the shamanistic leaders of ceremonies inside the Stone Age caves.

Music, like alcohol, can also arouse sexual passion. As Charles Darwin remarked a century and a half ago in his *Descent of Man:* "All these facts with respect to music and impassioned speech become intelligible to a certain extent, if we may assume that musical tones and rhythm were used by our half human ancestors, during the season of courtship." The biological foundation for Darwin's assertion may find confirmation in the genetic and neural blueprint of our brains, especially the hypothalamus of the limbic system. A colleague of mine at the University of Pennsylvania School of Medicine, Andrew Newberg, and his former associate Eugene D'Aquili have begun to elucidate how the hypothalamus responds to and coordinates the rhythms of the body, using the noninvasive technique of SPECT. They point out that sexual pleasure, too, is rhythmic at its core and under the control of the hypothalamus.

Following Newberg and D'Aquili's lead, we can make a case for religion's being a part of the biocultural heritage that we have received from the Stone Age. The prevalence of religion in cultures around the world today and in the past implies that the human brain is primed to acknowledge a power greater than itself. After all, the unconscious and conscious workings of our brains, as well as the forces of nature themselves, are invisible and might be controlled by agencies beyond our comprehension. In a mysterious world, inhabited by all kinds of fabulous creatures real and imagined, humans needed a way to navigate around the dangers and invoke any beneficent powers. Given the fluid, integrative capacity of the human brain, it reaches out for explanations of these mysteries. We first turn to authority figures—our parents and teachers, among others—but for many the ultimate answer comes from a god.

Newberg and D'Aquili investigated the religious propensity of the human brain by SPECT monitoring the "mystical states" of Tibetan monks and Catholic nuns. They hypothesize that the hypothalamus can be put into overdrive by intense inward concentration, as well as by the mind-altering effects brought on by an alcoholic beverage, a hard-driving melody, frenetic spinning like a Sufi worshipper, or a sexual orgasm. First, one might experience ecstasy from the rush of neurotransmitters along the activated neural pathways. Then, as the hippocampus applies the brakes, as it were, to keep the organism from collapsing from exhaustion, one particular area of the cortex kicks in. The researchers note a marked inhibitory response in the right posterior inferior parietal lobule (the area of our cortex behind and a little above our right ear), which they believe gives us our sense of separation from the physical world. If that boundary is blurred by impulses from the hypothalamus as it tries to offset an emotional high, Newberg and D'Aquili claim, one will experience, like the monks and nuns in the experiment, a sense of oneness and absorption into a unitary being.

It is a huge leap from SPECT scans of the parietal lobe to unveiling the neural and cultural complexity of a mystical state. Yet, based on the available scientific data, Newberg and D'Aquili have begun to make sense of the give and take between the primitive nervous system—dominated by emotions and rhythms—and the brain's overlying cortex, which mediates consciousness and symbolic thought. Future investigations will likely uncover many more pathways of interconnectivity and neurotransmitter release, showing how the modern human brain is turned on or off by alcohol, sex, music, and religion, either separately or in combination with one another.

In *The Varieties of Religious Experience,* William James argued that nearly every human being has experienced a religious impulse. James focused on those individuals—the mystics, seers, and prophets, as well as many artists, musicians, and writers—who have gone through a transforming experience to become "twice-born." James went on to make the broader claim that "the sway of alcohol over mankind is unquestionably due to its power to stimulate the mystical faculties of human nature." Stone Age shamans probably belonged to the same family of the regenerated.

WHAT NEXT?

Our dueling fascination and consternation with alcoholic beverages will surely continue. Despite their dangerously addictive potential, they have been sanctioned by tradition, just as music and religion have been. The sorghum beer cultures of sub-Saharan Africa, the *chicha* cultures of the Americas, and the wine cultures of the Middle East and Asia all have roots stretching back millennia. It could be argued, however, that any fermented beverage culture must tread a fine line between harnessing the benefits of alcohol and avoiding its damaging effects.

From a very positive perspective, a mind-altering fermented beverage holds out the promise of individual and cultural renewal by encouraging and nourishing creativity and innovation of unusually imaginative individuals—

"shamanistic spirits"—who are able to transcend traditions and think outside the box. Intriguingly, the Latin root for *spirit* may derive from a Proto-Indo-European root meaning "to blow," which some linguists suggest should be understood in the sense of "to play a flute." Could this word, which also connotes the invisible workings of the human mind, be a holdover from the time that our ancestors played flutes, spurred on by fermented beverages, at Geissenklösterle and Isturiz in Europe, Jiahu in China, Caral in Peru, Pecos in New Mexico, and elsewhere?

My approach to alcoholic beverages and human culture differs dramatically from deterministic views of our biocultural past, which emphasize environmental, economic, or utilitarian causes for social transformations. I envision a more open-ended process in which the "pleasure cascade" in humans was activated by innovative ideas and discoveries, helped along by the consumption of an alcoholic beverage. By altering normal consciousness, humans envisioned new ways of symbolically representing the world around them, whether in art, music, poetry, the clothes and jewelry they wore, or rational explanations of how the world worked, which owed much to serendipitous insights and seemingly accidental events.

Fermented beverages played a direct role in both military conquest and the transfer of culture and technology from one area to another. The wine trade was one of the principal incentives for the Phoenicians, and later the Greeks and Romans, to expand their influence in the Mediterranean. Where wine went, other cultural elements eventually followed, even where another fermented beverage had long held sway. The earliest alphabetic inscriptions in Greek, which was derived from Phoenician, were poetic compositions on wine vessels. The Celts in Europe might have eschewed wine at first, but after they had imported some of the most stupendous Greek and Etruscan bronze vessels for their Nordic grog, they were gradually won over to wine and the more "civilized" ways of the south. Wherever we look on Earth, peoples were often first drawn to the cultures of their more technologically advanced neighbors or colonizing powers by the fermented beverages that the latter drank. The European explorers of the so-called Age of Discovery from the fifteenth to the seventeenth century were only one of the most recent examples: their ships were stocked with rum and sherry, which they traded to African chieftains for spices and slaves.

From this perspective, the Chinese, who were technologically in advance of so many other peoples, might well have preempted the Europeans as conquerors of the New World. Political and military prowess depended only partly on natural resources and what plants and animals were available to be domesticated, as Jared Diamond contends in *Guns, Germs and Steel;* rather, once a people had achieved a certain level of development, their future success depended on the myriad contingent factors of history and culture. When the Ming Dynasty gave up on its ambitious plans of maritime trade in the fifteenth century A.D., the world was left wide open for the Europeans, who had obtained most of their knowledge and technology from Asia, to become its rulers.

As archaeological and biomolecular investigations advance, we can expect to learn much more about our species' special relationship with fermented beverages. The consumption of alcohol in some regions about which we currently know little or nothing—including New Guinea, India, sub-Saharan Africa, Australia and the Pacific islands—will be investigated and possibly filled in. We may at last know whether the North American and Australian native peoples truly lacked fermented beverages or, more likely, concocted some of their own from a sweet fruit, tree resin, or other plant source. We should eventually be able to trace the movement of domesticated plants and ideas about beverage making across central Asia.

We can also anticipate many new insights about how alcohol affects the human body and brain. Because we are biological products of our past—more than 99 percent of which took place during the Palaeolithic period—many of the dietary ills of modern society, including obesity, diabetes, and alcohol and drug addiction, can be traced to the disparity between this Palaeolithic heritage and our modern lifestyles. Our bodies and brains are adapted to the moderate consumption of food and drink, which we inherited from the Stone Age; so when we overindulge in a fermented beverage, we suffer the physiological and psychological consequences.

Much more will also be learned about early plant domestication. The Eurasian grape was the first fruit to have its DNA fully sequenced, and the Eurasian grape was chosen because of our research that showed how early it had likely been domesticated for large-scale winemaking. Genetic microarrays, which enable thousands of genes to be tested at one time, will speed up the process of distinguishing between domesticated and wild traits in other species of plants.

Finally, we can look forward to many more re-creations of ancient beverages and new taste sensations, based on the biomolecular archaeological evidence. Bringing these delectable ancient beverages back to life transports us to an ancient time and teaches us more about the earliest methods of natural product fermentation. After a recent trip to Peru, where I observed (and tasted) traditional fermented beverages made from all manner of vegetables, fruit, and cereals—including purple, yellow and white maizes, quinoa, pepper-tree berries, freeze-dried potatoes, cornstalk juice, manioc, peanuts, and mesquite pods—the prospects for re-creating more ancient drinks appear very bright.

My synthetic vision of our species and its relationship to alcoholic beverages may or may not take hold in the academic and popular imagination, and we may not find conclusive evidence to show how much human cultures owe to these drinks. I am encouraged, however, by the ever more sensitive tools now available to biomolecular archaeologists seeking clues to our biological and cultural heritage.

Prehistory teaches us to persevere in our quest for knowledge. Twenty-six thousand years ago at Dolní Věstonice and the nearby site of Pavlov in the modern Czech Republic, humans made the earliest known fired-clay objects on Earth: naked female figurines ("Venuses") and animal figurines representing bears, lions, and foxes. The figurines were made the same way that they would be today—by mixing the clay with a temper (powdered bone in this instance) and firing it in a kiln. The people at these sites also adorned their bodies with ocher and beads made from carved mammoth bones, the teeth of arctic foxes, and shells. They wove grasses and other fibers into the first clothes, as revealed by the distinctive impressions left on clay. These finds gleam like a light in the darkness of the Palaeolithic period and then disappear. The art and bodily ornament endured, but the truly innovative element of their culture—making an artificial product from clay—was lost and would not be rediscovered until thousands of years later in East Asia. Similarly, I believe that Pliny the Elder's dictum—*in vino veritas* (in wine there is truth)—will ultimately prevail in showing how our species' intimate relationship with fermented beverages over millions of years has, in large measure, made us what we are today.

SELECT BIBLIOGRAPHY

GENERAL

Both, F., ed. 1998. *Gerstensaft und Hirsebier: 5000 Jahre Biergenuss.* Oldenburg: Isensee.

Buhner, S. H. 1998. *Sacred and Herbal Healing Beers: The Secrets of Ancient Fermentation.* Boulder, CO: Siris.

Crane, E. 1983. *The Archaeology of Beekeeping.* Ithaca, NY: Cornell University.

———. 1999. *The World History of Beekeeping and Honey Hunting.* New York: Routledge.

De Garine, I., and V. de Garine, eds. 2001. *Drinking: Anthropological Approaches.* New York: Berghahn.

Dietler, M., and B. Hayden, eds. 2001. *Feasts: Archaeological and Ethnographic Perspectives on Food, Politics, and Power.* Washington, DC: Smithsonian.

Douglas, M., ed. 1987. *Constructive Drinking: Perspectives on Drink from Anthropology.* Cambridge: Cambridge University Press.

James, W. 1902. *The Varieties of Religious Experience: A Study in Human Nature.* New York: Modern Library.

Jordan, G., P. E. Lovejoy, and A. Sherratt, eds. 2007. *Consuming Habits: Global and Historical Perspectives on How Cultures Define Drugs.* London: Routledge.

Koehler, C. 1986. "Handling of Greek Transport Amphoras." In *Recherches sur les amphores grecques,* ed. J.-Y. Empereur and Y. Garlan, 49–56. Athens: École Française d'Athènes.

McGovern, P. E. 2006. *Ancient Wine: The Search for the Origins of Viniculture.* Princeton: Princeton University Press.

Rätsch, C. 2005. *The Encyclopedia of Psychoactive Plants: Ethnopharmacology and Its Applications.* Rochester, VT: Park Street.

Rudgley, R. 1999. *The Encyclopedia of Psychoactive Substances.* New York: St. Martin's.

Schultes, R. E., A. Hofmann, and C. Rätsch. 1992. *Plants of the Gods: Their Sacred, Healing, and Hallucinogenic Powers.* Rochester, VT: Healing Arts.

Völger, G., ed. 1981. *Rausch und Realität: Drogen im Kulturvergleich.* Cologne: Rautenstrauch-Joest-Museum.

Wilson, T. M., ed. 2005. *Drinking Cultures: Alcohol and Identity.* Oxford: Berg.

ONE. *HOMO IMBIBENS*

Berg, C. 2004. World Fuel Ethanol: Analysis and Outlook. www.distill.com/World-Fuel-Ethanol-A&O-2004.html.

Dudley, R. 2004. "Ethanol, Fruit Ripening, and the Historical Origins of Human Alcoholism in Primate Frugivory." *Integrative and Comparative Biology* 44 (4): 315–23.

Eliade, M. 1964. *Shamanism: Archaic Techniques of Ecstasy,* trans. W. R. Trask. New York: Bollingen Foundation.

Johns, T. 1990. *With Bitter Herbs They Shall Eat It: Chemical Ecology and the Origins of Human Diet and Medicine.* Tucson: University of Arizona Press.

Lewis-Williams, J. D. 2005. *Inside the Neolithic Mind: Consciousness, Cosmos and the Realm of the Gods.* London: Thames & Hudson.

Nesse, R. M., and K. C. Berridge. 1997. "Psychoactive Drug Use in Evolutionary Perspective." *Science* 278 (5335): 63–67.

Rudgley, R. 1999. *The Lost Civilizations of the Stone Age.* New York: Free Press.

Siegel, R. K. 2005. *Intoxication: The Universal Drive for Mind-Altering Substances.* Rochester, VT: Park Street.

Stephens, D., and R. Dudley. 2004. "The Drunken Monkey Hypothesis." *Natural History* 113 (10): 40–44.

Sullivan, R. J., and E. H. Hagen. 2002. "Psychotropic Substance-Seeking: Evolutionary Pathology or Adaptation?" *Addiction* 97 (4): 389–400.

Turner, B. E., and A. J. Apponi. 2001. "Microwave Detection of Interstellar Vinyl Alcohol $CH_2=CHOH$." *Astrophysical Journal Letters* 561: L207–L210.

Wiens, F., et al. 2008. "Chronic Intake of Fermented Floral Nectar by Wild Treeshrews." *Proceedings of the National Academy of Sciences USA* 105 (30): 10426–31.

Zhang, J., and L. Y. Kuen. "The Magic Flutes." *Natural History* 114 (7): 42–47.

Berger, P. 1985. *The Art of Wine in East Asia*. San Francisco: Asian Art Museum.

Hawkes, D., trans. 1985. *The Songs of the South: An Ancient Chinese Anthology of Poems by Qu Yuan and Other Poets*. Harmondsworth: Penguin.

Henan Provincial Institute of Cultural Relics and Archaeology. 1999. *Wuyang Jiahu* (The site of Jiahu in Wuyang County). Beijing: Science Press.

————. 2000. *Luyi taiqinggong changzikou mu* (Taiqinggong Changzikou tomb in Luyi). Zhengzhou: Zhongzhou Classical Texts.

Huang, H. T. 2000. *Biology and Biological Technology*, part 5, *Fermentation and Food Science*, vol. 6 of J. Needham, *Science and Civilisation in China*. Cambridge: Cambridge University Press.

Karlgren, B., trans. 1950. *The Book of Odes*. Stockholm: Museum of Far Eastern Antiquities.

Li, X., et al. 2003. "The Earliest Writing? Sign Use in the Seventh Millennium B.C. at Jiahu, Henan Province, China." *Antiquity* 77 (295): 31–44.

Lu, H., et al. 2005. "Culinary Archaeology: Millet Noodles in Late Neolithic China." *Nature* 437: 967–68.

McGovern, P. E., et al. 2004. "Fermented Beverages of Pre- and Proto-historic China." *Proceedings of the National Academy of Sciences USA* 101 (51): 17593–98.

McGovern, P. E., et al. 2005. "Chemical Identification and Cultural Implications of a Mixed Fermented Beverage from Late Prehistoric China." *Asian Perspectives* 44: 249–75.

Paper, J. D. 1995. *The Spirits Are Drunk: Comparative Approaches to Chinese Religion*. Albany: State University of New York Press.

Schafer, E. H. 1963. *The Golden Peaches of Samarkand: A Study of T'ang Exotics*. Berkeley: University of California Press.

Warner, D. X. 2003. *A Wild Deer amid Soaring Phoenixes: The Opposition Poetics of Wang Ji*. Honolulu: University of Hawai'i Press.

THREE. THE NEAR EASTERN CHALLENGE

Aminrazavi, M. 2005. *The Wine of Wisdom: The Life, Poetry and Philosophy of Omar Khayyam*. Oxford: Oneworld.

Balter, M. 2005. *The Goddess and the Bull*. New York: Free Press.

Braidwood, R., et al. 1953. "Symposium: Did Man Once Live by Beer Alone?" *American Anthropologist* 55: 515–26.

Curry, A. 2008. "Seeking the Roots of Ritual." *Science* 319 (5861): 278–80.

Grosman, L., N. D. Munro, and A. Belfer-Cohen. 2008. "A 12,000-Year-Old Shaman Burial from the Southern Levant (Israel)." *Proceedings of the National Academy of Sciences USA* 105 (46): 17665–69.

Heun, M., et al. 1997. "Site of Einkorn Wheat Domestication Identified by DNA Fingerprinting." *Science* 278 (5341): 1312–14.

Hodder, I. 2006. *The Leopard's Tale: Revealing the Mysteries of Çatal Höyük.* London: Thames & Hudson.

Joffe, A. H. 1998. "Alcohol and Social Complexity in Ancient Western Asia." *Current Anthropology* 39 (3): 297–322.

Katz, S. H., and F. Maytag. 1991. "Brewing an Ancient Beer." *Archaeology* 44 (4): 24–33.

Katz, S. H., and M. M. Voigt. 1986. "Bread and Beer: The Early Use of Cereals in the Human Diet." *Expedition* 28 (2): 23–34.

Kennedy, P. F. 1997. *The Wine Song in Classical Arabic Poetry: Abū Nuwās and the Literary Tradition.* Oxford: Oxford University Press.

Kislev, M. E., A. Hartmann, and O. Bar-Yosef. 2006. "Early Domesticated Fig in the Jordan Valley." *Science* 312 (5778): 1372–74.

Kuijt, I., ed. 2000. *Life in Neolithic Farming Communities: Social Organization, Identity, and Differentiation.* New York: Kluwer Academic/Plenum.

McGovern, P. E., et al. 1996. "Neolithic Resinated Wine." *Nature* 381: 480–81.

Mellaart, J. 1963. "Excavations at Çatal Höyük, 1962." *Anatolian Studies* 13: 43–103.

Milano, L., ed. 1994. *Drinking in Ancient Societies: History and Culture of Drinks in the Ancient Near East.* Padua: Sargon.

Özdoğan, M., and N. Başgelen. 1999. *Neolithic in Turkey, the Cradle of Civilization: New Discoveries.* Istanbul: Arkeoloji ve Sanat.

Özdoğan, M., and A. Özdoğan. 1993. "Pre-Halafian Pottery of Southeastern Anatolia, with Special Reference to the Çayönü Sequence." In *Between the Rivers and over the Mountains: Archaeologica Anatolica et Mesopotamica Alba Palmieri Dedicata,* ed. M. Frangipane, 87–103. Rome: Università di Roma "La Sapienza."

———. 1998. "Buildings of Cult and the Cult of Buildings." In *Light on Top of the Black Hill: Studies Presented to Halet Çambel,* ed. G. Arsebük, M. J. Mellink, and W. Schirmer, 581–601. Istanbul: Ege Yayınları.

Özkaya, V. 2004. "Körtik Tepe: An Early Aceramic Neolithic Site in the Upper Tigris Valley." In *Anadolu'da Doğdu: Festschrift für Fahri Işık zum 60. Geburtstag,* ed. T. Korkut, 585–99. Istanbul: Ege Yayınları.

Russell, N., and K. J. McGowan. 2003. "Dance of the Cranes: Crane Symbolism at Çatalhöyük and Beyond." *Antiquity* 7 (297): 445–55.

Schmant-Besserat, D. 1998. "'Ain Ghazal 'Monumental' Figures." *Bulletin of the American Schools of Oriental Research* 310: 1–17.

Schmidt, K. 2000. "Göbekli Tepe, Southeastern Turkey: A Preliminary Report on the 1995–1999 Excavations." *Paléorient* 26 (1): 45–54.

Stol, N. 1994. "Beer in Neo-Babylonian times." In *Drinking in Ancient Societies: History and Culture of Drinks in the Ancient Near East,* ed. L. Milano, 155–83. Padua: Sargon.

Vouillamoz, J. F., et al. 2006. "Genetic Characterization and Relationships of Traditional Grape Cultivars from Transcaucasia and Anatolia." *Plant Genetic Resources: Characterization and Utilization* 4 (2): 144–58.

FOUR. FOLLOWING THE SILK ROAD

Bakels, C. C. 2003. "The Contents of Ceramic Vessels in the Bactria-Margiana Archaeological Complex, Turkmenistan." *Electronic Journal of Vedic Studies* 9: 1c. www.ejvs.laurasianacademy.com.

Barber, E. J. W. 1999. *The Mummies of Ürümchi.* New York: W. W. Norton.

De La Vaissière, É., and É. Trombert, eds. 2005. *Les sogdiens en Chine.* Paris: École Française d'Extrême-Orient.

Mair, V. H. 1990. "Old Sinitic *$m^{y}ag$*, Old Persian *maguš* and English 'magician.' " *Early China* 15: 27–47.

Olsen, S. L. 2006. "Early Horse Domestication on the Eurasian Steppe." In *Documenting Domestication: New Genetic and Archaeological Paradigms,* ed. M. A. Zeder et al., 245–69. Berkeley: University of California Press.

Rossi-Osmida, G., ed. 2002. *Margiana Gonur-depe Necropolis.* Venice: Punto.

Rudenko, S. I. 1970. *Frozen Tombs of Siberia: The Pazyryk Burials of Iron Age Horsemen,* trans. M. W. Thompson. Berkeley: University of California Press.

Rudgley, R. 1994. *Essential Substances: A Cultural History of Intoxicants in Society.* New York: Kodansha International.

Sarianidi, V. I. 1998. *Margiana and Protozoroastrism.* Athens: Kapon.

FIVE. EUROPEAN BOGS, GROGS, BURIALS, AND BINGES

Aldhouse-Green, M., and S. Aldhouse-Green. 2005. *The Quest for the Shaman: Shape-Shifters, Sorcerers and Spirit-Healers of Ancient Europe.* London: Thames & Hudson.

Behre, K.-E. 1999. "The History of Beer Additives in Europe: A Review." *Vegetation History and Archaeobotany* 8: 35–48.

Brun, J.-P, et al. 2007. *Le vin: Nectar des dieux, génie des hommes.* Gollion, Switzerland: Infolio.

Dickson, J. H. 1978. "Bronze Age Mead." *Antiquity* 52: 108–13.

Dietler, M. 1990. "Driven by Drink: The Role of Drinking in the Political Economy and the Case of Early Iron Age France." *Journal of Anthropological Archaeology* 9: 352–406.

Dineley, M. 2004. *Barley, Malt and Ale in the Neolithic.* Oxford: Archaeopress.

Frey, O.-H., and F.-R. Herrmann. 1997. "Ein frühkeltischer Fürstengrabhügel am Glauberg im Wetteraukreis, Hessen." *Germania* 75: 459–550.

Juan-Tresserras, J. 1998. "La cerveza prehistórica: Investigaciones arqueobotáni-cas y experimentales." In *Genó: Un poblado del Bronce Final en el Bajo Segre (Lleida)*, ed. J. L. Maya, F. Cuesta, and J. López Cachero, 241–52. Barcelona: University of Barcelona Press.

Koch, E. 2003. "Mead, Chiefs and Feasts in Later Prehistoric Europe." In *Food, Culture and Identity in the Neolithic and Early Bronze Age*, ed. M. P. Pearson, 125–43. Oxford: Archaeopress.

Long, D. J., et al. 2000. "The Use of Henbane (*Hyoscyamus niger* L.) as a Hallucinogen at Neolithic 'Ritual' Sites: A Re-evaluation." *Antiquity* 74: 49–53.

McGovern, P. E., et al. 1999. "A Feast Fit for King Midas." *Nature* 402: 863–64.

Michel, R. H., P. E. McGovern, and V. R. Badler. 1992. "Chemical Evidence for Ancient Beer." *Nature* 360: 24.

Miller, J. J., J. H. Dickson, and T. N. Dixon. 1998. "Unusual Food Plants from Oakbank Crannog, Loch Tay, Scottish Highlands: Cloudberry, Opium Poppy and Spelt Wheat." *Antiquity* 72: 805–11.

Nelson, M. 2005. *The Barbarian's Beverage: A History of Beer in Ancient Europe*. London: Routledge.

Nylén, E., U. L. Hansen, and P. Manneke. 2005. *The Havor Hoard: The Gold, the Bronzes, the Fort*. Stockholm: Kungl. Vitterhets Historie och Antikvitets Akademien.

Quinn, B., and D. Moore. 2007. "Ale, Brewing and *Fulachta Fiadh*." *Archaeology Ireland* 21 (3): 8–11.

Renfrew, C. 1987. *Archaeology and Language: The Puzzle of Indo-European Origins*. Cambridge: Cambridge University Press.

Rösch, M. 1999. "Evaluation of Honey Residues from Iron Age Hill-Top Sites in Southwestern Germany: Implications for Local and Regional Land Use and Vegetation Dynamics." *Vegetation History and Archaeobotany* 8: 105–12.

———. 2005. "Pollen Analysis of the Contents of Excavated Vessels: Direct Archaeobotanical Evidence of Beverages." *Vegetation History and Archaeobotany* 14: 179–88.

Sherratt, A. 1987. "Cups That Cheered." In *Bell Beakers of the Western Mediterranean: Definition, Interpretation, Theory and New Site Data*, ed. W. H. Waldren and R. C. Kennard, 81–106. Oxford: British Archaeological Reports.

———. 1991. "Sacred and Profane Substances: The Ritual Use of Narcotics in Later Prehistoric Europe." In *Sacred and Profane: Proceedings of a Conference on Archaeology, Ritual and Religion*, ed. P. Garwood, et al., 50–64. Oxford: Oxford University Committee for Archaeology.

Stevens, M. 1997. "Craft Brewery Operations: Brimstone Brewing Company; Rekindling Brewing Traditions on Brewery Hill." *Brewing Techniques* 5 (4): 72–81.

Stika, H. P. 1996. "Traces of a Possible Celtic Brewery in Eberdingen-Hochdorf, Kreis Ludwigsburg, Southwest Germany." *Vegetation History and Archaeobotany* 5: 81–88.

———. 1998. "Bodenfunde und Experimente zu keltischem Bier." In *Experimentelle Archäologie in Deutschland*, 45–54. Oldenburg: Isensee.

Unger, R. W. 2004. *Beer in the Middle Ages and the Renaissance.* Philadelphia: University of Pennsylvania Press.

Wickham-Jones, C. R. 1990. *Rhum: Mesolithic and Later Sites at Kinloch, Excavations 1984–1986.* Edinburgh: Society of Antiquaries of Scotland.

SIX. SAILING THE WINE-DARK MEDITERRANEAN

Adams, M. D., and D. O'Connor. 2003. "The Royal Mortuary Enclosures of Abydos and Hierakonpolis." In *Treasures of the Pyramids*, ed. Z. Hawass, 78–85. Cairo: American University in Cairo.

Aubet, M. E. 2001. *The Phoenicians and the West: Politics, Colonies, and Trade.* Cambridge: Cambridge University Press.

Bass, G. F., ed. 2005. *Beneath the Seven Seas: Adventures with the Institute of Nautical Archaeology.* London: Thames & Hudson.

Bikai, P. M., C. Kanellopoulos, and S. Saunders. 2005. "The High Place at Beidha." *ACOR Newsletter* 17 (2): 1–3.

Ciacci, A., P. Rendini, and A. Zifferero. 2007. *Archeologia della vite e del vino in Etruria.* Siena: Città del Vino.

Ciacci, A., and A. Zifferero. 2005. *Vinum.* Siena: Città del Vino.

Guasch-Jané, M. R., et al. 2006. "First Evidence of White Wine in Ancient Egypt from Tutankhamun's Tomb." *Journal of Archaeological Science* 33 (8): 1075–80.

Jeffery, L. H. 1990. *The Local Scripts of Archaic Greece: A Study of the Origin of the Greek Alphabet and Its Development from the Eighth to the Fifth Centuries B.C.* Oxford: Oxford University Press.

Jidejian, N. 1968. *Byblos through the Ages.* Beirut: Dar el-Machreq.

Long, L., L.-F. Gantés, and M. Rival. 2006. "L'Épave Grand Ribaud F: Un chargement de produits étrusques du début du Ve siècle avant J.-C." In *Gli etruschi da Genova ad Ampurias*, 455–95. Pisa: Istituti editoriali e poligrafici internazionali.

Long, L., P. Pomey, and J.-C. Sourisseau. 2002. *Les étrusques en mer: Épaves d'Antibes à Marseille.* Aix-en-Provence: Edisud.

McGovern, P. E., et al. 2008. "The Chemical Identification of Resinated Wine and a Mixed Fermented Beverage in Bronze Age Pottery Vessels of Greece." In *Archaeology Meets Science: Biomolecular Investigations in Bronze Age Greece; The Primary Scientific Evidence, 1997–2003*, ed. Y. Tzedakis et al., 169–218. Oxford: Oxbow.

McGovern, P. E., A. Mirzoian, and G. R. Hall. 2009. "Ancient Egyptian Herbal Wines." *Proceedings of the National Academy of Sciences USA* 106: 7361–66.

Morel, J. P. 1984. "Greek Colonization in Italy and in the West." In T. Hackens, N. D. Holloway, and R. R. Holloway, *Crossroads of the Mediterranean,* 123–61. Providence, RI: Brown University Press.

Pain, S. 1999. "Grog of the Greeks." *New Scientist* 164 (2214): 54–57.

Parker, A. J. 1992. *Ancient Shipwrecks of the Mediterranean and the Roman Provinces.* Oxford: British Archaeological Reports.

Parker, S. B. 1997 *Ugaritic Narrative Poetry.* Atlanta, GA: Scholars.

Ridgway, D. 1997. "Nestor's Cup and the Etruscans." *Oxford Journal of Archaeology* 16 (3): 325–44.

Stager, L. E. 2005. "Phoenician Shipwrecks and the Ship Tyre (Ezekiel 27)." In *Terra Marique: Studies in Art History and Marine Archaeology in Honor of Anna Marguerite McCann,* ed. J. Pollini, 238–54. Oxford: Oxbow.

Tzedakis, Y., and Martlew, H., eds. 1999. *Minoans and Mycenaeans: Flavours of Their Time.* Athens: Greek Ministry of Culture and National Archaeological Museum.

Valamoti, S. M. 2007. "Grape-Pressings from Northern Greece: The Earliest Wine in the Aegean?" *Antiquity* 81: 54–61.

SEVEN. THE SWEET, THE BITTER, AND THE AROMATIC IN THE NEW WORLD

Allen, C. J. 2002. *The Hold Life Has: Coca and Cultural Identity in an Andean Community.* Washington, DC: Smithsonian Institution.

Balter, M. 2007. "Seeking Agriculture's Ancient Roots." *Science* 316 (5833): 1830–35.

Bruman, J. H. 2000. *Alcohol in Ancient Mexico.* Salt Lake City: University of Utah Press.

Coe, S. D., and M. D. Coe. 1996. *The True History of Chocolate.* New York: Thames & Hudson.

Cutler, H. C., and M. Cardenas. 1947. "Chicha, a Native South American Beer." *Botanical Museum Leaflet, Harvard University* 13 (3): 33–60.

D'Altroy, T. N. 2002. *The Incas.* Malden, MA: Blackwell.

Dillehay, T. D. 2000. *The Settlement of the Americas: A New Prehistory.* New York: Basic Books.

———, et al. 2007. "Preceramic Adoption of Peanut, Squash, and Cotton in Northern Peru." *Science* 316 (5833): 1890–93.

———, et al. 2008. "Monte Verde: Seaweed, Food, Medicine, and the Peopling of South America." *Science* 320 (5877): 784–86.

Dillehay, T. D., and Rossen, J. 2002. "Plant Food and Its Implications for the Peopling of the New World: A View from South America." In *The First Americans: The Pleistocene Colonization of the New World*, ed. N. G. Jablonski, 237–53. San Francisco: California Academy of Sciences.

Erlandson, J. M. 2002. "Anatomically Modern Humans, Maritime Voyaging, and the Pleistocene Colonization of the Americas." In *The First Americans: The Pleistocene Colonization of the New World*, ed. N. G. Jablonski, 59–92. San Francisco: California Academy of Sciences.

Furst, P. T. 1976. *Hallucinogens and Culture.* San Francisco: Chandler & Sharp.

Goldstein, D. J., and Coleman, R. C. 2004. "*Schinus molle* L. (Anacardiaceae) *Chicha* Production in the Central Andes." *Economic Botany* 58 (4): 523–29.

Hadingham, E. 1987. *Lines to the Mountain Gods: Nazca and the Mysteries of Peru.* New York: Random House.

Hastorf, C. A., and S. Johannessen. 1993. "Pre-Hispanic Political Change and the Role of Maize in the Central Andes of Peru." *American Anthropologist* 95 (1): 115–38.

Havard, V. 1896. "Drink Plants of the North American Indians." *Bulletin of the Torrey Botanical Club* 23 (2): 33–46.

Henderson, J. S., et al. 2007. "Chemical and Archaeological Evidence for the Earliest Cacao Beverages." *Proceedings of the National Academy of Sciences USA* 104 (48): 18937–40.

Henderson, J. S., and R. A. Joyce. 2006. "The Development of Cacao Beverages in Formative Mesoamerica." In *Chocolate in Mesoamerica: A Cultural History of Cacao*, ed. C. L. McNeil, 140–53. Gainesville: University Press of Florida.

Jennings, J. 2005. "*La chichera y el patrón:* Chicha and the Energetics of Feasting in the Prehistoric Andes." *Archaeological Papers of the American Anthropological Association* 14: 241–59.

———, et al. 2005. " 'Drinking Beer in a Blissful Mood': Alcohol Production, Operational Chains, and Feasting in the Ancient World." *Current Anthropology* 46 (2): 275–304.

Kidder, A. V. 1932. *The Artifacts of Pecos.* New Haven: Phillips Academy by the Yale University Press.

La Barre, W. 1938. "Native American Beers." *American Anthropologist* 40 (2): 224–34.

Lothrop, S. K. 1956. "Peruvian Pacchas and Keros." *American Antiquity* 21 (3): 233–43.

Mann, C. C. 2005. *1491: New Revelations of the Americas before Columbus.* New York: Knopf.

McNeil, C. L., ed. 2006. *Chocolate in Mesoamerica: A Cultural History of Cacao.* Gainesville: University Press of Florida.

Moore, J. D. 1989. "Pre-Hispanic Beer in Coastal Peru: Technology and Social Context of Prehistoric Production." *American Anthropologist* 91 (3): 682–95.

Moseley, M. E. 1992. *The Incas and Their Ancestors: The Archaeology of Peru.* New York: Thames & Hudson.

————, et al. 2005. "Burning Down the Brewery: Establishing and Evacuating an Ancient Imperial Colony at Cerro Baúl, Peru." *Proceedings of the National Academy of Sciences* 102 (48): 17264–71.

Perry, L., et al. 2007. "Starch Fossils and the Domestication and Dispersal of Chili Peppers (*Capsicum* spp. L.) in the Americas." *Science* 315 (5814): 986–88.

Schurr, T. G. 2008. "The Peopling of the Americas as Revealed by Molecular Genetic Studies." In *Encyclopedia of Life Sciences* (www.els.ne).

Sims, M. 2006. "Sequencing the First Americans." *American Archaeology* 10: 37–43.

Smalley, J., and Blake, M. 2003. "Sweet Beginnings: Stalk Sugar and the Domestication of Maize." *Current Anthropology* 44 (5): 675–703.

Staller, J. E., R. H. Tykot, and B. F. Benz, eds. 2006. *Histories of Maize: Multidisciplinary Approaches to the Prehistory, Linguistics, Biogeography, Domestication, and Evolution of Maize.* Amsterdam: Elsevier Academic.

EIGHT. AFRICA SERVES UP ITS MEADS, WINES, AND BEERS

Arthur, J. W. 2003. "Brewing Beer: Status, Wealth and Ceramic Use Alteration among the Gamo of South-Western Ethiopia." *World Archaeology* 34 (3): 516–28.

Barker, G. 2006. *The Agricultural Revolution in Prehistory: Why Did Foragers Become Farmers?* Oxford: Oxford University Press.

Bryceson, D. F., ed. 2002. *Alcohol in Africa: Mixing Business, Pleasure, and Politics.* Portsmouth, NH: Heinemann.

Carlson, R. G. 1990. "Banana Beer, Reciprocity, and Ancestor Propitiation among the Haya of Bukova, Tanzania." *Ethnology* 29: 297–311.

Chazan, M., and M. Lehner. 1990. "An Ancient Analogy: Pot Baked Bread in Ancient Egypt." *Paléorient* 16 (2): 21–35.

Davies, N. de G. 1927. *Two Ramesside Tombs at Thebes.* New York: Metropolitan Museum of Art.

Edwards, D. N. 1996. "Sorghum, Beer, and Kushite Society." *Norwegian Archaeological Review* 29: 65–77.

Geller, J. 1993. "Bread and Beer in Fourth-Millennium Egypt." *Food and Foodways* 5 (3): 255–67.

Haaland, R. 2007. "Porridge and Pot, Bread and Oven: Food Ways and Symbolism in Africa and the Near East from the Neolithic to the Present." *Cambridge Archaeological Journal* 17 (2): 165–82.

Hillman, G. C. 1989. "Late Palaeolithic Plant Foods from Wadi Kubbaniya in Upper Egypt: Dietary Diversity, Infant Weaning, and Seasonality in a Riverine Environment." In *Foraging and Farming: The Evolution of Plant Exploitation,* ed. D. R. Harris and G. C. Hillman, 207–39. London: Unwin Hyman.

Holl, A. 2004. *Saharan Rock Art: Archaeology of Tassilian Pastoralist Iconography.* Walnut Creek, CA: AltaMira.

Huetz de Lemps, A. 2001. *Boissons et civilisations en Afrique.* Bordeaux: University of Bordeaux Press.

Huffman, T. N. 1983. "The Trance Hypothesis and the Rock Art of Zimbabwe." *South African Archaeological Society, Goodwin Series* 4: 49–53.

Karp, I. 1987. "Beer Drinking and Social Experience in an African Society: An Essay in Formal Sociology." In *Explorations in African Systems of Thought,* ed. I. Karp and C. S. Bird, 83–119. Washington, DC: Smithsonian Institution.

Lejju, B. J., P. Robertshaw, and D. Taylor. 2006. "Africa's Earliest Bananas?" *Journal of Archaeological Science* 33: 102–13.

Lewis-Williams, J. D., and T. A. Dowson. 1990. "Through the Veil: San Rock Paintings and the Rock Face." *South African Archaeological Bulletin* 45: 5–16.

Lhote, H. 1959. *The Search for the Tassili Frescoes: The Story of the Prehistoric Rock Paintings of the Sahara,* trans. A. H. Brodrick. New York: Dutton.

Maksoud, S. A., N. el Hadidi, and W. M. Wafaa. 1994. "Beer from the Early Dynasties (3500–3400 cal B.C.) of Upper Egypt, Detected by Archaeochemical Methods." *Vegetation History and Archaeobotany* 3: 219–24.

Mazar, A., et al. 2008. "Iron Age Beehives at Tel Rehov in the Jordan Valley." *Antiquity* 82 (317): 629–39.

McAllister, P. A. 2006. *Xhosa Beer Drinking Rituals: Power, Practice and Performance in the South African Rural Periphery.* Durham, NC: Carolina Academic.

Morse, R. A. 1980. *Making Mead (Honey Wine): History, Recipes, Methods, and Equipment.* Ithaca, NY: Wicwas.

Netting, R. M. 1964. "Beer as a Locus of Value among the West African Kofyar." *American Anthropolologist* 66: 375–84.

O'Connor, D. B., and A. Reid, eds. 2003. *Ancient Egypt in Africa.* London: University College London.

Pager, H. L. 1975. *Stone Age Myth and Magic as Documented in the Rock Paintings of South Africa.* Graz: Akademische.

Parkin, D. J. 1972. *Palms, Wine and Witnesses: Public Spirit and Private Gain in an African Farming Community.* Prospect Heights, IL: Waveland.

Phillipson, D. W. 2005. *African Archaeology.* Cambridge: Cambridge University Press.

Platt, B. 1955. "Some Traditional Alcoholic Beverages and Their Importance in Indigenous African Communities." *Proceedings of the Nutrition Society* 14: 115–24.

Platter, J., and E. Platter. 2002. *Africa Uncorked: Travels in Extreme Wine Territory.* San Francisco: Wine Appreciation Guild.

Sahara: 10.000 Jahre zwischen Weide und Wüste. 1978. Cologne: Museen der Stadt.

Samuel, D. 1996. "Archaeology of Egyptian Beer." *Journal of the American Society of Brewing Chemists* 54 (1): 3–12.

Samuel, D., and P. Bolt. 1995. "Rediscovering Ancient Egyptian Beer." *Brewers' Guardian,* December, 27–31.

Sangree, W. H. 1962. "The Social Functions of Beer Drinking in Bantu Tiriki." In *Society, Culture, and Drinking Patterns,* ed. D. J. Pittman and C. R. Snyder, 6–21. New York: Wiley.

Saul, M. 1981. "Beer, Sorghum, and Women: Production for the Market in Rural Upper Volta." *Africa* 51: 746–64.

Vogel, J. O., and J. Vogel, eds. 1997. *Encyclopedia of Precolonial Africa: Archaeology, History, Languages, Cultures, and Environments.* Walnut Creek, CA: AltaMira.

Wendorf, F., and R. Schild. 1986. *The Prehistory of Wadi Kubbaniya.* Dallas, TX: Southern Methodist University Press.

Wendorf, F., R. Schild, et al. 2001. *Holocene Settlement of the Egyptian Sahara.* New York: Kluwer Academic/Plenum.

Willis, J. 2002. *Potent Brews: A Social History of Alcohol in East Africa, 1850–1999.* Nairobi: British Institute in Eastern Africa.

NINE. ALCOHOLIC BEVERAGES

Acocella, J. 2008. "Annals of Drinking: A Few Too Many." *New Yorker,* May 26, 32–37.

Bowirrat, A., and M. Oscar-Berman. 2005. "Relationship between Dopaminergic Neurotransmission, Alcoholism, and Reward Deficiency Syndrome." *American Journal of Medical Genetics* 132B (1): 29–37.

Brochet, F., and D. Dubourdieu. 2001. "Wine Descriptive Language Supports Cognitive Specificity of Chemical Senses." *Brain and Language* 77: 187–96.

Castriota-Scanderberg, A., et al. 2005. "The Appreciation of Wine by Sommeliers: A Functional Magnetic Resonance Study of Sensory Integration." *Neuroimage* 25: 570–78.

Diamond, J. M. 1997. *Why Is Sex Fun? The Evolution of Human Sexuality.* New York: Basic Books.

———. 2005. *Guns, Germs, and Steel: The Fates of Human Societies.* New York: Norton.

Dick, D. M., et al. 2004. "Association of GABRG3 with Alcohol Dependence." *Alcoholism: Clinical and Experimental Research* 28 (1): 4–9.

Hamer, D. H. 2004. *The God Gene: How Faith Is Hardwired into Our Genes.* New York: Doubleday.

Mithen, S. J. 2006. *The Singing Neanderthals: The Origins of Music, Language, Mind, and Body.* Cambridge, MA: Harvard University Press.

Newberg, A. B., E. D'Aquili, and V. Rause. 2001. *Why God Won't Go Away: Brain Science and the Biology of Belief.* New York: Ballantine.

Nurnberger, J. I. Jr., and L. J. Bierut. 2007. "Seeking the Connections: Alcoholism and Our Genes." *Scientific American* 296 (4): 46–53.

Pandey, S. C., et al. 2004. "Partial Deletion of the cAMP Response Element-Binding Protein Gene Promotes Alcohol-Drinking Behaviors." *Journal of Neuroscience* 24 (21): 5022–30.

Standage, T. 2005. *A History of the World in Six Glasses.* New York: Walker.

Steinkraus, K. H., ed. 1983. *Handbook of Indigenous Fermented Foods.* New York: M. Dekker.

Strassman, R. 2000. *DMT: The Spirit Molecule; A Doctor's Revolutionary Research into the Biology of Near-Death and Mystical Experiences.* South Paris, ME: Park Street.

Thomson, J. M., et al. 2005. "Resurrecting Ancestral Alcohol Dehydrogenases from Yeast." *Nature Genetics* 37: 630–35.

Wolf, F. A., and U. Heberlein. 2003. "Invertebrate Models of Drug Abuse." *Journal of Neurobiology* 54: 161–78.

ACKNOWLEDGMENTS

THE SCOPE OF THIS BOOK goes far beyond what I attempted in my book *Ancient Wine*, which focused on the Middle East. That was like planting and tending a carefully laid-out vineyard. In attempting to sketch out a worldwide overview of fermented beverages, reaching back to the beginning of our species, and in trying to understand why humans have had a millennia-long love affair with these drinks, I felt more as though I was trying to tame a vast jungle in this book. To make sense of the lines of evidence from many diverse disciplines, I called on the advice of friends, colleagues, and fermented-beverage aficionados. They helped me to decipher the inner workings of the human brain. They directed my attention to small archaeological details buried in the literature that cried out for consideration. They taught me the intricacies of making and tasting alcoholic beverages. They helped me catalogue the vast resources of sugar-rich plants ripe for fermenting in every corner of the earth, which our ancestors ingeniously converted into delicious, mind-altering drinks.

Among others, I am indebted to the following archaeologists, archaeobotanists, chemists, enologists, foodies, geneticists, chocolatiers, historians, neuroscientists, physical anthropologists, beer makers, winemakers, and mead makers: Brian Anderson, Fredo Arias-King, Maria Aubet, Ginny Badler, Michael Balick, Steve Batiuk, Rostilav Berezkin, Sam Calagione, Phil Chase, Michael Chazan, Guangsheng Cheng, Mark Chien, Elizabeth

Childs-Johnson, Janet Chrzan, Elin Danien, Irina Delusina, the late Keith DeVries, Michael Dietler, Thomas Dillehay, Merryn Dineley, Paul Draper, Pascal Durand, Clark Erickson, Brian Fagan, Hui Fang, Gary Feinman, Nichola Fletcher, Mareille Flitsch, Mike Gerhart, David Goldstein, J. J. Hantsch, Harald Hauptmann, John Henderson, Ellen Herscher, Nick Hopkins, H. T. Huang, the late Michael Jackson, Ron Jackson, Justin Jennings, Chris Jones, Rosemary Joyce, John Kantner, Michael Karam, Diana Kennedy, Tony Kentuck, Eva Koch, Bob Koehl, Carolyn Koehler, Peter Kupfer, Karl Lamberg-Karlovsky, Al Leonard, Caryn Lerman, Li Liu, Huiqin Ma, Victor Mair, Daniel Master, Simon Martin, Jim Matthieu, Ami Mazar, James McCann, Jon McGee, Rod McIntosh, Steve Menke, Ian Morris, the late Roger Morse, Hugh Myrick, Reinder Neef, Max Nelson, Marilyn Norcini, Charles O'Brien, Rafael Ocete, John Oleson, Deborah Olzewski, Don Ortner, Ruth Palmer, Giancarlo Panarella, Fabio Parasecoli, Joel Parka, Brian Peasnall, Wayne Pitard, Greg Possehl, Maricel Presilla, Nancy Rigberg, Gary Rollefson, Mike Rosenberg, Gabriele Rossi-Osmida, Karen Rubinson, Kathleen Ryan, Ken Schramm, Fritz Schumann, Tad Schurr, Bryan Selders, Kirsten Shilakes, Richard Smart, Daniela Soleri, Larry Stager, Hans-Peter Stika, George Taber, Jigen Tang, André Tchernia, Sean Thackrey, Matthew Tomlinson, Jordi Tresserras, Jean Turfa, Anne Underhill, Michael Vickers, Mary Voigt, Alexei Vranich, Rich Wagner, Ellen Wang, Nina Wemyss, Fred Wendorf, Ryan Williams, Justin Willis, Warren Winiarski, Luke Wohlers, Jim Wright, Juzhong Zhang, and Xiuqin Zhou.

My greatest source of inspiration and help in exploring the world of ancient fermented beverages came from the dedicated corps of enthusiastic chemists who have served as research associates in the Biomolecular Archaeology Laboratory of the University of Pennsylvania Museum over the past thirty years, beginning with the late Rudy Michel and continuing with the late Don Glusker and Larry Exner and now with Gretchen Hall and Ted Davidson. They were backed up by other scientific colleagues in laboratories around the world, including Rosa Arroyo-García, the late Curt Beck, Eric Butrym, Gary Crawford, Wafik el-Deiry, James Dickson, Anne-Marie Hanssen, Gar Harbottle, Jeff Honovich, Jeff Hurst, Sven Isaaksen, the late Bob Kime, Joe Lambert, Rosa Lamuela-Raventós, Leo McCloskey, Naomi Miller, Armen Mirzoian, Robert Moreau, Mark Nesbitt, Andy Newberg, Alberto Nuñez, Chris Petersen, Michael Richards, Vernon Singleton, Ken Suslick, José Vouillamoz, Wenge Wang, Andy Waterhouse, Wilma Wetterstrom, José Zapater, "Jimmy" Zhao, and Daniel Zohary.

One's appreciation and understanding of fermented beverages can be enormously enhanced by traveling the world, tasting and talking as one goes. I have been most fortunate to visit some of the principal wine-producing areas of the world with the assistance of various local institutions and individuals: Italy (Associazione Nazionale Città del Vino), France (Musées Gallo-Romains de Lyon-Fourvière), Germany (University of Mainz), Spain (Fundación para la Cultura del Vino), and California (COPIA, the American Center for Wine, Food and the Arts, as well as many of the state's talented winemakers). Many other universities, institutions, and individuals have also eased my way along the fermented-beverage paths of the world, from China and Tibet to Turkey and Greece to California and New Mexico, with numerous stops in between. There is much left to explore.

In addition to being supported by the University of Pennsylvania and its museum, our research continues to receive backing from a wide range of institutions (most recently, the Abramson Cancer Center of the University of Pennsylvania, Cornell University, La Trobe University in Australia, and the Institute for Aegean Prehistory) and private individuals who have recognized the importance and fascination of fermented beverages in the development of human bioculture.

At the University of California Press, my editor, Blake Edgar, took an enthusiastic interest in the subject of ancient (and modern) fermented beverages by keeping me apprised of the latest research and shepherding the manuscript through the publication process. I am also extremely grateful to Erika Búky, Amy Cleary, Laura Harger, John Ricco, Lisa Tauber, and many other staff members and freelancers who have made the book a reality.

INDEX

African beverages, 13–16; additives, *232,* 234, 257; available ingredients, 13–16, *232,* 259–60, 263–64; beer in Egypt, 182, 186, 241–50; beer in sub-Saharan Africa, 250–59; Egyptian viticulture and winemaking, 166, 179, 180–81, 241, 262; fruit and palm wines, 259–64; grape wine in modern Africa, 262; honey beverages, 182, 234, 237–38, 240–41; millet beer, 251–52, 252–53, 255–56; modern *bouza,* 246–47. *See also* sorghum beer

agave, 219, 227

Aghios Kosmas, 185

agriculture: in Americas, 204–6; in Mediterranean, 162; in sub-Saharan Africa, 232. *See also* Neolithic revolution; plant domestication; viticulture and winemaking; *specific crops*

Ahasuerus, 114

Ahiram, 179

Ahnishinaubeg people, 229

Ahura Mazda, 118

'Ain Ghazal, 91–92

Akhenaten, 250

alcohol: animal attraction to, xiii, 2–5, 8–10, 11, 205, 266, 272; medicinal uses and benefits, 7, 75–76, 267; occurrence in nature, 2–4, 266; and origins of life on Earth, 1–2; psychotropic effects of, xi, xiii, 21–22, 267, 271–73, 275

alcohol content, wine vs. beer, 39

alcohol dehydrogenase (ADH), 5–6, 9

alcoholic beverage consumption. *See* fermented-beverage consumption

alcoholic beverage technology. *See* fermented-beverage technology

alcoholism, 8; genetic susceptibility to, 271, 273, 274

alcohol metabolism, 9, 274–75

alcohol production, current statistics, 6

aldehyde dehydrogenase 1 (ALDH1) gene, 274–75

Aleppo pine resin, 75, 185

Alexander the Great, 115, 118, 131, 239

Algeria: Tassili n'Ajjer paintings, 258–59

allspice, 218

Altai Mountains: Pazyryk *kurgan* burials, 123–25, *124–25,* 126–27

altered consciousness, 21–22, 102–3, 268, 278–79; artistic depictions of entoptic phenomena, 20–21, 140, 144, 236; hemp in Pazyryk *kurgan* burials, 123, *124–25,* 127; physiology of, 277–78; psychotropic effects of alcohol, xi, xiii, 21–22, 267, 271–73, 275; in shamanistic rituals, 21, 22, 26, 40–41, 229. *See also* mind-altering beverages; psychoactive plants and compounds

Althea, 120

Amanita muscaria. See fly agaric

Amarone, 195

Amazonia, 5, 205, 210, 226

Americas. *See* New World *entries; specific regions and sites*

γ-aminobutyric acid (GABA), 272

Amomyrtus luma, 203

Amorgos, 185

amphetamine, 210

amphoras, 36; from Mediterranean shipwrecks, 171–72, 174. *See also* containers; pottery

β-amyrin, 48, 49

Anabasis (Xenophon), 99

Anadenanthera, 226

Ananas bracteatus, 226. *See also* pineapples

anandamide, 120

Anatolia, Anatolian sites, 77–89; Çatal Höyük, 86–89; Çayönü, 80, 83, 85, 93; as center of innovation, 136; cult buildings, 77–78, 81, 93; Göbekli Tepe, 78, *79,* 80, 87; Gordion, 123–24, 131, 134–36, 151, 157; Hallan Çemi, 80, 81; honey in, 87; Körtik, 80, 81, 87; Nevali Çori, 77–78, 80, *80,* 85; viticulture and winemaking in, 82–84, 157–58, 175

ancestor worship and ceremonies, xi, 22, 26; Africa, 237–38, 251, 252, 257, 261–62, 264–65, 267; Americas, 206, 212, 221; China, 40–41, 56; Levant, 178, 179; Near East, 91, *92,* 161

Anchor Steam Brewery, 69

Ancient Wine (McGovern), 12, 131, 193

angel's trumpet, 226

animal domestication, 30; horse, 122–23. *See also* herding

Animal Master figure, 19, 20, *20*

animals: American mammal extinctions, 198–99; in Anatolian sculpture and carvings, 77–78, *79,* 80, *80,* 81, 86, 87; attraction to alcohol, xiii, 2–5, 8–10, 11, 205, 266, 272; attraction to cacao, 210; attraction to honey, 234–35; drunken monkey hypothesis, 8–10, 11, 205, 266; hybrid human-animal figures, 19, 20, *20,* 87, 236; on *kurgan* burial objects and mummies, 123, *124–25,* 125; in Palaeolithic art, 18–19, 81, 281; on Persian drinking vessels, 114. *See also specific animals*

annatto, 218

Annona muricata, 226–27

Anshan, 112

antioxidants, 49, 75, 76

Antoninus Pius, 175

Anyang, 46–49, *48*

apes, 8, 24–25; chimpanzees, 8, 9–10, 15, 235

Apis mellifera, 234. *See also* bees

apples, 143

aquavit, 144

Arabic poetry, 101–2, 103

Arachis, 204

Archestratus of Syracuse, 175

Archilochos, 158

Arda Wiraz, 118

Ariadne, 183

Aristotelia chilensis, 203

Arran, 138

Arrhenius, Birgit, 155

arrowroot, 226. *See also* manioc

art: Ahiram sarcophagus, 179; alcoholic beverages in, 17; Anatolian sculptures and carvings, 77–78, *79,* 80, *80,* 81; Bronze Age figurines from Denmark, 144; at Çatal Höyük, 86–88, *88;* cultic "ancestor" statues, 91, *92,* 93; depictions of honey hunters, 143, 235–37, *236;* drinking on Near Eastern cylinder seals, 70, *98–99,* 100, 113; Egyptian reliefs and paintings, 172, 181, 239, 243–44, 246, 247, *248;* Exekias cup, 183; goddess of

Myrtos figurine, 185; Mayan frescoes and vessels, 214, *215,* 221; Minoan frescoes, 188, 189; Neolithic tomb decorations in northern Europe, 140; Palaeolithic, 16–17, 18–22, 26, 162–63, 268, 281; Tassili n'Ajjer paintings, 258–59; Ugarit stela, 179

Artemisia, 49, 51, 52, 116

Artemisia argyi. See wormwood

Artemisia vulgaris. See mugwort

arts, 27

A'sā, al-, 101

Ashgrove, 138, 139, 145

Ashkelon, 170

Asia. *See specific regions and sites*

Asians, ALDH1 gene in, 274–75

Aspergillus, 52

Assyrians, 113, 134, 174, 190, 194

Astrocaryum standleyanum, 9

Atatürk Dam, 77

ATF (Bureau of Alcohol, Tobacco, and Firearms), 44

Athabascan people, 229

ATP (adenosine triphosphate), 5, 6

Atropa belladonna. See deadly nightshade

aurochs, 78, *79,* 87

Australia, 162, 200, 266, 280

Australopithecus afarensis, 7

Avesta, 117

ayahuasca, 226

Ayia Triada, 189

ayran, 96

Aztecs, 213, 217–21, 222, 228

Baal, 172, 175, 178, 183

Baalat-Gebal, 165

Baalbek, 175

Baal Cycle, 178–79

baboons, 3

Babylon, 99, 111

The Bacchae (Euripides), 184

Bacchic poetry, 101–3, 111

Bacchic rage, 184

Bacchus, 183

Bacchus temple, Baalbek, 175

bacteria: alcohol intolerance, 6, 21; in fermentation processes, 2, 5, 6, 35, 153

cereals: in Africa, 232, 241, 254–55, 260, 263; in Europe, 142–43; in Mediterranean, 162, 182. *See also* saccharification; *specific cereal crops*

ceremonial beverages and alcohol consumption, 262, 267; in Americas, 206, 221, 224–25, 226, 227; beer in Africa, 251, 252–53, 255–56, 257, 258–59; Dionysian festivals, 103–4, 183–84; Egyptian festivals, 165, 246; Eleusinian Mysteries, 189; Greek *kykeon*, 188–89, 190–91; mead in Kikuyu and Masai ceremonies, 237–38; northern Europe, 140, 147–48, 149, 158; palm wine in Africa, 261–62; Phoenician sailors, 172. *See also* ancestor worship and ceremonies; religion; shamanism

Cerro Baúl, 223–25

Cestus (Sextus Julius Africanus), 99

Chaco Canyon, 228

chamomile, 260

chang (Chinese herbal wines), 51, 52, 55

Changzikou tomb, 49, 51

Chardonnay, 176

Chasselas, 83

Chateau Jiahu, 42–46, *45*

Château Ksara, 176, 177

Chazan, Michael, 244–45

cheese, in Greek *kykeon*, 188, 190

chemical analyses. *See* residue analyses

Chen, Laoshi, 55

Cheng, Guangsheng, 37, 42, 43, 53

Chenopodium, 204

Cherchen, 121; Ürümchi mummies, 121, 136

cherries, 143

chewing. *See* mastication

chicha: associated pottery vessels, 207; cultural significance, 206–7; maize-based, 38–39, 206–8, 209, 220, 228; potato-based, 203, 280–81; suitable plants at Monte Verde, 203

chickens, 30

chickpea, 85

Chile: Monte Verde, 198, 199, 200, 202–4

chili peppers, *200*, 204; in cacao beverages, 217, 218; at Cerro Baúl, 224; in Theobroma re-creation, 222

Chimay, 129

chimpanzees, 8, 9–10, 15, 235

China, 28–58, 279–80; attitudes about intoxication, 51, 219; author's introduction to, 28–29; China–Near East technology transfer, 104, 128; Great Wall, 107; Indo-European influence in, 122; in Near Eastern writings, 60; Neolithic revolution in, 30, 40; Shang dynasty oracle bones, 32–33; Tang-era borrowings from Western cultures, 109–10; viticulture in, 39, 108, 126. *See also* Central Asia; Chinese beverages; Silk Road

China fir, 49

Chinese beverages: Chateau Jiahu re-creation, 42–46; fruits and honey in, 37, 38, 39, 53–54, 55; Jiahu grog, 37, 38–39, 103, 108, 269; Liangchengzhen grog, 55–57; poetry celebrating, 57–58; Shaoxing rice wine, 6, 52–54; Tang dynasty, 58; winemaking techniques, 51, 52–57; wines from Shang and Zhou tombs, 46–52; Xi'an tomb beverage, 47–48

Chinese date. *See* jujube

Chinese medicine, 49

Chinese poetry, 57–58

Chinese pottery, 30–31, 54–55, 56, 58

Chiribaya people, 226

chlorite, 81

chocolate, 210, 212. *See also* cacao; cacao beverages

Chomsky, Noam, 23

Chontalpa, 210, 212

chonta palm, 226

Christian ritual, wine in, xi, 268

CHRM2 gene, 273

chrysanthemum, 48–49, 51, 57, 58

Ciliegiolo, 194

Circe, 188

Cistercians, 129

Claviceps. See ergot

climate change, Neolithic revolution and, 205

cloudberries, 139, 143

clover, 144, 145, 240

fungi: ergot, 118, 189; hallucinogenic mushrooms, 117–18, 220, 229, 273; puffball
fungus, 235; for saccharification, 52
Funnel Beakers, 137, 146–47
funnels, 54, 65, 89, 185

GABA (γ-aminobutyric acid), 272
Gaia Estate Ritinitis, 75
Gallagher, Larry, 43, 44
Gamkrelidze, Thomas, 127
Gann, Thomas, 214
Garnacha, 196
Garstang, John, 242
Gaul, Gauls, 146; wine trade, 149, 150, 193
Gaza, 170, 175
Geissenklösterle flutes, 17, 18, 33–34, 35
Geller, Jeremy, 241, 242–43
General History of the Things of New Spain
(Sahagún), 217–18, 220
genetics: alcohol consumption and,
269–76; DNA analysis techniques,
xii, 280; language capacity and, 23
Genghis Khan, 105
Genó, 141
Geography (Strabo), 108, 234
Georgia, 80, 83. *See also* Transcaucasia
Gerhart, Mike, 43, 44
germander, 166
Germany (including archaeological sites):
Baden culture beakers, 137; Geis-
senklösterle flutes, 17, 18, 33–34, 35;
Hochdorf, *150*, 150–51, 152–53, 157;
Hohmichele and Glauberg, 152;
Lichterfelde, 147; Tacitus on German
drinking habits, 113; viticulture, 158
Gesher, 94
Geshtinanna, 100
gibbons, 8, 24
Gibraltar, 195, 196
Gilgal I, 93–94, 263
Gilgamesh epic, 61, 257
ginseng, 117
Giryama people, 262
Giza, 164, 244–45, 250
Glauberg, 152
glutamate, 272
glycolysis, 2, 5. *See also* fermentation

goats, 30
Göbekli Tepe, 78, *79*, 80, 87
Gobi Desert, 105, 106
Godin Tepe, 61–71, 104; barley beer,
66–71, 104; geographic setting, 62–63,
66; wine and winemaking facilities,
63–66, 111
God L, 222
gold artifacts: from European sites, 147–48,
151, 157; Incan drinking vessels, 207;
Nestor's cup, 187–88; Uluburun shipwreck, 174
golden eagle, 228
Goldstein, David J., 224
Gonur Depe/Gonur South, 115–16, 117, 119
Gordion: Midas tumulus, 123–25, 131,
134–36, 151, 157
gorillas, 8
Gossypium, 204
Gotland sites, 153–54, 155, 156
Gouais Blanc, 176
gourds, 12–13, 16, 214, 220–21, 224, 234,
237, 239, 251, 257, 260, 264
Gourliea decorticans, 226
grain. *See* cereals; malt; mashing techniques and facilities; *specific grain types*
Gram, Bille, 144, 156
grape, Eurasian *(Vitis vinifera)*, 12, 65, 280;
in Central Asia, 108, 109, 126, 128; domestication and earliest viticulture, 13,
76, 82–84, 111, 127; in Egypt, 166, 242;
in Europe, 143–44; in Levant, 175, 178;
in Mesopotamia, 62. *See also* grape
wine; viticulture and winemaking
grape hyacinth, 120
grapes, 94; American varieties, 227–28;
Central Asian Eurasian variety, 108;
for Chateau Jiahu re-creation, 43;
Chinese varieties, 38, 39, 55, 108; domestication of, 13, 39, 82, 111; from
Egyptian and Levantine sites, 166,
169, 175, 242, 243; on Exekias cup,
183; grapevine in Egyptian mythology,
165; in Jiahu grog, 37, 38, 108; at Myrtos, 184; at Persian sites, 112, 119; *Saccharomyces cerevisiae* on, 6, 38, 68; as
tartaric acid source, 37; wild grapes in

malt, malting, 242–43; maize, 209, 224; rice, 38, 43. *See also* barley malt
Malta, 189
mammal extinctions, American, 198–99
Manihot esculenta. See manioc
manioc, *200*, 204, 226, 227, 263
manzanita, 200, 227
MAO inhibitors, 273
maple, 156, 229
maps: Africa, *233;* Americas, *199;* Eurasia, *14–15;* Europe and Mediterranean, *132–33*
Mapuche people, 203
maqui, 203
Marchalina hellenica, 3
Marco Polo, 106, 107
mare's-milk, 123
Mare's Teat grape, 108
Margiana sites, 115–19
Mariesminde Mose, 147–48
marijuana. *See* hemp/marijuana
marjoram, 240
Marsala, 192
marzeah, 179
Masai people, 237–38, 252
mashing techniques and facilities, 68; ancient Egypt, 241, 242–43, *244–45,* 246, 247, 249–50, 257–58; Burkina Faso, *244–45,* 247, 249, 250, 256–58
mastication, saccharification by, 38–39, 203, 255; barley, 38, 68; maize, 206–7, 208–9; manioc, 226; rice, 38–39, 43; sorghum, 255
Matamala, Joan Carles, 141
maté, 214
mating behavior, 25–26; birds, 17, 18, 25, 35, *36;* gibbons, 24–25
Matopo Hills rock paintings, 235–36, *236*
Mauritania, fruit findings, 259
Maya, 213, 217; depictions of cacao and cacao beverages, 214–15, *215,* 221; Maize God, 221; Mayan chocolate vessels, 214; modern Lacandón Maya, 218, 227
Maya, Jose Luis, 141
Maytag, Fritz, 69
Mbuti people, 234

McPherson, Tara, 45–46
mead. *See* honey mead
meadowsweet, 138–39, 144
medicinal beverages and additives, *13,* 267; Africa, *232,* 260; China, 49–50, 55; ephedra, *13,* 116, 117, 119–20; Near East, 96; northern Europe, 120–21
medicinal plants and compounds: in Africa, 261; molluscan purple as, 273; at Monte Verde, 202; opium, 140; resins, 75, 155–56; in Shanidar Cave burials, 120–21; triterpenoids, 49. *See also* psychoactive plants
Mediterranean, 192, 194–95; fermented-beverage technology diffusion (map), *132–33;* prehistoric migrations and settlement patterns, 160–63. *See also specific regions and sites*
Mediterranean beverages: beer, 178, 182, 186–87; Etruscan grog, 190–92; *kykeon,* 187–89; *mulsum* and *omphacomelitis,* 158. *See also* Mediterranean shipping and trade; Mediterranean viticulture and winemaking
Mediterranean containers, in northern Europe, 147, 149, *150,* 151–53, 155, 156–57
Mediterranean shipping and trade, 36, 162–65, 279; between Etruria and Gaul, 193; between Levant and Crete, 182–83; between Levant and Egypt, 169–70, 175; Phoenician shipwrecks' wine cargoes, 171–72; wine trade with northern Europe, 149–50, 152, 156, 158
Mediterranean shipwrecks, 192, 194–95; Canaanite Uluburun wreck, 173–74, 180; Etruscan Grand Ribaud wreck, xiv, 192; Phoenician, 171–72
Mediterranean viticulture and winemaking, 157–58, 279; Abydos wine, 94, 166–70, *167;* Crete, 185–87; Egypt, 166, 179, 180–81, 241, 262; Italy, 191–92; Levant, 174–75, 178, 181, 186–87; modern Lebanon, 176
Mehrgarh, 128
Melipona, 218
Melissa, 166

New World beverages *(continued)*
  chichas, 38–39, 203, 206–8, 209, 220,
  228; honey in, 218, 227; maize-based,
  38–39, 206–9, 220, 228; maté, 214;
  mixed beverages, 209, 215, 217–18,
  222, 224, 225; modern, 215, 218,
  280–81; north of Mexico, 5, 227–30;
  psychoactive additions, 226, 227;
  pulque, 219, 220; Wari pepper tree
  wine, 223–26. *See also* cacao
  beverages
Nicotiana. See tobacco
Niepoort, Dirk van der, 181
Nigeria: Kofyar people, 251
Nile: delta royal winemaking industry,
  166, 181–82. *See also* Egypt
Nineveh, 113
Ning Baosheng, 34
Ninkasi (Sumerian beer re-creation), 69
Ninkasi (Sumerian goddess), 69, 246
Nitriansky Hrádok, 137
nixtamalization, 209
Nkang, 263
Noah hypothesis, 13, 82–84
nomadic steppe peoples, 122–27, 136
noodles, 30
noradrenalin, 119
Nordic grog, 138–40, 144, *145,* 146, 147,
  152–54, 156
Norse mythology, mead in, 148
North America, 227–30; absence of alcohol
  in, 227–29, 266, 280; human arrival,
  198–200, 205, 229–30; native grape
  varieties, 82; potlatch ceremonies, 148.
  See also Mexico
North Mains, 138
Nuñez, Alberto, 37
nut grass, 232
Nylén, Erik, 154–55
Nymphaea, 260

oak, 163, 173
Obedieh, 176
ocher pigment, 17, 22, 162, 268, 281
O'Connor, David, 163
octli, 219
Odin, 148

Odyssey (Homer), 188
Oenotia, 193, 194
oil palm, 260, 261
Ojibwa people, 229
okra, 257
oleanolic acid, 48
Olmecs, 212–13
Omar Khayyam, 102, 103, 111
Ōmiwa no Kami, 59
opioids, 272, 273
opium, 116, 120, 139, 140, 188, 273
Opuntia, 219, 226
oracle bones, 32–33, 51
orangutans, 8
organ-pipe cactus, 227
Origanum dictamnus, 189
"Origins and Ancient History of Wine"
  (conference), 73
Orkneys, 138
Oryza. See rice
Osiris, 165
Osmanthus fragrans, 51
Ōtomo no Tabito, 59
Ötzi, 155–56
Oval on the Citadel Mound. *See* Godin
  Tepe
Ovid, 134
Özkaya, Vecihi, 81

Paestum, xiv
Pakistan: Mehrgarh site, 128
Palaeolithic culture: art, 16–17, 18–22, 26,
  268; music and dance, 20, 23, 25–26.
  See also shamanism
Palaeolithic hypothesis, 11–13, 16–18, 205,
  268
palms, 9; Africa, 232, 264; Americas, 204,
  215, 226, 227; palm wine, 260–62.
  See also date palm
palmyra palm, 260
Panicum, 30. *See also* millet
Pantelleria, 195
Papaver somniferum. See opium; poppy
Parsagaedae, 112
Pasteur, Louis, xiii
pastoralists. *See* herding
Pavlov, 281

Quinn, Billy, 141, 142
quinoa, 204
Quinta do Passadouro, 181

radish, 69
ragwort, 120
raisin bush, 257
raisins, raisined wines, 96, 112, 166, 175, 195
Ramesses III, 240
raphia palm, 260
Raphia vinifera, 260
Rapi'uma texts, 174–75, 178, 179
Ras Beirut, 161–62
raspberries, 89
ratel, 234–35
rats, 10
rattles, 20, 33, 35, 40, 41
Raventós family, 196
rb marzeah, 179
Re, 246
red-crowned crane, 17, 35, *36*, 87
red ocher, 17, 22, 162, 268, 281
red pine, 3
red-tailed hawk, 228
Rekhmire tomb, 239
religion, religious ritual: alcoholic beverages and, xi, 19–22, 27, 267–68, 276; Aztec, 221; Buddhism, 107, 118–19, 268; Canaanite, 174, 178–79; diffusion along Silk Road, 107; Dionysos and Dionysian festivals, 183–84; Egyptian, 165, 246; Islam, 101, 118–19; Mayan mythology, 221–22; Minoan, 185, 189; mysticism and alcohol, 102–3; Norse mythology, 148; Phoenician, 172; sacred marriage ceremony *(hieros gamos)*, xiv, 96, 99–100; San mythology, 236–37; Shang dynasty oracle bones, 32–33; Sufism, 102–3; Wari, 224, 225; wine in Christian and Jewish ritual, xi, 268; Zoroastrianism, 115–20, 122. *See also* ancestor worship and ceremonies; ceremonial beverages; funerary rituals; shamanism
Renan, Ernst, 164
Rephaim texts, 174–75, 178, 179
Reshef, 172

residue analyses: Central Asian sites, 116, 119; Dynastic Egyptian sites, 166, 196; Jiahu beverage, 37–39; Mediterranean sites, 171–72, 184–85, 186, 188; Mesoamerican cacao vessels, 212–14, 217, 218; Mycenaean cup, 188; Myrtos jars, 184–85, 186; Near Eastern sites, 67–68, 69, 74–76, 81, 104, 134, 169; northern European sites, 138–39, 145, 151, 152, 153–54, 155, 156; Predynastic Egyptian sites, 241–42, 254
resinated beverages: Abydos wine, 94, 166–70, *167;* Anatolian wine, 74–76, 95; China and Japan, 47–48, 49, 51, 52, 55, 59; Etruscan grog, 191; Myrtos wine, 184–85; Near East, 74–76, 95, 269; from Phoenician shipwrecks, 171–72; Uruk, 100
resins, 3, 75, *232;* birch resins, 155–56; medicinal uses of, 75, 155–56. *See also* myrrh; resinated beverages
resveratrol, 76
retsina, 75, 185
Rhine, 158
Rhizopus, 52
Rhône, 158
rhubarb, 130
Rhum, 138, 139
rice: domestication of, 31, 58; preparation for sake, 58, 59; saccharification methods, 38–39, 43–44, 52, 55, 57, 59
rice beverages, 29; Chateau Jiahu re-creation, 42–46; Jiahu grog, 36–39; Liangchengzhen grog, 55; sake, 38, 44, 58, 59; Shang and Zhou dynasty China, 49, 51, 54; Shaoxing wine, 6, 52–54
Richards, Michael, 37
Richthofen, Ferdinand von, 106–7
Ridge Vineyards, 66
Rig Veda, 117
Río Azul, 217
Rites of Zhou (Zhouli), 51
robins, 4
Rollefson, Gary, 91
Roman drinking vessels: in northern Europe, 157. *See also* Mediterranean containers

Rome, Romans: attitudes toward Celtic
beverages, 146; wines and viticulture,
75, 158, 193–94
ron palm, 260
root crops. See tubers; *specific types*
rose, 240
rosemary, 120, 141
Rosenberg, Michael, 81
Rossi-Osmida, Gabriele, 119
roundworm, 272
Ruba'iyyat (Omar Khayyam), 102, 103
Rudenko, Sergei, 123, 125, 126
Rudgley, Richard, 139–40
rue, 188
rue, Syrian, 117
Rumex, 254, 260
Russia: horse nomads of steppes, 122–27
rye, ergot fungus on, 118, 189

saccharification, 38–39, 43–44, 52, 73,
268–69; barley, 38, 56, 68–69; maize,
206–7, 208–9; mastication as method
for, 38–39, 203; mold saccharification,
38, 43–44, 52, 53; as purpose of Irish
fulachta fiadh, 141–42; rice,
38–39, 43–44, 52, 55, 57; sprouting
and malting, 38, 43, 56, 68, 143, 209;
tubers, 203, 254; wheat, 85. See also
barley malt; malt; mashing;
mastication
Saccharomyces bayanus, 2
Saccharomyces cerevisiae, 2, 5–6, 38, 68, 209;
in honey, 234
sacred marriage ceremony *(hieros gamos),*
xiv, 96, 99–100
saffron, 130, 135, 188
Sagard, Gabriel, 227
sage, 166
Sagittarius B2N, 1
saguaro cactus, 219, 226, 227
Sahagún, Bernardino de, 217–18, 220
Sahara, *232;* fruits in, 259–60; Nabta Playa
site, 253–54, 255, 259, 263
Sahel, *232;* fruits in, 259; modern beer
making in Burkina Faso, *244–45,* 247,
249, 250, 256–58; palms and palm
wine in, 261; sorghum and millet

beers in, 255–56; sorghum in, 253–54,
255, 258–59
Saint Anthony's fire, 118
Saint Barnaby's thistle, 120
sake, 38, 44, 58, 59
Salamis, 190
saliva, for saccharification, 38, 203, 226.
See also mastication
salmonberry, 200
Salvia, 166
Samuel, Delwen, 250
Sangiovese, 194
San Lorenzo a Greve, 191
San Miguel brewery, 141
San Pedro cactus, 226
San people, 236–37
Santa Rita Corozal, 214
sapote, 215, 218
Sardinia, 189
Sargon II palace, 190
Sarianidi, Viktor, 115–17, 119
Satureja, 166
Sauer, Jonathan, 72
sausage tree, 234
savory, 166
Scala Dei, 196
scale insects, 3
Scandia, 157
Scandinavia: author's work in, 154; dancers
depicted in rock carvings, 144; Got-
land sites, 153–54, 155, 156; mixed bev-
erages in, 153–54; *Vitis vinifera* in, 143.
See also Denmark; Vikings
Schinus molle. See Peruvian pepper tree
Schmidt, Klaus, 78, 84–85
Scientific American, 71
Scirpus. See bulrushes
Scoblionkov, Deborah, 42
Scotch whisky, 138, 177
Scotland, Scottish sites, 137–39, 142–43, 145
Scottish & Newcastle, 250
Scythians, 125–26, 140–41
sealing techniques, xiii–xv, 63–64, 168, 170
seaweeds, 202
Sekhmet, 246
Selders, Bryan, 44, 222
Semillon, 176

yeasts, 2, 6, 87, 143; for Chateau Jiahu recreation, 44; insects as transporters, 6, 209, 260; New World *chicha*, 209. See also *Saccharomyces* entries
Yellow Emperor, 41–42
yerba-maté, 214
Yi li (Book of Conduct), 40
Yin. *See* Anyang
yogurt, 70, 96
yopo tree, 226
you jars, 49
Ystad, 157
yuca, 226. *See also* manioc
yucca, 209, 219
Yuchanyan Cave, 58
Yuezhi people, 108, 126

Zagros Mountains, xiv, 61, 63, 70; Hajji Firuz Tepe, 74–76; Neanderthal burials in, 120–21; viticulture in, 82, 97, 111, 112. *See also* Godin Tepe
Zea. See maize
Zerabar Lake, 111
Zeus, 183
Zhang, Juzhong, 29, *34, 36*
Zhang, Zhiqing, 49
Zhang Qian, 39, 108, 128
Zhao, Zhijun "Jimmy," 37, 38
Zhou dynasty China, 33, 40, 52, 54; attitudes about intoxication, 51, 219
Zhuangzhi (Book of Master Zhuang), 47
Zifferero, Andrea, 193
Zimbabwe: Matopo Hills rock paintings, 235–37, *236*
Ziziphus, 254, 259. *See also* jujube
Zoroastrianism, 115, 117, 122; *haoma*, 116, 117–20; Margiana fire temples, 115–17
Zosimus, 247
Zulu peoples, 251, 252

Text:	11.25/13.5 Adobe Garamond
Display:	Adobe Garamond, Vendetta Light
Indexer:	Thérèse Shere
Cartographer:	Ben Pease
Compositor:	Westchester Book Group
Printer and Binder:	Thomson-Shore, Inc.